THE GARDEN CONSERVANCY

1999

OPEN DAYS DIRECTORY

*The Guide to Visiting
America's Very Best
Private Gardens*

THE GARDEN CONSERVANCY

Cold Spring, NY

Published by The Garden Conservancy, Inc., 41 Albany Post Road, Post Office Box 219, Cold Spring, New York, 10516. (914) 265-2029.

GardenCons@aol.com. www.GardenConservancy.com

ISSN 1087-7738

ISBN 1-893424-00-6

Publisher's Cataloging-in-Publication

The 1999 Garden Conservancy open days directory : the guide to visiting America's very best private gardens. — 5th ed.
    p. cm
    Includes index

        1. Gardens—United States-Directories. 2. Botanical gardens—United States-Directories. 3. Arboretums – United States-Directories. 1. Garden Conservancy

      SB466.U65G37 1999   712'.07473
                                 QB198-1548

Open Days Program Coordinator, Laura Mumaw Palmer

Open Days Program Assistant, Erin E. Dempsey

Book production by Cross River Publishing Consultants, Inc., Katonah, NY 10536.

Fifth Edition

This book is printed on recycled paper.

Manufactured in the United States of America.

CONTENTS

ACKNOWLEDGEMENTS

The Garden Conservancy gratefully acknowledges

for its generous sponsorship of the 1999 Open Days Program.

We are grateful to all those who have made it possible to bring you the *1999 Open Days Directory.*

Our appreciation to the fine garden businesses who have supported this publication through their advertising. Please consult these pages for all of your gardening needs and tell the advertisers you saw them in the *Directory.*

Under the inspirational leadership of Janet Poor, a tireless group of Regional Representatives continue to recruit gardens around the country for your enjoyment.

Mrs. John N. Wrinkle & Mrs. A. Jack Allison Jr, Birmingham, Alabama; Mrs. Donald C. Williams & Nancy Swanson, Phoenix, Arizona; Mrs. Donivee Nash, Los Angeles, California; Sonny Garcia, Charmain Giuliani, Richard G. Turner Jr. & Tom Valva, San Francisco Bay Area, Calfornia; Mrs. Harvey D. Hinman,San Francisco Peninsula, California; Mrs. Gene Moore, Colorado Springs, Colorado; Mrs. Moses Taylor, Denver, Colorado; Page Dickey, Jane Havemeyer, Sara M. Knight, Penelope Maynard, Enid Munroe, & Melissa Orme, Connecticut & Southeastern New York; Mrs. Sidney Scott Jr. & Mrs. George P. Bissell Jr., Wilmington, Delaware; Mrs. Thomas S. Morse & Suzanne Tifft, Vero Beach, Florida; Mrs. William Huger, Atlanta, Georgia; Mrs. Charles E. Schroeder & Janet Meakin Poor, Chicago, Illinois; Ann Hobson Haack, New Orleans, Louisiana; Mrs. Clark F. MacKenzie, Baltimore, Maryland; Mrs. Adrian P. Reed, Chestertown, Maryland; Mrs. Henry S. Streeter, Boston, Massachusetts; Mrs. Robert G. Walker, South Darmouth, Massachusetts; John W. Trexler, Worcester, Massachusetts; Marie Cochrane, Ann Arbor, Michigan; Starr Foster, Bloomfield Hills, Michigan; Mrs. Bragaw Vanderzee, Grosse Pointe, Michigan; Mrs. Henry L. Sweatt, Minneapolis, Minnesota; Mrs. J. Duncan Pitney, New Jersey; Joanne Lenden, Albany, New York; Mrs. James T. Flynn, Lake Champlain, New York & Vermont; Lalitte Scott, Eastern Long Island, New York; Mrs. W. Stuver Parry, Akron, Ohio; Mrs. William R. Seaman, Cincinnati, Ohio; Karen K. Meyer, Columbus, Ohio; Mrs. James Woodhull & Barbara Rion, Dayton, Ohio; Mrs. Frank H. Goodyear & Mrs. Edward Starr III, Philadelphia, Pennsylvania; Mrs. Halbert Law & Mrs. John Stout, Chattanooga, Tennessee; Mrs. Albert M. Austin III & Mrs. David B. Martin, Memphis, Tennessee; James deGrey David, Jennifer Staub Mcyers, & Dr. Gordon L. White, Austin, Texas; Joanne S. Lawson, Mrs. J. Taft Symonds, & Mrs. Sellers J. Thomas Jr., Houston, Texas; Mrs. A. V. S. Olcott, Manchester, Vermont; Joanne S. Lawson, Mrs. John Macomber, Washington, D.C.; Barbara Flynn, Seattle, Washington; Mr. & Mrs. James Rufus Thomas II, Charleston, West Virginia; Mrs. Robert W. Braeger & Mrs. William Allis, Milwaukee, Wisconsin. (in alphabetical order by Open Day Area)

LAURA MUMAW PALMER
Coordinator
Open Days Program

ANTONIA F. ADEZIO
Executive Director
The Garden Conservancy

INTRODUCTION

WELCOME TO THE GARDEN CONSERVANCY'S *1999 Open Days Directory*, your personal invitation to visit hundreds of private gardens in the United States.

It couldn't be easier. We've asked our Garden Hosts to provide descriptions of their gardens, the dates and hours they welcome your visit, and detailed driving directions. You do the rest!

So plan your visit to see these wonderful gardens, whether they're in your neighborhood or make for an enticing weekend getaway.

WHAT IS THE OPEN DAYS PROGRAM?

The Open Days Program is the only national program that invites the public to visit America's very best, rarely-seen, private gardens.

HISTORY

In 1995, the Garden Conservancy published the first edition of the *Open Days Directory*, listing 110 private gardens in New York and Connecticut. Since then the Directory has evolved into a listing of hundreds of private gardens nationwide, with plans to continue its expansion.

The Open Days Program is modeled after similar programs abroad including England's popular "Yellow Book" and Australia's growing Open Garden Scheme.

The mission of the Open Days Program is to increase public appreciation and enjoyment of America's gardens in all their regional diversity, and to build an audience to support garden preservation in America.

HOW IS THE OPEN DAYS PROGRAM ORGANIZED?

Each Open Day area has at least one Regional Representative who works on a volunteer basis to recruit private gardens in his or her area and to assist with the promotion and advancement of the program.

The *Open Days Directory* is published and distributed by the Garden Conservancy.

If you are interested in learning more about the organization of Open Days throughout the United States, please contact The Garden Conservancy, Open Days Program, Post Office Box 219, Cold Spring, NY 10516. Telephone: 914/265-2029. Fax: 914/265-9620.

ADMISSIONS

A $4 admission fee is charged per garden. Visitors may purchase admission coupons through the Garden Conservancy at a discounted price (see order form on the last page of this *Directory*). Admission coupons remain valid from year to year.

Proceeds from the Open Days Program support the national preservation work of the Garden Conservancy, as well as local not-for-profit organizations designated by individual Garden Hosts.

GENERAL INFORMATION

The Garden Conservancy's Open Days Program is simply based on a Garden Host's willingness to share his or her garden with the public on various dates throughout the gardening season. We make every attempt to open a variety of gardens, within a reasonable driving distance of each other, on the same date. There are exceptions and you will note some gardens that we simply had to include but that are off the beaten path.

We are also pleased to provide listings of public gardens in each Open Day area to round out your day of garden visiting or to enjoy at other times of the year.

GARDEN LISTINGS

Those of you who have purchased the *Open Days Directory* in the past will notice some changes to its organization. This year we've arranged garden listings in the following sequence:
- alphabetically by state
- alphabetically according to Open Day Area (i.e. San Francisco Bay Area, Seattle & Vicinity, Dutchess & Columbia Counties)
- alphabetically by town or city
- alphabetically by garden name.

To help you locate a specific garden, we've indexed them by garden name in the back of the *Directory*. There is also a master calendar in the beginning of the *Directory* that lists all Open Days for the 1999 season.

MAPS

Each state section begins with a map of that state with its Open Days noted. Each Open Day listing is preceded by a map illustrating the gardens open on that specific day.

Directions given for each garden assume that garden visitors are traveling from the nearest major highway. In some cases, references from two starting points are given. Please travel with a local map.

Each private garden listing includes the name of the garden and its location. A description of the garden, the dates and times it is open, and driving directions are also included.

Public garden listings are marked with a ❖, and include the garden name, full address, contact information, a brief description of the garden, hours of operation, and driving directions. We encourage you to contact the site directly for more information.

Information in this *Directory* was to the best of our knowledge, correct at the time the *Directory* went to press. Since publication, some changes may have occurred. When possible, the Garden Conservancy will notify you of changes in advance; otherwise please take note of schedule changes posted at admission tables or check the Garden Conservancy's website prior to your visit. (GardenConservancy.com)

INFORMATION GATHERING

The information presented in the *Open Days Directory* is collected by Garden Conservancy staff and Regional Representatives around the country. We rely on Garden Hosts to provide information for their listings. Information for Public Garden listings is likewise gathered from the site's staff. The Garden Conservancy is not responsible for the accuracy of the information published within these listings.

Nominations to include gardens in the *Open Days Directory* are acceped. Please call or write for a survey form and nomination criteria.

Inquiries regarding the *Open Days Directory* should be directed to:

LAURA MUMAW PALMER, *Coordinator*
Open Days Program
The Garden Conservancy
P.O. Box 219
Cold Spring, NY 10516
Telephone: (914) 265-2029
Fax: (914) 265-9620

MESSAGE FROM THE CHAIRMAN

THE GREAT APPRECIATION OF BEAUTY, the enthusiasm, and the interest generated in 1998 by the Open Days Program was indeed rewarding. More than 50,000 garden visits were recorded — visits that have helped to support the crucial preservation efforts of the Conservancy and have supported other nonprofit organizations designated by garden hosts. Even more impressive than numbers, however, is the almost tangible level of excitement the program has engendered since its inception.

The Open Days Program has proven to be a fruitful and productive experience for all participants. Visitors are immensely appreciative of the singular opportunity to enjoy exceptional private gardens that otherwise would not be open to them. Garden hosts, who generously share their creativity and expertise, are tremendously impressed with the keen interest and knowledge of those who visit the gardens they have tended with such care. The Open Days Program has become an informal forum for the exchange of ideas and information, as well as a celebration of a mutual respect and love for nature and gardening.

Our dedicated group of Regional Representatives form the backbone of the Open Days Program. They skillfully and diligently direct the activities of the energetic committee members who worked with Garden Hosts throughout the United States to bring you the *1999 Open Days Directory*.

The millennium edition of the *Directory* will offer further expansion and refinements as we work to create a truly comprehensive compendium of private gardens of merit throughout our nation.

The *1999 Directory* is the harvest of the efforts of many dedicated individuals: the enterprising Regional Representatives and their hard-working committee members; gracious private and public garden hosts; and the staff of the Garden Conservancy.

The Open Days Directory is your passport to a spectrum of garden delights. We promise you will be enchanted, uplifted, awed, and fascinated — not to mention enlightened and inspired — by the beauty and diversity that awaits you on the other side of these garden gates.

JANET MEAKIN POOR, *Open Days Chairman*

THE GARDEN CONSERVANCY

WHY-AND HOW-DO WE CONSERVE GARDENS? The Garden Conservancy was founded to answer these questions, to provide the resources necessary to preserve many of Americaís finest gardens, and to open the gates of these exceptional gardens to the public for education and enjoyment.

Why do we conserve gardens? Anyone who gardens knows the fragile nature of the gardener's creation: Subject to the ravages of climate, weeds, erosion, pests, and other problems, even the most carefully designed gardens can vanish within just a few years when untended. When we lose an exceptional garden, we lose its beauty, but we also lose the lessons it can teach us about the gardener's era — its values, horticultural science, and aesthetic standards. We conserve beautiful gardens because they are a vital part of our nation's cultural heritage. Experts estimate that more than two-thirds of great American gardens have already been lost to the tides of time. As the first national organization devoted to garden preservation, The Garden Conservancy is working to stem that tide by identifying gardens of unusual merit across the nation-from a desert garden in California to a Japanese garden in New York-and working with their owners and other interested parties to insure the gardens' futures. Some of these gardens are national treasures, while others are important community resources; all merit conservation as part of our national legacy.

How do we conserve gardens? While the gardener is able to maintain the garden, it remains vibrant. But when the gardener can no longer invest the time, energy, and resources required, the garden and its beauty can perish. Saving a fine garden requires expertise, funding, and community support — resources The Garden Conservancy brings to bear in preserving great American gardens and opening them to the public. The Garden Conservancy works in partnership with individual garden owners as well as public and private organizations, and uses its legal, financial, and horticultural resources to secure each garden's future and to make it permanently accessible to the public.

THE PRESERVATION PROJECTS OF THE GARDEN
CONSERVANCY
1999 Garden Visiting Information
The Garden Conservancy is currently working toward the preservation of eighteen special gardens around the country. You are

welcome to visit and will find a full description, visiting information, and directions for the following projects in this edition of the *Directory*:

> Aullwood Garden MetroPark, Dayton, OH
> The Ruth Bancroft Garden, Walnut Creek, CA (San Francisco Bay Area)
> The Beatrix Farrand Garden at Bellefield, Hyde Park, NY
> The Chase Garden, Orting, WA
> Dumbarton Oaks Park, Washington, DC
> The Fells, John Hay National Wildlife Refuge, Newbury, NH
> Gibraltar, Wilmington, DE
> The Harland Hand Garden, El Cerrito, CA
> The James Rose Center, Ridgewood, NJ
> McKee Botanical Garden, Vero Beach, FL
> Peckerwood Garden, Hempstead, TX
> Springside, Poughkeepsie, NY
> Van Vleck House & Gardens, Montclair, NJ

You may also visit the following Garden Conservancy preservation projects not included in this edition of the *Directory*.

HISTORIC MORVEN, Princeton, NJ: Home to a signer of the Declaration of Independence and many of New Jersey's governors, the Morven landscape is a composite of 200 years of American history. Set amidst stately lawns and trees in downtown Princeton, a colonial revival garden is the focus of current preservation efforts. Call for more information (609) 683-4495.

THE JOHN P. HUMES JAPANESE STROLL GARDEN, Mill Neck, NY: Created for Ambassador and Mrs. John P. Humes in 1960, this four-acre Japanese garden uses sloping terrain, a pond and waterfall, moss terraces, and stepping stones to represent mountain streams flowing to the ocean. Tea ceremonies are held regularly in the teahouse. Open Saturdays and Sundays. 11:30 a.m. to 4:30 p.m. from mid-April through mid-October. For information about group tours and special events, please call (516) 676-4486.

THE MCLAUGHLIN GARDEN AND HORTICULTURAL CENTER, South Paris, ME: Bernard McLaughlin spent a lifetime creating and maintaining collections of lilacs, lilies, iris, hosta, and native wildflowers, comprising this three-acre perennial garden. Following McLaughlin's death, the community successfully rallied to preserve the garden and its 50-year old "open door" visiting tradition. Open daily, dawn to dusk, from spring through fall. For information on special events and educational programs throughout the season, please call (207) 743-8820.

MUKAI FARM AND GARDEN, Vashon Island, WA: Island Landmarks is working to save this site which represents a chapter in the early Japanese-American experience. In the midst of her family's prosperous strawberry farm a first-generation Issei woman created a Japanese-style garden, replete with "island" and waterfalls surrounded by pools filled with koi and waterlilies. Please call for more information, (206) 463-2445.

VAL VERDE, Montecito, CA: Acknowledged as Lockwood de Forest's masterwork, Val Verde is an original composition of classical and modern design ideas that dates from the 1920s and 1930s but prefigures much of contemporary landscape design. The current owner is taking steps to guarantee the preservation of this estate. Val Verde is not yet open to the public. For more information on arranging a private tour, please call (805) 969-1053.

1999 OPEN DAYS CALENDAR

MARCH
20 Texas: Houston Area

APRIL
10 & 11 Arizona: Phoenix Area
17 Florida: Vero Beach Area
   Louisiana: New Orleans
   Tennessee: Memphis Area
25 Connecticut
   Southeastern New York

MAY
1 California: San Francisco
   Peninsula Area
   Maryland: Baltimore Area
   New York: Suffolk County/
   Eastern Long Island
2 Connecticut
   Southeastern New York
8 & 9 California: San Francisco Bay
   Area
9 Delaware: Wilmington Area
15 California: Los Angeles Area
   Georgia: Atlanta Area
   Michigan: Ann Arbor Area
   New Jersey
   Pennsylvania: Philadelphia Area
   District of Columbia: Washington
   Area
16 Connecticut
   Southeastern New York
   Michigan: Bloomfield Hills Area
22 Georgia & Tennessee:
   Chattanooga Area
22 & 23 Massachusetts: Boston Area
29 Southeastern NewYork
30 Connecticut

JUNE
5 Ohio: Columbus Area
   Washington: Seattle Area
6 Maryland: Chestertown Area
12 New Jersey
   Vermont: Manchester &
   Woodstock Area
13 Connecticut
   Michigan: Grosse Pointe Area
   Southeastern New York

19 Illinois: Chicago Area
   Massachusetts: Worcester Area
   New York: Albany Area
   New York: Suffolk County/
   Eastern Long Island
   Ohio: Akron Area
   Ohio: Cincinnati Area
   West Virginia: Charleston Area
26.District of Columbia: Washington
   Area
27 Connecticut
   Illinois: Chicago Area
   Southeastern New York

JULY
10 Colorado: Denver Area
   Massachusetts: South Dartmouth
   Area
   Minnesota: Minneapolis Area
   Vermont: Manchester &
   Woodstock Area
11 Connecticut
   Southeastern New York
17 Colorado: Colorado Springs Area
   Michigan: Bloomfield Hills Area
   New York: Suffolk County/
   Eastern Long Island
18 Colorado: Denver Area
   Wisconsin: Milwaukee Area
25 Connecticut
   Illinois: Chicago Area
   Southeastern New York
31 New York: Lake Champlain Area

SEPTEMBER
11 New Jersey
12 Connecticut
   Southeastern New York
18 New York: Suffolk County/
   Eastern Long Island
25 Ohio: Dayton Area
   Texas: Austin Area

OCTOBER
9 & 10 Alabama: Birmingham Area
16 California: San Francisco Bay
   Area
17 Southeastern New York

ALABAMA

Birmingham

1999 ALABAMA OPEN DAYS

October 9 & 10: BIRMINGHAM AREA

Birmingham Area

BIRMINGHAM: *October 9 & 10, 1999*

Bromberg Garden, BIRMINGHAM, 1 P.M. – 5 P.M.

Brooke Garden, BIRMINGHAM, 1 P.M. – 5 P.M.

Diane & Eric Hansen Garden, BIRMINGHAM, 1 P.M. – 5 P.M.

Metz Garden, BIRMINGHAM, 1 P.M. – 5 P.M.

Louise & John Wrinkle, BIRMINGHAM, 1 P.M. – 5 P.M.

Bromberg Garden, BIRMINGHAM, AL

Fifty-five years ago Frank's mother and father began planting these three and one-half acres. Their passion was springtime as you'll notice by the cherry trees, forsythia, and dogwoods they nurtured on the front lawn. For the last eight years, Frank and I have worked to restore the gardens, as well as make them our own. The rose garden gives me flowers to share, and the perennial bed is filled with Frank's mother's treasures as well as my own touches of color. Our favorite place, though, is the secret garden tucked under a large oak. It's where I cool down after garden chores and listen to the music of the frog trio in the pond. It is a private haven we'll gladly share for an afternoon.

DATES & HOURS: October 9 & 10; 1 p.m. – 5 p.m.

DIRECTIONS: *From Highway 280 East,* exit at the Cahaba Heights overpass. Turn right onto Pump House Road. The house is approximatly .3 mile on the left at the intersection of Caldwell Mill Road and Pump House Road. Please park on Pump House Road.

Proceeds shared with The Birmingham Botanical Society.

Brooke Garden, BIRMINGHAM, AL

The approach to this garden, over a bridge and through a woodland setting, is only one aspect of what is in store for the visitor. The gravel drive opens out into a circular stone and gravel courtyard, which serves as the hub for several possible routes into other parts of the property. One is drawn up along the winding stone path with its colorful mixed border to the screen porch of the guesthouse. Here, one can see the charming herb garden, as well as a surprisingly stunning view across the pool and meadow garden to a distant ridge.

DATES & HOURS: October 9 & 10; 1 p.m. – 5 p.m.

DIRECTIONS: *From Highway 280 East or West,* take Cherokee Road east .9 mile. Take a left at the bridge directly across the street from Sherwood Road. Please park where directed.

Proceeds shared with First Look.

Diana & Eric Hansen, BIRMINGHAM, AL

This is a beautifully established garden, created by Eleanor and Georges Bridges. The house was built in 1921 and for sixty years Eleanor Bridges planted and Georges sculpted. Original sculpture remains in the garden along with thousands of surprise lilies, tulips, iris, daffodils, flowering trees, ballustrades, and fountains. Even when this garden is not in full bloom, the garden setting is a joyous place to be.

DATES & HOURS: October 9 & 10; 1 p.m. – 5 p.m.

DIRECTIONS: *From Highway 280* take the Mountain Brook/Hollywood Boulevard Exit. Turn left. Cross Highway 31 in Homewood. Continue on Oxmoor Road (West) 1.1 miles. Approaching Dawson Memorial Baptist Church on the right, turn left onto Edgwood Boulevard. The house is at the end of the second block, on the right, behind a high natural hedge. Please park on Edgwood Boulevard.

Proceeds shared with Birmingham Botanical Society.

Metz Garden, BIRMINGHAM, AL

My garden gives me pleasure, a challenge, and fun. It is located on a hill with a front door yard and back patio and without a lawn. Plants include roses, a variety of shrubs, trees, azaleas, ground covers, perennials, orchids, annuals, and large containers of tropicals. The back has raised vegetable beds (from compost) and herbs. The variety proves year-round interest.

DATES & HOURS: October 9 & 10; 1 p.m. – 5 p.m.

DIRECTIONS: *From Mountain Brook Village,* take Lane Park Road by Botanical Gardens, make a left at the traffic light at Country Club Road. Sterling Road is the middle street at the next intersection (approximately 2 miles). *From English Village,* take Fairstay Drive by Redmont Garden Apartments. Take the first left after the apartments and several houses.

Louise & John Wrinkle, BIRMINGHAM, AL

The original house and property were developed in 1938 by Louise's parents. Ten years ago, she and her husband moved back to her childhood home and extensively remodeled the house and grounds. A two-acre mature woodland garden features collections of hollies and vacciniums, as well as the ranunculus family. Southeastern natives and their Asian counterparts, many planted side by side for easy comparison, are subjects of equal interest. Guests may circulate freely among the upper gardens: a small boxwood parterre defined by a Belgian fence of native crab apple, a cutting garden, and an herb garden. A network of winding gravel paths leads visitors from these upper gardens to a wooded valley, where a brook flows year round.

DATES & HOURS: October 9 & 10; 1 p.m. – 5 p.m.

DIRECTIONS: *From Highway 280/I-459* take Exit 19 onto Lake Shore Drive. Turn right and go through two traffic lights. The road becomes Mountain Brook Parkway. Continue 1.1. miles to right onto Overbrook Road, then go .6 mile and make a left onto Beechwood. The house is on the corner of Beechwood and Woodhill. Please park along Woodhill and walk up the driveway.

Proceeds shared with Birmingham Botanical Gardens.

❖ The Advent Gardens, Cathedral Church of the Advent,

2017 SIXTH AVENUE NORTH, BIRMINGHAM, AL 35203. (205) 251-2324.
These gardens are an oasis in the heart of Birmingham's central business district. The larger, the Rector's Garden, is a courtyard framed by church buildings. A white garden, it also offers favorite Southern plantings, as well as fountains and statuary. The canopy of a giant oak invites visitors to garden benches for lunch, reading, and reflection. The Betty Turner Garden is an allée of Japanese maples underplanted with shade-loving perennials. The gardens are tended by the Advent's St. Fiacre Guild, volunteers who show their love of gardening in this much loved place.

DATES & HOURS: Year round, daily, 8 a.m. – 5 p.m.; Sunday, 8 a.m. – 1 p.m.

DIRECTIONS: *Located at* the corner of 6th Avenue North and 20th Street in downtown Birmingham.

❖ Birmingham Botanical Gardens,

2612 LANE PARK ROAD, BIRMINGHAM, AL 35223. (205) 879-1227.
Birmingham Botanical Gardens features sixty-seven acres of native and exotic plants. Major collections include camellia, cactus and succulent, rhododendron, iris, fern, lily, orchid, old-fashioned and modern roses, and sculpture. There is also a conservatory, plus vegetable and herb gardens. There is a renowned Japanese garden with an authentic teahouse and cultural performance pavilion. A horticultural library and ongoing horticultural programs are available. Attractive gift shop offers unusual garden items and flower-arranging supplies. Most areas are handicapped accessible.

DATES & HOURS: Year round, daily, dawn – dusk

DIRECTIONS: *From I-20/I-59* exit onto Highway 280 East. Take the Mountain Brook/Zoo/Gardens Exit. Turn left at traffic light onto Lane Park Road. The gardens are on the left. *From I-65 South,* take I-20 to I-59 East. Go 1 mile and turn right onto Route 280 East and follow above directions. *Heading north on I-65* take Exit 250 onto I-459 East. Take Exit 19 and go 3.5 miles on Route 280 West to the Zoo Exit. Turn left at the traffic light onto Lane Park Road. The gardens are on the left.

❖ Charles W. Ireland Sculpture Garden at The Birmingham Museum of Art,

2000 EIGHTH AVENUE NORTH, BIRMINGHAM, AL 35203. (205) 254-2565.
This multilevel sculpture garden is a unique space for the display of outdoor art. Welcoming you to this urban oasis is a lushly planted area shaded by towering water oaks. Beneath the oaks' central canopy is the striking installation, Blue Pools Courtyard, *by Valerie Jaudon. Sculpture by Rodin, Botero, and others lies directly ahead as you continue your way through this extraordinary space. The final focal point is the magnificent* Lithos II *waterwall by Elyn Zimmerman. Within the sculpture garden is the Red Mountain Garden Area, financed and maintained by The Red Mountain Garden Club since the garden's inception in 1956. Admission is free.*

DATES & HOURS: Year round, Tuesday through Saturday, 10 a.m. – 5 p.m.; Sunday, noon – 5 p.m.; Closed Mondays, New Year's Day, Thanksgiving & Christmas Day.

DIRECTIONS: *From I-20/I-59* take the 22nd Street Exit. Turn left onto 22nd Street, go one block, and turn right onto 8th Avenue North; go one block to 21st Street. The museum is on the corner of 21st Street and 8th Avenue North.

ARIZONA

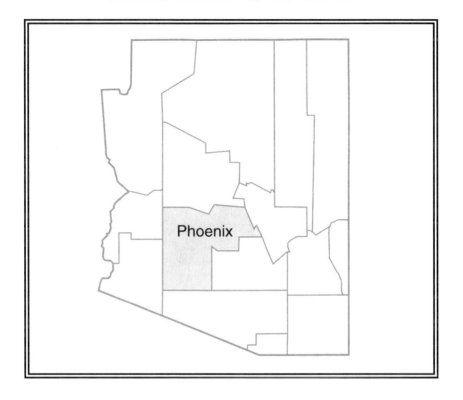

Phoenix

1999 ARIZONA OPEN DAYS

April 10 & 11: PHOENIX AREA

PHOENIX AREA:

April 10, 1999

Casa de Crozier, PHOENIX, 10 A.M. – 4 P.M.

Eclectic Garden, PHOENIX, 10 A.M. – 4 P.M.

Greg Trutza's Garden, PHOENIX, 10 A.M. – 4 P.M.

April 11, 1999

Lewis Gaarden, PARADISE VALLEY, 10 A.M. – 4 P.M.

Ventana, PARADISE VALLEY, 10 A.M. – 4 P.M.

Rancho Arroyo, PHOENIX, 10 A.M. – 4 P.M.

Greg Trutza's Garden, PHOENIX, 10 A.M. – 4 P.M.

Livia's Garden, SCOTTSDALE, 10 A.M. – 4 P.M.

Lewis Garden, PARADISE VALLEY, AZ

When working with the landscape architect, we agreed that we wanted the pool to feel like an irrigation holding pond in the desert, reminiscent of irrigation troughs found on old ranches and farms in Arizona. Surrounded by a wild garden of palo verdes, bottlebrush, creosote, and wildflowers, our garden attracts all manner of wildlife — hummingbirds, quail, lizards, an owl, and even an exuberant boy or two!

DATES & HOURS: April 11; 10 a.m. – 4 p.m.

DIRECTIONS: *Take Camelback to 32nd Street.* North on 32nd, turn east on Stanford, then north on Homestead to Harding. Turn right onto Harding.

Proceeds shared with Desert Botanical Garden.

Ventana, PARADISE VALLEY, AZ

A plethora of paths await your arrival. Meandering brick paths take you through five acres of once rocky desert to a lush green landscape made tranquil by the ever-present sound of falling water. With imagination in hand, I set out to create a variety of garden niches. From this concept evolved a koi water lily pond, herb and vegetable gardens, a citrus grove, a butterfly and hummingbird garden, cactus gardens, a rose garden combined with topiaries, a formal reflective pool, and a Santa Fe garden with wildflowers scattered throughout. Pieces of contemporary steel sculpture share space with whimsical stone animals. Additional structures, including a sunken tennis court, a greenhouse, a labyrinth garden shaded by elm trees giving harmony and peace, and a playground complete the space for family, friends, and nature.

DATES & HOURS: April 11; 10 a.m. – 4 p.m.

DIRECTIONS: *From Route 51* take the Glendale Avenue Exit onto Lincoln Drive. Take Lincoln Drive east to Tatum Boulevard (4800 E.). Take Tatum Drive north for 2.5 miles to Doubletree Road. Go east 1 mile to 56th Street. Turn south .6 mile to Mockingbird Lane eastbound (past the stop sign at Mockingbird Lane westbound). Turn left onto Mockingbird Lane and right at next street (Mummy Mountain Road). Proceed to the end of the road; the entrance to #8101 will be on the left.

Proceeds shared with Desert Botanical Garden.

Casa de Crozier, PHOENIX, AZ

Casa de Crozier, built in the 1920s, lies in the heart of the north central area. Our garden is a lush, romantic oasis with a Mediterranean ambiance, emphasized by abundant foliage. Six years ago, the property was abandoned, overgrown, and very disjointed. Using Rajah slate and pre-1900 Chicago used brick, a network of curving, winding walkways and planter beds were added. Shade-loving plants, an herb and cutting garden, two koi ponds, citrus, fig, and olive trees, and two outdoor barbeque areas add interesting and enchanting elements. Featured in December 1997s Phoenix Home and Garden, *our property is a constant source of pride and joy.*

DATES & HOURS: April 10; 10 a.m. – 4 p.m.

DIRECTIONS: *From Central Avenue in Phoenix,* go north on Central until Glendale Avenue. Approximately .3 mile north of Glendale, on Central Avenue, our home, #7215, is located on the east side of the street. The driveway entrance has low oleander hedges and cobblestone pillars. Parking is available across the street on Northview and on the nearby streets of Myrtle and Orangewood. Walk to the house via the bridle path.

Proceeds shared with Desert Botanical Garden.

Eclectic Garden, PHOENIX, AZ

Brick pathways encourage one to meander and experience the components of the Eclectic Garden. The stroll to the "Orchard" starts at the "Kitchen Garden," goes under the pergola heavy with roses and past "Cupid's Corner." As a backdrop to the pool there is the "Statue Garden" where animals and angels are posed in play. Peace and serenity are almost palpable in the "Oriental Garden," which includes a place for meditation, Chinese and Japanese accessories, and a goldfish-filled stream with a waterfall at each end. The "English Garden" is a source of color, aroma, and cuttings.

DATES & HOURS: April 10; 10 a.m. – 4 p.m.

DIRECTIONS: *The area is easily accessed from both I-17 and State 51 (Squaw Peak Freeway).* Take 7th Avenue to Butler (the traffic light between Northern and Dunlap Avenues). Go west on Butler to 11th Avenue (second street on right — stop sign in "Y" at intersection). North on 11th Avenue to first street on right (Why Worry Lane). Turn right (east) on Why Worry. The house is the first on the right.

Proceeds shared with The Arizona Humane Society.

Rancho Arroyo, PHOENIX, AZ

This one-acre virgin desert features a variety of cacti, creosote, palo verde, and ironwood trees. Some species of cacti and succulents from abroad were added by Hubert Earle, former owner and past director of Desert Botanical Garden in Phoenix. A recently restored 1925 adobe home and guesthouse are surrounded by elephant ear and blossoming desert plants. Groomed trails throughout.

DATES & HOURS: April 11; 10 a.m. – 4 p.m.

DIRECTIONS: *Glendale Avenue and 20th Street* (#6737 North 20th) reached by Squaw Peak Freeway (AZ. 51) from north and south and by Lincoln from the east and Glendale from the west. About 6 miles from downtown Phoenix and Scottsdale.

Proceeds shared with Desert Botanical Garden.

Greg Trutza's Garden, PHOENIX, AZ

With a central Phoenix location surrounded by historic neighborhoods, my garden has traditional elements woven with an experimental spirit. As a landscape architect, I have used these grounds as a constantly changing canvas of new plant selections, building materials, and design layouts to showcase our unique Phoenix lifestyle. The front yard has picket fences and English country gardens. The rear yard — with winding walks of used brick, numerous water features, and outdoor pavilions — invites escape. This garden has been featured in numerous local and national magazines.

DATES & HOURS: April 10 & 11; 10 a.m. – 4 p.m.

DIRECTIONS: *From Central Avenue in Phoenix,* go west on Thomas Road to 15th Avenue and turn right. Continue up 2 streets to West Earll Drive. (Phoenix Community College's football grandstands are on the right.) Turn left (west) onto West Earll Drive to #1523. It's the fifth house on the south side of the street with a used brick circular driveway and picket fence.

Proceeds shared with Desert Botanical Garden.

❖ Desert Botanical Garden,

1201 NORTH GALVIN PARKWAY, PHOENIX, AZ 85008. (602) 941-1217.
Surrounded by rugged red buttes, the Desert Botanical Garden's 145 acres comprise one of the most complete collections of desert flora in the world. The garden is home to more than 20,000 plants and is a renowned research facility. The exhibition "Plants and People of the Sonoran Desert" captures the life of the area's first inhabitants. Spring is an especially beautiful time to visit, when hundreds of varieties of wildflowers burst into bloom.

DATES & HOURS: October through April, daily, 8 a.m. – 8 p.m.; May through September, 7 a.m. – 8 p.m. Closed Christmas Day.

DIRECTIONS: *Take the McDowell Road* east to Galvin Parkway and turn south. The garden is on Galvin Parkway/64th Street just south of McDowell Road. The entrance is clearly marked on the east side of Galvin Parkway, and is just north of the Phoenix Zoo, in Papago Park.

Livia's Garden, SCOTTSDALE, AZ

Our landscaping echos the Mexican hacienda theme of our house. We love the intimate spaces that Chad Robert (Landscaping by André) helped us create — a "sala" (outdoor living room), ramada, pool area, and several fireplaces for cozy dining. It is a perfect setting for entertaining family and friends. The rose garden is our special pride, with a rose named for each of our grandchildren. Palms, agaves, cacti, and bougainvillea are enhanced by seasonal color, including a purple orchid tree — all complemented by a golf course view for "instant green."

DATES & HOURS: Sunday, April 11; 10 a.m. – 4 p.m.

DIRECTIONS: *Take Scottsdale Road (or Pima) to Pinnacle Peak Road* 1.6 miles east (or .4 mile west from Pima) to Pinnacle Peak Country Club Estates gatehouse (marked by a tall American flag) on the south side of the road. The gatehouse guard will direct you to our house.

Proceeds shared with Desert Botanical Garden.

❖ The Cactus Garden at The Phoenician,

6000 East Camelback Road, Scottsdale, AZ 85251. (602) 941-8200.
Up the steps, across from the main entrance to The Phoenician resort, the Cactus Garden is a small gem nestled against the tailend of Camelback Mountain. Flagstone pathways wind through a wide variety of well-marked cacti and succulents, punctuated by several pieces of bronze statuary.

DATES & HOURS: Year round, daily, dawn – dusk.

DIRECTIONS: *The entrance to The Phoenician is north off of Camelback Road,* between 56th and 64th Streets. Drive into the main entrance to the resort. The garden is directly across and up the steps.

❖ Boyce Thompson Arboretum,

37615 Highway 60, Superior, AZ 85273. (520) 689-2811.
Boyce Thompson Arboretum is Arizona's oldest and largest botanical garden, featuring plants of the world's deserts. Nestled at the base of Picketpost Mountain, the Arboretum was founded in the 1920s by mining magnate William Boyce Thompson. Encompassing 323 acres, are several miles of nature paths through the gardens — including the Cactus Garden, Taylor Family Desert Legume Garden, the Curandero Trail of medicinal plants. Ayer Lake is home to a variety of water fowl, as well as two species of endangered fish — the Desert Pupfish and Gila Topminnow. Other specialty gardens include the Wing Memorial Herb Garden, the Demonstration Garden and the Hummingbird/Butterfly Garden. There are surprises around every bend, from a streamside forest to towering trees. The Arboretum is a National Historic District and an Arizona State Park. Monthly special events are held September through May.

DATES & HOURS: Year round, daily, 8 a.m. – 5 p.m. Closed Christmas Day.

DIRECTIONS: *Take I-60/Superstition Freeway* east from Phoenix. The entrance is located on the south side of the highway, just west of Superior, Arizona.

CALIFORNIA

1999 CALIFORNIA OPEN DAYS

May 1: SAN FRANCISCO PENINSULA AREA
May 8 & 9: SAN FRANCISCO BAY AREA
May 15: LOS ANGELES AREA
October 16: SAN FRANCISCO BAY AREA

LOS ANGELES AREA: *May 15, 1999*

Merrill & Donivee Nash, ARCADIA, 10 A.M. – 4 P.M.

Watterson Garden, LOS ANGELES, 10 A.M. – 2 P.M.

Mr. & Mrs. Robert D. Volk, SAN MARINO, 10 A.M. – 4 P.M.

Clara's Rose Garden, SIERRA MADRE, 2 P.M. – 6 P.M.

Merrill & Donivee Nash, ARCADIA, CA

The home and garden is located in the Upper Rancho area of the historic Rancho Santa Anita, a neighborhood famous for its 200-to 300-year-old-oak trees. The garden is a constantly evolving entity whose backbone is several hundred roses — Austins, hybrid teas, and old English. A formal pool, tennis court, and Dumbarton Oaks-inspired summerhouse provide the framework for perennials, climbing roses, clematis, and many varieties of trees. This garden is designed with the opportunity of almost year-round outdoor living in mind, but is at its most beautiful during the roses' first bloom.

DATES & HOURS: May 15; 10 a.m. — 4 p.m.

DIRECTIONS: *From the west,* proceed east on 210 Freeway. Exit at Rosemead North/Michillinda. Proceed north on Michillinda, cross Foothill Boulevard, turn right onto Hampton Road. Continue to intersection of Hampton and Dexter Roads. The house is #1014 Hampton on the southwest corner of the intersection. *From the east,* proceed west on 210 Freeway. Exit at Baldwin Avenue. Proceed north on Baldwin, cross Foothill Boulevard, turn left at the second street/Hampton Road. Follow Hampton to the intersection of Dexter and Hampton. Follow as above.

Proceeds shared with The California Arboretum Association.

❖ The Arboretun of Los Angeles County,

301 NORTH BALDWIN AVENUE, ARCADIA, CA 91007. (626) 821-3222.
The Arboretum is a 127-acre horticultural and botanical museum jointly operated by the County of Los Angeles and the California Arboretum Foundation. The Arboretum has plants from around the world blooming in every season. It is a wildlife refuge, fish, turtles, ducks, geese, and other native and migrating birds enjoy the sanctuary of Baldwin Lake and the Tropical Forest. It is Old California with historic buildings dating from 1840 that show early California lifestyles. The Hugo Reid Adobe is a California state landmark, the century-old Queen Anne Cottage is a national landmark. The Arboretum staff has introduced more than 100 flowering plants to the California landscape and boasts tree collections from many countries.

DATES & HOURS: Year round, daily.

DIRECTIONS: *Off the 210 Freeway* exit on Baldwin Avenue. The Arboretum is in the San Gabriel Valley, freeway close to downtown Los Angeles, and right next door to Pasadena.

❖ **Descanso Gardens,** 1418 DESCANSO DRIVE, LA CAÑADA, FLINTRIDGE, CA 91012. (818) 952-4401. FAX: (818) 790-3295.

Descanso Gardens is a rare find — a woodland garden in the midst of California chapparral and Los Angeles urban sprawl. Here, in 160 acres, is an oasis of peace, beauty, and tranquility. Visitors stroll through the thirty-five-acre California Live Oak forest containing 50,000 camillia shrubs, the largest camellia forest in North America. They admire the beauty of the five-acre International Rosarium filled with more than 4,000 antique and modern roses, or relax beside flowing streams containing shimmering koi. Each spring, thousands of tulips and other bulbs highlight the month-long Spring Festival of Flowers. Descanso also contains a one-acre lilac grove where lilacs for warm winter climates originated. Visitors also enjoy viewing the California Native Plant Garden and hiking the chaparral trail surrounding the garden perimeter.

DATES & HOURS: Year round, daily (except Christmas), 9 a.m.– 4:30 p.m.

DIRECTIONS: Exit off the 210 Freeway onto Angeles Crest Highway. Turn south. Turn right on Foothill Boulevard and left on Descanso Drive.

Archibald Young / Martin — Watterson, LOS ANGELES, CA

This garden was designed by A.E. Hanson for Archibald & Editha Young in 1927 in the Andalusian style to match the George Washington Smith-designed hacienda. Originally on three acres, the present garden has been rescued by the current owners, George Martin & Jim Watterson. It includes mature palm trees; a 300-plus rose garden; a classic Mediterranean garden; a cactus garden; a seventy-year-old white wisteria arbor and colonnade; a hand-set Moorish-style rock-paved motor court; and a 7,000 square foot home and artist studio, and pool with pavilion.

DATES & HOURS: May 15; 10 a.m. – 2 p.m.

DIRECTIONS: *Exactly 1 mile south of the 210 Freeway* going south on San Rafael Avenue (from Colorado Boulevard). Take Linda Vista/San Rafael Exit from 210 Freeway east and San Rafael Exit from 210 Freeway west; or *exit Avenue 64 from #110 Pasadena Freeway* — take Avenue 64 north to La Loma Road. Make a right onto La Loma to San Rafael. Make a right onto San Rafael. The main gate is between La Loma Avenue and Hillside Terrace. Pasadena 91105.

Proceeds shared with The California Arboretum Foundation.

Mr. & Mrs. Robert D. Volk, SAN MARINO, CA

This one-acre property has a series of garden rooms, connected by a 150-foot allée. The traditional perennial border includes many Austin roses and herbaceous plants. A knot garden complements the Georgian Colonial architecture of the house, but surprises the viewer with its Mediterranean plant material. The pool garden has a purple border and a diverse collection of hydrangeas. Outside the library, there is a vivid perennial bed designed to attract hummingbirds and butterflies. These gardens were created over the last twenty years by the owners, working with landscape designers Robert Fletcher, Shirley Kerins, and Mark Bartos.

DATES & HOURS: May 15; 10 a.m. – 4 p.m.

DIRECTIONS: *From the Pasadena Freeway (110),* go to the end and proceed north on Arroyo Parkway .5 mile to California Boulevard. Turn right and proceed 1.9 miles to Allen Avenue. Turn right and proceed two blocks to Orlando Road and the entrance gates to the Huntington. Turn right and proceed .4 mile to the intersection of Avondale Road and Orlando Road. *From the Foothill Parkway (210),* take the Hill Avenue Exit, proceed south 1.1 miles to California Boulevard. Turn left and proceed .4 mile to Allen Avenue. Turn right and proceed as above.

Proceeds shared with The Huntington Botanical Gardens.

❖ The Huntington Library, Art Collections, & Botanical Gardens,

1151 OXFORD ROAD, SAN MARINO, CA 91108. (626) 405-2141.
FAX (626) 405-2260.

The former estate of railroad magnate Henry Huntington showcases over 14,000 species of plants in 150 acres of gardens. Highlights include a twelve-acre desert garden, a rose garden, Japanese garden, jungle garden, and ten acres of camellias. Art and literary treasures are displayed in historic buildings on the grounds. English tea is served in the Rose Garden Tea Room

DATES & HOURS: Tuesday through Friday, noon – 4:30 p.m.; Saturday & Sunday, 10:30 a.m. – 4:30 p.m.; Summer hours (June through August), Tuesday through Sunday, 10:30 a.m. – 4:30 p.m.

DIRECTIONS: *Located near the city of Pasadena,* approximately 12 miles northeast of downtown Los Angeles. From the downtown area, take the Pasadena Freeway (110) north until it ends and becomes Arroyo Parkway. Continue north on Arroyo for two blocks to California Boulevard, turn right and continue on California for 2 miles. Turn right at Allen Avenue and go straight for two short blocks to the Huntington gates. For recorded directions from other area freeways, call (626) 405-2274.

Clara's Rose Garden, SIERRA MADRE, CA

2,500 rose bushes surround this Georgian colonial home. Roses include Dolly Parton, Peace, Sheer Bliss, Charles de Mills, Souvenir de la Malmaison, and Paradise, which is an older rose of an opalescent lavender with a shocking pink magenta edge. There is a stunning view of the Climbing Peace roses that shower a wrought-iron gazebo poised on the edge of the lawn. Roses grow in colors from snowy white to vivid rose.

DATES & HOURS: May 15; 2 p.m. – 6 p.m.

DIRECTIONS: *Exit Baldwin Avenue* from the 210 Freeway. Go north to Foothill and turn left onto Foothill. Turn right on Baldwin. Go past Sierra Madre Boulevard and turn right onto Highland. Past Mt. Trail the house is on the right side, with big iron gates. Cross streets are Mt. Trail and Cañon. The house is #282 E. Highland Avenue.

Proceeds shared with the Arboretum of Los Angeles County.

SAN FRANCISCO BAY AREA: *May 8, 1999*

Blarry House, SAN FRANCISCO, 10 A.M. – 4 P.M.

Beatrice Bowles, SAN FRANCISCO, 10 A.M. – 2 P.M.

Genevieve di San Faustino, SAN FRANCISCO, 10 A.M. – 2 P.M.

Feibusch Garden, SAN FRANCISCO, 10 A.M. – 2 P.M.

Bill & Ilse Gaede, SAN FRANCISCO, 2 P.M. – 6 P.M.

Sonny Garcia & Tom Valva, SAN FRANCISCO, 10 A.M. – 6 P.M.

Marjory Harris, SAN FRANCISCO, 2 P.M. – 6 P.M.

Harry Stairs Garden, SAN FRANCISCO, 10 A.M. – 4 P.M.

Ted Kipping, SAN FRANCISCO, 10 A.M. – 4 P.M.

Miland-Sonenberg Garden, SAN FRANCISCO, 10 A.M. – 2 P.M.

May 9, 1999

Our Own Stuff Gallery Garden — Marcia Donahue, BERKELEY,
   10 A.M. – 4 P.M.

 Harland Hand Garden, EL CERRITO, 10 A.M. – 4 P.M.

Garden of Anderson Family, KENSINGTON,, 10 A.M. – 2 P.M.

Nor Rhyme Nor Reason, OAKLAND, 10 A.M. – 4 P.M.

Sharon & Dennis Osmond, OAKLAND, 10 A.M. – 4 P.M.

❖ The Ruth Bancroft Garden, WALNUT CREEK, 10 A.M. – 2 P.M.

SAN FRANCISCO BAY AREA: *October 16, 1999*

Maybeck Cottage — Garden of R. Raiche & David McCrory, BERKELEY, 2 P.M. – 6 P.M.

Our Own Stuff Gallery Garden — Marcia Donahue, BERKELEY, 10 A.M. – 4 P.M.

Saudade da Bahia — David Feix Garden, BERKELEY, 10 A.M. – 4 P.M.

 Harland Hand Garden, EL CERRITO, 10 A.M. – 4 P.M.

Sharon & Dennis Osmond, OAKLAND, 10 A.M. – 4 P.M.

Beatrice Bowles, SAN FRANCISCO, 10 A.M. – 2 P.M.

Miland-Sonenberg Garden, SAN FRANCISCO, 10 A.M. – 2 P.M.

Stevens Garden, SAN FRANCISCO, 10 A.M. – 2 P.M.

Garden of Torre San Gimignano, SAN FRANCISCO, 10 A.M. – 4 P.M.

 ❖ The Ruth Bancroft Garden, WALNUT CREEK, 10 A.M. – 2 P.M.

Maybeck Cottage — Garden of R. Raiche & David McCrory, BERKELEY, CA

The garden's collection encompasses nearly 3,000 types of plants from around the world. Emphasis here is on plants that thrive in Berkeley, with some pushing the cold tolerance a bit; plants with great foliage and year-round interest; and plants that tolerate deer. The plants are displayed in a heightened naturalistic style among constructions, or theaters, of found objects. Roger has developed and perfected the style he and David now market as "Planet Horticulture" under their firm of the same name.

DATES & HOURS: October 16; 2 p.m. – 6 p.m.

DIRECTIONS: *Get to Cedar Street* (4 blocks north of University Avenue or 4 blocks south of Gilman Street; both are exits from Highway 80). Proceed east, uphill, until Cedar Street ends at La Loma. Make a left onto La Loma. The second street on the right is Buena Vista at a four-way stop sign. Turn right onto Buena Vista and park along the road. Maybeck Twin Drive is the first left on Buena Vista. The first house up from the corner (not the corner house) is #1.

Our Own Stuff Gallery Garden — Marcia Donahue, BERKELEY, CA

My eighteen-year-old garden is a gallery where Mark Bulwinkle's sculpture in steel and mine in stone complement a large collection of unusual and sculptural plants. Their arrangement and interaction create an atmosphere many of my visitors and I find thrilling. Anne Raver wrote, "Art and nature are as intimately entangled here as lovers and nothing is sacred." To me, though, everything is sacred here, even sacred enough to poke fun at, and I love sharing it all with whomever is interested on Sunday afternoons.

DATES & HOURS: May 9, October 16; 10 a.m. – 4 p.m.

DIRECTIONS: *From I-80/580 by the San Francisco Bay,* take the Ashby Avenue/Berkeley exit. After 1.5 miles look for Shattuck Avenue. There are two gas stations at the intersection of Shattuck and Ashby. Cross Shattuck and turn right onto Wheeler Street. Look for the fourth house on the left, #3017 Wheeler Street. Please park on Wheeler or Emerson Streets.

Proceeds shared with The Strybing Arboretum.

Saudade da Bahia — David Feix Garden, Berkeley, CA

This garden expresses "Saudade," the Brazilian concept of sentimental longing, in this case a longing for the tropics. The illusion of being in some equatorial paradise is sustained by the misty clouds delivered on cue, bromeliads festooning the tree branches, and lush, abundant foliage. The garden is strongly influenced by the designer's travels in Brazil and Southeast Asia, and it combines Mediterranean and cool-growing subtropical plants with more than 300 species of bromeliad in a garden of line, texture, color, and contrasts.

DATES & HOURS: October 16; 10 a.m. – 4 p.m.

DIRECTIONS: *Located approximately one mile from the University Avenue Exit on I-80,* and two blocks west of the North Berkeley BART station at Sacramento Street and Delaware Street. Take the University Avenue Exit going east toward the hills/campus, cross San Pablo Avenue and turn left onto Chestnut Street. Continue for three short blocks on Chestnut, turn right onto Delaware Street and park along the road. The garden is located between Chestnut and West Street at #1294 Delaware Street.

Proceeds shared with The Ruth Bancroft Garden.

 ## Harland Hand Garden, El Cerrito, CA

Harland Hand's Garden was designed using the principals of fine art in a compositon of interesting combinations of foliage and floral color, texture, and form. Inspired by Nature and rock formations in the High Sierras, Mr. Hand sculpted concrete steps, paths, pools, and benches. The garden has been featured in various books, magazines, newspapers, and TV programs. The nearly half-acre garden is an environment to experience. Mr. Hand died in September, 1998, however his garden will continue to be open to the public by appointment. Information concerning his own book, The Composed Garden, *will also be available.*

DATES & HOURS: May 9, October 16; 10 a.m. – 4 p.m.

DIRECTIONS: *Take I-80 to El Cerrito,* Central Avenue Exit. Turn right onto Central Avenue. Turn left onto San Pablo Avenue. Turn right onto Moeser Lane. Go up the hill, to right on Shevlin Drive and proceed 1.5 blocks to the garden.

Proceeds shared with The Harland Hand Garden Trust.

Garden of Anderson Family, KENSINGTON, CA

The Anderson Family Garden is an exciting mixture of the old and new. First settled in the early 1920s by the Anderson family, the original garden surrounded a small cottage. That garden included a fruit orchard, rose gardens, and vegetable gardens. There was even a chicken coop. The current owner, Janet Anderson, grew up in this garden and later in life came back and retired here. Working with professional garden artists, the current garden design weaves together historic garden elements with an exotic collection of new plants, statuary, and urns. Don't miss the variety of bulbs, salvias, geraniums, palms, cycads, roses, bamboos, orchids, rhododendrons, and other unique plants!

DATES & HOURS: May 9; 10 a.m. – 2 p.m.

DIRECTIONS: *Kensington is in the hills between Berkeley and El Cerrito* in the East Bay. Take the Albany Exit (Buchanan Street Exit) off I-880N. This is the first exit north after Gilman Street Exit in Berkeley. Follow the road to the east past San Pablo Road up Marin Avenue. Take Marin Avenue to the Marin Circle (about 2 miles). Go around the circle and then up The Arlington. Follow The Arlington up to the town of Kensington. Just past the town grocery, make a "U"-turn and go back down about one-half block. Make the first right on Ardmore Road. Take Ardmore down about .25 mile and then park. Beverly Street is a small cul-de-sac on the right (it looks like a driveway and is easy to miss). Walk down to the garden from Ardmore Road.

❖ The Blake Garden of the University of California,

70 RINCON ROAD, KENSINGTON, CA 94707. (510) 524-2449.

This ten and one-half-acre garden was given to the University in the early 1960s by the Blake family. The garden was established when the house was designed and built in the early 1920s. It has a large display of plants ranging from drought-tolerant to more moisture-loving plants from places such as Asia. The garden is divided into the formal area, the drought-tolerant section, the Australian Hollow, the cut-flower section, and the redwood canyon.

DATES & HOURS: Year round, Monday through Friday, 8 a.m. – 4:30 p.m.. Closed on University holidays.

DIRECTIONS: *From I-80,* take the Buchanan Street off-ramp east to Buchanan Street. Follow Buchanan Street to a traffic circle. Take the third exit off of the circle, for Arlington Avenue. Travel 1.8 miles to Rincon Road on the left. Blake House is at 70 Rincon Road.

Nor Rhyme Nor Reason, OAKLAND, CA

Northern California is blessed with a climate in which an incredible diversity of plants can be grown. This one-acre garden exploits this diversity and replicates the jumble that experimenting with many species can create. Willy-nilly borrowing of many garden styles and irreverent mixtures of them bring delight.

DATES & HOURS: May 9; 10 a.m. – 4 p.m.

DIRECTIONS: *Turn off of I-580* at Golf Links Road and follow it for 2 miles into the hills. Turn right onto Caloden, which becomes Malcolm after one block, and turn left onto Ettrick Street. The address is #11205 Ettrick Street.

Sharon & Dennis Osmond, OAKLAND, CA

Mine is an intensively planted garden which relies heavily on foliage color and texture for year-round interest. It is small, intimate, and very personal. There are a number of mirrors in the garden that draw the garden visitor or viewer into the garden and make them a participant. There are also touches of what is simply preposterous or merely silly. Come here and enjoy yourself!

DATES & HOURS: May 9, October 16; 10 a.m. – 4 p.m.

DIRECTIONS: *Located in* the Rockridge area of Oakland, just two and one-half blocks from the Rockridge BART station, our house is at #5548 Lawton Avenue, and is easily reached by public transportation. Take College Avenue to Lawton. Turn east onto Lawton.

❖ Dunsmuir House & Gardens Historic Estate,

2960 PERALTA OAKS COURT, OAKLAND, CA 94605. (510) 615-5555.
John McLaren, designer of Golden Gate Park in San Francisco, is said to have assisted in designing the gardens at the Dunsmuir Estate for the Hellman family, who owned the estate from 1906 until the late 1950s. Today, the meadows and gardens are still graced with a wide variety of trees, including Camperdown elms, bunya-bunya, and hornbeam, which surround the turn-of-the-century Colonial Revival mansion.

DATES & HOURS: February through October, Tuesday through Friday, 10 a.m. – 4 p.m. Also open the first and third Sunday, May through September.

DIRECTIONS: *Located off I-580 East at the 106th Avenue exit.* Make three quick left turns to cross under the freeway, then turn right onto Peralta Oaks Drive. Follow signs to Dunsmuir. *From I-580 West,* exit at Foothill/MacArthur Boulevard and veer to the right onto Foothill Boulevard. Turn right onto 106th Avenue and right again onto Peralta Oaks Drive. Follow signs to Dunsmuir.

❖ Kaiser Center Roof Garden,

300 LAKESIDE DRIVE, OAKLAND, CA 94612. (510) 271-6197.

The Kaiser Center Roof Garden is a three and one-half-acre park located four floors above street level on top of the Kaiser Center Garage. The garden, designed by the San Francisco firm of Osmundson and Staley, was installed in 1960. Despite a busy urban setting, boundary hedges, winding paths, bermed plantings, and a reflecting pond give the garden a quiet, oasis-like quality. A large variety of specimen trees, shrubs, perennials, and annuals provide year-round horticultural interest.

DATES & HOURS: Year round, Monday through Friday, 7 a.m. − 7 p.m.

DIRECTIONS: *From San Francisco,* take the Bay Bridge to I-580 South (toward Hayward). One mile past the bridge, take the Harrison Street exit and turn right onto Harrison Street. Go straight through three traffic lights. Lake Merritt is on your left and the Kaiser Building is ahead to the right. Continue straight on Harrison and get into the right lane. Turn right onto 20th Street and make an immediate right into the parking garage. There is also street parking in the neighborhood. Take the garage elevator to Roof Garden level.

Blarry House, SAN FRANCISCO, CA

Blarry House is a continuing experiment with low-maintenance natives and exotics. Of special interest are the Proteaceae. Our small garden is on multilevels with views of the city and the San Francisco Bay. A pond (also known as the raccoon bath and smorgasbord) sits aside the requisite Gunnera. A country feel lends contrast to the reality of being in the middle of the city. Our dining room looks out onto a micro-farm of five chickens. Raccoons, skunks, hummingbirds, opossum and a variety of wild birds add to our rural fantasy.

DATES & HOURS: May 8; 10 a.m. − 4 p.m.

DIRECTIONS: *From Route 101,* take the Army/Cesar Chavez exit and go west on Cesar Chavez to Noe Street, travelling about ten blocks. Turn left onto Noe Street, which dead ends at Laidley. We are three houses to the left of the intersection of Laidley and Noe. The house is dark green. *From northbound I-280,* follow signs to the Bay Bridge but exit at San Jose Avenue. After the first traffic light on San Jose, turn left onto Dolores and immediately left onto 30th Street. Turn left onto Noe Street and follow directions from above. Please park along the street.

Proceeds shared with The Friends of the Urban Forest.

Beatrice Bowles, SAN FRANCISCO, CA

Harmony Hill is a secret garden in the heart of the city on historic Russian Hill. There is a wild woodland feeling, with a special emphasis on fragrant plants. Paths and stone stairs meander up steep slopes of rhododendron, daphne, azaleas, and ferns. Three generations have lived and gardened in this rustic arts-and-crafts-style retreat. Harmony Hill has been featured in Rosemary Verey's Secret Gardens *and* Gardens of San Francisco.

DATES & HOURS: May 8, October 16; 10 a.m. – 2 p.m.

DIRECTIONS: *From the East,* turn right off of California Street (corner of Grace Cathedral and Huntington Park) onto Taylor Street. Go six blocks to the corner of Taylor and Broadway. It is the first stairway north of Broadway on the west side with a green iron railing, #1629. Please park on the road or in the public lot by Grace Cathedral.

Genevieve di San Faustino, SAN FRANCISCO, CA

Our garden follows no particular form but is quite simply eclectic Mediterranean with independent spirit! We enjoy many experiments and have had many successes. With a lot of hard work and a bit of luck we forever bloom!

DATES & HOURS: May 8; 10 a.m. – 2 p.m.

DIRECTIONS: *Located in the Pacific Heights district* of San Francisco on Pierce Street between Broadway and Pacific Avenues. Please park along the street.

Feibusch Garden, SAN FRANCISCO, CA

Dennis Shaw solved the problem of my very steep hillside by terracing it with railroad ties. I am partial to succulents and there are many species of aloes, aeoniums, agaves, echeverias, ice plants and sedums. Combining these with grasses, phormiums, watsonias, grevilleas, and acacias make an interesting tapestry of textures and color. A bridge connects the garden to my house, which provides easy access. The garden is bold and strong, but provides a lovely sense of tranquility.

DATES & HOURS: May 8; 10 a.m. – 2 p.m.

DIRECTIONS: *Going south on I-280,* take the Monterey Boulevard exit and continue west on Monterey to Foerster. Turn right onto Foerster and head uphill to Los Palmos and continue to house #544 on the right. Please park along the street.

Bill & Ilse Gaede, SAN FRANCISCO, CA

Views of the downtown San Francisco skyline are framed by the hillside setting of this urban garden designed by Harland Hand. Pathways wander through beds planted with the wide variety of plants afforded by the mild year-round San Francisco climate. Plantings include orchids, succulents, cacti, rhododendrons, camellias, and ground covers. Incorporated into the design is a small man-made pool fed by a trickling waterfall cascading from one of the numerous rock formations located throughout the garden.

DATES & HOURS: May 8; 2 p.m. – 6 p.m.

DIRECTIONS: *From the Ferry Terminal Building* in downtown San Francisco, go up Market Street approximately 2.7 miles to Church Street. Turn left onto Church Street and go approximately .7 miles to 21st Street. Go right up the hill on 21st Street. The garden is at #3660 21st Street in the first block on the right hand side, approximately two-thirds of the way up the block.

Sonny Garcia & Tom Valva, SAN FRANCISCO, CA

Our garden is small but filled with many rare and unusual plants. It was a challenge to incorporate many good design ideas into such a small space. The emphasis in our garden is on foliage. Bold, textured, colored, and variegated plants are collected from all over the country. Intricate juxtapositions and dramatic combinations of colorful foliage keep the garden interesting year round. We are very honored to have our garden featured in books, magazines, and television, including "The Victory Garden" on PBS, Rosemary Verey's Secret Gardens, *and Sir Roy Strong's* Successful Small Gardens.

DATES & HOURS: May 8, October 16; 10 a.m. – 6 p.m.

DIRECTIONS: *From the north,* take Route 101 South to I-280 South. Take the Monterey Boulevard exit. Go .5 miles to Foerster Avenue. Turn left onto Foerster and right onto Flood Avenue. *From the south*, take Highway 280 North to the Ocean Avenue exit. Turn left onto Geneva Avenue and stay in the right lane. Turn left onto Ocean Avenue and immediately right onto Phelan Avenue. Follow Phelan Avenue around San Francisco City College. Turn left onto Gennessee and right onto Flood. Look for house #423.

Proceeds shared with The Strybing Arboretum.

Marjory Harris, SAN FRANCISCO, CA

In 1988 Harland Hand designed and built my garden on Mt. Davidson, the city's highest hill. The pie-shaped yard fans out to a width of sixty feet at the top, where there is a panoramic view of San Bruno Mountain and the Bay. The garden has seven levels, rising thirty feet over a length of eighty feet. Wildlife visit the three ponds and waterfall. Microclimates include bogs and scree, a shady fern walk, and a secret woodland garden. Around 2,000 mostly small plants fill cracks, crevices, and mounds, including many echeverias, salvias, brugmansias, cupheas, flowering maples, clematis, and thymes. Tom Chakas designed the rebar trees and vine holders. Daniel Arcos created the hummingbird mosaic.

DATES & HOURS: May 8; 2 p.m. – 6 p.m.

DIRECTIONS: *From Route 101* take I-280 (Daly City branch); take Monterey Boulevard exit; go down Monterey to Foerster; turn right onto Foerster; turn left onto Los Palmos. The house is #494. *From 19th Avenue:* Take 19th to Sloat Boulevard; turn east onto Sloat; left onto Portola; right onto Santa Clara (second right); take left fork onto Yerba Buena; turn left onto Hazelwood (a 90-degree turn, the sign is visible after you turn); take left fork onto Los Palmos. *From Market Street* head in the direction of Twin Peaks. Market Street becomes Portola Drive. After crossing the intersection of Woodside & O'Shaughnessy, Tower Market will be on the left (red awning). Pass Tower and turn left onto Fowler. Turn right onto Teresita; follow Teresita to Los Palmos, then turn right on Los Palmos to #494.

Proceeds shared with The Harland Hand Garden Trust.

Harry Stairs Garden, SAN FRANCISCO, CA

My house and garden sits on a little-known stairway in a part of town once known as Fairmount Heights, now it is commonly known as Noe Valley. The size of the lot is roughly one-half acre. Having the good fortune to live on such a large open property, I am able to create not one, but several different garden environments. My garden consists of four sections, all connected with bending pathways of various stepping stones. The upper section is the most formal, with a slate walkway and sitting areas around a lawn and trellises of climbing star jasmine and honeysuckle. The lower section has a slate sitting area surrounded by a variety of grasses. To the left of the grass area is a kidney-shaped rose garden and deck with chairs and reclining benches. The most spectacular part of the yard is the backdrop of Noe Valley, the San Francisco skyline, the Bay Bridge, and the East Bay hills framed by towering eucalyptus and cyprus trees. Gardening is my passion; the joy and happiness it brings me is shared with those who walk the stairs and take time out to stop and look.

DATES & HOURS: May 8; 10 a.m. – 4 p.m.

DIRECTIONS: *Take Noe Street* to the end (Laidley Street). Harry Street steps are directly across the intersection. Park and walk up.

Ted Kipping, SAN FRANCISCO, CA

This small garden is tucked behind a turn-of-the-century farmhouse and is filled to the brim with unusual plants. It is divided into various levels each featuring a different theme, including a meadow and a bog. The property is adjacent to a city park which has a wide variety of palms and other plants that overflow from the original garden.

DATES & HOURS: May 8; 10 a.m. – 4 p.m.

DIRECTIONS: *Going south on I-280,* take the Monterey Boulevard Exitand continue west on Monterey to Congo Street. Turn right onto Congo and then right onto Joost. Number 257 is on the right side. Please park along the street.

Miland – Sonenberg Garden, SAN FRANCISCO, CA

In what was a solid concrete patio, nearly surrounded by three-story residential buildings, this thirty-by-thirty-foot garden is an oasis of dense, highly diverse foliage and flowering plants. Once the original concrete was removed, the owners put back irregularly shaped pieces in a circle within the rectangle of the garden's perimeter, thus creating a mandala form. Full of art, real and kitsch, the garden is centered on a sculptural fountain adorned with skull-shaped rocks. The garden's verticality is emphasized by dozens of flowering vines that climb the neighboring walls, as well as a treehouse-like porch worked into the vine-covered stairwell. Cantilevered out from the porch floor is a massive, bronze hand of Buddha.

DATES & HOURS: May 8, October 16; 10 a.m. – 2 p.m.

DIRECTIONS: *Located in San Francisco's sunny Mission District,* the garden is at the eastern edge of the Noe Valley neighborhood. Fair Oaks is a small street running parallel to and between Dolores and Guererro, two north-south arterials. Number 117 is just off the intersection of 22nd Street and Fair Oaks. *From the Bay Bridge or Route 101,* take the Duboce Street off-ramp to Guererro. Turn left and go south to 22nd Street. Turn right and look for parking.

Proceeds shared with The Strybing Arboretum.

Stevens Garden, SAN FRANCISCO, CA

This is a collector's garden — a small city one at that — built on a rocky hillside site. There is really no theme to it, or plan. I collect alpines that will survive a damp location and many tree species, some dwarf, some bonsai and many in pots. Paths are river stones, thus there is no wheelchair accessibility.

DATES & HOURS: October 16; 10 a.m. – 2 p.m.

DIRECTIONS: *Just a few blocks from the Strybing Arboretum.* From the arboretum, go south on Ninth Avenue to Parnassus. Make a left (east) past the University of California Medical Center. The first right after the Medical Center is Willard. Make a right onto Willard and proceed up a steep hill. At the top of the hill, go right onto Belmont. At the top, make a left onto Edgewood. We are #183.

Garden of Torre San Gimignano, San Francisco, CA

The Torre, designed by architects Jeremy Kotas, Skip Shaffer, and Christina Francavillese, was built in 1990 to be an integral part of its terraced garden. It is located on the primary street of the historic Fairmount Tract, laid out in 1864 to be the city's first suburb for country homes. Situated on the north-facing slope of Miguel Hill, the site provides a panoramic view of the skyline of downtown San Francisco. As the Torre is on the sheltered, leeward side of the city's hilly spine, the setting provides a haven for subtropical plants. After entering the portal from Laidley Street, one mounts three flights of stairs through a rock garden to enter the foyer. One continues up a helical stairway through the atrium with a side garden to the living room and dining room to the back garden with a serpentine stairway leading to the top patio terrace, with an unobstructed view of downtown. The garden's informal layout is based on a design created by Roger Scharmer but modified and executed by the owners of the Torre —William Gregory and Richard L. Ingraham.

DATES & HOURS: October 16; 10 a.m. – 4 p.m.

DIRECTIONS: *Travel south on Market Street.* Turn left onto Noe Street and left onto Laidley Street. Or take I-280 into the city, exiting onto San Jose. Proceed to 30th Street and turn left. Proceed up 30th Street to Noe Street. Turn left up the final block of Noe and turn left onto Laidley Street. The Torre's address is #140 Laidley Street. Please park along the street.

❖ The Japanese Tea Garden,

Golden Gate Park, San Francisco, CA 94117. (415) 831-2700.
The Japanese Tea Garden in Golden Gate Park, the oldest public Japanese garden in the United States, dates from 1894. Created for the California Mid-Winter Exposition to represent a Japanese village, the five-acre stroll garden includes a drum bridge, a teahouse, a pagoda, a gift shop, two gates built for the 1915 Panama Pacific Exposition, and a Temple Belfry Gate (or Shoronomon). The garden also has a notable collection of beautiful stone lanterns and a large bronze Buddha cast in 1790.

DATES & HOURS: April through October, daily, 9 a.m. – 5:30 p.m.; November through March, daily, 8:30 a.m. – 5 p.m.

DIRECTIONS: Located in the center of Golden Gate Park near the DeYoung Museum and Academy of Sciences on Hagiwara Drive.

❖ The Strybing Arboretum and Botanical Gardens,

9TH AVENUE AND LINCOLN WAY, SAN FRANCISCO, CA 94122. (415) 661-1316. *The Strybing Arboretum and Botanical Gardens sprawl over fifty-five acres and features plants from all over the world. 7,000 species hailing from Chile, Australia, Cape Province, and New Zealand show their colors in the Primitive Plant Garden, the Moon-Viewing Garden, and the Garden of Fragrance. You can stroll on your own or take a free guided tour offered by the Strybing Arboretum Society. If you are still not sated, stop by the Helen Crocker Russell Library of Horticulture, a free reference library, open daily 10 a.m. – 4 p.m.(except major holidays).*

DATES & HOURS: Monday through Friday, 8 a.m.– 4:30 p.m.; Weekends and holidays 10 a.m.– 5 p.m. Free Admission (donation encouraged).

DIRECTIONS: *Located in Golden Gate Park,* at the corner of Ninth Avenue and Lincoln Way.

 ## ❖ The Ruth Bancroft Garden,

P.O. BOX 30845, WALNUT CREEK, CA 94598. (925) 210-9663. *The Ruth Bancroft Garden rises above the status of a collection to an exceptional demonstration of the art of garden design. Working primarily with the dramatic forms of her beloved succulents, Mrs. Bancroft has created bold and varied compositions in which the colors, textures, and patterns of foliage provide a setting for the sparkle of floral color.*

DATES & HOURS: Open for Directory visitors on May 8, October 16; 10 a.m.– 2 p.m. Otherwise, open by appointment only.

DIRECTIONS: *Just north of Highway 24,* exit I-680 on Ygnacio Valley Road. Follow Ygnacio Valley Road 1.5 miles to Bancroft Road. Turn left, pass Stratton. At the end of wooden fence turn right into #1500 Bancroft Road.

SAN FRANCISCO PENINSULA AREA: *May 1, 1999*

Gene & Chuck Pratt, ATHERTON, 10 A.M. − 2 P.M.

Joan & Mo Sanders, ATHERTON, 10 A.M. − 2 P.M.

The Tuffli Garden, ATHERTON, 2 P.M. − 6 P.M.

Debby & Rob Ruskin, PALO ALTO, 10 A.M. − 2 P.M.

Gene & Chuck Pratt, ATHERTON, CA

We have been personalizing our one-acre property since moving in over ten years ago. Our passion for aesthetics is evident in the abundance of artistic detail that enhances the stucco walls, stone terrace, massive California live oaks, coast redwoods, arbors, and water features found throughout our garden. We are constantly evaluating, upgrading, and refining our inviting and comfortable garden rooms.

DATES & HOURS: May 1; 10 a.m. – 2 p.m.

DIRECTIONS: *From Highway 101,* take the Marsh Road/Atherton Exit heading west. Marsh Road ends at Middlefield Road. Turn left onto Middlefield Road and continue a few blocks to an elementary school on the corner of Encinal. Turn right onto Encinal and proceed to #166. Please note that parking is prohibited on the south side of the street.

Joan & Mo Sanders, ATHERTON, CA

A one-acre garden that is enhanced with more than 200 rose bushes, citrus plants, and herbs. Redwood trees, gleditsia, and birch predominate, but others include fruit trees and Japanese maples. A small formal garden with arches displays various clematis and climbing roses. Look for an Archie Held waterfall sculpture near the pergola in the rear garden. The garden is part of a subdivision of the old Flood summer estate.

DATES & HOURS: May 1; 10 a.m. – 2 p.m.

DIRECTIONS: *Take Highway 101* to the Marsh Road Exit. Go west on Marsh to its end and turn left onto Middlefield Road and left again onto James. Take the second right off James and look for 156 Hawthorn.

The Tuffli Garden, ATHERTON, CA

As second generation owners of this garden we are midway through an exciting multi-year redesign necessitated by the loss of the 400-year-old oak tree which had canopied the entire back of our property. We retained Jonathan Plant, who designed a garden which is in the tradition of the English plantsman's garden, incorporating formal elements in a rich tapestry of plant collections. Ours is a garden for all seasons with camellias, cherries, magnolias, spring bulbs, roses, hydrangeas, perennials, and dramatic autumn color.

DATES & HOURS: May 1; 2 p.m. – 6 p.m.

DIRECTIONS: *Take Route 101 to Woodside Road/Route 84.* Go west to El Camino Real (or take Route 280 to Woodside Road/Route 84 and go east to El Camino Real). Take El Camino Real south for .7 mile. Turn right and go west on Selby Lane, which is the first right turn in Atherton. Our cul-de-sac, also called Selby Lane, is the third cul-de-sac on the right after Austin Avenue (at a stop sign). It is .7 mile from El Camino Real. Please park along the street.

❖ Allied Arts Guild,

75 ARBOR ROAD AT CAMBRIDGE, MENLO PARK, CA 94025. (650) 322-2405.
One of the San Francisco Peninsula's most enduring institutions is Allied Arts Guild with its shops and arts and craft studios nestled in a California landmark setting of mission-style buildings and Spanish gardens. The gardens, reminiscent of those of Granada, provide an oasis of graciousness and serenity to those who come to shop, lunch, or simply bathe in their charm. The Guild benefits Packard Children's Hospital.

DATES & HOURS: Year round, Monday through Saturday, 10 a.m. – 5 p.m.

DIRECTIONS: *Take Highway 101* to University Avenue, turnoff in Palo Alto and drive west on University Avenue to El Camino Real. Travel north for 1 mile to Menlo Park's Cambridge Avenue. Turn west onto Cambridge and follow to the end which is the Allied Arts Guild parking lot.

Debby & Rob Ruskin, PALO ALTO, CA

This active family garden was designed by the owner, a lover of plants, wildlife, cozy spaces, water, stone, and peaceful relaxation. The living areas include a redwood deck and gazebo, a brick patio surrounding a lap pool, gravel paths, and raised rock beds nestled into lush greenery punctuated with roses, daylilies, and other perennials.

DATES & HOURS: May 1; 10 a.m. – 2 p.m.

DIRECTIONS: *From Highway 101,* take the Embarcadero West/Stanford Exit and proceed to Walnut Drive (after a traffic light at Louis Road). Turn right onto Walnut and right again onto Walter Hays. Continue around the "U" to #174 Walter Hays.

❖ The Elizabeth F. Gamble Garden Center,

1431 WAVERLEY STREET, PALO ALTO, CA 94301. (650) 329-1356.
This two-acre urban garden, located 40 miles south of San Francisco, surrounds a turn-of the-century house and carriage house. The formal gardens have been restored from the original plans. The working gardens include experimental demonstrations and displays.

DATES & HOURS: Year round, daily, dawn – dusk.

DIRECTIONS: *From Route 101,* exit on Embarcadero West. Turn left onto Waverley Street. The parking lot is on the left. *From U.S. 280,* exit on Page Mill Road East, cross El Camino and continue on Oregon Expressway. Turn left onto Waverley Street. The house is on the corner of Waverley and Churchill. The parking lot is north of the house.

❖ Emma Prusch Farm Park,

647 SOUTH KING ROAD, SAN JOSE, CA 95116. (408) 926-5555.

Emma Prusch Farm Park offers visitors opportunities for recreation and to learn about San Jose's agricultural past. The park's forty-seven acres feature San Jose's largest barn; more than 100 community and school garden plots; acres of open grass perfect for picnicking, kite flying, games, and relaxing; a rare fruit orchard featuring a strawberry tree, wild pear tree, and a raisin tree; a grove of international trees; close encounters with farm animals – everything from sheep, pigs, steer, ducks, chickens, geese, and rabbits; and old farm equipment displays. In addition, there are school tours, environmental education classes, and summer camps, as well as year-round special events.

DATES & HOURS: Year round, daily, 8:30 a.m. – dusk.

DIRECTIONS: *From Highway 101,* take the Story Road East Exit. Turn left at King Road and left at the next traffic light into the driveway. *From Route 680,* take the King Road Exit and turn left onto King Road. Proceed one-half block and turn right into the driveway. *From Route 280,* take the King Road Exit and turn right. Proceed to the next traffic light and turn right into the driveway.

❖ Filoli, CANADA ROAD, WOODSIDE, CA 94062. (650) 364-8300 EXT. 507.

Filoli is a 654-acre estate. It is a registered State Historical Landmark and is listed on the National Register of Historic Places. Sixteen acres of formal gardens are divided into a number of separate garden rooms.

DATES & HOURS: Mid-February through October, Tuesdays through Saturdays, 10 a.m. – 2 p.m. Please call for docent-led tours every Tuesday and Wednesday.

DIRECTIONS: *Located approximately 25 miles south of San Francisco off Highway 280.* Edgewood Road Exit.

COLORADO

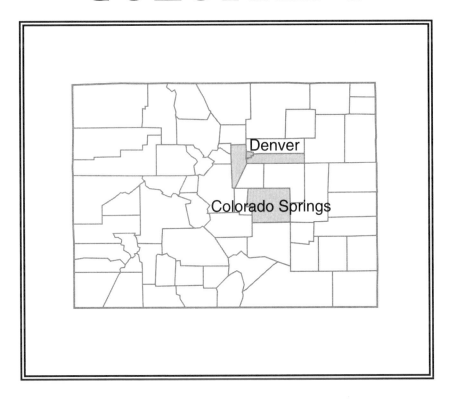

1999 COLORADO OPEN DAYS

July 10 & 18: DENVER AREA
July 17: COLORADO SPRINGS AREA

COLORADO SPRINGS AREA: *July 17, 1999*

A Discovery Hypothesis, COLORADO SPRINGS, 10 A.M. – 4 P.M.

tawto'ma Gardens, COLORADO SPRINGS, 10 A.M. – 2 P.M.

The Henson's Faux Rock & Waterfall Habitat Room, MANITOU SPRINGS,
     10 A.M – 4 P.M.

A Discovery Hypothesis, COLORADO SPRINGS, CO

This is not an orderly, groomed garden. It has no lawn, no vantage point where you can see the whole area. Its paths and thickets require exploration, so that every few steps reveal new surprises. It's a sheltering habitat for deer, raccoons, skunks, squirrels, birds, snakes, as well as humans — a habitat for both native and experimental plants — a memory habitat for artistic wood, special rocks, and craft items that the owners have gathered in their travels. And it provides settings for Gernot's sculptures and waterscapes. It's a garden for creative activity, reflective contemplation, and serene repose.

DATES & HOURS: July 17; 10 a.m. – 4 p.m.

DIRECTIONS: *Find West Colorado Avenue.* Go west on Colorado Avenue, almost to Manitou Springs. At Columbia Road (the one after 36th), turn right (north) and go three blocks to the arterial stop at Holly Street. Turn right (east) onto Holly. The very first left is Dahlia Street. Turn left (north) onto Dahlia and go one-half block to #418 Dahlia Street.

Proceeds shared with The Horticultural Art Society of Colorado Springs.

tawto'ma Gardens, COLORADO SPRINGS, CO

The tawto'ma gardens are on the west side of Colorado Springs overlooking the Garden of the Gods National Park at the foot of famous Pike's Peak. The gardens surround a home primarily built of the pink sandstone found in the Garden of the Gods. The gardens contain an extensive variety of plant materials, both perennial and annual varieties, with an abundance of roses of all types. The designs include a butterfly garden, cutting garden, herb garden, shaded woodland garden, water features and a rose court. An outstanding horticultural display in a breathtaking natural setting!

DATES & HOURS: July 17; 10 a.m. – 2 p.m.

DIRECTIONS: *From I-25* exit Fillmore westbound. Turn north onto Mesa Road, pass the xeriscape demonstration garden at the water treatment facility and pass the Garden of the Gods Club on the left. The fourth left past the water treatment facility, before the overlook to the park, is the pink stone entrance, approximately .5 mile from Fillmore. *From 30th Street at the Garden of the Gods Visitor Center* travel north several hundred yards, turn right at Mesa Road and proceed up hill to the first gate on the right, #3450 Mesa Road.

❖ Cheyenne Mountain Zoo, 4250 CHEYENNE MOUNTAIN ZOO ROAD, COLORADO SPRINGS, CO 80906. (719) 633-9925.

The Cheyenne Mountain Zoo is located at 7,000 feet on the side of Cheyenne Mountain. The horticultural efforts are focused on native plants, theme gardens, and naturalized exhibits. Two favorite gardens are the Hummingbird Garden and the Butterfly Garden. The Hummingbird Garden was featured in a book, Hummingbird Gardens, *and supplies many opportunities to see these wonders up close. In Asian Highlands, Siberian tigers are featured in a large naturalistic exhibit. The area is also home to some unusual trees and shrubs. Primate World, with a large outdoor gorilla exhibit, has been used in an experimental prescribed fire. Lion's Lair was landscaped using a combination of grasses and perennials to give the feeling of the open savanna. Your trip to the zoo will feel like a trip to the Great Rocky Mountains.*

DATES & HOURS: Year round, daily, 9 a.m. – 5 p.m.

DIRECTIONS: *From I-25,* take Exit 138 and drive west for 2.8 miles to the Broadmoor Hotel. Turn right at the hotel and follow signs from there.

❖ The Colorado Springs Xeriscape Demonstration Garden, 2855 MESA ROAD, COLORADO SPRINGS, CO 80904. (718) 448-4651. FAX (718) 448-4599.

The Xeriscape Demonstration Garden was designed in response to the need to conserve water. Since one-half of all water used annually is applied to lawns and gardens, planting with water conservation in mind was the goal. We are a demonstration garden where all members of the community can come to see that xeriscape can be a beautiful, low-water use addition to their yards. The view from the garden is also quite an attraction as we overlook the Garden of the Gods.

DATES & HOURS: Year round, daily, 10 a.m. – 4 p.m.

DIRECTIONS: *Take Interstate 25* to Fillmore Exit. Go west, pass Coronado High School, and proceed to the next traffic light. This is Mesa Road. Turn right onto Mesa Road and go about .5 mile to the entrance.

❖ Garden of the Gods Visitor Center,

1805 NORTH 30TH STREET, COLORADO SPRINGS, CO 80904. (719) 634-6666. *"Where the Garden Comes Alive." The red rocks of Garden of the Gods have served as a landmark to travelers for over 3,000 years. Imagine towering sandstone rock formations against a backdrop of snow-capped Pikes Peak and brilliant blue skies. That's the view from the beautiful Garden of the Gods Visitors Center. The Garden of the Gods is a unique biological melting pot where several life zones converge. The grasslands of the Great Plains meet the pinyon-juniper woodlands characteristic of the American Southwest, and merge with the mountain forests skirting 14,100-foot Pikes Peak. Around the Visitor Center can be found the various native gardens that naturally blend with this park that has been designated as a National Natural Landmark.*

DATES & HOURS: June 1 – August 31, daily, 8 a.m. – 8 p.m.; September 1 – May 31, daily, 9 a.m. – 5 p.m.

DIRECTIONS: *From Denver go south on I-25.* Take Exit 146 onto Garden of the Gods Road. Turn left onto 30th Street and go .25 mile. The Visitor Center will be on your left.

❖ Starsmore Hummingbird Garden, 2120 SOUTH CHEYENNE

CAÑON ROAD, COLORADO SPRINGS, CO 80906. (719) 578-6146. *The garden at the Starsmore Discovery Center, which is the visitor's center for North Cheyenne Cañon Park, has been turned into a hummingbird garden by the Friends of Cheyenne Cañon volunteers. The original plantings of shrubs in several garden beds at the front of the center are gradually being filled in with flowering perennials, which attract hummingbirds and are native to the area. The Cañon is a natural magnet for Broadtail and Rufous Hummingbirds every summer.*

DATES & HOURS: June through August, daily, 9 a.m. – 5 p.m.

DIRECTIONS: *Exit I-25 at Exit 140B (South Tejon Exit)* and turn right on Tejon. Tejon becomes Cheyenne Boulevard. Travel 3 miles west on Cheyenne Boulevard. Follow "Seven Falls" signs and "Starsmore Discovery" signs to South Cheyenne Cañon Road. Park in lot.

The Henson's Faux Rock & Waterfall Habitat Room,
MANITOU SPRINGS, CO

Mary Henson, floral designer, and George Henson, sculptor/painter, have created a three-story faux rock grotto complete with waterfall and Mayan ruins that form a small rainforest room. At mid-level is a balcony that serves as their dining room, jutting out into this warm, humid habitat. The twenty-six foot waterfall tumbles into a small pool surrounded by bamboo, giant elephant ear, angel's trumpet, schefflera, plumeria, and other tropical flora. The rock ledges are home to many varieties of orchids and bromeliads.

DATES & HOURS: July 17; 10 a.m. – 4 p.m.

DIRECTIONS: *Take Highway 24 West* to the first Manitou exit. Turn right immediately onto Garden of the Gods Place (which dead ends into El Paso Boulevard). Turn left on El Paso Boulevard, go one block and turn right onto Rockledge Lane. Go one block to #328 which is a Mexican-style dwelling with a two-story plant room adjacent to the driveway.

Proceeds shared with The Manitou Springs Garden Club.

DENVER AREA:

July 10, 1999

Hope & Edward Connors Garden, CHERRY HILLS VILLAGE, 10 A.M. – 2 P.M.

The City Garden of Clari & Bob Davis, DENVER, 10 A.M. – 2 P.M.

The Connor Garden, DENVER, 10 A.M. – 4 P.M.

The Leonard Leonard Office Gardens, DENVER, 10 A.M. – 4 P.M.

Warren Garden, DENVER, 10 A.M. – 4 P.M.

Weiss' Garden, DENVER, 10 A.M. – 4 P.M.

Weckbaugh, ENGLEWOOD, 10 A.M. - 2 P.M.

Alpenridge, LITTLETON, 10 A.M. – 2 P.M.

July 18, 1999

Stylers' Garden, GREENWOOD VILLAGE, 10 A.M. – 2 P.M.

The Brunk Gardens, GREENWOOD VILLAGE, 10 A.M. – 2 P.M.

Hope & Edward Connors Garden,

CHERRY HILLS VILLAGE, CO

Started in 1970 on a former winter wheat field, herb, perennial, water, cutting, and rock gardens are all maintained by the owner. This garden is largely an experiment in what will grow in semi-arid Arapahoe County — much does.

DATES & HOURS: July 10; 10 a.m. – 2 p.m.

DIRECTIONS: *We are just west of Holly Street,* .5 mile south of Holly Street and .5 mile north of Belleview Avenue. Our address is #4 Cantitoe Lane.

The City Garden of Clari & Bob Davis, DENVER, CO

Small garden — front courtyard containing shade material. Driveway with our perennials. Perennial border with shade material bordering four-foot fence. Side and back garden also containing a large variety of shade plants. Garden is thirty-six years old. Designed and maintained by the owners.

DATES & HOURS: July 10; 10 a.m. – 2 p.m.

DIRECTIONS: *Colorado or University Boulevard –* 6th Avenue east to Hudson Street. Hudson Street north to #778 Hudson.

The Connor Garden, DENVER, CO

This garden has evolved from a passion for colors, shapes, textures, and fragrances. Although the garden is small, each year more turf disappears and more garden is created — ornamental trees are planted, more varieties of roses, lilies, clematis, peonies, groundcovers, hostas, delphinium, and small shrubs appear. Recently, chairwalls, raised beds, and a water garden have been added in back; in the front, the garden has doubled in size.

DATES & HOURS: July 10; 10 a.m. – 4 p.m.

DIRECTIONS: *From Colorado Boulevard,* go east on Sixth Avenue until you come to Grape Street on your right (14 blocks east). Turn right and look for a two story brick house in the middle of the block on your left.

The Leonard Leonard Office Gardens, DENVER, CO

The purpose of the gardens is to surround the patio sitting area with a relaxing environment away from the office. Sound is provided by five waterfalls: three in the North Garden, and two in the South. Visually, the North Garden is undulating, with a few rock outcrops softened by low ground covers. On the other hand, the South Garden, functionally a four-plus foot hill topped by three pines blocking the neighboring view, consists of sheer sedimentic moss rock walls, cut by the waterway and sewn with balanced plantings of vegetables, herbs, perennials, and evergreens. The South Garden was my twenty-fifth wedding anniversary gift to my wife.

DATES & HOURS: July 10; 10 a.m. – 4 p.m.

DIRECTIONS: *On Downing Street,* third building north of Fourth Avenue, # 420, east side. The garden is in the backyard. Park on Fourth Avenue or Downing Street.

Proceeds shared with The American Red Cross.

Warren Garden, DENVER, CO

Brick paths lead the eye around the house to a not-quite circular brick patio in the rear. Growing areas are planted with a wide variety and size of textured shrubs and plants. Shade trees minimize the western sun, providing shady areas for the eye and wildlife. A selection of evergreens on the sides "warm" the yard in winter. It is an intimate, relaxed haven in the city.

DATES & HOURS: July 10; 10 a.m. – 4 p.m.

DIRECTIONS: *South Humboldt Street* is located opposite the south end of Washington Park across from the tennis courts. A main intersection is Downing Street and Louisiana Avenue. Going east of Louisiana, South Humboldt Street is three blocks from the intersection with Downing Street. Coming west on Louisiana, South Humboldt Street is one block after the Franklin Street traffic light at the beginning of Washington Park, just past South High School.

Proceeds shared with Intercommunity Care Givers.

Denver Area

Weiss' Garden, DENVER, CO

Come into my "Secret Garden." Enter in the front through the antique iron gates into my peaceful sanctuary of shade plants and tumbling waters. Sit down, rest, and feel the tranquility wash over you. Now, follow the path through another shade garden around to the north side of the house. Notice the varied foliage interspersed amongst the blooming perennials. Pass over the driveway and enter through the iron gates to our terraced backyard "getaway." Perfect for entertaining favorite friends while fountain sounds and birds bathing calm you. Plants, trees, and shrubs display their finery from early spring through fall in my "secret garden." Relax and enjoy the beauty.

DATES & HOURS: July 10; 10 a.m. – 4 p.m.

DIRECTIONS: *Take Colorado Boulevard* to 3rd Avenue and turn east onto 3rd Avenue. (This is the "Hilltop" area which is just east of Colorado Boulevard from the Cherry Creek area.) Continue east five blocks to Clermont Street Parkway. Turn north and continue for one long block. Our house is on the corner of 4th Avenue and Clermont Street on the southeast corner. It is a Mediterranean-style house with an antique orange tile roof, #390 Clermont Street Parkway.

❖ Denver Botanic Gardens,

1005 YORK STREET, DENVER, CO. 80206. (303) 331-4000. FAX (303) 331-4013. *Denver Botanic Gardens is an urban oasis. Stroll through the world-renowned Rock Alpine Garden, or visit the Japanese, Herb, Vegetable, or Water – Smart gardens, to name a few. The gift shop offers books, gifts, live plants, and more. Helen Fowler Library has an extensive collection of horticultural books and catalogs. Special events and plant shows are planned throughout the year.*

DATES & HOURS: Year round, daily, 9 a.m. – 5 p.m., with extended evening hours May through September.

DIRECTIONS: *Located five minutes east of the downtown area* and accessible by major RTD bus routes. *From Interstate 25,* exit east on Sixth Avenue. Proceed east to Josephine Street. Turn north onto Josephine Street. The parking lot is on the left side of Josephine, between 9th and 11th Avenues.

Weckbaugh Garden, ENGLEWOOD, CO

This cottage garden of an amateur plant lover, slowly developed over many years without professional help as to design. There are plantings of peonies, daylilies, a shade garden, a pergola, and pool with aquatic plants. Much self-saving of annuals and the spreading of perennials have created a naturalistic effect. Now under quite a bit of renovation.

DATES & HOURS: July 10; 10 a.m. – 2 p.m.

DIRECTIONS: *From Denver,* starting at 1st Avenue and Speer Boulevard, proceed south on University Boulevard (past Hampden Avenue) to Quincy. Turn left (east) onto Quincy to South Monroe Lane (just west of Kent-Denver football field). Turn right onto Monroe Lane to the post-and-rail fence with a sign noting #4501 South Monroe Lane.

Stylers' Garden, GREENWOOD VILLAGE, CO

The Stylers' Garden has several different areas, although the focus is clearly on water gardening. Several ponds and other small water gardens display their extensive collection of aquatic and bog plants, including the giant Victoria water lily. Other features include annual and perennial gardens, a whimsical outdoor bedroom, rose garden, window boxes and container gardens, and several large xeriscape features, such as a thirty-foot koi and a six-foot dragonfly.

DATES & HOURS: July 18; 10 a.m. – 2 p.m.

DIRECTIONS: *From I-25,* take the Orchard Road Exit and go west on Orchard Road to Monaco Street, approximately 1.5 miles. Turn right onto Monaco Street and then turn right at the first street, Ida Avenue. We are the third house on the right, #6583 East Ida Avenue.

The Brunk Gardens, GREENWOOD VILLAGE, CO

Shaded by a windrow of hackberry, ash, and honey locusts, we have created many gardens within our garden. The garden's main focal point is the waterfall that cascades into two large ponds. The ponds provide for the peaceful coexistence of koi and many plants. Our garden is a continual collection of perennials and annuals in formal beds and others in a woodland setting. From the Romantic Garden, decked in pink-and-white, shade-loving perennials and annuals, to our newest addition, the Grass Garden, there is a garden to please everyone.

DATES & HOURS: July 18; 10 a.m. – 4 p.m.

DIRECTIONS: *I-25 to Orchard.* Go west on Orchard to Monaco. Make a right on Monaco to Ida (the first left). Enter the garden through the double gate on the right, before you reach Kearney Street.

Alpenridge, LITTLETON, CO

Alpenridge has three rock gardens, each with a different exposure. The perennial border is best viewed from the west deck. A protected garden on the north side of the house has rhododendrons, bloodroots, and trilliums. A large dry xeric garden, featuring a buffalo grass garden planted with thousands of bulbs and shrubs, demonstrates that gardening with limited water does work. Different kinds of ornamental grasses dot the various gardens. A large passion-flower vine blooms all summer in a protected southern exposure.

DATES & HOURS: July 10; 10 a.m. – 2 p.m.

DIRECTIONS: *From I-70,* take I-25 South to Santa Fe Drive. Travel south on Santa Fe Drive and at the next light after Bowles, go west on Church Street. Travel south on Prince Street and east on Ridge Road for about three blocks to #1952.

❖ Chatfield Arboretum,

8500 DEER CREEK CANYON ROAD, LITTLETON, CO 80123.
(303) 973-3705. FAX (303) 973-3705.

Chatfield Arboretum's 700 acres wind along Deer Creek, encompassing several distinct High Plains habitats. Nature trails thread around wetlands and prairie ecosystems. Educational stops along the trails explain surrounding vegetation and encourage wildlife watching. A nineteenth-century farmstead has been restored to present an authentic view of pioneer life on the Colorado High Plains. Chatfield Arboretum is run by Denver Botanic Gardens.

DATES & HOURS: Year round, daily, 9 a.m. – 5 p.m.

DIRECTIONS: *Located just southwest of the Wadsworth Boulevard and C-470 intersection.* Proceed south on Wadsworth from this intersection to the second traffic light and turn right (west) onto Deer Creek Canyon Road. The Arboretum entrance gate is .4 mile on the left.

❖ Hudson Gardens,

6115 SOUTH SANTA FE DRIVE, LITTLETON, CO 80120.
(303) 797-8565. FAX (303) 797-3650.

A thirty-acre Regional Display Garden accenting sixteen individual gardens. Historic Rose Garden, Rock Garden Canyon, Water Gardens, Demonstration Gardens, Butterfly Bank. Excellent perennial and shrub collections for zones 4 and 5 climate. Gardens are labeled and individual handouts are available. Large summer sculpture displays. Educational program, space rentals, and a gift shop.

DATES & HOURS: Year round, daily, 10 a.m. – one hour before sunset.

DIRECTIONS: *From C-470* north on South Santa Fe Drive 2.5 miles, on left, opposite gas station. *Or .5 mile south on South Santa Fe Drive* from Bowles Avenue/Littleton Boulevard junction to South Santa Fe Drive on right.

CONNECTICUT

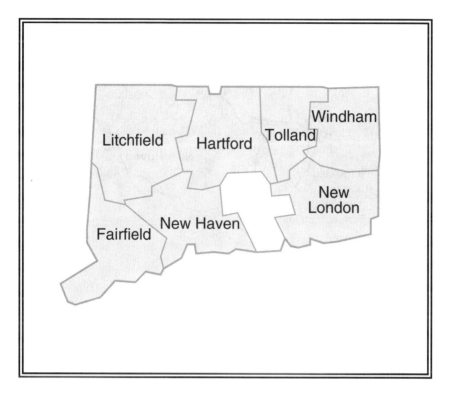

1999 CONNECTICUT OPEN DAYS

May 2: FAIRFIELD & NEW HAVEN COUNTIES,
TOLLAND & WINDHAM COUNTIES

May 16: FAIRFIELD & NEW HAVEN COUNTIES,
HARTFORD COUNTY, TOLLAND & WINDHAM COUNTIES

MAY 30: FAIRFIELD & NEW HAVEN COUNTIES

June 13: FAIRFIELD & NEW HAVEN COUNTIES, HARTFORD COUNTY,
LITCHFIELD COUNTY, NEW LONDON COUNTY,
TOLLAND & WINDHAM COUNTY

June 27: FAIRFIELD & NEW HAVEN COUNTIES, LITCHFIELD COUNTY,
NEW LONDON COUNTY, TOLLAND & WINDHAM COUNTIES

July 11: FAIRFIELD & NEW HAVEN COUNTIES, LITCHFIELD COUNTY, NEW
LONDON COUNTY, TOLLAND & WINDHAM COUNTIES

July 25: FAIRFIELD & NEW HAVEN COUNTIES, LITCHFIELD COUNTY

September 12: FAIRFIELD & NEW HAVEN COUNTIES, LITCHFIELD COUNTY

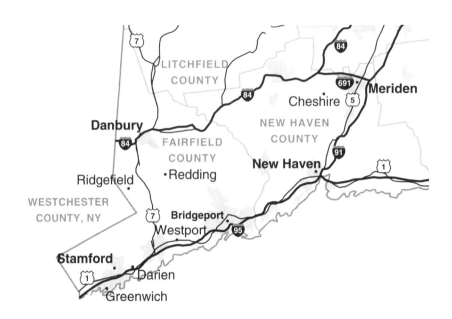

FAIRFIELD & NEW HAVEN COUNTIES:

May 2, 1999

Ruth & Jim Levitan, STAMFORD, 10 A.M. – 6 P.M.

Paul Held & Jane Sherman, WESTPORT, 10 A.M. – 6 P.M.

May 16, 1999

Nicholas Nickou, BRANFORD, one guided tour at 10 A.M.

Maggie & Michael Daly, FAIRFIELD, 10 A.M. – 4 P.M.

Sarah & Jonathan Seymour, FAIRFIELD, 10 A.M. – 6 P.M.

Highstead Arboretum, REDDING, guided walks every two hours beginning
at 10 a.m.

Joel & Ellie Spingarn, WEST REDDING, 10 A.M. – 4 P.M.

Jane Bescherer, WILTON, 2 P.M. – 6 P.M.

May 30, 1999

Peonies at Poverty Hollow, REDDING RIDGE, 9 A.M. – 6 P.M.

Henriette Suhr, Mt. Kisco, NY will be open on May 29.

June 13, 1999

Enid & Harry Munroe, FAIRFIELD, 2 P.M. – 6 P.M.

Sarah & Jonathan Seymour, FAIRFIELD, 10 A.M. – 6 P.M.

Stonybrooke, GREENWICH, 10 A.M. – 2 P.M.

David Barnhizer, RIDGEFIELD, 10 A.M. – 4 P.M.

Melissa Orme, RIDGEFIELD, 10 A.M. – 6 P.M.

Anita & Jim Alic, WESTPORT, 10 A.M. – 6 P.M.

Barbara Carr, WESTPORT, 10 A.M. – 6 P.M.

Hughes – Sonnenfroh, WEST REDDING, 2 P.M. – 6 P.M.

June 27, 1999

Enid & Harry Munroe, FAIRFIELD, 2 P.M. – 6 P.M.

Katie Brown, GREENWICH, NOON – 6 P.M.

Mr. & Mrs. Philip H. McCaull, GREENWICH, 10 A.M. – 2 P.M.

Susan Cohen, RIVERSIDE, 10 A.M. – 2 P.M.

July 11, 1999

Enid & Harry Munroe, FAIRFIELD, 2 P.M. – 6 P.M.

Sarah & Jonathan Seymour, FAIRFIELD, 10 A.M. – 6 P.M.

Barlow Cutler–Wotton, WESTPORT, 10 A.M. – 2 P.M.

Two Rivers, WESTPORT, 10 A.M. – 4 P.M.

July 25, 1999

George Trecina, MERIDEN, 10 A.M. – 2 P.M., guided tour at 10 A.M.

Sandra & Richard Bergmann, NEW CANAAN, 10 A.M. – 4 P.M.

Donna Clark, RIDGEFIELD, 10 A.M. – 4 P.M.

September 12, 1999

Florence & John Boogaerts, COS COB, 2 P.M. – 6 P.M.

Enid & Harry Munroe, FAIRFIELD, 2 P.M. – 6 P.M.

Stonybrooke, GREENWICH, 10 A.M. – 2 P.M.

Simon & Rosita Trinca, GREENWICH, 2 P.M. – 6 P.M.

George Trecina, MERIDEN, 10 A.M. – 2 P.M., guided tour at 10 A.M.

Joseph Keller, RIDGEFIELD, 10 A.M. – 6 P.M.

Barlow Cutler–Wotton, WESTPORT, 10 A.M. – 2 P.M.

Nickolas Nickou, BRANFORD, CT

This garden features many species and varieties of mature rhododendrons and azaleas. In addition, there are many rare trees and shrubs from China and Japan, coupled with woodland flowering plants and ferns.

DATES & HOURS: May 16; one guided tour at 10 a.m. No wandering alone.

DIRECTIONS: *From I-95,* take Exit 55 onto Route 1. Go east .4 mile to a right onto Featherbed Lane; continue to end. Turn left, go 200 feet, then right onto Griffing Pond Road, which runs into Sunset Hill Drive. (Ignore the first right onto Sunset Hill Drive.) The yellow hydrant on the left marks the driveway, #107 on mailbox. Please park along the road.

❖ Bible Garden at St. Paul's Church,

174 WHISCONIER ROAD, BROOKFIELD, CT 06804. (203) 775-9587.

In the Spring of 1997, members of St. Paul's Church designed and created a Bible Garden in front of the church to grow only herbs and flowers mentioned in the Bible, thereby forging a link between today and those distant and hallowed times. The garden is designed in the shape of a cross, forty feet by forty feet, with flagstone paths and a circle in the center. The plants are all identified as to their place in the Bible and labeled accordingly. Behind the church is a columbarium (burial ground) for church members. A traditional New England stone wall surrounds the maintained gardens. A ten-foot granite cross highlights the center of the garden.

DATES & HOURS: Year round, daily, dawn – dusk.

DIRECTIONS: *Located .25 miles north* of the intersection of Routes 25 & 133 in Brookfield.

❖ Brookfield Historical Society Museum Garden,

165 WHISCONIER ROAD, BROOKFIELD, CT 06804. (203) 740-8140.

Designed by Dr. Rudy J. Favretti, this nineteenth-century herb garden complements the 1876 museum it adjoins. The focal point is a sundial surrounded by coral bells and thyme. There is a brick walk throughout the property. The garden was created and is maintained by the Brookfield Garden Club.

DATES & HOURS: Year round, daily, dawn – dusk.

DIRECTIONS: *Located on the corner of Routes 25 & 133 in Brookfield.*

Florence & John Boogaerts — Mianus Dawn,

COS COB, CT

This tiny, steep site overlooking the Mianus River is an exuberant combination of her lavish Gertrude Jekyll perennials and his Edward Lutyens architectural stonework. The garden is a sequence of terraces carved into the wooded hillside: a fern grotto, niches and ramps, a flower garden, a boxwood parterre, a potager, a grape arbor, and an espalliered apple orchard.

DATES & HOURS: September 12; 2 p.m. – 6 p.m.

DIRECTIONS: From *I-95*, take Exit 4, turn onto Indian Field Road (north, towards Greenwich). Travel .7 mile, turn right (Mobil station) onto East Putnam Avenue. Travel .5 mile, turn left (Gulf station) onto Orchard Street, bear right at triangle, turn right at next intersection, Valley Road. Travel 1.6 miles, after second stop sign, fourth house, #316, on left. *From Merritt Parkway, Exit 33, Eastbound* (New Haven) bear right onto Den Road, at Roxbury Road turn left at stop sign (1.7 miles) to Westover Road; *Westbound* (to NYC), right on Den Road (.5 mile) to Bangall Road, turn left, continue w/red barn horse farm on the right (.5 mile), to Riverbank Road, turn left, cross over Merritt. Riverbank Road becomes Westover Road. Go 1.7 miles to Mianus Road, turn right. Mianus Road becomes Valley Road. Go 1.7 miles to #316 on right. Please park along road.

❖ The Garden Education Center of Greenwich & Montgomery Pinetum,

BIBLE STREET, COS COB, CT 06807. (203) 869-9242.

The 102-acre pinetum, formerly the estate of renowned plant collector Colonel Robert H. Montgomery, now a town of Greenwich park open to the general public, contains fine conifers, rock gardens, and woodland trails. The Garden Education Center has an auditorium/gallery, library, two garden shops, and a teaching greenhouse.

DATES & HOURS: Montgomery Pinetum: year round, daily, 8:30 a.m. – dusk. Garden Education Center: September – December, closed Sundays; January – June, closed Saturdays and Sundays. Closed July and August.

DIRECTIONS: *From I-95* take Exit 4/Indian Field Road. Follow Indian Field Road to end at traffic light. Turn right onto Route 1/Post Road/Putnam Avenue. At fourth traffic light turn left onto Orchard Street. Proceed .2 mile and turn right onto Bible Street. Follow Bible Street .7 mile; the entrance is on your left.

❖ Bates – Scofield House,

45 OLD KINGS HIGHWAY NORTH, DARIEN, CT 06820. (203) 655-9233.

The herb garden, adjacent to the Bates-Scofield house museum, was planted and is maintained by the Garden Club of Darien. It contains more than thirty varieties of culinary, medicinal and strewing herbs known to have been used in Connecticut in the eighteenth century.

DATES & HOURS: Year round, daily, dawn – dusk.

DIRECTIONS: *Take I-95* to Exit 13. Turn left onto Post Road. At the second traffic light, turn left onto Brookside Road. Bear right at curve; the house and parking lot are on the left.

Maggie & Michael Daly, FAIRFIELD, CT

Thirty-three years ago this four acres was dense wet woods. Much work has been slowly done to clear and drain the property. The house is surrounded by terraces, perennial gardens, a rose garden, garden pool, and a vegetable garden. Two beautiful meadows, one to the south and one to the north, have since been acquired. Lovely views and great privacy are the strengths of this property.

DATES & HOURS: May 16; 10 a.m. – 4 p.m.

DIRECTIONS: *From the south* take Exit 19 off of I-95. Turn left at end of ramp and go straight to Post Road (Route 1). At the first light turn left; at the second light turn right. Go to the end of Hulls Highway then turn right on Hulls Farm Road. The third left is Redding Road, the third driveway on the left is #155. The mailbox is opposite the driveway. *From the north,* take Exit 21 off of I-95. At bottom of ramp, go straight crossing Mill Plain Road. Take an immediate right onto Sturges Road. Bear left over a stone bridge, right at the end of the bridge. The road leads into Brousou. Oliver Nursery is on your left. Follow Brousou, bearing left at the grocery store. Take the third left at Governor's Lane and turn right onto Redding Road, #155, first driveway on your left.

Proceeds shared with The Kennedy Center, Trumbull, CT.

Enid & Harry Munroe, FAIRFIELD, CT

Our beautiful, informal, shade and mixed border gardens change throughout the season as we experiment with perennials, herbs, shrubs, ground covers, ornamental grasses, and tropical plants. We have more than 100 container plants, many with "black" foliage or blooms. The gardens were an inspiration for Enid Munroe's book, An Artist in the Garden: a Guide to Creative and Natural Gardening.

DATES & HOURS: June 13, June 27, July 11, September 12; 2 p.m. – 6 p.m.

DIRECTIONS: *From the Merritt Parkway,* take Exit 42/Westport/Weston. Turn left at end of ramp onto Weston Road. Bear left as road forks to right, keeping Daybreak Nursery greenhouse on the right. Turn left at the "T" onto Cross Highway. At third stop sign, make a sharp right onto Sturges Highway. Take the second left onto Fleming Lane. The house, #131, is the second on the right. Please park along street.

Sarah & Jonathan Seymour, FAIRFIELD, CT

Though we still consider our gardens to be woodland gardens we have thinned out the trees over the years from deep shade to partial shade. This has allowed us to add an herb/vegetable garden, some sun-loving perennials and what is becoming for Sarah a new passion, viburnums and hydrangeas. As of this writing we are planning a squash patch, and the hosta collection is always growing. To all the people who have come year after year to visit, a heartfelt thank-you for appreciating what we have tried to accomplish here and, of course, we would love to see you again. To those who are new to the Conservancy tours, come wander in the gardens, chat with Roger Raymond the beekeeper; pet our beloved cats and dogs and you just have to see Jonathan's stone birdhouses. As always, we are proud to say that we do all our own design, planting, and stonework.

DATES & HOURS: May 16, June 13, July 11; 10 a.m. – 6 p.m.

DIRECTIONS: *From the Merritt Parkway,* take Exit 44/Fairfield, from New York take a right off ramp onto Congress Street; from New Haven take a left off ramp, left at light, go under Merritt and right onto Congress Street. Follow Congress approximately 2.25 miles to Cross Highway. Turn left. At first stop sign, go left onto Redding Road. Driveway is .3 mile on the left, just past Melin Drive. There are five mailboxes across street from driveway. The house, #1534, is third on left up driveway. Please park along Seymour section of driveway.

❖ Connecticut Audubon Birdcraft Museum,

40 UNQUOWA, FAIRFIELD, CT 06430. (203) 259-0416.

America's oldest private songbird sanctuary was founded in 1914. The five-acre sanctuary (originally fourteen acres), planted to attract birds with trees and shrubs, was designed by Mabel Osgood Wright (1859-1934), a pioneering American conservationist, photographer, and author. Demonstration plantings to attract birds and a butterfly meadow restoration are in progress.

DATES & HOURS: Year round, Tuesday through Friday, 10 a.m. – 5 p.m.; Saturday & Sunday, noon – 5 p.m.

DIRECTIONS: *Take I-95 to Exit 21/Mill Plain Road.* Go north on Mill Plain Road for .5 miles to stop sign. Turn right onto Unquowa Road and proceed for .5 miles to parking entrance immediately on left after I-95 overpass.

Katie Brown, GREENWICH, CT

We bought a charming old carriage house in 1994 with wonderful old trees, but not a flower in the place. Since I am a landscape designer, the only thing to do was to rip out overgrown shrubs and plant lots of flowers. Over the last three years this has been a labor of love. An entry bank spills over with fairy roses, daylilies, and hydrangeas inviting you to an upper terrace bordered by David Austin roses, nepeta, and lavender. Below, a rose-covered pergola leads to the pool garden, which is a combination of grasses, perennials, heather, and plants chosen specifically for their interesting shape, color, and texture.

DATES & HOURS: June 27; noon – 6 p.m.

DIRECTIONS: *From Hutchinson River Parkway north,* take Exit 30/King Street. Turn left at the stop sign and go approximately 1.4 miles (St. Paul's Catholic Church will be on the right). Turn right onto Sherwood Avenue. Go to the end of Sherwood. Turn left onto Riversville Road. Number 399 is exactly .5 mile on the right. Just past the house go left on Hycliff Road and park. Walk right on Riversville Road and #399 is the first house on the left.

Mr. & Mrs. Philip H. McCaull, GREENWICH, CT

Walking this beautiful property, you will be reminded of an English manor house, yet there are distinctively southern touches. Interesting specimen trees, a boxwood garden, a wildflower garden, a vegetable garden, an unorthodox herb garden, and a cutting garden of roses, lilies, and annuals grace the grounds and flagstone patio. A pond, stables, and pool complete this paradise.

DATES & HOURS: June 27; 10 a.m. – 2 p.m.

DIRECTIONS: *From the Merritt Parkway,* take Exit 28/Round Hill Road. Go south 1 mile. The house, #221, is on the east side of the road. Park along Round Hill Road.

Proceeds shared with The Breast Cancer Alliance.

Stonybrooke, GREENWICH, CT

Twenty-five years ago, we fell in love with this property of waterfalls, rock outcroppings, and open space as Caleb Mead had, 250 years before us, when he built his sawmill on the Stony Brooke. Today, only the dam is left, but the stunning terrain is a harmonious background for the perennial gardens, specimen plantings, and vistas, set off by rolling, natural lawn. Stonybrooke is serene and restorative in all seasons. It is about 75% wheelchair-accessible.

DATES & HOURS: June 13, September 12; 10 a.m. – 2 p.m.

DIRECTIONS: *From the Merritt Parkway,* take North Street Exit south toward town. Just short of 1 mile, Taconic Road goes off sharply to the left. Just past Byfield Lane, Stonybrooke begins at the S-curve and bridge. Please park on Byfield. There are a few parking places farther along near the main entrance.

Proceeds shared with Green Fingers Garden Club.

Simon & Rosita Trinca, GREENWICH, CT

This garden evokes the great American meadow with mass plantings of grasses and other perennials. The bleached colors which remain in the winter remind us of our homeland – Australia. There is also a lily pool.

DATES & HOURS: September 12; 2 p.m. – 6 p.m.

DIRECTIONS: *The house, #364,* is on the corner of North Street and Doubling Road. Please park along Doubling Road.

❖ Pardee Rose Garden,

180 PARK ROAD, HAMDEN, CT 06517. (203) 946-8142.

The Pardee Rose Garden covers about three acres in East Rock Park. The rose beds are laid out geometrically, leading to a three-tiered central brick rose garden, and are planted with 1,500 rose bushes. More than 400 named varieties are currently grown. There are two greenhouses, as well as annual and perennial flower plantings.

DATES & HOURS: Year round, daily, dawn – dusk.

DIRECTIONS: *From I-95* take I-91 to New Haven. Take Exit 5 and continue north on State Street for 2 miles. Turn left onto Farm Road. The garden is 1 block up the hill.

George A. Trecina, MERIDEN, CT

A professional landscape designer's display and trial gardens with one-third acre of continuous mixed borders, containing more than 300 varieties of woody plants and perennials, some unusual. The planting schemes are enhanced with an assortment of annuals, tender perennials, and container plantings with a decidely tropical theme. The sloping front yard — structured with paths, walls, and stairways — features a white garden and a "wild" garden. Some plants are offered for sale.

DATES & HOURS: July 25, September 12; 10 a.m. – 2 p.m. Guided tour at 10 a.m.

DIRECTIONS: *From I-91* take Route 691 west to Exit 6/Lewis Avenue. Turn right to end. Go right on Hanover Street to the first traffic light. Turn left onto Columbus Avenue and go to second stop sign. Turn left onto Prospect Avenue and then make the first right onto Spring Street to the fourth house on the right, #341. *From I-84*, take Route 691 east to Exit 5/Chamberlain Highway. Go right to the end. Turn left onto West Main Street to the first traffic light. Turn right onto Bradley Avenue and go to the first stop sign. Turn left onto Winthrop Terrace and past the traffic light onto Columbus Avenue. Continue from Columbus Avenue as above. Please park along Spring Street.

Sandra & Richard Bergmann, NEW CANAAN, CT

This architect's modernist garden with highly-ordered geometry is an extension to the 1836 Greek Revival-style house. An abstract but formal composition using a series of stepped terraces merges, joins, and enfolds space on the one-third-acre lot. Keeping to the minimalist theme, abundant summer annuals are limited to two colors. The serene, landscaped rooms are formalized by yew parterres, serial hedges, stone and painted brick walls, a bosk of pruned crab apple trees, a topiary folly of cones and pyramids, raked gravel, and other French and Italian elements. Its geometry contrasts with the thick, random woodland plantings of mature pines and hemlocks. A screen of European beech separates the entry court from the landmark building.

DATES & HOURS: July 25; 10 a.m. – 4 p.m.

DIRECTIONS: *From I-95,* take Exit 11 at Darien. Turn left if coming from New York (right if coming from New Haven) onto Post Road. Go to Mansfield Avenue, turn left. Mansfield becomes South Avenue* in New Canaan and dead-ends at Elm Street. Turn left at Elm Street and go one block. The railroad station is at the intersection. Turn right onto Park Street intersection. We are the first house on the left at the corner of Park and Seminary. *From the Merritt Parkway,* take Exit 37 at Darien and turn left onto South Avenue. Follow directions above.* Please park across the street at the free municipal parking lot.

❖ New Canaan Nature Center,

144 OENOKE RIDGE ROAD, NEW CANAAN, CT 06840. (203) 966-9577.
Two miles of trails crisscross natural areas of this forty-acre site, providing access to unusual habitat diversity – including wet and dry meadows, two ponds, wet and dry woodlands, dense thickets, and an old orchard and cattail marsh. Highlights include a bird and butterfly garden, a large herb garden, a wildflower garden, a naturalists' garden, a small arboretum, and a 400-foot solar greenhouse.

DATES & HOURS: Year round, daily, dawn – dusk.

DIRECTIONS: *Take Exit 37 off the Merritt Parkway* and follow Route 124 through town. Located on Route 124, 1 mile north of the New Canaan town center.

Highstead Arboretum, REDDING, CT

Set on thirty-six acres of Connecticut woodland, meadow, wetland, and ledge, Highstead Arboretum is home to special collections of laurel and deciduous azaleas. In May, take in the fragrance and color as you are guided through the azalea collection. Fenced for protection from deer, this collection showcases fourteen species of deciduous azalea. June will bring the glory of the laurel in bloom. In addition to the natural growth of mountain laurel on the property, a collection representing three of the seven laurel species (nearly four dozen cultivars to admire) is displayed in the Kalmia Garden.

DATES & HOURS: May 16. Guided walks only at 10 a.m., noon, 2 p.m., 4 p.m.

DIRECTIONS: *From I-95/Merritt Parkway,* take Route 15 to Route 7 north. Follow to Route 107. Turn right and go 6 miles. Cross Route 53. Pass a police station, an elementary school, and the Redding Country Club. Take the second driveway on the left after the Country Club, #127 Lonetown Road. Follow signs into arboretum. Follow signs for parking.

The Peonies at Poverty Hollow, REDDING RIDGE, CT

More than 425 varieties of peonies (tree, herbaceous, and intersectional) flourish among ledges, mature trees, stone walls, and winding paths on several acres of hillside and plateau. Shade gardens and small seating groups are scattered along the way for quiet overviews and reflection. As a Country Living *cover story in 1996 and featured again in 1998, this property continues to evolve. A bed of native peonies from France and another from England have been added recently. In the March 1999 issue of* Connecticut Magazine, *garden columnist Rea Lukar Duncan suggests that perhaps nowhere else in a private garden is there such a variety of peonies. A member of the Board of Directors of the American Peony Society, author/owner R. Kennard Baker devotes much of his time to this love of earth and beauty.*

DATES & HOURS: Special Open Day on May 30; 9 a.m. – 6 p.m.

DIRECTIONS: *From the Merritt Parkway/Exit 44.* Head north on Route 58 (Blackrock Turnpike) to the stop sign at the Episcopal Church and Church Hill Road (exactly 10 miles). Turn right onto Church Hill Road, travel down a steep and winding hill. Bear right onto Poverty Hollow Road and over the bridge where an officer will direct parking. *From Georgetown,* follow Route 107 through all its gyrations to Redding Nursery. Exit right onto Cross Highway. Follow past blinking traffic light to intersection with Route 58 (Blackrock Turnpike). Cross over Route 58 onto Church Hill Road and follow as above.

Proceeds shared with The American Peony Society and The Bedford Garden Club

David Barnhizer, RIDGEFIELD, CT

The house is a circa 1750 saltbox set on an unfinished railroad spurline. An eighteen-foot granite cliff, from which splashes a recirculating waterfall, provides dramatic focus to the naturalistic gardens created by Stamats Landscaping Design. There are many native shrubs as well as woodland perennials such as rodgersia, ligularia, hosta, ferns, foamflower, and epimedium.

DATES & HOURS: June 13; 10 a.m. – 4 p.m.

DIRECTIONS: *From the intersection of Route 35 and Route 123,* travel north on Route 35/South Salem Road. Go .6 mile to mailbox that reads #153 on right. *From the intersection of Route 35 and Route 33* at the landmark fountain, go south on Route 35/South Salem Road. Go 1.4 miles to mailbox that reads #153 on the left. Please park on grass shoulder of Route 35 or on Old South Salem Road.

Proceeds shared with The Weir Preserve.

Donna Clark, RIDGEFIELD, CT

Romantic, English-style gardens are in an informal country setting. Follow the flowing lines of the gardens to find many varieties of old favorites and the very newest perennials and annuals intertwined with whimsical sculptures. These ever-changing gardens are a continuous creation from the heart. Stepping through a garden gate into the vegetable and cutting gardens, you are welcomed by three miniature donkeys who will come to the fence with the encouragement of carrots pulled from the garden.

DATES & HOURS: July 25; 10 a.m. – 6 p.m.

DIRECTIONS: *From Route 35,* turn onto Route 116/North Salem Road. The house, #264, is 1 mile from that intersection on the right. Please park in the driveway or across the street on Wooster Heights Road.

Joseph H. Keller — Garden of Ideas, RIDGEFIELD, CT

Ten years ago, this spot was covered with Kentucky bluegrass and poison ivy-infested woods. Today, a fine collection of both woody and herbaceous ornamental plants grow here alongside a stunning natural marsh. A large raised-bed vegetable garden produces a bounty of delicious edibles from April through November. Stroll through shade and sun, ponder poetic verse displayed along the way, and relax in one of many secluded nooks. Other points of interest include hand-built cedar structures, whimsical statuary, unusual annuals, water features, and lots of birds and bugs.

DATES & HOURS: September 12; 10 a.m. – 6 p.m.

DIRECTIONS: *From Route 35* in Ridgefield, take Route 116 for 2.9 miles. The house, #647, is on the left. *From Route 121* in North Salem, take Route 116 into Connecticut. The house is on the right, 1.3 miles from the New York border. Please park in the paved parking area.

Melissa Orme, RIDGEFIELD, CT

This formal, four-square perennial garden is planted for interest year-round. There is also a crabapple allée, an herb parterre, and a path winding through a small meadow.

DATES & HOURS: June 13; 10 a.m. – 6 p.m.

DIRECTIONS: *From Ridgefield Center,* take Main Street/Route 35 North. At the blinking light take North Salem Road/Route 116 west 2 miles. The house, #482, is on the right. *From I-684,* take Exit 7/Purdys. Follow North Salem Road/Route 116 east through North Salem, NY, into Ridgefield, CT, 8.8 miles. The house, #482, is on the left, just past Barlow Mountain Road. Park across the road through stone posts.

❖ Ballard Park & Garden,

ROUTE 35, MAIN STREET, RIDGEFIELD, CT 06877.
This semiformal garden was donated in 1964 to the town of Ridgefield by Mrs. Edward L. Ballard. It is maintained by the Ridgefield Garden Club. It is a garden of long bloom period perennials, compact shrubs, and easy-care annuals. The park has a Fletcher Steele-designed pergola.

DATES & HOURS: Year round, daily, dawn – dusk.

DIRECTIONS: *Entrance in middle of town on Route 35.* Park at Grand Union. Entrance to the park on North end.

❖ Keeler Tavern Museum — Cass Gilbert House & Garden, 132 MAIN STREET, P.O. BOX 204, RIDGEFIELD, CT 06877. (203) 438-5485.

A "Charleston Garden" is what architect Cass Gilbert called this garden setting that he designed circa 1910. A garden house looks down on a sunken garden with brick walls, arches, and a reflecting pool. The award-winning flower beds have been restored and are maintained by the Caudatowa Garden Club, using more than 100 varieties of annuals and perennials.

DATES & HOURS: Year round, daily, dawn – dusk.

DIRECTIONS: *At the intersection of Route 33 and Route 35.*

Susan Cohen, RIVERSIDE, CT

Overlooking a tidal inlet, this small, sloping property has been shaped over the past twenty years by its current owners, who first removed overgrown shrubs and vines to create a garden in harmony with its waterfront setting. Susan Cohen, a landscape architect, created a fountain grotto from the old foundation walls of a derelict boathouse, regraded parts of the land and designed flowering borders to surround the house. Four raised beds provide growing space for vegetables, herbs, and roses.

DATES & HOURS: June 27; 10 a.m. – 2 p.m.

DIRECTIONS: *From I-95,* take Exit 5. Turn right onto Post Road/Route 1. Turn right again at the first intersection onto Sound Beach Avenue. Follow into Old Greenwich. Turn right at the light onto West End Avenue. A Mobil station will be on the right. At the small traffic circle, go left onto Riverside Avenue. There is a boatyard on the left. Make a left onto Marks Road and then the first left onto Perkely Lane. The house, #7, is the second on the right. Please park on Marks Road beyond Perkley Lane.

Ruth & Jim Levitan, STAMFORD, CT

This unique, one-acre woodland garden is covered by dogwoods and azaleas blooming over a carpet of old fashioned spring perennials and biennials. It was created over a forty-year period by the owners, both dedicated amateur gardeners.

DATES & HOURS: May 2; 10 a.m. – 6 p.m.

DIRECTIONS: *From the Merritt Parkway,* take Exit 35/High Ridge Road. Go 50 yards north and turn left onto Wire Hill Road. Proceed about .7 mile, go over a small bridge, and make the first right onto Red Fox Road. Go up the hill one block and take the first left onto Wake Robin Lane. The house, #26, is the second on the second block. Please park in the street.

❖ Bartlett Arboretum,

151 BROOKDALE ROAD, STAMFORD, CT 06903-4199. (203) 322-6971.
This sixty-three-acre garden is a living museum embracing natural woodlands, perennial borders, flower gardens, and an educational greenhouse. The arboretum offers a wide variety of programs and courses, a plant information service, and guided tours.

DATES & HOURS: Year round, daily, 8:30 a.m. – dusk.

DIRECTIONS: *From the Merritt Parkway* take Exit 35. Take High Ridge Road/Route 137 North for 1.5 miles to Brookdale Road on left.

❖ Stamford Museum & Nature Center,

39 SCOFIELDTOWN ROAD, STAMFORD, CT 06903. (203) 322-1646.

The Stamford Museum and Nature Center's 118 acres include woodland trails and a 300-foot boardwalk winding along a stream to provide a trail walk experience for parents with strollers, the elderly, and people in wheelchairs. A garden with plants indigenous to Connecticut is at the boardwalk entrance. On the early-New England farm, herbs and vegetables grow. The setting for the entire property includes flowering trees, shrubs, and ground covers, as well as a small lake, a waterfall, a marble fountain, and sculpture.

DATES & HOURS: Year round, Monday through Saturday & holidays, 9 a.m. – 5 p.m.; Sundays, 1 p.m. – 5 p.m.

DIRECTIONS: *From I-95* take Exit 7 to Washington Boulevard/Route 137 North to Merritt Parkway. Located .75 mile north of Exit 35 on the Merritt Parkway at the junction of High Ridge Road (Route 137) and Scofieldtown Road.

❖ Boothe Memorial Park — Wedding Rose Garden,

MAIN STREET, PUTNEY, STRATFORD, CT 06497. (203) 381-2046.

A brick pathway, lined with seasonal perennials, annuals, and shrubs, leads to the exuberant Wedding Rose Garden. Separated into two garden rooms, the Wedding Garden has a restored fountain and displays Love, Honor, and Cherish roses. The Rainbow Room features a colorful explosion of thirty-four varieties. Climbing roses on trellises and an arbor enclose the garden.

DATES & HOURS: Year round, daily, dawn – dusk.

DIRECTIONS: *From I-95 West* take Exit 38/Merritt Parkway. Continue to Exit 53. Go south on Route 110 to Main Street, Putney which forks to the right. Head south on Main Street for .25 mile to the park on the left. *From I-95 East* take Exit 33. Follow Ferry Boulevard, bear left at fork, and go under thruway. Bear right onto East Main Street/Route 110 to its end (Main Street Putney). Go .7 mile to the park on the right.

Anita & Jim Alic, WESTPORT, CT

This secluded woodland property was developed by eclectic collector gardeners. Evolved from a Connecticut "jungle" and turned into a series of loosely defined rooms, it includes an entry garden, an extensive rose garden, a shade garden, a shrub garden, a perennial and grass garden, and pool plantings.

DATES & HOURS: June 13; 10 a.m. – 6 p.m.

DIRECTIONS: *From the Merritt Parkway,* take Exit 42. Go north on Route 57, 1 mile to first light/Lyons Plain Road. Turn right. Go 200 yards, then bear right onto Coleytown Road. Go .5 mile to North Avenue and turn left. Snowflake Lane is 200 yards ahead on the right. The house, #6, is at the end of Snowflake Lane on the right. Please parallel park on grass along road.

Barbara Carr, WESTPORT, CT

We purchased the property in June of 1972. The weekend we moved in, a freak storm caused the nearby tidal pond to overflow its banks. Our house appeared to be a floating island. When the waters receded, plant damage was obvious. In my determination to bring things back to life, I learned to garden and to love it. My garden is fun, whimsical, and full of wonderful specimen plants. It brings me great pleasure, and I hope that you will enjoy your visit. It was recently featured in Time-Life's Designing Beds and Borders.

DATES & HOURS: June 13; 10 a.m. – 6 p.m.

DIRECTIONS: *From I-95 North,* take Exit 19/Southport. At end of ramp, turn right onto Center Street. Go to intersection and make a right onto Pequot Avenue. Make first right onto Westway Road. At the intersection, make a left onto Westway Road/Westport Road. Look for #31 on the mailbox. *From I-95 South,* take Exit 19/Southport to stoplight. Go right onto Post Road. Just before Pequot Motel make a left onto Center Street. Go under I-95 overpass and follow directions above. Please park on one side of the street only.

Barlow Cutler – Wotton, WESTPORT, CT

A country garden with open vistas across a lawn under a canopy of seventy-five-year-old apple trees to perennial borders and meadow gardens with mowed paths and screening by shrubs and trees. July's meadows are ablaze with yellow-gold heliopsis and red monarda. September highlights the billowing, white "sweet" clematis climbing through the shrubs and the tall, tender salvias in maroon, purple, and deep blue. Bordering the lawn under the apple trees are dark green yews with gnarled trunks, planted as seedlings by the gardener's mother in 1931.

DATES & HOURS: July 11, September 12; 10 a.m. – 2 p.m.

DIRECTIONS: *From the Merritt Parkway,* take Exit 41. Turn south onto Route 33. Follow to junction of Route 57 (traffic light). Turn right onto King's Highway north. Pass a cemetery. The garden is at the top of the hill, across from a long white picket fence. Look for a stone wall and #79 on the mailbox. The house is a grey-shingled colonial on the right. Please park across the street in front of the white picket fence.

Proceeds shared with The Aspetuck Land Trust.

Paul Held & Jane Sherman, WESTPORT, CT

Sloping terrain and dappled sunlight make a perfect environment for growing some precious, rare plants. This garden includes a delightful mix of shrubs and ground covers, both alpine and woodland. It is home of the largest collection of Primula sieboldii *in North America and Europe. It is also home for the American Hepatica Association. Hepatica is a woodland flower treasured by adults and children alike.*

DATES & HOURS: May 2; 10 a.m. – 6 p.m.

DIRECTIONS: *Take the Merritt Parkway* to Exit 42. Go under the parkway if coming from the north; turn left off exit if coming from the south. Go to Route 136 and go north to the first stop sign, which is North Avenue. Make a right onto North Avenue and go .3 mile to #195 on the tree or mailbox. Please park on the street on the dirt curb.

Two Rivers, WESTPORT, CT

"Two Rivers" was built on a 1774 foundation. The gardens overlook the point where the Aspetuck and Saugatuck Rivers meet to begin their journey to Long Island Sound. This very special property has been awarded a Certificate of Achievement by the National Wildlife Federation. The property is enhanced by garden rooms planted with 10,000 spring bulbs. The two acres consist of a shade and woodland garden with many wildflowers, large perennial borders with an emphasis on native plantings, an evergreen garden, and a white garden which illuminates the pool at night. The gardens are accented with colorful annuals and interesting containers. Elements of formal and natural design are incorporated in each area. Spaces are created by architectural elements as trellises, arbors, patios, picket fences, garden gates, birdhouses, stone steps, stone walls, and ironworks.

DATES & HOURS: July 11; 10 a.m. – 4 p.m.

DIRECTIONS: *From the Merrit Parkway,* take Exit 42. Proceed north on Route 57 toward Weston. At the three-way traffic light (after .7 mile) make a left on Ford Road. We are the white house on the right corner, #51.

Hughes–Sonnenfroh Gardens, WEST REDDING, CT

For a husband and wife team (arborist and landscape designer), this home feels like a little piece of heaven. With all the work, we still both rejoice in the changes in our garden with each passing day. After a year off for construction and improvements, Tim and I look forward to sharing our garden with you again. Two years ago there was such an abundance of questions concerning deer control, this year I'll be ready with a list for you all. See you on June 13, 1999.

DATES & HOURS: June 13; 2 p.m. – 6 p.m.

DIRECTIONS: *From Route 84,* take Exit 3/Route 7 South. Go 3 miles to traffic light at junction of Route 35. Bear left through light, continuing on Route 7 South. Go 1.5 miles. At third traffic light turn left onto Topstone Road. Go .25 mile, down hill, cross railroad tracks and bear left up hill continuing on Topstone Road for .5 mile. Take second left onto Chestnut Woods Road. The house, #54, is the second on the right. The three dogs are big and harmless! Please park along driveway or the north side of Chestnut Woods Road.

Proceeds shared with the Redding Garden Club.

Joel & Ellie Spingarn, WEST REDDING, CT

This is a plant-lover's garden, planted and tended by owners. Of special interest are dwarf conifers, alpines, trough gardens, and wall gardens, which include some uncommon plants.

DATES & HOURS: May 16; 10 a.m. – 4 p.m.

DIRECTIONS: *From I-95,* take Route 7 North. Proceed several miles to traffic light at junction of Routes 7 and 107. Turn onto Route 107 and go about 2 miles. Turn right onto Beeholm Road. The house, #39, is on the corner of Beeholm Road and Route 107.

Jane Bescherer, WILTON, CT

My small corner of paradise is a two-acre garden that starts at the top of a hill and gradually works its way down through stone steps, rose arbors, new stone walls, irises, sundials, herbs, old stone walls, peonies, bird baths, old roses, crab apple trees, and lilacs. It is a work in progress on an unfinished canvas.

DATES & HOURS: May 16; 2 p.m. – 6 p.m.

DIRECTIONS: *From intersection of Routes 33 & 7 in Wilton,* take Route 33 North toward Ridgefield. From traffic light at white Congregational Church, continue just over 2 miles and turn right on Nod Hill. Take next right onto Olmstead Hill and right again onto English Drive. The house, #38, is the second driveway on the left. Park along English Drive.

Proceeds shared with the Wilton Garden Club.

❖ Weir Farm National Historic Site,

735 NOD HILL ROAD, WILTON, CT 06897. (203) 834-1896.

From 1882 to 1919, Weir Farm was the summer home of the American Impressionist painter J. Alden Weir. Sixty acres have been preserved of the landscape that inspired Weir and his contemporaries — Childe Hassam, John Twachtman, and Albert Pinkham Ryder. A self-guided tour allows visitors to explore the sites where some of their paintings were done. Guided tours are available of the art studios and the circa 1915 restored rustic enclosed garden. A Colonial Revival sunken garden, built by Weir's daughter in the 1930s, was rehabilitated in the spring of 1998 and is adjacent to the visitor center.

DATES & HOURS: Call for tour schedule.

DIRECTIONS: *From I-84* take Exit 3/Route 7 South. Follow for 10 miles into the Branchville section of Ridgefield and turn right at light onto Route 102 West. Take the second left onto Old Branchville Road. Turn left at the first stop sign onto Nod Hill Road. Follow for .7 mile; the site is on the right and the parking is on the left.

❖ Wilton Old Town Hall, 63 RIDGEFIELD ROAD, WILTON, CT 06897.

Historic Old Town Hall (1832) is the major civic project of the Wilton Garden Club. Of special interest is the Mary Comstock Wildflower Garden and the award-winning, fieldstone-framed grotto garden, featuring native plants. There is always something of interest relative to bloom, foliage, texture, and shape.

DATES & HOURS: Year round, Monday through Friday, dawn – dusk.

DIRECTIONS: *Parking entrance* to garden is behind the Old Town Hall accessed by Belden Hill Road. The building is located at 69 Ridgefield Road (Route 33) in Wilton. Turn left at intersection heading north on Route 33 onto Belden Hill Road, and left at the sign into the parking lot.

HARTFORD COUNTY:

May 16, 1999

Brad & Toni Easterson, SOUTH GLASTONBURY, 10 A.M. – 2 P.M.

June 13, 1999

Brad & Toni Easterson, SOUTH GLASTONBURY, 10 A.M – 2 P.M.

Sara M. Knight, WEST HARTFORD, June 13, 10 A.M. – 2 P.M.

❖ Hill – Stead Museum's Sunken Garden,

35 MOUNTAIN ROAD, FARMINGTON, CT 06032. (860) 677-4787.

This Colonial Revival country house, now a museum, was the former home of Alfred Atmore Pope and his wife, Ada Brooks Pope. The sunken garden is based on a circa 1916 design by Beatrix Jones Farrand and features more than seventy-five varieties of perennials and other flora in the texture, foliage, and color combinations (blues, pinks, whites, purples and grays) preferred by Farrand.

DATES & HOURS: May through October, Tuesday through Sunday, 10 a.m. – 5 p.m.; November through April, 11 a.m. – 4 p.m. The last house tour begins one hour prior to closing.

DIRECTIONS: *From I-84* take Exit 39. Go straight past the traffic light at the end of the exit to the traffic light at the intersection of Route 10. Turn left onto Route 10 South/Main Street and at the next traffic light turn left onto Mountain Road. The entrance is .25 mile on the left.

❖ Elizabeth Park Rose & Perennial Gardens,

ASYLUM AVENUE, HARTFORD, CT 06105. (860) 242-0017.

This 15,000-specimen rose garden is the oldest municipal rose garden in the country. Other gardens include perennials, rock gardens, heritage roses, and annual displays. The Lord & Burnham greenhouses offer seasonal displays.

DATES & HOURS: Gardens: Year round, daily, dawn – dusk. Greenhouse only: Monday through Friday, 8 a.m. – 3 p.m.

DIRECTIONS: *From I-84* take Exit 44 for Prospect Avenue. Head north on Prospect. The Park is on the corner of Prospect and Asylum Avenues.

Brad & Toni Easterson, SOUTH GLASTONBURY, CT

Once the site of an old mill, this garden runs along a brook for 300 feet. It encompasses a series of perennial, shrub, and mixed borders with emphasis on native material, naturalistic plantings, and organic gardening practices. The south garden has an extensive collection of ornamental grasses.

DATES & HOURS: May 16, June 13; 10 a.m. – 2 p.m.

DIRECTIONS: *From Hartford* take Route 2 east to Route 17 to South Glaston-bury. At the Congregational Church, turn right onto High Street. Travel .25 mile to the brook. The house is #124. Please park on High Street.

Sara M. Knight, WEST HARTFORD, CT

This garden was developed over a twenty-year period. It boasts hostas under a giant yew along the driveway, a front cottage garden, and a heather bed. A formal area with roses is near the pool. There is also a small hexagonal herb garden, a forty-foot perennial border with a long blooming span, and a short woodland walk with rhododendrons and azaleas, underplanted with myrtle and wildflowers.

DATES & HOURS: June 13; 10 a.m. – 2 p.m.

DIRECTIONS: *From I-84,* take the Park Road/West Hartford Center Exit. Turn left at light at end of ramp. Go straight past five lights. Road changes names from Park to Sedgwick to Mountain and bends around to the right. High Farms Road is second left after the fifth light. The house, #18, is the third on the right. Park along the street.

❖ Gardens at the Noah Webster House,

227 SOUTH MAIN STREET, WEST HARTFORD, CT 06107. (860) 521-5362.
The Noah Webster House has a raised-bed teaching garden planted with herbs and other plants available to the Websters during the middle of the eighteenth century. A small demonstration plot of vegetables is also grown. Plants are labeled, so visitors may guide themselves through the garden.

DATES & HOURS: Year round, daily, dawn – dusk.

DIRECTIONS: *Located 1 mile south of I-84* off of Exit 41. Follow signs at the end of the exit and travel for 1 mile. The museum is on the left.

LITCHFIELD COUNTY:

May 16, 1999

❖ Shoyoan Teien—The Freeman Family Garden, MIDDLETOWN, 10 A.M. – NOON.

June 13, 1999

Martha A. & Robert S. Rubin, CORNWALL, 10 A.M. – 4 P.M.

Dan & Joyce Lake, LITCHFIELD, 2 P.M. – 6 P.M.

John N. Spain, MIDDLEBURY, 10 A.M. – 6 P.M.

Linda Allard's Garden, WASHINGTON, 10 A.M. – 4 P.M.

Mr. & Mrs. J. Winston Fowlkes III, WASHINGTON, 10 A.M. – 2 P.M.

George Schoellkopf, WASHINGTON, 2 P.M. – 6 P.M.

June 27, 1999

Maywood Gardens, BRIDGEWATER, 10 A.M. – 2 P.M.

Eduard & Susan Muszala, BRIDGEWATER, 2 P.M.– 6 P.M.

Mr. & Mrs. David Stoner, LITCHFIELD, 2 P.M. – 6 P.M.

Wm. Mitchell Van Winkle, LITCHFIELD, 10 A.M. – 4 P.M.

John N. Spain, MIDDLEBURY, 10 A.M – 6 P.M.

May Brawley Hill, WARREN, 10 A.M. – 2 P.M.

Charles Raskob Robinson & Barbara Paul Robinson, WASHINGTON,
        2 P.M. – 6 P.M.

Gael Hammer, WASHINGTON DEPOT, 10 A.M. – 4 P.M.

Rita & Steve Buchanan, WINSTED, 10 A.M. – 6 P.M.

July 11, 1999

Steepleview Gardens, COLEBROOK, 10 A.M. – 4 P.M.
Alton Peters, FALLS VILLAGE, 2 P.M. – 6 P.M.
Bunny Williams, FALLS VILLAGE, 2 P.M. – 6 P.M.
Lee Link, SHARON, 2 P.M. – 6 P.M.
Kathleen & James Metz, SHARON, 2 P.M. – 6 P.M.
Plum Creek Farm, SHARON, 2 P.M. – 6 P.M.
Georgia Middlebrook, WASHINGTON, 2 P.M. – 6 P.M.
George Schoellkopf, WASHINGTON, 2 P.M.– 6 P.M.
John & Julia Scott, WEST CORNWALL, 10 A.M. – 4 P.M.
Michael Trapp, WEST CORNWALL, 10 A.M. – 6 P.M.

July 25, 1999

Steepleview Gardens, COLEBROOK, 10 A.M. – 4 P.M.
Jane Havemeyer, ROXBURY, 10 A.M. – 4 P.M.
Peter Wooster, ROXBURY, 2 P.M. – 6 P.M.

September 12, 1999

Marveen & Michael Pakalik, COLEBROOK, 2 P.M. – 6 P.M.
Bunny Williams, FALLS VILLAGE, 2 P.M. – 6 P.M.

❖ Bellamy – Ferriday House & Garden,

9 MAIN STREET NORTH, BETHLEHEM, CT 06751. (203) 266-7596.

The Ferriday Garden is a romantic, nine-acre landscape comprised of interesting woody and herbaceous plants. The garden was initially designed circa 1920 and developed through the early 1980s. Since 1992, the Antiquarian and Landmarks Society staff have been busy restoring the large collections of lilacs, old roses, peonies, and perennials. A formal yew and chamaecyparis parterre connect an orchard and meadow, creating a pleasing stroll through the garden.

DATES & HOURS: May through October; Wednesday, Saturday, & Sunday; 11 a.m. – 4 p.m.

DIRECTIONS: *From I-84* take Exit 15/Southbury. At exit ramp take Route 6 east for 13 miles to Route 61. Go left onto Route 61 North. At intersection of Routes 61 and 132, stay on Route 61 and take the first left into the driveway.

Maywood Gardens, BRIDGEWATER, CT

This property displays gardens of various design. Included are a formal rose garden, perennial garden, woodland garden, annual garden, and a large green-house complex.

DATES & HOURS: June 27; 10 a.m. – 2 p.m.

DIRECTIONS: *From I-84* take Exit 9 and travel north on Route 25 toward Brookfield Village. Turn right onto Route 133 east (toward Bridgewater), cross over Lake Lillinonah Bridge and take the first right after the bridge onto Wewaka Brook Road. Travel .75 mile and turn right onto Beach Hill Road to the end. Turn right onto Skyline Ridge. Travel .5 mile and turn right onto Cooper Road. Park on the right across from the greenhouse complex.

Edward & Susan Muszala, BRIDGEWATER, CT

This former parsonage is set amid a delightful mix of perennial gardens, a rose garden, and extensive shade plantings, all accented by garden sculptures and architectural pieces.

DATES & HOURS: June 27; 2 p.m. – 6 p.m.

DIRECTIONS: *From the center of Bridgewater* (village store on your left) turn right at the stop sign. Turn right at the first road on the right (Hut Hill Road). The house is the first on the right, #9

Marveen & Michael Pakalik, COLEBROOK, CT

One lovely, open, sunny acre with distant views of the Berkshires, this garden features three long herbaceous perennial/shrub borders, each devoted to the seasons. A lovely all-white woodland garden blends with native flora. A stone patio features unusual container plantings.

DATES & HOURS: September 12; 2 p.m. – 6 p.m.

DIRECTIONS: *From Route 8 north or Route 44 west,* travel to Winsted, then take Route 183 north to Colebrook. At intersection of Routes 182 and 183, turn left and go to top of hill. The house, #46, is the first white house on the right. *From 44 east to Norfolk,* bear left at Texaco station and take Route 182 approximately 4 miles (just past Route 182A) to top of hill. The house, #46, is a white house on the left. Please park on the street.

Steepleview Gardens — Kathy Loomis, COLEBROOK, CT

Our gardens at Steepleview were created in a former cow pasture at the top of a sunny hill to showcase an everchanging rainbow of floral colors that complement one another. Interesting plant habits and foliage textures are featured in the more than twenty cottage style gardens displaying hundreds of different hybrid daylilies, stunning six-foot spikes of delphinium, and a very large collection of familiar and unusual perennials. Butterflies and hummingbirds are frequent garden visitors, lured to the flowers planted specifically to attract them. Bright beautiful colors are the main theme of the gardens at Steepleview.

DATES & HOURS: July 11, July 25; 10 a.m. – 4 p.m.

DIRECTIONS: *From Winsted, CT:* Coming through Winsted on Route 44, turn right onto Route 183 (Colebrook Road). Continue for approximately 3 miles to the four-way intersection with Route 182. There is a large barn on the left. Turn left onto Route 182. Steepleview Gardens will be at the third house on the left. (Gray farmhouse at top of hill.) *From Norfolk:* Coming through Norfolk on Route 44, turn left onto Route 182 just before George's Norfolk Garage. Travel approximately 4 miles. Look for the Pinney Street sign on the right. Do not take this road, but begin counting houses after it. Steepleview Gardens will be the third house on the right. Please park on the road.

Proceeds shared with The Colebrook Historical Society.

Garden of Martha A. & Robert S. Rubin, CORNWALL, CT

This land must have been a settler's nightmare back in the eighteenth century: a steep north facing hillside of glacial ledge, scattered stones, watery chasms, and bog. The woods of maple, oak, and ash were too dense to get a wagon through. But there was water in a fast flowing stream, plenty of rock to build walls and foundations, wood for a house, a barn, an icehouse, a shed. So it became a farm. Today, the land offsets its geological irregularities in more aesthetic ways. It bestows a glorious view and features winding, hidden footpaths through woodlands and over streams to distant ponds and waterfalls. It has bowed to its human caretakers by allowing gardens of vegetables, shrubs and flowers, an orchard, berry patches, and a contemplative garden surrounding a Japanese teahouse. But all that human hands have rendered accede to the natural aspect that made it possible. Martha Adams Rubin is the author of Countryside, Garden and Table.

DATES & HOURS: June 13; 10 a.m. – 4 p.m.

DIRECTIONS: *Take Connecticut Route 7* to Cornwall Bridge. At Cornwall Bridge, bear right onto Route 4 (or left if you are coming from the north). In about 4 miles at a flashing stop light continue straight ahead onto Route 43. In another 4 miles you will see a cemetery on the right and a Civil War monument on the left. Just beyond turn right onto Hautboy Hill Road. The Rubin house is .6 mile on the left, #74. *Alternate:* On Route 63 drive 6 miles north of Goshen, CT and turn left onto Hautboy Hill Road (or right if you are coming from the north). The Rubin house is .3 mile on the right.

Mr. & Mrs. Alton E. Peters, FALLS VILLAGE, CT

Next to the entrance of this typical, late eighteenth-century Connecticut farmhouse and nearby red barn is a small herb garden enclosed by a low box hedge. A perennial border follows a serpentine stone wall, and across the stream that runs through the property is a field of wildflowers. The most recent addition, designed by Michael Trapp, is a walled garden which surrounds a teahouse and a small pool.

DATES & HOURS: July 11; 2 p.m. – 6 p.m.

DIRECTIONS: *From I-84,* take Route 7 north to Falls Village. Turn right at the blinking light onto Route 126. Continue on Route 126 for 1.8 miles until just before Route 126 ends. Turn right into a driveway marked by two pillars and lined by pear trees. Please park in front or along the road.

Bunny Williams, FALLS VILLAGE, CT

Various gardens surround nineteenth-century buildings. A sunken formal garden has mixed borders and a small reflecting pool. Walkways lead to a potager filled with unusual groupings of pots. The potager connects to a new conservatory. There is a newly established woodland garden and a new vegetable garden and orchard to enhance a recently completed outdoor building.

DATES & HOURS: July 11, September 12; 2 p.m. – 6 p.m.

DIRECTIONS: *From Route 7 north,* go to Falls Village. Turn left at the blinking light onto Main Street/Route 126. Bear right (still on Route 126). Go to stop sign at Point of Rocks Road. The driveway is directly ahead. Please park in field adjacent to house.

Dan & Joyce Lake, LITCHFIELD, CT

Blessed as we are with thirty-two acres of diverse terrain and the ownership of a horticultural business, we have used our surroundings to develop a variety of naturalistic ponds, wetlands, forest, and rock gardens. While most of our gardens are two to four years old, viewers can enjoy perennial beds, both sunny and shady, a large Locust arbor, grass garden, and pondside expressions. Although in its nascent stages, a 700' woodland stroll garden is available for the visionary. We have extensive amounts of native mountain laurel and have many large boulders in our landscape. We have a landscaped container nursery with an allée and a formal design with tasteful garden accents.

DATES & HOURS: June 13; 2 p.m. – 6 p.m.

DIRECTIONS: *In Litchfield,* at stop light on Route 202 by Stop & Shop turn onto Milton Road. After .25 mile fork right onto Beach Street. Go 2 miles, and Horticultural Center is on the right. There are stone columns, stone walls and large maple trees. We are 2 miles from Milton Road; 2.25 miles from Route 202.

Proceeds shared with Habitat for Humanity.

Mr. & Mrs. David Stoner, LITCHFIELD, CT

The garden is only twelve years old and could best be described as informal cottage style. It overlooks a pond and Prospect Mountain. In addition to perennial beds, there are more than sixty roses and fifty peonies, and a variety of small trees and shrubs. The vegetable garden is large and beautiful.

DATES & TIMES: June 27; 2 p.m. – 6 p.m.

DIRECTIONS: *From the west,* take Route 202 east through Bantam to the first left (north) across from La Cupola Restaurant. Follow to Maple Street and go north for .75 miles. The house, #183, is on the west side of the street. Please park in driveway or along street.

Proceeds shared with The Bellamy-Ferriday House.

Wm. Mitchell Van Winkle, LITCHFIELD, CT

This garden boasts some 200 rose bushes of all kinds — old garden roses, newer shrub roses, hybrid tea roses, and climbing roses, to name but a few — and one of the best views in Litchfield.

DATES & HOURS: June 27; 10 a.m.– 4 p.m.

DIRECTIONS: *From the center of Litchfield,* travel west on Route 202. At first traffic light, turn right onto North Lake Street. At first fork, bear left, go over top of hill. Number 293 is a gray-shingled house on the left near the road. Please park on east side of North Lake Street.

❖ Laurel Ridge Foundation, WIGWAM ROAD, LITCHFIELD, CT.

This display of the genus Narcissus was planted over approximately ten acres in 1941. The original 10,000 daffodils have naturalized for the past fifty years. The current owners have maintained the display and welcome visitors to drive by and share its splendor.

DATES & HOURS: April through May, daily, dawn – dusk.

DIRECTIONS: *Take Route 118 east* from Litchfield to Route 254. Turn right onto Wigwam Road. The planting is about 1 mile on the left.

❖ **White Flower Farm,** P.O. Box 50, Route 63, Litchfield, CT 06759. (860) 567-8789; Fax (860) 496-1418.

White Flower Farm is best known as a mail-order nursery, but it's also a great place to visit. In addition to the working nursery, the grounds are home to an impressive collection of mature trees and shrubs. There are also numerous display gardens featuring perennials, tender perennials and annuals, bulbs and roses. Tour maps are available at the Visitor Center or the Store.

DATES & HOURS: Daily, 9 a.m. – 6 p.m., April – October; 10 a.m. – 5 p.m. November – March.

DIRECTIONS: *The garden is located on State Route 63;* it's .7 mile north of Route 109, and 3.3 miles south of Route 118. Watch for the signs, and please park in the lot just north of the store.

John N. Spain, Middlebury, CT

Garden areas include a rock garden, an outdoor (winter hardy) cactus garden, a planted wall, troughs, and a woodland garden. The rock garden combines dwarf conifers with hardy cacti and many conventional rock garden plants. There is also a landscaped greenhouse of cacti and succulents.

DATES & HOURS: June 13, June 27; 10 a.m. – 6 p.m.

DIRECTIONS: *From I-84 West,* take Exit 17. Go straight on Route 64 to second traffic light. Turn right onto Memorial Drive. At end, turn left onto Kelly Road. Go .25 miles to the second street on the right, Three Mile Hill Road. Continue on Three Mile Hill Road to the third street on the right, Bayberry Road. The house, #69, is the second on the right. Please park along the road.

❖ Shoyoan Teien – The Freeman Family Garden,

WESLEYAN UNIVERSITY, THE MANSFIELD FREEMAN CENTER FOR EAST ASIAN STUDIES, 343 WASHINGTON TERRACE, MIDDLETOWN, CT 06459-0435. (860) 685-2330. WWW.WESLEYAN.EAST.EDU

Shoyoan Teien is a Japanese-style viewing garden designed and built by Stephen Morrell in 1995. Inspired by the "dry landscape" aesthetic, the garden's raked gravel riverbed evokes the prominent bend in the Connecticut river as it flows through wooded hills near Middletown. Japanese tea ceremonies are periodically performed in the adjacent tatami room.

DATES & HOURS: Open Days Event with Stephen Morrell: May 16, 10 a.m. – noon. Weekends during the academic year: Saturday, Sunday 2:00 p.m. – 5 p.m. Call for specific open dates.

DIRECTIONS: *From the north,* take I-91 South to Exit 22 (left exit) to Route 9/Exit 15 and follow the signs to Wesleyan. *From the south,* take I-95 to I-91 North/Exit 18 or take the Merritt/Wilbur Cross Parkway (Route 15) to Route 66 East and follow the signs to Wesleyan. *From the northeast,* take the Massachusetts Turnpike/I-90 West to I-84 West to Hartford; I-91 South to Exit 22 South (left exit); south on Route 9 and follow signs to Wesleyan/ Exit 15. *Or, take I-95 South* through Providence, R.I. to Route 9 North/Exit 15, and follow signs to Wesleyan.

❖ Hillside Gardens,

515 LITCHFIELD ROAD (ROUTE 272), NORFOLK, CT 06058. (860) 542-5345. *Hillside Gardens is home to horticulturists Fred and Mary Ann McGourty. Their extensive garden, set around an old farm with stone walls, has more than twenty borders arranged with imaginative plant combinations. There are also areas for trial and evaluation of new perennials. The associated nursery specializes in a wide range of choice and uncommon plants.*

DATES & HOURS: May 1 through September 15, daily except holidays, 9 a.m. – 5 p.m.

DIRECTIONS: *Located on Route 272,* 2.5 miles south of the center of Norfolk.

Jane Havemeyer, ROXBURY, CT

This is a small garden in progress which the owner/gardener seeks to keep in harmony with the style, scale, and setting of an old Connecticut farmhouse. The present picture includes a personal version of an old-fashioned parlor garden, a small kitchen herb garden, and pots and perennials defining a terrace and edging the house — along with a nice view of the valley.

DATES & HOURS: July 25; 10 a.m. – 4 p.m.

DIRECTIONS: *Take I-84* to Exit 15/Southbury. Go north on Route 6/Route 67 for 1.5 miles to traffic light, where Route 67 splits off to the left. Turn left, continue on Route 67 towards Roxbury for 4.7 miles to Squire Road. Turn left onto Squire Road continuing for 1.3 miles to end of road at stop sign. Turn left onto South Street and continue for 1 mile to Mallory Road. Turn left. It is the second house on left, a tan farmhouse with black shutters. Please park in small pull-in at front of house or continue to barn driveway, the next left.

Proceeds shared with The Gertrude Jekyll Garden at the Glebe House.

Peter Wooster, ROXBURY, CT

This one-quarter acre garden is enclosed by a fence and densely planted, with an eye toward collecting. We only want one of everything.

DATES & HOURS: July 25; 2 p.m. – 6 p.m.

DIRECTIONS: *From I-84,* take Exit 15 at Southbury. Go north on Route 67/6 for 1.5 miles to stop light where Route 67 turns left. Follow Route 67, going left towards Roxbury for 4.5 miles to Squire Road. Turn left and continue for .5 mile to Apple Lane. Turn right and continue .6 mile up hill to top. The garden is on the right just past yellow barn. Please park along road.

Proceeds shared with The Gertrude Jekyll Garden at the Glebe House.

❖ Painter Ridge Perennials,

35 PAINTER RIDGE ROAD, ROXBURY, CT 06783. (860) 355-3844.

These country perennial gardens bloom continually from May to November. Included are fruit trees, old-fashioned lilacs and roses, herbaceous perennials, and an organic vegetable garden. Owners are in the process of creating a maze throughout a two-and-one-half to three-acre plot. Plants and cut flowers are available for sale.

DATES & HOURS: May through October, daily, 10 a.m.– 4 p.m.

DIRECTIONS: *From Roxbury/Southbury,* take Route 67 to Route 317 to Painter Hill Road to Painter Ridge Road, approximately 3 miles. *From Washington/Woodbury,* take Route 47 to Painter Ridge Road.

Lee Link, SHARON, CT

Three stone walls cascade down a sunny hillside. The space between each is planted with perennial borders which bloom with the flowering seasons of spring and summer. One level is set off by a water garden, which reflects a winter conservatory on the hill behind it.

DATES & HOURS: July 11; 2 p.m. – 6 p.m.

DIRECTIONS: *From the junction of Routes 7 and 112,* turn onto Route 112. Go about 2 miles on Route 112 until you see a sign "Entrance to Lime Rock Race Track." Turn left onto White Hollow Road and travel 2.5 miles. The house, #99, is on the right, opposite a white fence.

Kathleen & James Metz, SHARON, CT

Cobble Pond Farm features both formal and informal herbaceous borders. Several garden rooms, in a pastoral setting, are defined and accented by stone walls, hedges, clipped yews, sweeping lawns, mature trees, flagstone paths, and open fields. The fifteen acres were designed by the Olmsted Brothers firm. The secret garden in the Italian style, sunken garden, and pergola continue to reflect the plan.

DATES & HOURS: July 11; 2 p.m.– 6 p.m.

DIRECTIONS: *Take I-84* to Route 22 north to Route 343 in Amenia, New York. Turn right onto Route 343 and go 5 miles to Sharon Clock Tower. At the four-way stop sign turn right onto South Main Street. Go .9 mile and turn left onto West Woods Road. The entrance is the third driveway on the left. Please park on West Woods Road.

Plum Creek Farm, SHARON, CT

Over 100-foot perennial border planned for summer-long flowering as well as foliage texture and color interest. The grounds overlook a three-tiered formal garden with vistas to a pond with a geyser and a view of a folly in the woods. A walking path runs from the formal garden past a hillside planted with hostas, the upper pond with geyser, a waterfall to lower pond, and a long shrub border. A woodland/fern walk crosses a bridge, passes the folly, and meanders along a stream before crossing a second bridge and returning to the house.

DATES & HOURS: July 11; 2 p.m. – 6 p.m.

DIRECTIONS: *From Route 7* proceed to the intersection of Route 4 at Cornwall Bridge, cross bridge and take Route 4 toward Sharon (up hill) for 2 miles. The driveway is on the right with white gates and small white bridge beyond. Follow driveway to top of hill. *From the intersection of Routes 41 and 4* at Clocktower in Sharon, take Route 4 toward Cornwall Bridge for 5.8 miles. The driveway is on the left. Follow as above.

❖ Cricket Hill Garden,

670 WALNUT HILL ROAD, THOMASTON, CT 06787. (860) 283-1042.
A visit to this garden/nursery has been likened to stepping into a scroll painting of Chinese tree peonies. See more than 100 named varieties of tree peonies in an array of colors, flower forms, and fragrances.

DATES & HOURS: May through June, Wednesday through Sunday, 10 a.m. – 4 p.m.

DIRECTIONS: *Take I-95 or I-84* to Route 8 North. Go to Exit 38/Thomaston, turning left at the bottom of the ramp onto Main Street. Turn left at the third traffic light onto Route 254. Go .5 mile on Route 254 to a blinking yellow light. Turn left onto Walnut Hill Road. Go up hill 1 mile and see our sign on the right.

May Brawley Hill, WARREN, CT

My garden includes a fenced, old-fashioned perennial garden in front of a barn, perennial borders around the house, a potager, a woodland garden featuring species primula, and a pond.

DATES & HOURS: June 27; 10 a.m. – 2 p.m.

DIRECTIONS: *From Kent/Route 7,* take Route 341 east toward Warren. Take the third left after Warren town line onto Brick School Road. Bear right at fork. The house, #184, is 1 mile on left past fork. *From Warren/Route 45 north,* take the fourth left onto Brick School Road. Bear left at stop sign. The house, #184, is 1 mile further on the right. Please park along the road.

Linda Allard's Garden, WASHINGTON, CT

High on a hillside, with a panoramic view of the Litchfield Hills, this garden has old world charm. Surrounded by stone walls covered with espaliered fruit trees and climbing roses and hydrangeas, the garden is partly formal and partly potager. A lush rose arbor filled with pale pink and white roses interwoven with clematis separates the two. Boxwood hedges define the white formal garden enhanced by a variety of green textures. Geometric beds overflowing with fruits, vegetables, herbs and flowers are a true depiction of potager. This part of the garden changes yearly; plantings are worked by color and color combination.

DATES & HOURS: June 13; 10 a.m. – 4 p.m.

DIRECTIONS: *From Washington Green* – at Gunn Memorial Library turn onto Wykeham Road. Follow for about 1.5 miles until Old Litchfield Road forks left. Stay right on Wykeham for about .25 mile. As you go up a small hill, you will approach a red barn on the right side of the road. The entrance to the garden is opposite the red barn. Number 156 is on the stone wall; proceed through the gate to the garden.

Mr. & Mrs. J. Winston Fowlkes III, WASHINGTON, CT

This garden, designed and maintained by Nancy McCabe for the last nine years, consists of long perennial borders and a woodland garden. Two terraces are richly planted.

DATES & HOURS: June 13; 10 a.m. – 2 p.m.

DIRECTIONS: *From Washington Green*, take Wyksham Road for approximately 2 miles, bearing right at fork. Turn right onto East Street, passing a complex of barns and horses, and follow 1 mile to the end. At stop sign, turn left and then an immediate right onto Potash Hill Road. Follow to the end. The house, #72, is a barn with a three-car garage. Please park on road.

Georgia Middlebrook, WASHINGTON, CT

Sprainbrook Farm, with its 1750 house, features a silver-foliage herb garden surrounding an old sundial, a crow's-foot-pattern colonial garden, a salad/herb garden under espaliered pear trees, a collection of old roses near a pond, and a large perennial border. A collection of Bill Heise metal sculptures sets off the gardens, as do five bridges over waterways. There is a pond trail and a developing wildflower garden.

DATES & HOURS: July 11; 2 p.m. – 6 p.m.

DIRECTIONS: *From I-84,* take Exit 15. Go 5 miles through Southbury and Woodbury to Route 47. Turn left toward Washington. Go 4.5 miles to Nettleton Hollow Road. Bear right at fork and continue 2.5 miles to #204. *From the north,* take Route 109 going east through Washington Depot, follow to Nettleton Hollow Road, 2.3 miles from Depot. Turn right and continue 2 miles to #204. Please park off road or along road shoulder.

Charles Raskob Robinson & Barbara Paul Robinson,
WASHINGTON, CT

Brush Hill, included in Rosemary Verey's book The Secret Garden *and* House & Garden *(October 1997), is set between an eighteenth-century Connecticut farmhouse and barn amidst old stone walls. The garden includes a rose walk featuring old roses and climbers, a fountain garden planted in yellows and purples, herbaceous borders, and a terraced garden planted in hot colors leading up to a garden folly, through a woodland arch to a developing woodland walk with waterfalls. There is an old Lord & Burnham greenhouse along with a white wisteria-draped bridge over the pond with water lilies and grass borders.*

DATES & HOURS: June 27; 2 p.m. – 6 p.m.

DIRECTIONS: *From I-84,* take Exit 15 at Southbury. Take Route 6 north to intersection of Route 47. Turn left. Go 4 miles, pass Woodbury Ski Area on left, and make right onto Nettleton Hollow Road. Go 4.1 miles, pass intersection of Wykeman and Carmel Hill Roads, and take next sharp left onto Clark Road (dead end). The house, #88, is the first and only one on left. Please park along Clark Road before driveway.

George Schoellkopf, WASHINGTON, CT

A true plantsman's garden, filled with striking combinations of unusual plants in an eclectic and distinctive design.

DATES & HOURS: June 13, July 11; 2 p.m. – 6. p.m.

DIRECTIONS: *From I-84,* take Exit 15 at Southbury. Take Route 6 north through Southbury and Woodbury. Turn left onto Route 47 north. Go 4 miles, pass Woodbury Ski Area on left and turn right onto Nettleton Hollow Road. Go 1.7 miles. The house is on the right. Please park along road.

Gael Hammer, WASHINGTON DEPOT, CT

This is a cottage garden designed to engulf the house with flowers and shrubs, which provide different spaces for outdoor living. Special areas include oversize borders, a grass garden, a white moon garden, an enormous "step" garden, and container gardens on an old-fashioned porch and a sunny deck.

DATES & HOURS: June 27; 10 a.m. – 4 p.m.

DIRECTIONS: *From Route 109,* travel to Washington Depot. Take River Road .5 mile from town. Park in front of the house.

John & Julia Scott, WEST CORNWALL, CT

About four acres with upper mill pond, waterfall, stream, and lower pond shrubberies, herbaceous borders, and terraced gardens leading to lower pond at garden.

DATES & HOURS: July 11; 10 a.m. – 4 p.m.

DIRECTIONS: *Take Route 7* to Route 128 in West Cornwall. Turn east for 1-2 miles after covered bridge. Take first left, by Cornwall School (Cream Hill Road). Number 52 is on the right side (red board fence.)

Michael Trapp, WEST CORNWALL, CT

This Old World garden is intimate, with cobbled paths, terraced gardens, raised perennial beds, and reflecting pools. Overlooking the Housatonic River, the property has a distinct French/Italian flavor.

DATES & HOURS: July 11; 10 a.m. – 6 p.m.

DIRECTIONS: *From Route 7,* take Route 128 east through the covered bridge into West Cornwall. Continue on Route 128, taking the second left onto River Road. The house, #7, is yellow with gray trim. It is the first on the left and sits behind the Brookside Bistro. Please park in front or along the road.

Rita & Steve Buchanan, WINSTED, CT

This one-acre garden, started in 1993, has been featured in the Litchfield County Times, Country Living Gardener, *and other publications. Surrounding a pond and bordered by a creek and woodland, it includes stone-walled terraces filled with large drifts of perennials, native wetland wildflowers and shrubs, and unusual broadleaf evergreens and conifers. There is a greenhouse and kitchen garden. The Buchanans write and illustrate garden books and have done all the work on this garden themselves.*

DATES & HOURS: June 27; 10 a.m.– 6 p.m.

DIRECTIONS: *From Route 44,* (west of Winsted) go north on Colebrook Road/Route 183. Go 2.1 miles. The house, #317, is on the west side of the road. Please park in driveway or along the road.

❖ Gertrude Jekyll Garden at the Glebe House Museum,
HOLLOW ROAD, WOODBURY, CT 06798. (203) 263-2855.

In 1926 the famed English horticultural designer and writer Gertrude Jekyll was commissioned to plan an "old-fashioned" garden to enhance the newly created museum dedicated to the election of America's first Episcopal bishop. Although small in comparison with other elaborate designs she completed in England and Europe, the Glebe House garden includes 600 feet of classic English-style mixed border and foundation plantings, a small formal quadrant, and an intimate rose allée.

DATES & HOURS: April through November, Wednesday through Sunday, 1 p.m. – 4 p.m.

DIRECTIONS: *From I-84* take Exit 15. Take Route 6 East for ten minutes to the town of Woodbury. Look for the junction of Route 317. Take Route 317 to the fork, bear left and the Glebe House Museum is 100 yards ahead.

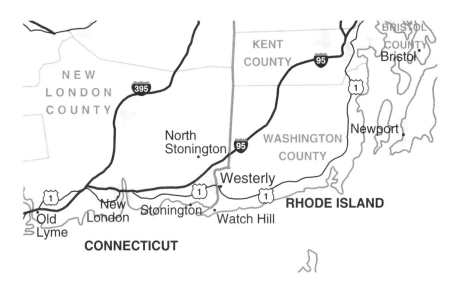

NEW LONDON COUNTY:

June 13, 1999

Barbara & Peter Block — Stewart Hill, North STONINGTON, 10 A.M. – 2 P.M.

Ruth Perry, OLD LYME, 10 A.M. – 2 P.M.

Mr. & Mrs. Juan O'Callahan, STONINGTON, 10 A.M. – 2 P.M.

Mrs. Frederick C. Paffard, STONINGTON, 10 A.M. – 2 P.M.

June 27, 1999

Ruth Perry, OLD LYME, 10 A.M. – 2 P.M.

Mrs. Frederick C. Paffard, Jr., STONINGTON, 10 A.M. – 2 P.M.

July 11, 1999

Barabara & Peter Block — Stewart Hill, NORTH STONINGTON, 10 A.M. – 2 P.M.

Mr. & Mrs. Thomas Moore, STONINGTON, 10 A.M. – 4 P.M.

PLEASE NOTE: *The following gardens in Watch Hill, Rhode Island are also open on this day.*

The Garden at Graigie Brae, WATCH HILL, 10 A.M. – 4 P.M., *page 363*

Mr. & Mrs. Thomas D. O'Connor-Bayberry Ridge, WATCH HILL,

10 A.M.– 4 P.M., *page 364*

❖ Connecticut College Arboretum,

WILLIAM STREET, NEW LONDON, CT 06320. (860) 439-5020.

The Connecticut College Arboretum was established in 1931. In addition to being a recreation area, the arboretum serves the college and the public with a unique blend of horticulture, conservation, and ecological research. Self-guided tour pamphlets are located in a box on the notice board inside the main entrance. The primary collection is of eastern North American native woody plants.

DATES & HOURS: Year round, daily, dawn – dusk.

DIRECTIONS: *From I-95 northbound* take Exit 83: left at the traffic light at end of ramp onto Williams Street. Turn right onto Route 32 North at the first traffic light (top of hill, at Coast Guard Academy). Turn left into the college main entrance at the second traffic light. *From I-95 southbound:* Exit 84N at end of Goldstar Bridge (over Thames River between Groton and New London) which becomes Route 32. Turn left at second light into the main college entrance. *From I-395 southbound:* take Exit 78 (on the left) onto connector to Route 32 South. College entrance is about 2.5 miles south. Turn right at second traffic light into college main entrance.

Barbara & Peter Block — Stewart Hill, NORTH STONINGTON, CT

Nature and history are the grand designers of our garden. When we started gardening here nine years ago the die was cast by hills, rock outcroppings, a second-growth oak forest, and beautiful stone walls creating outdoor rooms, large and small. Originally part of a 600-acre farm, we have cultivated four acres beginning with a perennial border planted in 1990. Since then gardens have popped up everywhere, dictated by stone, sun, slope, and soil. The perennial garden shares the sunny and flat lower levels of the property with a fenced cutting garden of raised beds featuring many unusual annuals started from seed. From there, a stone walkway meanders up through a rock garden of roses, heaths and heathers, creeping phlox, and dwarf conifers. In the upper sections close to the house, rivers of grass float through a woodland garden planted with many native trees and shrubs. Nearby is a pond area with a natural waterfall, a "fireside" garden and meadow.

DATES & HOURS: June 13, July 11; 10 a.m. – 2 p.m..

DIRECTIONS: Take I-95 to Exit 92. At traffic light at end of ramp turn left onto Route 2W. Continue through traffic circle, past shopping center on right, to first traffic light. Turn right. Proceed through stop sign into village of North Stonington. Pass Town Hall and hardware store on right (becomes Wyassup Road). The house is #273 Wyassup Road, 2.8 miles at a curve on the left. It has a green gate and "Stewart Hill" on stone wall.

Ruth Perry, OLD LYME, CT

Visit a cottage garden with a sense of humor. There is a rose garden, an herb garden, a bog garden, and lots of perennials. A developing formal garden is the most recent addition.

DATES & HOURS: June 13, June 27; 10 a.m. – 6 p.m.

DIRECTIONS: *From I-95*, take Exit 70/Old Lyme. Turn onto Route 156 North. Go approximately 5 miles to the intersection of Route 156 and Nehantic State Forest. The Perry garden is on the right. Please park along Park Road.

Mr. & Mrs. Juan O'Callahan, STONINGTON, CT

This four-acre seaside garden consists of grass with trees and border gardens along stone walls. There are six large cutting beds with a variety of flowers and bulbs, and four large rose beds enclosed in a yew hedge. A "secret garden" is built into the rock ledge next to the seawall. The greenhouse holds succulent plants in the summer. The view of Watch Hill, Sandy Point, and Fishers Island is spectacular.

DATES & HOURS: June 13; 10 a.m. – 2 p.m.

DIRECTIONS: *From I-95,* take Exit 91/Stonington Borough Village. At end of ramp, if coming from north, turn left; south, turn right. Go .25 mile, turn left onto North Main Street. Follow for about 2 miles across Route 1 to stop sign and turn left onto Trumbell Street. At next stop sign, turn right over the bridge (railroad tracks) into the village. Follow Water Street to Church Street (Noah's Restaurant), turn left. Go two blocks, then turn left into Orchard Street. Turn right at next block onto East Grand Street. Follow to end – Salt Acres, #20. Park on the grass under the trees on the left side of the road.

Proceeds shared with Pregnancy Support Center, Inc.

Mrs. Frederic C. Paffard Jr., STONINGTON, CT

A ninety-year-old boxwood hedge one-quarter-mile long, a rose arbor, and an old-fashioned garden are highlights. There is also a formal perennial garden edged with boxwoods, and a water garden. Interesting old outbuildings, a greenhouse, vegetables, a natural pond with resident otters and blue herons, and a meadow are adjacent. English boxwood and perennials will be available for sale, with ten percent of the proceeds to be donated to the Garden Conservancy.

DATES & HOURS: June 13, June 27; 10 a.m. – 2 p.m.

DIRECTIONS: *From I-95,* take Exit 91. Go south to North Main Street, then left toward Stonington Borough. Go about 1.5 miles to #389 North Main Street. *From Route 1,* turn north on North Main Street at traffic light. Number 389 is second driveway on right. Please park anywhere.

Mr. & Mrs. Thomas F. Moore, STONINGTON, CT

This special garden includes an English-style spring garden, a green boxwood and wildflower garden, a white garden, a rose garden and a summer garden. It also includes a vegetable patch and cutting garden. The gardens were designed by owners and B & B Landscaping, Mystic, CT.

DATES & HOURS: July 11; 10 a.m. – 4 p.m.

DIRECTIONS: *From I-95,* take Exit 91. Turn right at exit ramp. Take first left onto North Main Street going to Stonington Borough. Go 1 mile to box #523 on left. Turn up lane; sign says "Moore." *From Route 1,* turn north on North Main Street at traffic light. Number 523 is fourth driveway on right. Please park in driveway.

TOLLAND & WINDHAM COUNTIES:

April 25, 1999

R. W. Redfield, SCOTLAND, 10 A.M. – 6 P.M.

May 2, 1999

R. W. Redfield, SCOTLAND, 10 A.M. – 6 P.M.

May 16, 1999

Harriet & Frank Sornberger, SCOTLAND, 10 A.M. – 4 P.M.

June 13, 1999

Westminster Gardens, CANTERBURY, 2 P.M. – 6 P.M.
Harriet & Frank Sornberger, SCOTLAND, 10 A.M. – 4 P.M.

June 27, 1999

Westminster Gardens, CANTERBURY, 2 P.M. – 6 p.m.

July 11, 1999

David & Julia Hayes, COVENTRY, 10 A.M. – 6 P.M.
Lt. Col. Paul G. (U.S.A., Ret.) & Mrs. Ann B. Hennen, POMFRET,
     10 A.M. – 4 P.M.

Westminster Gardens —
Eleanor B. Cote & Adrian P. Hart, CANTERBURY, CT

The area surrounding the house has border plantings of dwarf evergreens, rhododendrons, azaleas, other shrubs, and perennials. There is also a stone terrace with a waterfall. The back area is approximately three acres. It has nearly an acre of woodland gardens with crushed stone walkways, 230 different varieties of hostas, and many astilbes, pulmonarias, ferns and other shade-loving plants. The remaining area has twenty gardens planted wih tall bearded iris, Japanese iris, Siberian Iris, daylilies, peonies, ornamental grasses, shrubs, various perennials, and some annuals.

DATES & HOURS: June 13, June 27; 2 p.m. – 6 p.m.

DIRECTIONS: *From I-395 South,* take Exit 89. Turn right at the bottom of ramp. Follow Route 14 about 6 miles to the stop sign at the bottom of the hill. Turn right. Go over bridge to four-way stop at intersection of Routes 169 & Route 14. Go straight on Route 14. *From 1-395 North,* take Exit 83A. Turn left at bottom of ramp. Follow Route 169 for approximately 10 miles to intersection of Route 169 & 14. Turn left onto Route 14/Westminster Road. Number 26 is the second house on the left after the Mobil station. Park along the road.

David & Julia Hayes, COVENTRY, CT

Sculptor David Hayes, whose work is found in many public and private collections in this country and in Europe, lives and works on this old farm. Hayes displays his completed works in an old orchard, by the pond, in a large hayfield, and behind the house. They are in or near informal gardens of herbs, wildflowers and ferns, roses (mostly old roses), annuals, and vegetables. Wear comfortable shoes as the paths are not all smooth.

DATES & HOURS: July 11; 10 a.m. – 6 p.m.

DIRECTIONS: *From I-84,* take Exit 59/Route 384. Follow Route 384 8 miles to end. Take Route 44 about 3.5 miles, then turn right into Silver Street (signs there for Caprilands and Hale Homestead). Follow about 2 miles to end, turning left onto South Street (go to right at fork after Hale Homestead). Go 4.5 miles to #905. Please park along street. The driveway is available for those with walking difficulties.

Proceeds shared with East Catholic High School Scholarship Fund.

❖ Caprilands Herb Farm,

534 SILVER STREET, COVENTRY, CT 06238. (860) 742-7244.

More than thirty world-famous theme gardens illustrate the use of shrubs, annual flowers, herbaceous plants, vegetables, and herbs in numerous creative and decorative arrangements and settings. Highlights include a bird and butterfly garden, a large herb garden, a wildflower garden, a naturalists' garden, a small arboretum, and a 400-foot solar greenhouse displaying many herbal varieties suitable for northern gardens. The gardens are framed by a sheep meadow with a flock of Scottish Blackface sheep, complementing the dyers' and weavers' gardens.

DATES & HOURS: Year round, daily except holidays, 9 a.m. – 5 p.m. (10 a.m. in the winter months).

DIRECTIONS: *The farm is on Silver Street* in North Coventry, south of Routes 44 and 31. Route 31 is accessed from I-84. Route 44 is accessed from I-384E.

Lt. Col. Paul G. (U.S.A., Ret.) & Mrs. Ann B. Hennen,

POMFRET, CT

These gardens, in various degrees of formality, cover three acres. Oriental and Occidental influences, coupled with appropriate garden ornaments and statuary, are present. Featured are perennial borders, stone pathways, a woodland path and brook garden, ponds with fountains, shrubs and natural borders, a bonsai display, a rock garden, and more. Work on new gardens and other projects may be in progress during visit.

DATES & HOURS: July 11; 10 a.m. – 4 p.m.

DIRECTIONS: *From I-84,* take Exit 69/Route 74 south to Route 44. Take Route 44 east to the four-way stop at the intersection of Routes 44, Route 169, and Route 97. Turn right onto Route 44 toward Putnam. The Pomfret Post Office is a short distance from the intersection on the right. The house, #52, is the second past the post office. Park on premises or at the post office lot.

Proceeds shared with The Pomfret Historical Society.

R. W. Redfield, SCOTLAND, CT

This large woodland garden includes a small stream bordered with candelabra primroses. The higher ground includes native and exotic woodland plants. There is also a sunny area with creeping phlox and other sun-lovers. Mature, slow-growing conifers and a raised bed area constructed in an old barn foundation are additional features.

DATES & HOURS: April 25, May 2; 10 a.m. – 6 p.m.

DIRECTIONS: *From the center of Scotland* (opposite the Green), Brook Road leaves Routes 14 & 97 between Congregational and Roman Catholic churches. Follow Brook Road approximately 1.8 miles to #379 on the left side of the road. Please park in the yard on lawn.

Harriet & Frank Sornberger, SCOTLAND, CT

Large granite outcrop with alpines and conifers. Woodland garden. Troughs and large stone raised beds with alpines. Long perennial border against stone walls. Sloping rock garden in center of lawn. Raised beds for delphiniums and vegetables.

DATES & HOURS: May 16, June 13; 10 a.m. – 4 p.m.

DIRECTIONS: *From Route 6,* take Route 97 South/Pudding Hill Road 2.8 miles to #426. *From Route 14,* go east to Route 97 North/Pudding Hill Road 2 miles to #426. Please park along driveway or on the west side of the road.

❖ Bowen House, Roseland Cottage,

556 ROUTE 169, WOODSTOCK, CT. (860) 928-4074.

The gardens were laid out in 1850 as part of the landscape of Henry Bowen's summer "cottage" built in 1846. Boxwoods border the twenty-one beds of annuals and perennials, forming a "parterre" garden. Landscape designer Andrew Jackson Downing's theories inspired the design of the ribbon and carpet-bedding plantings. Noteworthy trees and shrubs include a tulip tree, a Japanese maple, a Chinese wisteria, and old-fashioned roses.

DATES & HOURS: Year round, daily, dawn – dusk.

DIRECTIONS: *From I-395* take Exit 97 for Route 44 West for 1 mile. Go west on Route 171 for 3 miles and north on Route 169 for 1 mile. House is on the left.

DELAWARE

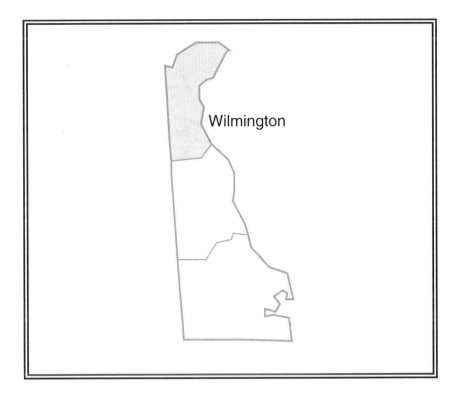

Wilmington

1999 DELAWARE OPEN DAYS

May 9: WILMINGTON AREA

WILMINGTON AREA: *May 9, 1999*

Meown Farm, CENTREVILLE, 10 A.M. – 2 P.M.

Mt. Cuba, GREENVILLE, 10 A.M. – 6 P.M.

Larke Stowe, WILMINGTON, 10 A.M. – 4 P.M.

 ❖ Gibraltar, WILMINGTON, by appointment only.

PLEASE NOTE: *The following gardens in Pennsylvania are participating as part of the Wilmington Area Open Day.*

Glenderro Farm, COATESVILLE, PA, 10 A.M. – 4 P.M., *page 358*

Runnymede, COATESVILLE, PA, 10 A.M. – 4 P.M., *page 359*

Primrose Paths, FAIRVILLE, PA, 10 A.M. – 2 P.M., *page 359*

Meown Farm, CENTERVILLE, DE

Approaching Meown Farm, one cannot help but notice the stone barn with its unique water tower. Designed in 1931 by Wilmington architect Albert Ely Ives, it originally housed the riding stable of Mrs. Isabella Mathieu du Pont Sharp. Today her son, Mr. Bayard Sharp, resides at Meown. Located among the rolling hills of northern Delaware, the property is enhanced by an orchard, rose garden, perennial border, cutting garden, and vegetable garden. The greenhouse, erected in 1969, contains some winners of the Philadelphia Flower Show awards.

DATES & HOURS: May 9; 10 a.m. – 2 p.m.

DIRECTIONS: *From the south,* take I-95 to Wilmington. Take Exit 7/Delaware Avenue/Route 52 and proceed straight ahead for three blocks to a dead end. Turn left onto Route 52 North. This street will change its name three times: Delaware Avenue, Pennsylvania Avenue, and Kennett Pike. Travel for 6 miles, before entering the Town of Centerville. Turn right onto Center Meeting Road. Meown is the second driveway on the right. *From the north,* take I-95 to Exit 7B and proceed one block to a traffic light, turning right onto Route 52 North. Follow as above. Please park in front of the greenhouse.

Proceeds shared with The Delaware Center for Horticulture.

Mt. Cuba, GREENVILLE, DE

The woodland gardens at Mt. Cuba have, for more than three decades, been the focus of Mrs. Pamela Copeland's interest in native plants and conservation. Most of the plants in this internationally renowned, naturalistic garden are native to the Piedmont region of the eastern United States. Mt. Cuba is located in the dramatic Piedmont countryside of northern Delaware. The gardens exemplify the beauty and integrity that are created when a single hand and mind, working over time, dictate the style and form of a landscape.

DATES & HOURS: May 9; 10 a.m. – 6 p.m.

DIRECTIONS: *From Route 141,* turn west onto Barley Mill Road at the traffic light at that intersection. Drive 3.9 miles on Barley Mill Road. Go past a four-way stop sign, over a bridge, and across railroad tracks, past Barley Mill Stables on the right, past Mt. Cuba Road (Road #261), around a sharp corner and into a valley with a split-rail fence on the right. Look for painted white rocks at the main drive on the right. Please proceed up drive without turning.

Proceeds shared with The Delaware Center for Horticulture.

❖ University of Delaware Botanic Gardens, Department of Plant & Soil Sciences, NEWARK, DE 19717. (302) 831-3651.

The mission of the University of Delaware Botanic Gardens is to promote general interest in plants. Education in all its facets is the top priority of the gardens. There are collections for all seasons of the year. The gardens are a Holly Society of America Test Arboretum and have a good selection of mature hollies. Beginning in early to mid-April, the magnolias begin to flower and offer early visitors a spectacular display. The viburnums brighten the spring garden with their attractive and sometimes fragrant flowers. The herbaceous garden provides a great deal of summer color and many examples of annual and perennial plants for the home garden. The plant interest continues into the autumn with vibrant fall foliage and colorful fruit of the trees and shrubs.

DATES & HOURS: Year round, daily, dawn – dusk.

DIRECTIONS: *From I-95 South,* take Route 896 north for 1.5 miles. *From the north,* take Route 896 south to College Avenue, .5 miles south of the light at Park Place. The University of Delaware Botanic Gardens is located on the University of Delaware campus in Newark, Delaware, on the grounds surrounding Townsend Hall, Worrilow Hall and Fischer Greenhouse/Laboratory. It is on South College Avenue across from the Chrysler assembly plant and adjacent to the ice skating rinks.

Larke Stowe, WILMINGTON, DE

Larke Stowe is situated on twenty acres with a view of a pond and azalea hill as you approach the house. The more formal gardens near the house to the east include an herb garden, an espaliered crab apple tree, terrace, and perennial beds. A charming grandchildren's bath house is near the pool. Cutting garden boxes and a small greenhouse are north of the house.

DATES & HOURS: May 9; 10 a.m. – 4 p.m.

DIRECTIONS: *Take I-95* to Wilmington, DE. Exit at Delaware Avenue/Route 52 North. Follow Route 52/Pennsylvania Avenue North to Route 100 (2.2 miles). Turn right on Route 100/Montchanin Road. Go 2.3 miles to crossroad with a four-way stop sign. Turn left, staying on Route 100/Montchanin Road. Go 1.2 miles to residence on the right, #2800 on the mailbox post. Please park in the driveway.

❖ **Gibraltar,**

2501 PENNSYLVANIA AVENUE, WILMINGTON, DE 19806. (302) 651-9617.
Gibraltar was designed by the landscape architect Marian Cruger Coffin between 1916 and 1925 for Isabella du Pont Sharp and Hugh Rodney Sharp, Sr. Coffin considered Gibraltar to be the best of her many commissions, and it is perhaps the most intact of her extant works today. Typical of the European-influenced design so prevalent during the early twentieth century in America, the estate has become one of Wilmington's few remaining urban open spaces. Formal elements like the Italian Garden, the Boxwood Walk, and the Bald Cypress Allée leading to a Belvedere, are set within a dramatically sloping English Parkscape. An extensive collection of statuary and garden ornaments is displayed throughout the site. Stone and extensive wrought iron work of the highest caliber completes the design.

DATES & HOURS: Currently undergoing restoration. Tours available by appointment, open hours to begin in 1999. Call for details.

DIRECTIONS: *I-95 into Wilmington.* 52 North/Pennsylvania Avenue, approximately 1.2 miles. Turn right at Greenhill Avenue. Entrance immediately on right.

❖ **Goodstay Gardens, University of Delaware Wilmington Campus,**

2600 PENNSYLVANIA AVENUE, WILMINGTON, DE 19806. (302) 573-4450.
The property dates from the 1700s. The tudor-style gardens, with gravel paths and boxwood-lined rooms, were described by artist Howard Pyle from his boyhood in the 1850s and were preserved and enhanced by Ellen du Pont Wheelwright and her husband, noted landscape architect Robert Wheelwright, in the 1920s. The gardens also feature a magnolia allée terminating in a circular reflecting pool, and small woodland garden with stream. Mrs. Wheelwright bequeathed the property to the University of Delaware in 1968. The Friends of Goodstay Gardens help enhance and maintain the gardens.

DATES & HOURS: Year round, daily, dawn – dusk.

DIRECTIONS: *From I-95,* take the Delaware Avenue Exit and bear left onto Pennsylvania Avenue. After the light at Pennsylvania Avenue and Greenhill Avenue, turn left through entrance in white fence. Parking is available in front of Goodstay Center. Please follow signs to garden entrance. *From Route 52:* Route 52 becomes Pennsylvania Avenue. After passing light at Rising Sun Lane, turn right at the second entrance to the Wilmington Campus.

❖ Hagley Museum,

ROUTE 141, WILMINGTON, DE 19807. (302) 658-2400.

Hagley Museum is where the du Pont story begins in the Brandywine Valley and features the original du Pont mills, estate, and gardens. Set on 235 acres along the Brandywine River, Hagley offers demonstrations and restorations for visitors of all ages, including a workers' community, and Eleutherian Mills, the first du Pont family home built in America. Adjoining the home is the E. I. du Pont Restored Garden, where the glory of the many du Pont gardens that grace the Brandywine Valley began.

DATES & HOURS: March 15 through December 30, daily, 9:30 a.m. – 4:30 p.m.; winter hours, January through March 14, weekends 9:30 a.m. – 4:30 p.m.; weekdays, guided tour 1:30 p.m.

DIRECTIONS: *From the South,* take I-95 to Exit 5B for Newport. Follow Route 141 North for 7 miles. After crossing Route 100, watch for Hagley's main entrance to the left. *From the North,* take I-95 South to Exit 8B for West Chester. Follow Route 202 north, also called Concord Pike, for 1.3 miles. Stay in the left lane and turn left onto Route 141. Follow Route 141 south for 2 miles, get into the right lane and turn right onto Tyler-McConnell Bridge. Shortly after crossing the bridge, watch for Hagley's main entrance on the right.

❖ The Rockwood Museum,

610 SHIPLEY ROAD, WILMINGTON, DE 19809. (302) 761-4340.

A gardenesque landscape with large specimen trees surrounds a rural Gothic manor house. A walled garden within landscaped grounds is home to several varieties of climbing roses, which bloom simultaneously with catawba rhododendrons. Sixty-five acres of woodlands with trails buffer this tranquil and beautiful haven.

DATES & HOURS: Year round, daily, 10 a.m.– dusk

DIRECTIONS: *From I-95 North or South,* take Exit 9/Marsh Road and follow brown museum signs to gate at 610 Shipley Road.

❖ Winterthur Museum, Garden & Library,

WINTERTHUR, DE 19735. (302) 888-4600 OR (800) 448-3883.

The Winterthur Garden is one of the best examples of naturalistic design supported by a plant collection that is arranged to achieve color combinations. The garden has a romantic ambiance and invites people to walk among the plants and the dramatic land forms. The Winterthur landscape represents an idealized vision of an American farm and forest. For more information, please see The Winterthur Garden: Henry Francis du Pont's Romance with the Land, *by Denise Magnani.*

DATES & HOURS: Year round, Monday through Saturday, 9 a.m. – 5 p.m.; Sunday, noon – 5 p.m. Closed Thanksgiving, Christmas, and New Year's Day.

DIRECTIONS: *Located on Route 52,* 6 miles northwest of Wilmington, 5 miles south of Route 1, and 30 miles southwest of Philadelphia, Pennsylvania.

DISTRICT OF COLUMBIA

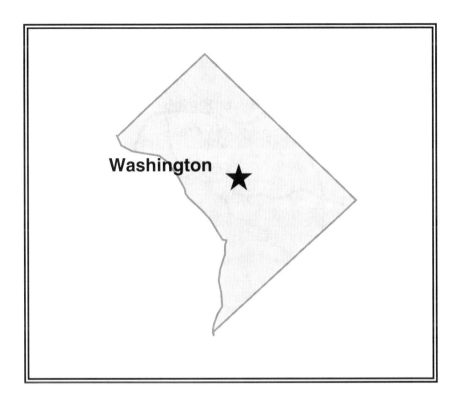

1999 DISTRICT OF COLUMBIA OPEN DAYS

May 15: WASHINGTON AREA
June 26: WASHINGTON AREA

WASHINGTON AREA:

May 15, 1999

John & Caroline Macomber, WASHINGTON DC, 10 A.M. – 4 P.M.

Mr. & Mrs. Eric Weinmann, WASHINGTON DC, 10 A.M. – 4 P.M.

 ❖ Dumbarton Oaks Park, WASHINGTON DC, 2 P.M – 6 P.M.

PLEASE NOTE: *The following gardens in Maryland and Virginia are participating as part of the Washington Area Open Day.*

May 15, 1999

Nancy Vorhees, BETHESDA, MD, 10 A.M. – 2 P.M., *page 180*

Gay & Tony Barclay — ORCHARD FARM, Potomac, MD, 10 A.M. – 4 P.M.,
        page 181

The Olson Garden, POTOMAC, MD, 10 A.M. – 4 P.M., *page 181*

Carole Ottesen's Garden, POTOMAC, MD, 2 P.M. – 6 P.M., *page 182*

June 26, 1999

The Sexton – Borgiotti Garden, CHEVY CHASE, MD, 10 A.M. – 4 P.M., *page 180*

Robert Moore & Frank Kirste, SILVER SPRING, MD, 10 A.M. – 4 P.M., *page 183*

Hilltop Cottage, McLEAN, VA, 10 A.M. – 4 P.M., *page 399*

John & Caroline Macomber, WASHINGTON, DC

The design of this narrow garden reflects the serene Federal style of the house; its simple lines are accentuated by a water runnel and a line of river birch, which unite three seating areas. The plantings are designed to be more cultivated near the house and to have a more woodland character at the far end: Trees, shrubs, and a selection of bulbs and perennials are planned especially for fall, winter, and spring interest.

DATES & HOURS: May 15; 10 a.m. – 4 p.m.

DIRECTIONS: *The garden is in central Georgetown* and can be reached from main roads such as Canal Road from the west, Wisconsin Avenue from the north, and Pennsylvania Avenue or M Street from the east. Number 2806 is on the south side of N Street, between 28th and 29th Streets.

Proceeds shared with The Georgetown Garden Club.

Mr. & Mrs. Eric Weinmann, WASHINGTON, DC

Our three-acre garden within the city has developed over the last twenty years. We have created a sweep of lawn, herbaceous borders enclosed by a trellis, a trompe l'ocil allée of willows, vegetable and cutting gardens, and a shade garden. A wide pebble terrace runs the length of the house.

DATES & HOURS: May 15; 10 a.m. – 4 p.m.

DIRECTIONS: *From Route 495 west,* take the Connecticut Avenue exit. Go south on Connecticut Avenue to Nebraska Avenue. Turn right and go around Ward Circle and take a left on Nebraska Avenue. Number 3244 is just beyond the fourth light on Nebraska Avenue at the corner of Foxhall Road. Please park on Nebraska Avenue opposite the house.

❖ Dumbarton Oaks Gardens & Dumbarton Oaks Park,

1703 32ND STREET, NW, WASHINGTON, DC 20007. (202) 339-6401.

The Dumbarton Oaks Gardens and Dumbarton Oaks Park were designed as one project by noted landscape architect Beatrix Farrand in cooperation with her clients, Mr. & Mrs. Robert Woods Bliss, who purchased the property in 1920. The design, mostly completed in the 1920s and 1930s, progressed from formal terraced gardens near the house, to an informal, naturalistic landscape in the stream valley below, with designed views between them. In 1940, the Blisses gave the house and related formal gardens to Harvard University as a research center and conveyed the twenty-seven-acre, naturalistic landscape to the National Park Service. Dumbarton Oaks Park is managed by the Rock Creek Park Division of the National Capital Region of the National Park Service.

DATES & HOURS: Daily, April through October, 2 p.m. – 6 p.m.; November through March, 2 p.m. – 5 p.m.

DIRECTIONS: *Garden entrance:* Located at R and 31st Streets, NW, 1.5 blocks east of Wisconsin Avenue. Please park along the street. *Park Entrance:* North on Lovers Lane from R Street, east of 31st Street; Lovers Lane runs between the Dumbarton Oaks Gardens east wall and the west edge of Montrose Park. Entrance is on the left at the bottom of the hill.

❖ Tudor Place Historic House & Museum Garden,

1644 31ST STREET, NW, WASHINGTON, DC 20007. (202) 965-0400.

Tudor Place's five-and-one-half-acre garden retains its original Federal period flavor while it reflects the evolution of 180 years of family ownership by descendants of Martha Washington. The extensive, sloping South Lawn has centuries-old specimen trees surrounded by nineteenth-century shrubberies. The formal north garden is divided into rooms with box circle and "flower knot" that date from the earliest design.

DATES & HOURS: Monday through Saturday, 10 a.m. – 4 p.m.; Sundays in April, May, September, and October, 12:30 p.m. – 4 p.m. Closed major holidays.

DIRECTIONS: *Located between* Q and R Streets in Georgetown, a twenty-minute walk from Dupont Circle or Foggy Bottom Metrorail Stops. Metrobus stops are nearby at Q and 31st Streets and Wisconsin Avenue. Street parking only.

❖ United States National Arboretum,

3501 NEW YORK AVENUE, NE, WASHINGTON, DC 20002. (202) 245-2726.
This is America's arboretum, on 440 acres of meadows and wooded hills in the
heart of the city. There are extensive collections of native and Asian plants in
natural settings. The National Herb Garden and the Bonsai and Penjing
Museum are world renowned, as is the Gotelli collection of dwarf conifers.
Azalea and magnolia displays are among the largest of their kind, and spectacular in the spring.

DATES & HOURS: Year round, daily, 8 a.m. – 5 p.m. Closed Christmas Day.

DIRECTIONS: *Located in* northeast Washington, D.C., off New York Avenue
(Route 50) and Bladensburg Road. Gates are located on the New York Avenue
service road and on R Street, off Bladensburg Road. Parking is free.

❖ Washington National Cathedral — Bishop's Garden,

MASSACHUSETTS & WISCONSIN AVENUES, NW, WASHINGTON, DC 20016-5098.
(301) 986-1290.
*The Bishop's Garden, often described as an "oasis in the city," includes a rose
garden, two perennial borders, a yew walk, three herb gardens, the bishop's lawn
and the shadow house. Tours are offered by All Hallows Guild, founded in 1916
to maintain and beautify the gardens and grounds of the cathedral. Plants are
based on Christian myths and legends, on historical interest, or are native to
America. The gardens were designed by Frederick Law Olmsted, Jr.*

DATES & HOURS: Year round, daily, dawn – dusk. Tours offered without
reservation, April through October, Wednesdays, 10:30 a.m. Group tours offered
by reservation only.

DIRECTIONS: *Take Massachusetts Avenue NW* to Cathedral Close (at intersection of Wisconsin Avenue NW). Turn onto Cathedral Grounds (Close) at South
Road. Gardens are entered through arch (on foot) approximately 300 feet from
Wisconsin on South Road. Self-guided garden tour brochure available in herb
cottage gift shop nearby.

FLORIDA

Vero Beach

1999 FLORIDA OPEN DAYS

April 17: VERO BEACH AREA

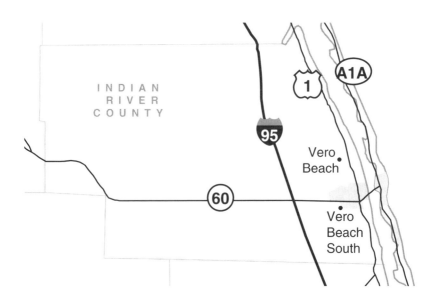

VERO BEACH: *April 17, 1999*

❖ The Garden at the Garden Club of Indian River, VERO BEACH,
    10 A.M. – 2 p.m.

The Gardens of Gracewood, VERO BEACH, 10 A.M. – 2 p.m.

Sally Ann & George Isham, VERO BEACH, 10 A.M. – 2 p.m.

Klein Garden, VERO BEACH, 10 A.M. – 2 p.m.

Lincoln Garden, VERO BEACH, 10 A.M. – 2 p.m.

Mangrove Gardens at Carwill Oaks, VERO BEACH, 10 A.M. – 2 p.m.

Alex & Marty Ross, VERO BEACH, 10 A.M. – 2 p.m.

Thai Tropical, VERO BEACH, 10 A.M. – 2 p.m.

 ❖ McKee Botanical Garden, VERO BEACH, 9:30 A.M. – 11 A.M.

Klein Garden, VERO BEACH, FL

Featured is a suburban Florida garden scheme with multiple target gardens within a large enclosed courtyard. Owners have interacted with mangroves surrounding their gardens and have incorporated an orchid house, a rose garden, and an herb garden. The owners fully maintain the gardens and grounds. This residence has also been designated as a Certified Florida Yard. Landscape architect Dan Ford assisted in the creation of this garden.

DATES & HOURS: April 17; 10 a.m. – 2 p.m.

DIRECTIONS: *From the south,* 3 miles north of Beachland Boulevard, Vero Beach on A-1-A to Bermuda Bay west entrance. Once past guard gate follow road between two small lakes to stop sign. Turn right, then an immediate left to end of cul-de-sac.

Lincoln Garden, VERO BEACH, FL

The garden features a European-style garden with an upper grass terrace leading to a lower terrace swimming pool, a pebble motor court extending into house foundation, and solid Japanese yew hedge.

DATES & HOURS: April 17; 10 a.m. – 2 p.m.

DIRECTIONS: *Take A-1-A to Fred Turk Drive.* Go to gate of John's Island at end of road, first house on right. From the north, go to main gate and ask for directions to Lincoln house.

Proceeds shared with McKee Botanical Garden.

Mangrove Gardens at Carwill Oaks, VERO BEACH, FL

Located on the Indian River, our garden encompasses mangroves, wetlands, lagoons, spoil islands, and upland grounds accessible by a series of walkways, bridges, and paths. Enter the mangroves and view a mini-rainforest. Following the paths and walkways you will arrive in the "kitchen garden" located along the river. Proceeding along the river you come to the "panther's lair" island and a large lagoon. It is our hope that our gardens will demonstrate to all who come that mankind and mangroves cannot only successfully coexist, but flourish — and that with careful planning this precious ecosystem can be preserved. The landscape architect is Dan Ford of The Landscape Design Studio.

DATES & HOURS: April 17; 10 a.m. – 2 p.m.

DIRECTIONS: *Take Route 60 east* to A-1-A north to the blinking light (approximately 3 miles north of the intersection of Route 60 and A-1-A). Turn left (west) into John's Island entrance and follow the guard's directions to the home. NOTE: Visitors will be admitted at the gate only by showing the guard a copy of the *Directory.*

Alex & Marty Ross, VERO BEACH, FL

One of the principal things that attracted us to our house was its location on a small canal off the Indian River. The site had all the advantages of being near open water, but it was peaceful, private, and protected. It reminded me, oddly enough, of the lagoon at my family's home in northern Minnesota. "Lagoon," then, was the key word that guided Warren McCormick as he designed the property; lagoon-like it certainly is, with its free-form pool, shady glades, and lush natural plantings.

DATES & HOURS: April 17; 10 a.m. – 2 p.m.

DIRECTIONS: *Off A-1-A,* just over 1 mile south of the 17th Street Bridge, turn right into the Little Harbour subdivision. Turn left onto Little Harbour Drive. Follow the road to its end on a cul-de-sac. Our home, #1310, is the yellow dormered story-and-a-half on the cul-de-sac.

Proceeds shared with The Saginaw Art Museum.

Thai Tropical, VERO BEACH, FL

Landscape architect Dan Ford created a small tropical paradise with a winding pathway that weaves through a water garden and bog area. You will appreciate many bromeliads, orchids, and Hawaiian ti plants. Rest on benches and enjoy the eastern serenity of water, wind, and nature. Pool and gardens are enhanced by Balinese and Thai stone and wood sculptures.

DATES & HOURS: April 17; 10 a.m. - 2 p.m.

DIRECTIONS: *On A-1-A* a little over 1 mile south of the 17th Street Bridge. Ten Coins – Corona Lane #1455

Proceeds shared with McKee Botanical Garden.

❖ Garden at the Garden Club of Indian River,

VERO BEACH, FL

Guests cross an oriental bridge from the parking area, walk through wrought-iron gates to find within our garden's serpentine walls not only quiet spaces planted with native trees and shrubs — areas to quietly contemplate nature — but also areas specifically planted to attract butterflies. Areas shaded by century-old live oaks blend many foliages, all identified. A paved terrace is surrounded by a sitting wall to view statuary, a bubbling fountain, and a birdbath.

DATES & HOURS: April 17; 10 a.m. – 2.p.m.

DIRECTIONS: *On the corner of 17th Avenue and 26th Street,* north of the library and on the mainland (west of the RR tracks) within the city of Vero Beach. *From State Road 60* go north on 17th Avenue 6 blocks. *From I-95* go east on State Road 60 eight miles to 14th Avenue, turn left, go 6 blocks to 26th Street and turn west 2 blocks and enter the club's parking area on 26th Street.

❖ **McKee Botanical Garden,**

350 US 1, Vero Beach, FL 32962-2905. (561) 794-0601.

The garden is now eighteen acres of what was originally an eighty-acre tropical hammock along the Indian River. McKee Botanical Garden was originally designed by landscape architect William Lyman Phillips in the early 1930s. Phillips created the basic infrastructure of streams, ponds, and trails. Native vegetation was augmented with ornamental plants, and for years McKee Jungle Gardens was one of Florida's most popular attractions. The garden went into decline during the 1970s due to competition from new large-scale attractions. The land, all but the last eighteen acres, was sold to condominium developers, but fortunately, the historic core of the garden remains. Plans are underway to reopen in 1999 as a public botanical garden but during 1999 the garden will be under full construction.

DATES & HOURS: April 17; 9:30 a.m. – 11 a.m.

DIRECTIONS: *The garden is located at 350 South US 1,* at the southern gateway to Vero Beach, on the mainland. It is two hours southeast of Orlando and one hour north of West Palm Beach.

GEORGIA

Lookout Mountain & Chattanooga, TN Area

Atlanta

1999 GEORGIA OPEN DAYS

May 15: Atlanta Area
May 22: Lookout Mountain & Chattanooga, TN Area

ATLANTA AREA: *May 15, 1999*

Jane & Dameron Black, ATLANTA, 10 A.M. – 4 P.M.
Hugh & Mary Palmer Dargan, ATLANTA, 10 A.M. – 4 P.M.
Franklin's Outhouse Garden, ATLANTA, 10 A.M. – 4 P.M.
The Garden of Ryan Gainey, DECATUR, 10 A.M. – 4 P.M.

Jane & Dameron Black, ATLANTA, GA

The garden is laid out with classical as well as modern elements. A gracious porch frames a dramatic axis that terminates in a grove of hardy palms. Other elements include an enclosed lawn, a formal pond, a hot-colored border, and a hidden swimming pool. Additional points of interest are a garden structure (circa 1881) and a pair of English lead statues. Exotic as well as native plantings reinforce the formal elements.

DATES & HOURS: May 17; 10 a.m. – 4 p.m.

DIRECTIONS: *From I-75,* take Exit 107/West Paces Ferry, and travel east on West Paces Ferry for 1.5 miles to Northside Drive. Turn left and go .6 mile and turn right onto Valley Road. Travel 1.1 miles and the house, #80, is on the right.

Proceeds shared with The Atlanta Botanical Garden.

Hugh & Mary Palmer Dargan, ATLANTA, GA

Visitors won't be surprised to learn that this couple spent many years gardening in Charleston, for the influence of that city's courtyard garden is obvious. In the front garden, dubbed The Perennial Sweep, boxwood balls anchor the arabesque curves of the planted borders. The backyard garden has a charming blue and white theme, carried out not only in the plantings, but in well chosen garden accessories. Hand-painted tiles created by the Dargans show that this is very much an artist's garden.

DATES & HOURS: May 15; 10 a.m. – 4 p.m.

DIRECTIONS: *From I-85 South* turn right onto Lenox Road. Turn left onto Buford Highway and then right onto Sidney Marcus Boulevard. Go .3 mile and turn right onto Lindbergh Drive. Go .7 mile and turn right onto Forrest Way. The garden is at #2595 Forrest Way.

Franklin's Outhouse Garden, ATLANTA, GA

This is a small in-town garden which has been developed over the last thirteen years. Key elements include a white lattice fence that provides enclosure for the garden, a large stone terrace for entertaining, a small grass area surrounded by six-foot perennial and annual flower beds, a fountain and fish pond, a wildflower area, planted pots which add interest and color, and a screened garden house which is fondly referred to as the "Outhouse." The garden provides an extensive collection of flowering trees and shrubs selected for seasonal interest and fragrance.

DATES & HOURS: May 17; 10 a.m. – 4 p.m.

DIRECTIONS: *From I-75* take Exit 10A (Northside Drive/Route 41North). Go .6 mile to Collier Road. Turn right on Collier Road and travel .1 mile to Cottage Lane. Turn left and the house, #2060, is on the left. Please park along the road.

The Garden of Ryan Gainey, DECATUR, GA

The garden has an extensive plant collection, beautifully integrated into rooms and thoughtfully designed to show classic garden style yet exuberant color. The garden has received national and international publicity and has been featured on HGTV (an eight-part series for PBS), The Victory Garden, *and* Audrey Hepburn's Gardens of the World.

DATES & HOURS: May 17; 10 a.m. – 4 p.m.

DIRECTIONS: *From I-75/I-85* (south of the center of Atlanta), take the Freedom Parkway Exit. Do not exit at Carter Center, but stay on Freedom Parkway until it dead ends on Ponce De Leon. Turn right on Ponce De Leon. When Scott Boulevard splits off to the left, bear right and stay on Ponce De Leon. At the third street on the right, turn right onto Drexel and then left at the next street. This is Emerson and the house, #129, will be on the left. Please park along the road.

Proceeds shared with The Cherokee Garden Library of the Atlanta History Center.

❖ Atlanta Botanical Garden,

1345 PIEDMONT ROAD, ATLANTA, GA 30309. (404) 876-5859.

At the Atlanta Botanical Garden you will find collections of roses, herbs, summer bulbs, ornamental grasses, conifers, and much more. A highlight of any trip to the garden is a tour through the Dorothy Chapman Fuqua Conservatory. Inside are collections of exotic tropical plants such as palms, cycads, ferns, orchids, and epiphytes. The adjacent Desert House showcases Old World succulents, including botanical rarities.

DATES & HOURS: Year round, Tuesday through Sunday, 9 a.m. – 6 p.m.

DIRECTIONS: *From I-75/I-85* take the 14th Street Exit and proceed east until it dead ends on Piedmont Avenue. Turn left and the garden entrance will be .5 miles on the right.

❖ The Atlanta History Center,

130 WEST PACES FERRY ROAD, ATLANTA, GA 30305. (404) 814-4000.

Thirty-three acres of beautiful gardens, woodlands, and nature trails show the horticultural history of the Atlanta region. Gardens include the Mary Howard Gilbert Memorial Quarry Garden with native plants, wildflowers, bridges, and a stream; the Tullie Smith Farm gardens featuring period vegetables, flowers, herbs, and antique species rarely seen elsewhere; the Swan House gardens featuring formal boxwoods and classical statuary; the Swan Woods Trail, labelled for nature study; the Garden for Peace featuring the Soviet Georgian sculpture "The Peace Tree"; the Frank A. Smith Memorial Rhododendron Garden featuring dozens of species of rhododendrons and azaleas; and the Cherry-Sims Asian-American Garden featuring species from the southeastern United States and their Asian counterparts, including many cultivars of Japanese maples.

DATES & HOURS: Year round, Monday through Saturday; 10 a.m.– 5:30 p.m. Sunday, noon – 5:30 p.m.

DIRECTIONS: *From I-75* take the West Paces Ferry Road Exit. The Center is located 2.6 miles east of the Interstate in Buckhead.

LOOKOUT MOUNTAIN, GA/
CHATTANOOGA, TN AREA: *May 22, 1999*

Susan & Steven Bradley, LOOKOUT MOUNTAIN, GA, 2 P.M. – 6 P.M.

PLEASE NOTE: *The following gardens in Tennessee are participating as part of the Chattanooga Area Open Day.*

Holmberg Garden, CHATTANOOGA, TN, 2 P.M. - 6 P.M., *page 367*
McDonald-Elder Garden, CHATTANOOGA, TN, 10 A.M. - 4 P.M., *page 367*
The Garden at Skillet Gap, CHATTANOOGA, TN, 2 P.M. - 6 P.M., *page 368*
Mr. & Mrs. Edward L. Mitchell, LOOKOUT MOUNTAIN, TN, 2 P.M. – 6 P.M.,
    page 368
Teeta's Garden, LOOKOUT MOUNTAIN, TN, 2 P.M. – 6 P.M., *page 369*
Warner's Garden, LOOKOUT MOUNTAIN, TN, 2 P.M. – 6 P.M., *page 369*

Steven & Susan Bradley, LOOKOUT MOUNTAIN, GA

Our garden is a six-acre Appalachian mountain, contemporary stroll garden. Visitors enter along the drive through a shrub-and fern-filled corridor. An open lawn with native trees features several pieces of sculpture and a Japanese maple collection. The house overlooks a hillside planting of spring blooming Siberian iris and Exbury azaleas. Later in the summer, flowering shrubs and plants that attract butterflies enliven this hillside. There are also sun and shade borders of perennials. Extensive woodland paths wind through a fern and rhododendron glen, beside a wet water stream and waterfall to a living mountain spring. Wild geranium drifts further down the mountainside to a large plantation of Mayapple.

DATES & HOURS: May 22; 2 p.m. – 6 p.m.

DIRECTIONS: *From Teeta's Garden,* (see Lookout Mountain, TN) go left to the blinking traffic light. Turn right on Scenic Highway. Drive 2.5 miles. Parking is on the right in the Scotland Yard/Covenant College soccer field parking lot. The house is on the left at #13,292 Scenic Highway. The house number is on the mailbox post.

Proceeds shared with Chattanooga Area Food Bank.

ILLINOIS

Chicago

1999 ILLINOIS OPEN DAYS

June 19 & 27, July 25: CHICAGO AREA

CHICAGO:

June 19, 1999

Mettawa Manor, METTAWA, 10 A.M. − 4 P.M.

Hélène & Thomas James, WILMETTE, 10 A.M. − 4 P.M.

Penny & Jim De Young, WINNETKA, 10 A.M − 4 P.M.

Mike & Becky Murray, WINNETKA, 10 A.M − 4 P.M.

Jane & Don Perkins, WINNETKA, 10 A.M − 4 P.M.

June 27, 1999

Pam Armour, LAKE FOREST, 10 A.M. − 4 P.M.

Camp Rosemary, LAKE FOREST, 10 A.M. − 4 P.M.

A Garden on old "Meadow Lane," LAKE FOREST, 10 A.M. − 4 P.M.

House in the Garden, WINNETKA, 10 A.M − 4 P.M.

July 25, 1999

A Garden on old "Meadow Lane," LAKE FOREST, 10 A.M. − 4 P.M.

Mettawa Manor, METTAWA, 10 A.M. − 4 P.M.

❖ Garfield Park Conservatory,

300 NORTH CENTRAL PARK AVENUE, CHICAGO, IL 60624. (312) 746-5100.
The historic Garfield Park Conservatory, built in 1907 by Jens Jensen, is one of the largest conservatories of its kind in the world. Its eight exhibit houses display plants — some several centuries old — found in climates that range from rainforest to desert. Along with hosting five flower shows a year, the Conservatory offers guided tours for schools and other groups, and a variety of community and educational activities.

DATES & HOURS: Year round, daily, 9 a.m. – 5 p.m.

DIRECTIONS: *From I-290 Eisenhower Expressway* exit at Independence/Exit 26A and go north. Take Independence to Washington Boulevard and turn right. Take Washington east to Central Park Avenue. Turn left onto Central Park going north. Parking is located at the corner of Lake Street and Central Park Avenue.

❖ Grandmother's Garden, FULLERTON AVENUE (2400 NORTH) AND STOCKTON DRIVE (50 WEST), CHICAGO, IL 60624. (312) 747-0740.

Wide, undulating, island beds of annuals, perennials, and grasses are set off by broad expanses of lawn weaving the gardens together. These lovely, free-form beds are a fine counterpoint for the formal plantings at the Lincoln Garden across the street.

DATES & HOURS: Year round, daily, dawn – dusk.

DIRECTIONS: *Take Fullerton Avenue* to Stockton Drive. The garden is located on the west side of Stockton Drive, south of Fullerton, near the entrance to the Lincoln Park Zoo.

❖ The Lincoln Garden, CHICAGO, IL (312) 747-0698.

Set amid a broad expanse of lawn in Lincoln Park, these gardens are at the foot of a handsome sculpture of Abraham Lincoln (1897). The six raised beds were established in 1989 and measure thirty feet by 360'. There are eighty varieties of perennials. Annuals are added to provide seasonal color and interest. The six segments have alternating warm and cool color schemes. The gardens remain standing in the winter, with the hardy perennials and ornamental grasses giving form and color to the landscape.

DATES & HOURS: Year round, daily, dawn – dusk.

DIRECTIONS: *North State Parkway* at North Avenue (1600 North) just east of the Chicago Historical Society.

❖ Michigan Avenue Plantings, CHICAGO, IL (847) 733-0140.

Stretching thirty city blocks, these island beds fill Michigan Avenue with big, bold, and beautiful seasonal plantings designed by Douglas Hoerr Landscape Architecture. Tulips underplanted with violas herald spring. Masses of annuals, perennials, and grasses celebrate summer. Kale and chrysanthemums added to the fall-blooming perennials and grasses announce fall, creating a stunning effect for miles along this stately avenue. These plantings are funded and maintained by The Michigan Avenue Streetscape Association, a not-for-profit organization of Michigan Avenue property owners and merchants.

DATES & HOURS: Year round, daily, dawn – dusk.

DIRECTIONS: *From the north* take Lake Shore Drive south to Michigan Avenue Exit. Central median planters from 11th Street north to Oak Street.

❖ The Rosenbaum Garden, CHICAGO, IL (312) 747-0698.

The gardens were designed to complement the existing old trees in this small city park overlooking Lake Michigan. Handsome flowering trees and shrubs give form and structure to the perennial plantings. Vibrant masses of daffodils in the spring give way to sweeps of colorful perennials and grasses in summer and fall. Lovely benches invite contemplation and repose.

DATES & HOURS: Year round, daily, dawn – dusk.

DIRECTIONS: *Take Lake Shore Drive* south to the Michigan Avenue Exit. Turn left at the first traffic light, which is Oak Street.

❖ The Shakespeare Garden, EVANSTON, IL (847) 864-0655.

Designed by Jens Jensen in 1915 and surrounded by the original hawthorn hedges planted in 1920, the garden is romantic, secluded, and especially beautiful in June and July when its eight flower beds are filled with roses, lilies, pansies, artemisia, herbs, campanula, forget-me-nots, and daisies, all evocative of Shakespeare's poetry. Listed on the National Register of Historic Places in 1988, this garden is said to have been "loved into existence" by the members of the Garden Club of Evanston, who continue to care for it seventy-nine years later.

DATES & HOURS: Year round, daily, dawn – dusk.

DIRECTIONS: *From either the north or the south enter Evanston* along Sheridan Road and proceed to Garrett Place (2200 North). Park on Garrett Place (about mid-campus), east of Sheridan Road. The garden is reached by a bluestone walk on the east side of the Howe Chapel (on the north side of the street). Enter along this walk; the garden is not visible from either Sheridan Road or Garrett Place.

❖ Chicago Botanic Garden,

1000 LAKE COOK ROAD, GLENCOE, IL 60022. (847) 835-5440.

The garden, a living museum, covers 385 acres and features twenty-one specialty gardens including a rose garden, a waterfall garden, an English walled garden, a bulb garden, a three-island Japanese garden, a fruit and vegetable garden, prairies, lagoons, and the 100-acre Mary Mix McDonald Woods. Nine islands on seventy-five acres of waterways and six miles of shoreline are distinguishing features of this "garden on the water." The living collections include more than 1.2 million plants, representing 7,000 plant types. Demonstration gardens showcase plants best suited for the Midwest. Research trial gardens hold plants being evaluated for performance in Chicago's environment. Conservation areas feature native and endangered flora of Illinois. Facilities include classrooms, an exhibit hall, an auditorium, a museum, a library, production and education greenhouses, the Daniel F. & Ada L. Rice Plant Resource Center, an outdoor pavilion, a carillon, food service, and a gift shop. Services include adult education, programs for schoolchildren, tram tours of the Garden, horticultural therapy and plant information. Owned by the Forest Preserve District of Cook County and managed by the Chicago Horticultural Society.

DATES & HOURS: Year round, daily, 8 a.m. – dusk. Closed Christmas Day.

DIRECTIONS: *Lake Cook Road* in Glencoe is located one-half mile east of the Edens Expressway. *From Chicago,* Metra trains (312-322-6777) and PACE buses (847-364-PACE) bring visitors to the Garden's entrance.

Pam Armour, LAKE FOREST, IL

When we settled here, the property was bare but for a few oaks, a wonderful Scotch pine, and some elm trees along the street, which soon died. Over the years, new plantings have shielded us from the street and gardens have emerged. Under the tree canopy, woodsy, shade-loving plants are used in curving borders. Where sun prevails, a shrub rose border is strengthened by handsome conifers and shrubs, accented with roses and perennials, as well as apples, grapes, and clematis. Two large topiaries anchor the round rose/perennial formal garden.

DATES & HOURS: June 27; 10 a.m – 4 p.m.

DIRECTIONS: *From Route 41,* take the Lake Forest Exit. Go east on Deerpath Road to Sheridan Road. Turn left onto Sheridan. After passing Woodland Road, note the red brick school where Sheridan curves left. Spruce Avenue forks off to the right. The #630 is on a tree on the left; the house is secluded behind a woodsy border. Please park on Spruce Avenue.

Camp Rosemary, LAKE FOREST, IL

This garden was designed by Rose Standish Nichols in the 1920s and is made up of wonderful garden rooms partitioned by pines, yews, and boxwood hedges. A sweeping lawn and luscious container plantings at the front steps are the first hints of the delightful discoveries inside: a charming box-edged parterre, a thyme garden, an urn brimming with roses, perennials, and annuals set against an ancient yew hedge affectionately called "the couch." Other areas include a chapel-like white garden with two reflecting pools, a vine-and-rose entwined pergola garden, three exuberant borders surrounding a small pool, an enchanting cottage garden, and a small herb garden.

DATES & HOURS: June 27; 10 a.m. – 4 p.m.

DIRECTIONS: *From Route 41,* take the Deerpath Road Exit going east (right). Proceed through town, over the tracks to the stop sign at Sheridan Road. Turn right. Go .5 mile, past Lake Forest College, past blinking yellow light, past Rosemary Road on the right. Go one-half block to Rosemary Road on the left. Turn left. Number 930 is in the middle of the block on the left. Please park in the front driveway area.

A Garden on Old "Meadow Lane," LAKE FOREST, IL

We moved into the big brick house with seven acres of land east of our present residence in 1954. The house was built in 1930 and planted in the English manner. Some white pines, spruce, and American elms still stand. Today on our remaining two and one-half acres, a large garden has matured around a smaller passive solar house built in 1984. Landscape architect Anthony Tyznik's beautiful design forms the bones of this garden, incorporating the existing tennis court and swimming pool and adding a pond in the northwest corner below wetland cottonwoods. More trees were planted, an orchard with espalliered apples and bee hives, borders, and shade gardens, the most recent of which is in an opening carved by lightning which ripped apart old spruce trees. Cut into benches, they surround a campfire. Another shade garden surrounds tombstones inscribed with Shakespearean verse where we buried two family dogs. Currently, landscape architect Frank Haas has served as my mentor and muse. Like Capability Brown, he improves everything his roving eye touches. We have a big green lawn which is not entirely weed-free and practice integrated pest management. My teachers are many books and especially the land itself.

DATES & HOURS: June 27, July 25; 10 a.m. – 4 p.m.

DIRECTIONS: *Take Route 41* to Westleigh Road in Lake Forest; go east on Westleigh to Green Bay Road. Turn left onto Green Bay and continue about .5 mile beyond stoplight at Deerpath to Laurel Avenue. Turn west onto Laurel to a narrow, unmarked cross street where you turn south and follow cul-de-sac to last house, #285 West Laurel Avenue. Park on one side of Laurel Avenue west of Green Bay Road and walk to house.

Proceeds shared with Madoo Conservancy.

Mettawa Manor, METTAWA, IL

The house and grounds were built in 1927 as a family compound. The current owners, only the second in the Manor's rich history, have been working for the past eight years on a ten-year plan to refurbish some garden areas and create new ones. The centerpiece of the garden is a newly built, walled, English-style garden with forty-foot perennial borders on either side of a sunken lawn that leads to a spring walk and rose room centered on an old fountain. Outside the east gate is a golden garden and an orchard/meadow underplanted with twenty thousand narcissi and bordered by a fenced potager/cutting garden and a circular herb garden. The 35-acre property has two ponds, a woodland garden, an eight-acre prairie, and a parkland of specimen trees.

DATES & HOURS: June 19, July 25; 10 a.m. – 4 p.m.

DIRECTIONS: *Take the Edens Expressway/I-94* to the Milwaukee Tollway/Route 94. Exit at Route 60 West/Town Line Road and follow .5 mile to special parking set aside in the W.W. Grainger parking lot directly east of Mettawa Manor. Further instructions on arrival.

❖ Anderson Gardens,

340 SPRING CREEK ROAD, ROCKFORD, IL 61107. (815) 877-2525.
Anderson Gardens is located on a five-acre site which contains an authentic Japanese pond strolling garden, a guesthouse, a teahouse, a gazebo, and four waterfalls. Lanterns, bridges, a stone pagoda, water basins, and gates are also part of this award-winning garden. A Japanese garden provides a place of meditation and contemplation.

DATES & HOURS: May through October, Monday through Saturday, 10 a.m.– 4 p.m.; Sunday, noon – 4 p.m.

DIRECTIONS: *From the East:* Take I-90 West to Rockford. Exit at Business 20/East State Street. Go west (right) on Business 20 to Mulford Road. Turn north (right) on Mulford Road and drive to Spring Creek Road. Turn west (left) on Spring Creek Road and drive 3 miles to the garden entrance at Parkview Avenue and Spring Creek Road. Turn north (right) into parking lot. *From the North:* Take I-90 East to Rockford. Exit at Riverside Boulevard. Go west (right) on Riverside Boulevard to Mulford Road. Turn south (left) on Mulford Road and drive to Spring Creek Road. Turn west (left) on Spring Creek Road and drive 3 miles to the garden's entrance at Parkview Avenue and Spring Creek Road. Turn north (right) into parking lot.

Hélène & Thomas James, WILMETTE, IL

This garden surrounds a Greek Revival-style house, once a simple farmhouse built in 1876. On the property there are some very old deciduous trees (oaks, elms, beeches) and evergreens. Under their canopy, shade-loving shrubs and perennials are planted in large, curving borders. Where sun prevails, more than thirty shrub roses (Blanc Double de Coubert, Rosa Mundi, Königin von Dänemark) *bloom at the end of June with other perennials, climbing hydrangeas, wild geraniums, and hostas. A small herb and vegetable garden is nestled against the old grey barn. The garden has been featured in* Midwest Gardens *by Pamela Wolfe.*

DATES & HOURS: June 19; 10 a.m. − 4 p.m.

DIRECTIONS: *From Edens Expressway/I-94* take the Lake Avenue Exit if travelling northbound or the Skokie Road Exit to Lake Avenue if travelling southbound. Proceed east on Lake Avenue approximately 2.5 miles. Cross the railway track at Green Bay Road. Continue east to 12th Street. Turn left. Drive to #1128 Greenwood Avenue in the middle of the block. Park on the street.

Penny & Jim De Young, WINNETKA, IL

Designed by the architect Edwin Clark, this brick English Tudor house, built in 1927, is complemented by a sweeping bent lawn, shagbark hickory trees, and a har-tru tennis court. Flowering crab apple trees, Sargent crabs, pagoda dogwoods, Japanese tree lilacs, Washington hawthorns, witch hazel, several varieties of viburnum, a unique azalea, a fringe tree, and a Magnolia tripetala *highlight this property. Ground covers of* Euonymus vegetus, Euonymus coloratus *and* pachysandra *complement many of the above plantings. Pink and white peonies are prominent in four sizable mixed borders, and each bed features a variety of annuals and perennials, that provide a colorful tapestry throughout the seasons. Spaced in the beds are* hibiscus, buddleia, cotinus, *and* caryopteris. *The rose garden, set around a circular pool, displays tea and floribunda roses, while shrub roses line the bed to the north of the tennis court. A variety of unique daylilies dominates the west side of the tennis court, and climbing the tennis court fence are an espaliered pear and an unusual selection of clematis.*

DATES & HOURS: June 19; 10 a.m. – 4 p.m.

DIRECTIONS: *From the Edens Expressway/I-94 North* exit at Willow Road East and follow to Hibbard Road. Turn right and go south on Hibbard Road to Hill Road. Turn left and travel east on Hill Road to stop sign at Locust Street. Cross Locust and continue east to the bend on the road; just past the bend, turn right onto Indian Hill Road. Number 22 Indian Hill Road is the third house on the right. The driveway is just before a three-way stop sign. *From the Edens Expressway/I-94 South,* exit at Lake Avenue East. Take Lake Avenue to Hibbard Road. Turn left and go north on Hibbard to Hill Road. Turn right and travel east on Hill Road to stop sign at Locust Street. Follow directions above. Please park along the road.

House in the Garden, WINNETKA, IL

This relaxing garden, framing an eighteenth-century French manor house, is designed classically as well as with universal accessibility for people with all physical abilities. The garden consists of seven outdoor rooms: a sixteenth-century style pergola, a secret garden, a honey locust allée, a provincial fountain woodland setting, a medallion with a pleached lindens entrance court, a cherry tree circle service court, and a hicks yew-bordered open lawn with a fountain and beech tree. A wonderful place to read poetry or meditate!

DATES & HOURS: June 27; 10 a.m. - 4 p.m.

DIRECTIONS: *Exit Edens Expressway/I-94* at Tower Road. Make two right turns onto Tower Road. Proceed East on Tower to Burr (one block before Green Bay Road). Turn right onto Burr and go two blocks. Enter the property through two pillars across from Hubbard Woods School. Go to the second driveway.

Mike & Becky Murray, WINNETKA, IL

A secluded summer garden in a naturalistic style surrounds a stone-terraced swimming pool. The plantings include broadleaf and evergreen trees and shrubs, perennials, a collection of container gardens, and a vine-covered pergola.

DATES & HOURS: June 19; 10 a.m. − 4 p.m.

DIRECTIONS: *From the north,* take the Edens Expressway/I-94 south to the Tower Road Exit. Go east on Tower Road for 1.4 miles to Hibbard Road (three-way stop). Turn right onto Hibbard. Take the first left onto Kent Road. It is the last house on the left. *From the South,* take the Eden Expressway/I-94 to Willow Road East Exit. Continue east on Willow Road for .75 mile to Hibbard Road. Go left on Hibbard to Kent Road (.8 mile). Turn right onto Kent Road. It is the last house on the left. Please park along Kent Road.

Jane & Don Perkins, WINNETKA, IL

This handsome property is graced by many mature trees. A well-established border of shrubs shields the house from the road. Featured in the backyard is a sixty-five-foot mixed border of shrubs, vibrantly colored annuals, and perennials. A rose-and-clematis bower finds its niche in this full border as well. Close to the house, there is a formal parterre with a fountain and a terrace rose garden.

DATES & HOURS: June 19; 10 a.m. – 4 p.m.

DIRECTIONS: *From Edens Expressway/I-94 North,* exit at Willow Road. Take Willow Road east to Hibbard Road. Go south on Hibbard to Winnetka/Hill. Travel east on Hill to stop sign at Locust. Continue east to the second house on the north.

❖ Craig Bergman's Country Garden, 700 KENOSHA ROAD, BOX 424, WINTHROP HARBOR, IL 60096. (847) 746-0311.

A garden center and perennial farm dedicated to the art of fine gardening. One thousand-one hundred herbaceous perennials hardy to the Midwest and 700 annuals and tender plants are offered in a park-like setting. There are five demonstration gardens: Sun Garden devoted to full-sun perennials grouped around a clematis bower; Shade Garden in the shadow of two giant Bur Oaks; Rock Garden comprised of plants which prefer a hot and dry situation; Rose and Herb Garden enclosed in a Belgian Fence of espaliered apple trees; Autumn Garden with rustic fencing and footbridge dedicated to plants which come into peak color during the fall. Refreshments and antique garden ornaments available in the Tea House.

DATES & HOURS: April 21 through October 23, 8 a.m. – 4 p.m. Closed Monday and Tuesday.

DIRECTIONS: *Located about one hour from Chicago or Milwaukee.* Take I-294 and exit east on Route 173. Continue east to Kenosha Road. Turn left and travel about 1.5 miles north. Garden center located on west side of street, set back in a meadow.

LOUISIANA

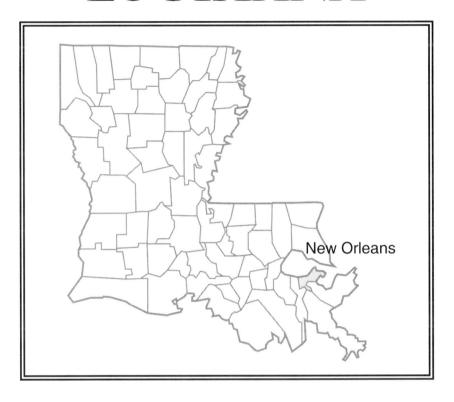

New Orleans

1999 LOUISIANA OPEN DAY

April 17: NEW ORLEANS

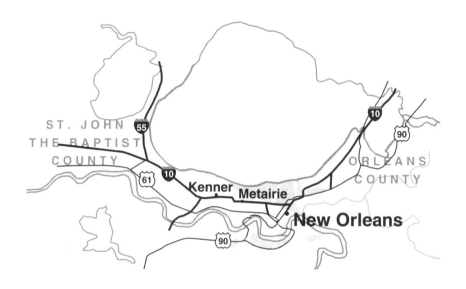

NEW ORLEANS: *April 17, 1999*

Mr. & Mrs. Prescott Dunbar, NEW ORLEANS, 10 A.M. – 4 P.M.

Mr. & Mrs. Richard W. Freeman Jr., NEW ORLEANS, 10 A.M. – 4 P.M.

Mr. & Mrs. James O. Gundlach, NEW ORLEANS, 10 A.M. – 2 P.M.

Ann Hobson Haack, NEW ORLEANS, 10 A.M. – 4 P.M.

Wendy & Boatner Reily's Garden, NEW ORLEANS, NOON – 5 P.M.

Mrs. Frank Strachan, NEW ORLEANS, 10 A.M. - 4 P.M.

Mr. & Mrs. Prescott Dunbar, NEW ORLEANS, LA

This garden, a quarter city block, wraps around a classically colonnaded 1850 Greek Revival house framed by two 150-year-old live oak trees. Daturas (brugsmanias now) and roses are among the highlights in the various borders. A large bauhinia tree dominates the patio, with its yellow-and-white rose and boxwood parterre. There is a secret white garden and a red border of rubber trees, palms, grasses, roses, and other perennials. A collection of young magnolias completes the garden.

DATES & HOURS: April 17; 10 a.m. – 4 p.m.

DIRECTIONS: *Driving from downtown New Orleans or the Greater New Orleans/Mississippi River Bridge Expressway,* take St. Charles Avenue to First Street. Turn left toward the river and go one block to Prytania. Turn right. The house is located on the corner of Second Street and Prytania. Please park along the road.

Mr. & Mrs. Richard W. Freeman, Jr., NEW ORLEANS, LA

Our garden surrounds a New Orleans "raised cottage," which was designed in 1895 by architect Thomas Sully. The most interesting features of the garden are the roses, which cover the low iron fence and trellis, and the sculpture placed around the yard.

DATES & HOURS: April 17; 10 a.m. – 4 p.m.

DIRECTIONS: *Henry Clay Avenue* can be reached from St. Charles Avenue. We are four blocks from St. Charles. From the French Quarter, take St. Charles (or streetcar) uptown about twenty minutes. The traffic light before Henry Clay is State Street. Turn left on Henry Clay. Number 1234 is on the corner and has a rounded porch.

Proceeds shared with Longue Vue Gardens.

Mr. & Mrs. James O. Gundlach, NEW ORLEANS, LA

Our home, in New Orleans' Garden District, is in the classic Greek Revival style and dates from 1853-1854. There is an addition in the Italianate style dating from 1869. The formal entrance has a two-tiered flower bed that leads to a free-flowing side garden. One-hundred-year-old boxwood and large magnolia trees provide a curtain of privacy. The cast-iron archway is covered with bougainvillea. Plants include rare varieties of camellias, sweet olive trees, crape-myrtles, a Chinese fringe tree, a parsley hawthorne tree, clethra, Burford holly, shell ginger, coppertone plants, oak leaf and lace cap hydrangeas, Chinese palms, agapanthus, and a variety of tropical plants. A focal point on the patio is an intriguing bit of southern Americana, a plant bed made from the brick foundation of the old cistern.

DATES & HOURS: April 17; 10 a.m. – 2 p.m.

DIRECTION: *Driving from downtown New Orleans or the Greater New Orleans/Mississippi River Bridge Expressway* take St. Charles Avenue to First Street. Turn left toward the river and go three blocks to Chestnut Street. Turn right and travel one block. The house is on the corner of Philip and Chestnut. Please park along the road.

Ann Hobson Haack Garden, NEW ORLEANS, LA

On a busy street at the back of the house is a garden hidden from view. Through the iron gates down one side of the property is a narrow path leading to the garden. This small rectangular garden with a central tapis vert *is edged by a deep border of fragrant southern plants. The border includes sweet olive, cape jasmine, roses,* Magnolia fuscata, *herbs, and vines of stephanotis and confederate jasmine. The garden adjoins an old flagstone terrace with pots for strawberry guava, lemon, and lime trees.*

DATES & HOURS: April 17; 10 a.m. – 4 p.m.

DIRECTIONS: *Driving from downtown New Orleans or the Greater New Orleans/Mississippi River Bridge Expressway,* take St. Charles Avenue to Jackson Avenue. Go one-half block past Jackson and make a U-turn on St. Charles back to Jackson Avenue. (No left turn is permitted at Jackson.) Turn right at Jackson and go three and one-half blocks. The house is between Chestnut and Camp Streets on the right.

Wendy & Boatner Reily's Garden,
NEW ORLEANS GARDEN DISTRICT, LA

The house was built as a villa, in 1850, but our garden wasn't developed until after 1910. The tall brick wall, live oak trees and hollies give privacy in the middle of the city. Old native roses, Old Blush and Mme. Carriere, climb on the Chinese trellis. On the house side is a small parterre planted in patterns of seasonal color. In the middle is a sundial from Versailles surrounded by pots of color. On the end is a tub (that was originally in the house) made from a single piece of Carrara marble and filled with Calla lilies. There is a boxwood knot-garden along the lawn. Many different azaleas form the other borders with Indian hawthorn, camellias, dogwood, crepe myrtle, and magnolia. Splashing water is a large part of our garden as it masks the traffic sounds. The terrace has pots of gem magnolia and ivy. A walled garden surrounds the guest house filled with cleyera, sweet oive, azaleas, impatiens, begonias, and petunias.

DATES & HOURS: April 17; noon – 5 p.m.

DIRECTIONS: *Driving from downtown New Orleans or the Greater New Orleans Miss River Bridge Expressway,* take St. Charles Avenue to First Street. Turn left toward the river and go one block to Prytania Street. Turn left and go one block to Philip Street. The house is in the next block, #2221 Prytania Street, on the left. Please park on the street.

Mrs. Frank Strachan, NEW ORLEANS, LA

Flanked by olive trees, an iron gate is the entry to these grounds, which surround the double-galleried Greek-Revival style house where Confederate President Jefferson Davis died. The garden has evolved over the past seventy years. The forty-five-year-old plan of garden rooms by Umberto Innocenti is apparent. The rose garden and plantings of indigenous and exotic materials can be observed and reflected in the pilastered mirrors of a teahouse facing the croquet lawn. Beyond the high garden wall are the orchid house, potting shed, and bathhouse for the swimming pool area, which features palms and plumbago.

DATES & HOURS: April 17; 10 a.m. – 4 p.m.

DIRECTIONS: *Driving from downtown New Orleans or the Greater New Orleans/Mississipi River Bridge Expressway,* take St. Charles Avenue to First Street. Turn left towards the river and go four blocks to #1134 First Street, on the corner of Camp Street, in the Garden District.

❖ Beauregard – Keyes House,

1113 CHARTRES STREET, NEW ORLEANS, LA 70124. (504) 523-7257.

Built by Joseph Le Carpentier in 1826, the Beauregard – Keyes House is at the corner of Chartres and Ursuline Streets. The original garden was described as a "jungle." The present garden is a formal parterre and consists of ferns, lilies, and irises. Two cast iron sofas under the iron arbor have a statue of St. Francis between them, and in the center of the garden is a cast iron fountain. The garden is designed to have seasonal blooms against a background of various evergreens.

DATES & HOURS: Year round, Monday through Saturday, 10 a.m. – 3 p.m.

DIRECTIONS: *Located opposite the Old Ursuline Convent* on Chartres Street in New Orleans.

❖ Longue Vue House & Gardens,

7 BAMBOO ROAD, NEW ORLEANS, LA 70124-1065. (504) 488-5488.

Longue Vue House and Gardens is an historic city estate created by Mr. & Mrs. Edgar B. Stern during the period 1939-42. Mr. Stern was a very successful cotton broker in New Orleans who married Edith Rosenwald, daughter of Sears & Roebuck entrepreneur Julius Rosenwald, in 1921. The house and gardens reflect the collaborative artistic and design vision of the Sterns, as well as that of Ellen Biddle Shipman, one of the leading landscape designers of the period, and the architects William and Geoffrey Platt.

DATES & HOURS: Year round, Monday through Saturday, 10 a.m. – 4:30 p.m. Sunday, 1 p.m. – 5 p.m. Closed major holidays.

DIRECTIONS: *From the I-10 Expressway,* take Exit 231A to Metairie Road or take Canal Street & Metairie Road buses.

❖ The New Orleans Botanical Garden,

CITY PARK, #1 PALM DRIVE, NEW ORLEANS, LA 70124. (504) 483-9386.

The New Orleans Botanical Garden in historic City Park is a rare and valuable surviving example of public garden design dating from the WPA and Art Deco periods of the 1930s. Having undergone major restoration during the last decade, it preserves the original work of three noted men: architect Richard Koch; landscape architect William Wiedon; and artist-sculptor Enrique Alferez. An extensive plant collection is featured in its numerous garden rooms.

DATES & HOURS: Year round, Tuesday through Sunday, 10 a.m. – 4:30 p.m.

DIRECTIONS: *From I-10 West,* take Metairie Road/City Park Exit, turn left onto City Park Avenue. *From I-10 East,* take I-610 to Canal Boulevard Exit, turn left onto City Park Avenue. *From I-10 Crescent City Connection,* take Metairie Road/City Park Exit, turn right onto City Park Avenue. *From the French Quarter,* drive-up Esplanade Avenue, over Bayou St. John, turn right on Wisner Avenue, enter at Wisner and Friedrichs.

MARYLAND

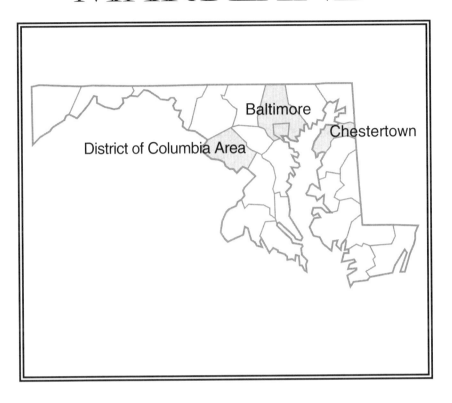

1999 MARYLAND OPEN DAYS

May 1: BALTIMORE AREA
May 15 & June 26: DISTRICT OF COLUMBIA AREA
June 6: CHESTERTOWN AREA

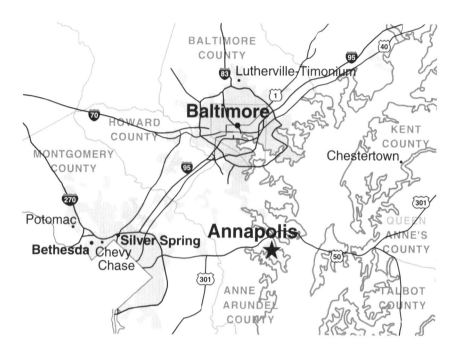

BALTIMORE AREA: *May 1, 1999*

Kathy & Joe Hardiman, BALTIMORE, 11 A.M. – 4 P.M.

Penney & A.C. Hubbard, BALTIMORE, 11 A.M. – 4 P.M.

Garden of Ann & Syd King, BALTIMORE, 11 A.M. – 5 P.M.

Tyrconnell, BALTIMORE, 11 A.M. – 4 P.M.

Jean & Sidney Silber, LUTHERVILLE, 11 A.M. – 4 P.M.

❖ The William Paca House & Garden,

186 PRINCE GEORGE STREET, ANNAPOLIS, MD 21401. (410) 263-5553.

Twenty years ago this two-acre site was a hotel and parking lot. The walled and terraced garden is the re-creation of the eighteenth-century town residence of William Paca, a Maryland signer of the Declaration of Independence, based on historical and archaeological research. The two-story octagonal summer house at the foot of the garden is the focal point of the four formal parterres, planted with historically accurate flowers, shrubs, and trees. An elegant Chinese-style bridge crosses the spring-fed ornamental pond surrounded by informal plantings. Herb, vegetable, and fruit gardens reflect the practical aspects of town life, as do the other outbuildings on the site.

DATES & HOURS: March through December, daily, 10 a.m. – 4 p.m. Sunday, noon – 4 p.m. Call for winter hours. Closed Thanksgiving, Christmas Eve, & Christmas Day.

DIRECTIONS: *Take Route 50* to Exit 24. Turn onto Rowe Boulevard, toward Annapolis. At the end of Rowe Boulevard, turn left onto College Avenue. At the first traffic light, turn right onto King George Street and at the bottom of the hill right onto Randall Street. At the traffic light, turn right onto Prince George Street. The garden entrance is through the William Paca House. Two hour parking is available on Prince George Street.

Kathy & Joe Hardiman, BALTIMORE, MD

Our gardens have evolved to connect our contemporary house to the surrounding naturally wooded nine-acre site. A lap pool overlooks a casual meadow garden that eventually disappears into the woods. Walking trails meander through the gardens that lead on one side to a stream and on the other to a native wildflower dell. Tier after tier of texture provide year-round interest with unusual trees, shrubs, ornamental grasses, and perennials.

DATES & HOURS: May 1; 11 a.m. – 4 p.m.

DIRECTIONS: *From the Baltimore Beltway/ I-695,* take Exit 25/Charles Street. Continue south on Charles Street to the fourth traffic light (fifth light if coming from the east). Turn right onto Bellona Avenue and go .4 mile to a right onto Bowen Mill Road. Bear right down the hill to #8, driveway on the left. Please park along the street.

Penney & A.C. Hubbard, BALTIMORE, MD

When it comes to plants we have always had a hard time saying "No." That is why our garden is an assemblage of many different trees, shrubs, and perennials. There are conifers for color variety, including blue spruce, golden chamaecyparis and brilliant Hinoki cypress. There are more than 150 varieties of daylilies, fifteen Japanese umbrella pines (Sciadopitys verticillata), *a collection of Japanese maples, lots of bulbs and a variety of ground covers. The natural setting of our garden includes several stone walls and garden pathways. There are interesting boulders and a stone wall from which water cascades into a swimming pool.*

DATES & HOURS: May 1; 11 a.m. – 4 p.m.

DIRECTIONS: *From I-695* take Exit 25 south (Charles Street) toward Baltimore to Bellona Avenue. Turn right onto Bellona Avenue and continue to Wine Spring Lane (approximately 1 mile, just past Joppa Road traffic light). Turn left (an angled turn) onto Wine Spring Lane and go to first road. Turn right onto Sherwood Avenue. Go to Walnut Hill Lane, turn left, and go up curved lane to #1408 on the left.

Proceeds shared with The Maryland Horticultural Society.

Garden of Ann & Syd King, BALTIMORE, MD

"It's like looking at a blueprint of a garden," said one visitor as he looked down at our garden more than fifty feet below the full-length living room windows. On facing hillsides, with a chain of man-made "lakes" between, our garden is situated among a stand of towering Tulip trees, accented by native dogwoods. Guests may visit the front garden at street level and view the lower gardens from the house or rear deck, also at street level, or they may follow mulched paths which wind down the hillside and lead to the various areas of the main gardens, featuring ferns, hostas, and a wide variety of other shade-loving perennials, shrubs, and trees. The gardens have been developed and are maintained by the owners.

DATES & HOURS: May 1; 11 a.m. – 5 p.m.

DIRECTIONS: *Approach from Ruxton Road,* which runs between Bellona Avenue and Falls Road. Coming From Falls Road, go .4 mile and turn right onto Darnall Road. *From Bellona Avenue,* go 1 mile and turn left onto Darnall. Go up Darnall to second street and turn right onto Ridgecrest Court. Number 2007 is at the bottom of the hill on the left.

Proceeds shared with The Maryland Horticultural Society.

Tyrconnell — Garden of Paul & Karen Winicki,

BALTIMORE, MD

Tyrconnell is an Italian-style garden designed by Arthur Folsom Paul in the early 1920s. The garden has remained, almost eighty years later, virtually intact despite the changes in ownership. Inspired by Villa d'Este, it features a quarter-mile boxwood allée, fountains, a stone grotto, and many beautiful vistas among twenty-two acres of woodland greenery. We feel very fortunate to have current stewardship of this unique property. Woodbury Lane intersects Charles Street at Brown Memorial Church.

DATES & HOURS: May 1; 11 a.m. – 4 p.m.

DIRECTIONS: *Tyrconnell is located at #120 Woodbrook Lane* just off of the 6300 block of North Charles Street, 3 miles south of Beltway Exit 25 and 1.2 miles north of Northern Parkway.

❖ Cylburn Arboretum & Park,

4915 GREENSPRING AVENUE, BALTIMORE, MD 21209. (410) 396-0180.

Cylburn Arboretum & Park covers 176 acres with large wildflower trails, a butterfly garden, collections of magnolias and maples, and an All-American Selections Display Garden. There are nature trails through the wooded areas and wildflower preserves. On the second floor of the Central Building is a bird museum. An annual rare plant sale on the Saturday before Mother's Day is an event not to be missed.

DATES & HOURS: Year round, daily, 6 a.m. – 9 p.m.

DIRECTIONS: *From I-695,* take the exit for Route 83 South to Northern Parkway. Go west on Northern Parkway to a left on Greenspring Avenue.

Jean & Sidney Silber, LUTHERVILLE, MD

Our thirty-eight-year-old garden of about three acres is primarily in a woodland. Mossy paths shaded by towering oaks are enclosed by mature rhododendrons and a variety of ericaceous plants. In the open sunny areas of the garden, two ponds provide a focus for beds of perennials, annuals, ornamental grasses, and specimen trees. Our long-term interest in sculpture is evident throughout the garden.

DATES & HOURS: May 1; 11 a.m. – 4 p.m.

DIRECTIONS: *From the Baltimore Beltway/ I-695* take Exit 22, Greenspring Avenue. Go north approximately 2.75 miles to Woodland Drive. Turn right onto Woodland Drive and go .7 mile to #11515 on your right. (Look for 3 mailboxes within a split rail fence.) We are the first driveway on the left at the top of the hill. *If going south on I-83 from York, PA,* take Exit 17, Padonia Road and bear right (west) onto Padonia. Proceed approximately 2.6 miles to Falls Road (traffic light). Here, Padonia becomes Broadway Road. Cross Falls Road and proceed on Broadway Road .7 mile to Woodland Drive. Turn left and proceed .5 mile to #11515 as above.

Proceeds shared with The Cylburn Arboretum Association.

❖ Ladew Topiary Gardens,

3535 JARRETTSVILLE PIKE, MONKTON, MD 21111. (410) 557-9466.
This historic manor house was built over three centuries. Twenty-two acres of formal topiary and flowering gardens are on the 250-acre estate of the late Harvey Ladew. These are the most renowned topiary gardens in America.

DATES & HOURS: Mid-April through October 31, Monday through Friday, 10 a.m.– 4 p.m. Saturday & Sunday, 10:30 a.m. – 5 p.m.

DIRECTIONS: *From I-95 North or South,* take Exit 74 to Route 152/Mountain Road northwest until the dead end at Route 146/Jarrettsville Pike. Turn left onto Jarrettsville Pike. The gardens are .5 miles on the left.

❖ Brookside Gardens,

1800 GLENALLAN AVENUE, WHEATON, MD 20902. (301) 949-8230.

A fifty-acre public display garden developed and operated by the Maryland-National Capital Park and Planning Commission in Montgomery County, Maryland. Indoors, two conservatories feature colorful seasonal displays accented by lush green tropical plants year round. Outdoors, eleven formal gardens contrast with the casual beauty of naturalistic settings.

DATES & HOURS: Year round, daily, dawn – dusk. Closed Christmas Day.

DIRECTIONS: *From the Beltway (I-495),* take Exit 31A North to Georgia Avenue. Travel 3 miles on Georgia and turn right onto Randolph Road. At the second traffic light on Randolph, turn right onto Glenallan Avenue. Brookside Gardens is .25 miles on the right.

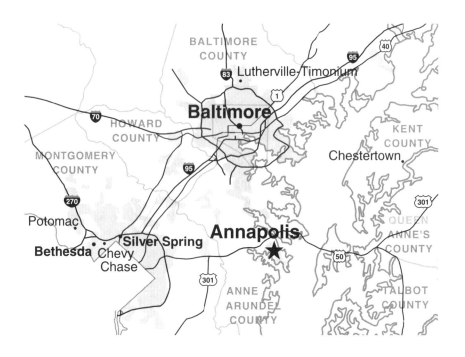

CHESTERTOWN AREA: *June 6, 1999*

Baymeath Farm, CHESTERTOWN, 10 A.M. − 4 P.M.

Marnie & Bill Flook, CHESTERTOWN, 10 A.M. − 4 P.M.

Near Water — John & Betsy Ray, CHESTERTOWN, 10 A.M. − 4 P.M.

The Reward, CHESTERTOWN, 10 A.M. − 4 P.M.

River House, CHESTERTOWN, 10 A.M. − 4 P.M.

Swan Cover, CHESTERTOWN, 10 A.M. − 4 P.M.

The Wickes House & Garden, CHESTERTOWN, 10 A.M. − 4 P.M.

Baymeath Farm, CHESTERTOWN, MD

In the Eastern Shore farm country, our grounds are designed to take advantage of mature woods, enhanced by meadow and water views. Planting around the house is for three season interest — fall, winter, and spring. At the kitchen we have a flowery herb garden and nearby, an enthusiastic perennial garden. There is a series of magnolia, azalea, and daffodil walks, from which a naturalized woodland path eventually leads to a marsh garden still being developed along the shore.

DATES & HOURS: June 6; 10 a.m. – 4 p.m.

DIRECTIONS: *In Chestertown,* Cross Street will become Quaker Neck Road/Route 289. Stay on Quaker Neck Road into the farm country for 6.8 miles. Our drive will be on the right about 2.5 miles past the Pomona General Store in the middle of a long hedge row. Number 5804 is on the mail box, and the drive leads to a brick house set against the woods.

Marnie & Bill Flook, CHESTERTOWN, MD

The Flook garden, situated on East Langford Creek, off of the Chester River, consists of a series of gardens including several woodland areas planted with wildflowers, rhododendrons, and other ericaceous shrubs; sunny borders planted with small trees, shrubs, perennials, grasses, and bulbs; a vegetable garden; and four plant boxes planted with dwarf shrubs and rock garden plants.

DATES & HOURS: June 6; 10 a.m. – 4 p.m.

DIRECTIONS: *Continue on Route 291 to MD 20* at the foot of the hill. Turn right and head toward Rock Hall on MD 20. (Radcliffe Mill, a garden shop, will be on the right.) After about 2 miles, turn left onto MD 446 (signs also read: Langford; Broad Neck Road). Continue on MD 446 for 6 miles to Lovely Lane. Turn left onto Lovely Lane and go about .6 mile until pavement ends, then, bearing left (do not enter Orchard Point and Rock Point Farms) continue a few hundred yards to "Flook" sign. Park in the field next to the road.

Near Water — John & Betsy Ray, CHESTERTOWN, MD

Near Water is a seven-acre garden in a rural setting. Primarily the gardens are inward-looking, with only one major vista across flat farm and woodland to the Chester River. The garden is composed of two distinct areas: the parkland and the various smaller garden areas which include a mounded rock garden overlooking a pond; a sunken garden; a hidden garden in a woodland; a sundial garden with pergola, doric temple and boxwood parterre; a double herbaceous border; an allée with statuary; two croquet courts with a two-story summer house; and an Italianate garden overlooking the parkland.

DATES & HOURS: June 6; 10 a.m. – 4 p.m.

DIRECTIONS: *Turn left at the traffic light and follow Route 213* past Washington College, about 1 mile to the traffic light at Cross Street (Route 289). Turn right onto Cross Street and follow it past the traffic light at High Street (the main street in Chestertown) and on out of town where it makes several sharp turns and becomes Quaker Neck Road (still Route 289). The Armory and then the Chester River will be on the left. Continue on Route 289 for about 9 miles, passing Pomona (small store and gas station on the right) where the road curves to the left. At the "Y" continue to the left on Cliff City Road (not Land's End Road). The first 2 houses on the left are the Rays'. Park along the road on the grass shoulder.

The Reward, CHESTERTON, MD

Situated on Langford Creek, the grounds of The Reward, (circa 1740), have evolved since 1970 around earlier boxwood plantings. The intention has been to create intimate areas surrounding the house and outbuildings while preserving the views of the surrounding fields and river. The winter garden, centered on an orangery, is one of several projects designed by William H. Frederick, Jr. for the owners.

DATES & HOURS: June 6; 10 a.m. – 4 p.m.

DIRECTIONS: *Leave Chestertown by way of Cross Street/*Route 289 South, this becomes Quaker Neck Road (still Route 289) when you get outside of Chestertown. Continue on Route 289 to Pomona (a one-store community). Stay left on Langford-Pomona Road. Go 1.1 miles to Walnut Point Road on right. Turn right. Go 1 mile to The Reward on the left.

River House, CHESTERTOWN, MD

Overlooking the Chester River, the garden at River House (1784) is simple and elegant in form and structure, appropriate to the context of the site and the house, which is the finest example of an early Federal-period townhouse in Kent County. Enter through the picket fence gate at the side of the house and find a cool, soft expanse of lawn, flower beds and boxwood, broken up by walks of old brick. Framed by eighteenth-century walls, plant material includes golden rain trees, holly, magnolia, Korean box, roses, lavender, and masses of spring daffodils, tulips and iris. Visitors always enjoy seeing the monumental piazzas on the back of the historic house.

DATES & HOURS: June 6; 10 a.m. – 4 p.m.

DIRECTIONS: *In Chestertown from Route 213 South,* the North Water Street garden of the River House will be on the left side of the bridge that you cross. This is the northwest side of the Chester River. *From Route 213 North,* cross bridge and continue past Water Street. Make a "U"-turn at traffic light and head south on Route 213; turn right onto Water Street.

Swan Cove, CHESTERTOWN, MD

Swan Cove, built in 1954 in a style reminiscent of early New York Dutch Colonial homes, is situated on a bend in the Chester River. A formal garden, pool and pavilion, gazebo and caretaker's cottage are positioned around the main house and linked by a series of terraces — all of which have been designed to take advantage of the sweeping views and vistas. The gardens are anchored by mass plantings of boxwood, which not only delineate separate garden rooms but also create a sense of unity and timelessness. A lead fountain with a swan base is the focal point of the formal garden. Visible from the entrance hall, it leads the eye through the wrought iron archway that frames the view to the woodland edge.

DATES & HOURS: June 6; 10 a.m. – 4 p.m.

DIRECTIONS: *From the Chestertown side of the bridge,* going north on Route 213, turn left at the first traffic light onto Cross Street (Route 289 South). Continue on Cross Street through town for 2 miles to gray brick entrance piers on the left marked "#7641, The Housley's Swan Cove."

The Wickes House & Garden, CHESTERTOWN, MD

The garden at the Wickes House (circa. 1769) is located in the heart of the historic district of Chestertown. The town was laid out in 1707. The walled, informal English garden has many winding brick walkways, giving the visitor access to a perennial garden, a rose garden, cutting garden, and a small herb garden. They are set within a backdrop of ornamental trees and shrubs, crape-myrtle, boxwood, and azaleas. A good place to relax and let the rest of the world roll by.

DATES & HOURS: June 6; 10 a.m. – 4 p.m.

DIRECTIONS: *The house is located in the heart of the Chestertown Historic District* at 102 High Street.

Proceeds shared with The Historical Society of Kent County.

DISTRICT OF COLUMBIA AREA:

May 15, 1999

Nancy Voorhees, BETHESDA, 10 A.M. – 2 P.M.

Gay & Tony Barclay — Orchard Farm, POTOMAC, 10 A.M. – 4 P.M.

The Olson Garden, POTOMAC, 10 A.M. – 4 P.M.

Carole Ottensen's Garden , POTOMAC, 2 P.M. – 6 P.M.

June 26, 1999

The Sexton – Borgiotti Garden, CHEVY CHASE, 10 A.M. – 4 P.M.

Robert Moore & Frank Kirste, SILVER SPRING, MD, 10 A.M. – 4 P.M.

PLEASE NOTE: *The following gardens in the District of Columbia and Virginia are participating as part of the Washington, DC Area Open Day.*

May 15, 1999

John & Caroline Macomber, WASHINGTON, DC, 10 A.M. – 4 P.M., *page 129*

Mr. & Mrs. Eric Weinmann, WASHINGTON, DC, 10 A.M. – 4 P.M., *page 129*

❖ Dumbarton Oaks Park, WASHINGTON, DC, 2 P.M. - 6 P.M., *page 130*

June 26, 1999

Hilltop Cottage, MCLEAN, VA, 10 A.M. – 4 P.M., *page 399*

Nancy Vorhees' Garden, BETHESDA, MD

My garden is an exuberant gem! The garden has a very well thought out basic structure overlaid with a lush and exotic mix of color, texture, size, and shape. You feel enclosed in this small, lovely, sumptuous space, rather like a jewel in a velvet-lined box. It is a multi-use area and very much a child's garden. The vine-covered garage is a focal point and has been converted into a storage shed and yoga studio. A twelve-foot-high cedar play tower is tucked behind three spectacular ten-foot-high oak leaf hydrangeas.

DATES & HOURS: May 15; 10 a.m. – 2 p.m.

DIRECTIONS: *Head northwest on Massachusetts Avenue* (toward Bethesda); continue through Westmoreland Circle (this is the DC/MD line, and Western Avenue spokes out to the right). Turn right onto Newport Avenue and right again onto Allan Road. The house is the third on the left. *From I-495,* take the River Road exit toward Washington. Go 4 to 5 miles and then turn right onto Western Avenue. Go .3 mile and turn right onto Allan Road. The house is three blocks down on the right.

The Sexton-Borgiotti Garden, CHEVY CHASE, MD

Patterned after English gardens I found enchanting during a tour in the 1980s, my garden is a charming blend of formal spaces with informal plants, which bloom from May into November and provide a riot of color. Herbaceous borders blend in with azaleas, rhododendrons, and holly trees, which serve as backgrounds. In the front garden, dominated by an imposing magnolia tree, there are two small conifer gardens. A unique foundation planting at the house features New York ferns, dwarf mugo pines, upright yews, blue star junipers, and Japanese blood grass. At the rear of the house, the garden is perfect for walking and meditating. Garden rooms are articulated by stone work — one area abounds with a sea of bogged rhubarb. Bulbs, ferns, and benches line a charming woodland walk. A swimming pool at the center reflects the many plants and trees surrounding it, and a few whimsical sculptures add surprises throughout.

DATES & HOURS: June 26; 10 a.m. – 4 p.m.

DIRECTIONS: *From Route 495/the Beltway,* take the River Road Exit heading toward Washington, DC. At the seventh traffic light you will be at the Kenwood Country Club. Stay in the left lane, pass the tennis courts, and turn left immediately onto Dorset Avenue. Go two blocks to top of hill and turn right onto Highland Drive. The garden is at the second house on the right, #5822.

Gay & Tony Barclay — Orchard Farm, POTOMAC, MD

Our American cottage garden wraps around an old farmhouse on five acres and gives us a wonderful excuse for combining old-fashioned perennials with some modern cultivars. Informal and idiosyncratic, a hornbeam hedge defines a garden room behind the house. The pocket herb garden is around the corner. Roses are everywhere!

DATES & HOURS: May 15; 10 a.m. – 4 p.m.

DIRECTIONS: *From Route 495,* take the River Road Exit toward Potomac. Pass traffic lights at Bradley Lane, Falls Road, and Piney Meeting House Road. At the yellow warning sign (deer) on right, signal left and turn into driveway at first green mailbox, #11600 River Road. Please park in the driveway.

The Olson Garden, POTOMAC, MD

The Olson Garden is situated on a beautiful country estate, nestled within a vast wooded area. Entering the front garden, the fragrance of the fleece vine intertwined in a trellis of flaming trumpet vine and the sound of trickling water welcomes you. Brilliant color combinations are interspersed through waves of ornamental grasses, reminiscent of the country slopes flowing to the cultured garden. As you pass under the arch, you find yourself in a little paradise where the fragrant autumn clematis welcomes you. A glimpse through the crape myrtles carpeted by liriope and daffodils reveals the interplay between the intricate layers of the peaceful bosque, the shimmering water below, and the grand woods beyond. Discover the hot tub hidden within a ring of tall elegant grasses. The comfort and shade of the wisteria canopy provides a view from the breakfast nook into the perennial garden. Its colorful year-round display can also be viewed from indoors. Don't miss this colorful country excursion to the Olsen Garden, sculpted by Corinna and Nicolien of European Garden Design.

DATES & HOURS: May 15; 10 a.m. – 4 p.m.

DIRECTIONS: *Take the Beltway* to exit at River Road North (south of Route 270). Follow River Road North to Falls Road (about 5 miles). Make a left on Falls Road, take the third right, Alloway Drive. The entrance to the property is in the second block, on the left, second to the last driveway. The house is on top of the hill. Park on the side of the road past the two stone entrance pillars.

Carole Ottesen's Garden, POTOMAC, MD

Continually a work in progress, my garden's great challenge has been to achieve unity using my unruly mob of heterogeneous plants. Strategies include grouping like with like and massing ground covers — often ferns. Through an iron gate (talented local gatesmith) the garden path — flanked by shaded beds of native and exotic azaleas and wildflowers, including rare trilliums and medicinals — climbs uphill to a sunny center. Here, native field flowers, sedums, ornamental grasses, and lilies reign. The path continues through moss lawn, culminating in challenging dry shade.

DATES & HOURS: May 15; 2 p.m. – 6 p.m.

DIRECTIONS: *From Route 495,* exit onto River Road. Proceed toward Potomac Village (approximately 3 miles) NW. Turn right at stop light onto Falls Road (Exxon station on right). Turn left at first traffic light, South Glen Road. Go 1.4 miles to #11400 on the left side. Look for fieldstone fence posts and a red mailbox at driveway entrance. If you reach the one-lane bridge, you've gone too far.

Robert Moore & Frank Kirste, SILVER SPRING, MD

The colors in my garden match and clash. To those who look shocked at "a clash," I respond "a good clash is better than a bad match" and more often than not, there is agreement. A vegetable and herb garden share space with annuals in front of a greenhouse of cuttings and orchids. Pleached hornbeans wall in a Fern Walk with whimsical irrigation heads. Water features and fun sculptures take the visitor along pathways to a conifer collection, beds of perennials and annuals and overflowing pots and urns with unique and colorful annuals. Vines that attract hummingbirds cover arbors and a garden shed. Hostas thrive under an architectural cherry which provides a canopy for a dogwood nestled in vinca. Chairs and benches throughout provide for relaxation and views of rooms that make up my Victorian-Japanese-Cottage garden.

DATES & HOURS: June 26; 10 a.m. – 4 p.m.

DIRECTIONS: *From Baltimore:* Route 95 to Route 495 (Beltway) to Silver Spring. Take Georgia Avenue exit. South to Silver Spring. Just past the second traffic light on Georgia Avenue, bear to the right onto 16th Street. Proceed down Route 410. At the second traffic light, turn right onto Sundale. Go 2 blocks and turn right onto Spencer. Go up hill, and house and garden is on the second block of Spencer on right. *From Connecticut Avenue NW:* From DC direction, take a right onto Route 410 (E-W Hwy.) just before traffic light; from Route 495 (Beltway) direction turn left onto Route 410. At the fourth traffic light turn left onto Sundale and proceed as above. Park on opposite side of street from house or on Leonard, the cross street. Do not park in front of house (you will block view of the garden from the house).

MASSACHUSETTS

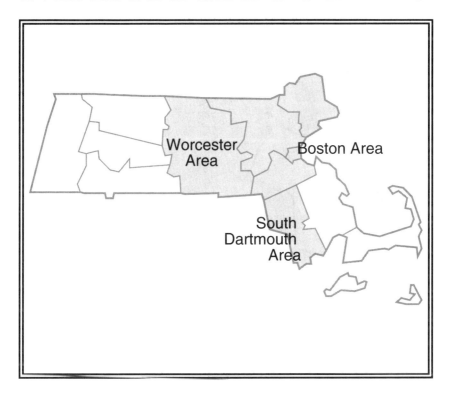

1999 MASSACHUSETTS OPEN DAYS

May 22 & 23: BOSTON AREA
June 19: WORCESTER AREA
July 10: SOUTH DARTMOUTH AREA

BOSTON AREA: *May 22, 1999*

The Georgaklis Garden, BROOKLINE, 9 A.M. – 5 P.M.

The Jane & Hooker Talcott Garden, BROOKLINE, 9 A.M. – 5 P.M.

Ashby Garden, CHESTNUT HILL, 9 A.M. – 5 P.M.

Benka Garden, CHESTNUT HILL, 9 a.m. – 5 p.m.

Greville Garden, CHESTNUT HILL, 9 A.M. – 5 P.M.

McKey's Garden, CHESTNUT HILL, 9 A.M. – 5 P.M.

Susan & Dudley Dumaine, WESTON, 9 A.M. – 5 P.M.

Parker Garden, WESTON, 9 A.M. – 5 P.M.

Pine Rock — The Friedlander Garden, WESTON, 9 A.M. – 5 P.M.

Spencer – Scott Garden, WESTON, 9 A.M. – 5 P.M.

BOSTON AREA: *May 23, 1999*

Sea Meadow, BEVERLY FARMS, 9 A.M. – 5 P.M.

Nancy Britz — The Village Gardener, HAMILTON, 9 A.M. – 5 P.M.

Ship Oak Farm, HAMILTON, 9 A.M. – 5 P.M.

The Garden of Mr. & Mrs. Oliver Wolcott, HAMILTON, 9 A.M. – 5 P.M.

Southgate Garden II, MANCHESTER, 9 A.M. – 5 P.M.

The Garden at 9 Friend Street, MANCHESTER–BY–THE–SEA, 9 A.M. – 5 P.M.

The Rocks, MANCHESTER–BY–THE–SEA, 9 A.M. – 5 P.M.

Silsby Garden, MANCHESTER–BY–THE–SEA, 9 A.M. – 5 P.M.

Grey Gulls, MARBLEHEAD, 9 A.M. – 5 P.M.

Kearney Garden, MARBLEHEAD, 9 A.M. – 5 P.M.

Low Woods, MARBLEHEAD, 9 A.M. – 5 P.M.

Gardens of Donald & Beverly Seamans, MARBLEHEAD, 9 A.M. – 5 P.M.

Spruce Cottage, MARBLEHEAD, 9 A.M. – 5 P.M.

Randall Weiting Garden, SALEM, 9 A.M. – 5 P.M.

North Star — Mr. & Mrs. John Goldsmith, SWAMPSCOTT, 9 A.M. – 5 P.M.

❖ The Sedgwick Gardens, LONG HILL RESERVATION

572 ESSEX STREET, BEVERLY, MA 01915. (978) 921-1944.

This 114-acre estate with five acres of gardens contains more than 400 species of trees, shrubs, bulbs, and perennials, many of them unusual. There are notable Japanese maples, weeping cherries, rhododendrons, azaleas, tree peonies, shrub roses, clematis, and stewartias. A property of the Trustees of Reservations.

DATES & HOURS: Year round, daily, 8 a.m. – dusk. Tours available by appointment.

DIRECTIONS: *Take Route 128* to Exit 18. Go left on Route 22/Essex Street towards Essex for one mile (bearing left at the fork) to brick gateposts and sign on left.

Sea Meadow, BEVERLY FARMS, MA

Sea Meadow is an informal, family place for all ages. Our rambling, shingled home looks southeast across a sloping lawn, meadows, a pond with wildfowl, wetlands, and woods to the ocean. A terrace with an ancient wisteria vine, roses, bulbs, and a large Cornus kousa *connects the house to an herb garden, a bed of heather, perennials, wildflowers, a vegetable garden, and blooming trees and shrubs. An intriguing rock garden under a thirty-foot glacial rock face has a secret path leading to the gazebo. Grassy trails take you through the wetlands to the dunes. We've made inviting areas from which to enjoy the beauty of the natural site.*

DATES & HOURS: May 23; 9 a.m. – 5 p.m.

DIRECTIONS: *From Route 128,* take Exit 17. Turn right onto Grapevine Road. Continue 1.3 miles, passing Chapman's Greenhouse on the right. At the grave-yard turn right onto Haskell Street. Go .4 mile to the end of the street. Turn left onto Hale Street/Route 127. Go .1 mile. Take the first right between stone gate posts, #675. Cross railroad tracks. Bear left at fork. Pass pond on the left; the driveway faces you. Please park in the driveway.

The Georgaklis Garden, Brookline, MA

In my garden I have tried to stretch the blooming season from early spring to late, late fall with many perennials and annuals throughout. My garden is a series of rooms and an outdoor extension of our home where we can enjoy dining, entertaining, or just quiet meditation. It has also been a wonderful backdrop for my sculpture. Even though the city is encroaching upon us, my garden still maintains its quietude.

DATES & HOURS: May 22; 9 a.m. – 5 p.m.

DIRECTIONS: *From Route 128* take Route 9 east to Brookline Village close to Boston line. Turn right at light at Dunkin Donuts and fire station onto High Street. Go to the end of High Street (past two stop signs). Turn left onto Chestnut Street. Follow Chestnut, bearing right. Continue straight onto Goddard Avenue (approximately 1 mile). Jamaica Pond is on your left. Follow Goddard for 200 yards, Hellenic College on your left — George Lane across the street from the College.

The Jane & Hooker Talcott Garden, Brookline, MA

Our garden is a series of pleasant, relaxing areas. It opens with a diverse rock-bordered perennial bed on a terrace, sloping down to the main lawn and sitting area. There you will find beds planted with peonies and a display of hostas, an ilex-bordered vegetable garden, and a frog pond surrounded by lily beds framed with yew. The property also includes dogwoods and flowering fruit trees.

DATES & HOURS: May 22; 9 a.m. – 5 p.m.

DIRECTIONS: *Take Route 9 east to Route 128.* Leave the Atrium shopping mall on your right, and the Chestnut Hill Mall on your left. Continue through Hammond Street with large CVS store on left. Go 1.25 miles from Hammond Street through four traffic lights. Go right on Lee Street. Proceed .3 mile, turn right on Warren Street. Number 420 is the third house on the left. Please park along the road.

❖ Mount Auburn Cemetery,

580 MOUNT AUBURN STREET, CAMBRIDGE, MA 02138. (617) 547-7105.
Mount Auburn Cemetery, founded in 1831, is America's first landscaped cemetery. One hundred and seventy-four acres contain more than 5,000 native and exotic trees identified and tagged. Many important and famous people are buried here. A fascinating place to visit and wonderful for bird-watching. Audio tour available for rent or purchase.

DATES & HOURS: Year round, daily, 8 a.m. – 5 p.m. (7 p.m. during the summer).

DIRECTIONS: *The entrance is on Mount Auburn Street* near the boundary of Cambridge and Watertown, approximately 1.5 miles west of Harvard Square, just west of Mount Auburn Hospital and Fresh Pond Parkway. The cemetery is easily reached by public transportation from Harvard Square (Number 71 or 73 bus).

Ashby Garden, CHESTNUT HILL, MA

In 1988 we retained landscape architect Thomas Wirth to redesign our small suburban garden. He created a series of outdoor rooms, surprises as the visitor rounds each corner, and curving shapes in grass or stone bounded by the straight lines of walls, fences, and paths. The view from inside the house was also an important part of the design. Shrubs and perennials were chosen to provide privacy, contrasting textures, continuous bloom from April to October, and color interest in the autumn. Special features include drystone walls, granite steps and patio, and a small pool beside natural outcroppings of Roxbury Puddingstone.

DATES & HOURS: May 22; 9 a.m. – 5 p.m.

DIRECTIONS: *From Route 128/I-95,* go east on Route 9 for 3 miles, passing the Chestnut Hill Mall. At the Chestnut Hill Shopping Center, make a left at the major traffic light onto Hammond Street.* Turn right at the first stop sign onto Middlesex Road. Take the third right onto Norfolk Road and the first left onto Crafts. Number 41 is the fifth house on the right. *From Boston,* go west on Route 9 for 5 to 6 miles. As you approach the Hammond Street turnoff, you will pass Norfolk Road, Dunster Road, and the Longwood Cricket Club tennis courts. At the Hammond Street traffic lights, turn right onto Hammond Street (you will see CVS and a Gulf Station ahead on the right). Follow the directions above.*

Proceeds shared with The Garden Club of America's Garden History & Design Scholarship Fund.

Benka Garden, CHESTNUT HILL, MA

Our garden was designed by Arleyn Levee to provide spaces to share with passersby as well as spaces to give us privacy and quiet. Perennial borders with peonies, irises, and roses dominate the front yard, with a bluestone walk leading to a wisteria overhanging the front porch. Behind the house is a bluestone terrace with espaliered cotoneaster, as well as azaleas, rhododendrons, and ornamental trees. At the rear of the property, down a short flight of steps, is a small woodland garden with broadleaf evergreens, tiarella, epimedium, *and* mertensia.

DATES & HOURS: May 22; 9 a.m. − 5 p.m.

DIRECTIONS: *From Route 9* (heading west): Turn right on Hammond Street (before CVS Drugstore). Pass Longwood Cricket Club and at stop sign turn right onto Middlesex Road. Drive 4 short blocks until you see a "one-way, do not enter" sign. Turn right onto Circuit Road. The house is fifth on the left. *From Route 9 (heading east):* Make left turn onto Hammond Street. Proceed as above.

Proceeds shared with Chestnut Hill Garden Club — Houghton Garden Fund.

Greville Garden, CHESTNUT HILL, MA

This eight-year-old city garden under a canopy of mature oak trees on one-half acre contains a series of garden rooms encircling the house. The garden is designed for year-round interest, starting with early bulbs in the rock garden, May bulbs in the parterre, and shrubs and perennials continuing throughout the year.

DATES & HOURS: May 22; 9 a.m. − 5 p.m.

DIRECTIONS: *From Route 128,* take Route 9 east toward Boston. Turn right onto Hammond Street.* Glenoe Road is the third street on the left. Look for #20, the second house on the left. *From Boston,* take Route 9 West/Boylston Street and turn left on Hammond Street. Follow directions above.*

McKey's Garden, CHESTNUT HILL, MA

Our garden consists of four distinct areas: a terraced lawn is surrounded by gardens of mixed flowering shrubs, specimen trees, a variety of smaller plant material and sitting areas paved with bluestone. Fieldstone steps lead down to a woodland setting featuring viburnums, azaleas, native shrubs, and shade trees; an intimate clearing contains woodland and bog plants; and an enclosed Georgian garden with mixed borders, fountain, and screened sitting room comprises the fourth area.

DATES & HOURS: May 22; 9 a.m. – 5 p.m.

DIRECTIONS: *From West:* From Route 128 take Route 9 east to Chestnut Hill. At fifth set of lights turn right off Route 9 onto Hammond Street. Proceed to Woodland Road intersection (Beaver Country Day School on your right). Turn right onto Woodland. Laurel Road will be your first left. Proceed to fourth house on right, #45. *From East:* Proceed west on Route 9 (Boylston Street) to intersection of Hammond Street (Longwood Cricket Club on right). Turn left onto Hammond Street and proceed to Woodland and Laurel Road as above.

❖ Garden in the Woods of the New England Wildflower Society,

180 HEMENWAY ROAD, FRAMINGHAM, MA 01701. OFFICE, (508) 877-7630. RECORDED INFORMATION, (508) 877-6574

Garden in the Woods, New England's premier wildflower showcase, displays the largest landscaped collection of native plants in the Northeast. Forty-five acres with woodland trails offer vistas of wildflowers, shrubs, and trees. Sixteen hundred varieties of plants, including more than 200 rare and endangered species, grow in protective cultivation. Largest wildflower nursery in New England.

DATES & HOURS: April 15 through June 15, daily with extended hours in May to 7 p.m.; June 16 through October 31, Tuesday – Sunday, 9 a.m. – 5 p.m. Last admission to garden trails, one hour before closing.

DIRECTIONS: *From the North, South and East:* Take Route 128 to Route 20 west; go 8 miles on Route 20 to Raymond Road (second left after traffic lights in South Sudbury); 1.3 miles to Hemenway Road. *From the West:* Take the Massachusetts Turnpike/Exit 12 to Route 9 East; go 2.4 miles to Edgell Road (Route 9 overpass); 2.1 miles to traffic lights; take a right onto Water Street and a left onto Hemenway Road. Follow garden signs.

Nancy Britz — The Village Gardener, HAMILTON, MA

My twin obsessions are daylilies and conifers. This is a five-acre national display garden of the American Hemerocallis Society, planted with over 1,000 registered cultivars. Many seedlings come from my extensive hybridizing program. The conifer gardens have more than 200 cultivars in several areas, including a rock garden of miniature and dwarf conifers planted with interesting companions. There are beds of shade plants, including hostas, astilbes, brunnera, rhododendrons, azaleas, hydrangeas, and various dicentras, as well as three sunny perennial beds and a large koi pond.

DATES & HOURS: May 23; 9 a.m. - 5 p.m.

DIRECTIONS: *Sagamore Farm Road* runs east from Route 1A about 5.5 miles north of Route 128 (Exit 20-Hamilton), and .3 mile south of the Ipswich/Hamilton line. A landmark is a white oval "Daylilies" sign on a white post in a bed of daylilies.

Ship Oak Farm, HAMILTON, MA

The name of the farm comes from the timber that was cut here for the shipbuilders of nearby Essex. The house dates from 1760. When purchased by the present owners the whole property was in disrepair. There were no lawns or gardens, just pastures and lovely old trees. Shrubs, ground covers, native plants, and an eighty-foot perennial border were added as well as a vegetable garden in an old paddock by the barn. Most of the plants are gifts from friends, neighbors, and the Arnold Arboretum. A great many species of birds are attracted to the garden. The garden was awarded a gold medal by the Massachusetts Horticultural Society in 1995.

DATES & HOURS: May 23; 9 a.m. – 5 p.m.

DIRECTIONS: *Route 128* to Exit 20 onto Route 1A north to Wenham. At church in Wenham, turn left onto Arbor Street and proceed through overhead light where Arbor becomes Highland Street (you are now in Hamilton). Watch for large equestrian complex on left. Just beyond is Gail Avenue on right (roosters on gateposts). Come to end of Gail Avenue (drive very slowly). *If traveling on Route 1A from north* turn right by library and community house onto Asbury Street. Continue to end and turn right at traffic light.

The Garden of Mr. & Mrs. Oliver Wolcott,

HAMILTON, MA

From the terrace of a seventeenth-century house, one looks out on a long herbaceous border backed by an old stone wall. Beyond an arch covered with clematis is a peony walk with a wrought-iron gate and fence at the end. Espaliered pears separate this more formal walk from the vegetable garden.

DATES & HOURS: May 23; 9 a.m. – 5 p.m.

DIRECTIONS: *From Route 128 take Exit 20 North.* Go through North Beverly and Wenham on Route 1A. Cross the railroad tracks in Hamilton and proceed 2 miles. A sign, #918, marks the house on the left. If you come to a sharp left turn, you have gone too far.

❖ Arnold Arboretum of Harvard University,

125 THE ARBORWAY, JAMAICA PLAIN, MA 02130. (617) 524-1718.

The 265-acre Arnold Arboretum displays North America's premier collection of more than 14,000 hardy trees, shrubs and vines. The grounds were planted and designed by the Arboretum's first director, Charles Sprague Sargent, and America's first landscape architect, Frederick Law Olmsted. Highlights include crab apple, conifer, lilac, rhododendron and bonsai collections.

DATES & HOURS: Year round, daily, dawn – dusk.

DIRECTIONS: *From Storrow Drive* take the Fenway/Park Drive Exit. Follow signs to the Riverway, which becomes the Jamaicaway and then the Arborway/ Route 1. *From I-95/Route 128 exit* onto Route 9 East. Follow Route 9 for 7 miles to the Riverway/Route 1 South. *From the Southeast Expressway/Route 93* take Exit 11/Granite Avenue/Ashmont onto Route 203. Follow past Franklin Park. This site is also accessible by public transportation. Please call for details.

Southgate Garden II, MANCHESTER, MA

A small (less than one-half acre) garden, built on a very wet area, so wet in fact that it was dug out to form a pond. When we bought the house in 1982, there was no garden at all. Robert Mackintosh designed the contours of the garden from the back of the house to the edge of the pond. May plantings will include azaleas, rhododendrons, bulbs, double-file viburnum, etc. Clematis should be in bloom also. If the garden is looking good, much of the credit should go to my faithful and respected garden assistant, Debi Bulloch — a great gardener.

DATES & HOURS: May 23; 9 a.m. – 5 p.m.

DIRECTIONS: *From Route 128,* headed north: Past exits to Essex, Beverly Farms. Turn off Route 128 at School Street Exit, Manchester. Continue slowly down School Street at the mandated speed of 25 mph, to #22, on your right, a small yellow house. Parking may be difficult; carpools are recommended. Parking may be available behind town hall and in a small lot at the junction of Washington Street and Norwood Avenue.

Proceeds shared with Manchester Women's Club Scholarship fund.

The Garden at 9 Friend Street, MANCHESTER-BY-THE-SEA, MA

The first garden at 9 Friend Street was laid out in 1928 for the present owner's grandfather. Mr. Frederick Rice, a floral and garden designer and lecturer, has made major changes during the past fifteen years. The English cottage-style garden, ablaze with color and awash with texture, is laid out in a series of rooms furnished with an extraordinary variety of perennials, annuals, roses, vines, and deciduous and evergreen shrubs. Brick and stone patios have been constructed for outdoor living. There are two fish ponds, a pavilion, and a teahouse. The garden was featured in the 1996 summer issue of Country Home — Country Gardens *magazine.*

DATES & HOURS: May 23; 9 a.m. – 5 p.m.

DIRECTIONS: *Route 128* north to Exit 15, School Street, Manchester, MA. Right onto School Street at the end of the exit. Pass Essex County Club on the left and through the blinking yellow light — cemetery on left, down hill. Friend Street is the second right beyond Sacred Heart Catholic Church. The house, #9, is gray with black shutters, on the right — the only house on the street with a white picket fence. Please park on Friend Steet or in lot behind Sacred heart Church.

Proceeds shared with The Manchester Council on Aging.

The Rocks, MANCHESTER-BY-THE-SEA, MA

The Rocks is a turn-of-the-century estate that has been restored over the past three years. It enjoys spectacular ocean views from the new seawall walk. The use of fairly mature plant material merges old gardens into new, deceiving most visitors into believing the site was largely untouched by the intense reconstruction of the magnificent house. A stroll garden over granite, lawn, cobblestone, and pebble presents beautiful views in every direction. The garden offers the opportunity to see fine details in limestone, brick, granite, and wrought-iron. Garden ornaments and lovely pots filled with colorful annuals personalize the three-acre garden. Across Harbor Street is a parterre garden behind a handsome green trellis fence.

DATES & HOURS: May 23; 9 a.m. – 5.p.m.

DIRECTIONS: *North on Route 128* to Exit 16 (Pine Street/Manchester). Proceed on Pine Street to the end at the center of Manchester. Take a right onto Route 127 for about .75 mile. Take a left onto Harbor Street at The Old Corner Inn. Cross a bridge over the railroad tracks to a stop sign. The Rocks is immediately straight ahead through stone pillars. Park on Harbor Street.

Silsby Garden, MANCHESTER-BY-THE-SEA, MA

A very personal garden over the last twenty years. The thinned woodland lends a cathedral-like setting to a myriad of pathways from which a wide variety of woodland shrubs and perennials may be viewed. The spine of the garden is a stream with numerous bridge crossings. The garden is my laboratory, the inspiration for plant combinations I use in my professional designs. Extensive mulching and close planting allow the garden to thrive with minimal mainte-nance. Visitors are welcome onto our deck to enjoy the view of the boxwood quatre foil *and gazebo vista.*

DATES & HOURS: May 23; 9 a.m. – 5 p.m.

DIRECTIONS: *North on Route 128* to Exit 15 (School Street/Manchester). Right off exit ramp toward Manchester. Take third left onto Lincoln Street. Take a left at end of Lincoln onto Route 127. Take second left onto Forest Street and continue to bear left at next intersection. Forest Street will become Loading Place Road. Follow to last property on left (Deck House) at end of road, #26 .

Grey Gulls, MARBLEHEAD, MA

Set above a rocky coastline this collector's garden presents a diverse array of uncommon bulbs and perennials, heirloom vegetables and distinctive containers. Hedges and (in winter) a wattle fence are necessary to protect the garden from the elements. Channing Blake landscaped the property between 1990 and 1992 creating a modern design of sinuous beds in harmony with the surrounding curves of shore and sea.

DATES & HOURS: May 23; 9 a.m. – 5 p.m.

DIRECTIONS: *Take Route 128* to Exit 25 (Route 114 East). At the fourth traffic light in Marblehead take a right onto Ocean Avenue. Cross the causeway and stay to the right for 1.5 miles to traffic circle. Bear right at traffic circle and go to #429 Ocean Avenue (number painted on rock). House is on right, park on street.

Kearney Garden, MARBLEHEAD, MA

Six years ago, half of this garden was a thicket of juniper and Norway maple. Randall Wieting has transformed it into rolling lawns surrounding rocky outcrops. The planting is primarily trees and shrubs, accented by perennials. Come up on the deck for a view of the Boston skyline across the bay.

DATES & HOURS: May 23; 9 a.m. – 5 p.m.

DIRECTIONS: *From Marblehead,* cross the causeway to Marblehead Neck. Bear left at the fork in the road, then take first right (Flint Street). The house is 200 yards on the right.

Low Woods, MARBLEHEAD, MA

Low Woods is a naturalist's waterfront property designed in the 1880s. One would guess it was designed by the Olmsted firm; however the actual landscape architect is unknown. The two-acre property includes a teahouse surrounded by Juniperus virginiana, bayberries, blueberries, and honeysuckle. There are multiple terraces and winding paths leading the visitor to breathtaking water views and restful gardens.

DATES & HOURS: May 23; 9 a.m. – 5 p.m.

DIRECTIONS: *Take Route 128* to exit 25 (Route 114 East). At the fourth traffic light in Marblehead take a right onto Ocean Avenue. Cross the causeway and stay to right for 1.5 miles to traffic circle. Bear right at traffic circle and follow long stone wall to first opening to right, #405 Ocean Avenue. The grey house sits high up. A large copper beach is evident from the road. Park along the road.

Gardens of Donald & Beverly Seamans, MARBLEHEAD, MA

A walk through the garden is full of surprises. You come upon bronze sculptures of animals, birds, and children nestled in the natural settings — or as fountains recirculating water in the pool. Entering the path from the driveway that leads to the house is a small rock garden. To the right is a vegetable and cutting garden. To the left is a glade of pachysandra with rhododendrons. Beside the house are pools with a mermaid fountain flowing into a small upper pool, which flows into a lower pool with water lilies and goldfish. Two bronze children pour buckets of recirculating water on either end. Over this pool is a bridge which leads to two gardens. Follow a rocky path to the right and find a Daylily Garden, clematis, a dwarf Japanese cut leaf maple, a shade garden containing ferns and hosta, and a variety of heather on a low ledge. Go straight after the bridge to view the harbor, note the semi-circular flower garden backed by Rosa rugosa. Beyond is a natural field where viburnum, witch hazel, blueberry bushes and wildflowers grow. A gazebo sits on a rock terrace with thyme, lavender, and daisies. The perfect place to stop and rest.

DATES & HOURS: May 23; 9 a.m. – 5 p.m.

DIRECTIONS: *From Route 128* east, take Route 114 east to end (in Marblehead). Go right on Route 129 for one block. At light, turn left on Atlantic Avenue. Go past big church on left and turn right on Chestnut Street (at hardware store). At top of hill, turn right on Harbor View. The house is #10, on the water side of the street.

Spruce Cottage, MARBLEHEAD, MA

A nearly 100-year-old white spruce stands guard over a one and one-half acre garden that we have worked for twenty years. Our sculpture gallery opens onto an English-style perennial garden and a pool of grass. We have created an oasis using various hedge forms and unusual trees and shrubs. A Magnolia grandiflora, *a crape-myrtle, and an eighteen-foot clump of bamboo smother the cottage.*

DATES & HOURS: May 23; 9 a.m. - 5 p.m.

DIRECTIONS: *Take Route 114* off Route 128. Travel east on Route 114. At the first traffic light in Marblehead turn left on West Shore Drive. Approximately 1.5 miles after cemetery, turn right on Green Street. A yew hedge and a rose bed with sign "Spruce Cottage" mark the entrance to the garden.

❖ The 1768 Jeremiah Lee Mansion Gardens,

170 WASHINGTON STREET, MARBLEHEAD, MA 01945. (781) 631-1768.

The beautiful gardens now surrounding the Jeremiah Lee Mansion are designed after eighteenth-century models. They feature an herb garden, a sunken octagonal sundial garden, a large upper terrace with a colorful perennial border, and a spacious lower garden with a variety of trees, shrubs, vines, groundcovers, and wildflowers. The gardens have been designed and maintained by volunteers from the Marblehead Garden Club since 1938.

DATES & HOURS: Year round, daily; dawn – dusk.

DIRECTIONS: *From Boston,* take Route 1A North to Route 129 East through Swampscott. Continue several miles on Atlantic Avenue into the business district of Marblehead. Turn left at the Texaco gas station, and take the next right onto Washington Street. Bear left at fork, drive up hill and down. The Jeremiah Lee Mansion will be on the left, a large grey building.

Randall Wieting Garden, SALEM, MA

A ten-year-old garden situated on a salt marsh, with large perennial gardens and a koi pond. There are many ornamental grasses, and with luck, all the Siberian iris will be out.

DATES & HOURS: May 23; 9 a.m. – 5 p.m.

DIRECTIONS: *From Route 128* go east on Route 114 to Salem, where it joins Route 1A. Continue on 114/1A. At Salem State College, bear right on Route 1A when Route 114 goes straight. Number 14 Buchanan Road is off Lincoln Road, which is off Route 1A/Loring Avenue opposite alumni house of Salem State College (South Campus).

North Star — Mr. & Mrs. John Goldsmith,

SWAMPSCOTT, MA

A pine grove and gathering of blue spruce hide the surprises that await the visitor. A contemporary house of dramatic proportions embraces gardens and lawns planted in great splashes of old-fashioned trees, shrubs, and perennials.

DATES & HOURS: May 23; 9 a.m. – 5 p.m.

DIRECTIONS: *From Boston:* Follow Route 1A to Route 129. In the town of Swampscott, take the right fork at the Citgo station onto Puritan Road. Follow .9 mile to Galloupes Point on right. At bottom of hill is #55.

❖ Lyman Estate – The Vale,

185 LYMAN STREET, WALTHAM, MA 02154. (617) 891-4882.

The Lyman Estate, known as The Vale, is one of the finest examples in the United States of a country property laid out according to the principles of eighteenth-century English naturalistic design. The greenhouses were built from 1800 to 1930, and contain century-old camellias and grapevines, as well as tropical and subtropical plants. Unusual plants available for sale year round. Please call for the dates of specialty sales. The Vale is a property of the Society for the Preservation of New England Antiquities.

DATES & HOURS: Greenhouse and grounds open Monday – Saturday; 9:30 a.m.– 4 p.m.

DIRECTIONS: *Take Route 128* to Exit 26/Route 20 East to Waltham/Boston. Follow Route 20 (it becomes Main Street) through the center of Waltham about 1.7 miles. At the Kentucky Fried Chicken, turn left onto Lyman Street. Follow Lyman .5 miles to a rotary and bear immediately right into the Estate driveway (check for a SPNEA sign).
NOTE: Access to grounds is limited if a wedding is in progress.

Susan & Dudley Dumaine, WESTON, MA

Gardens featuring exuberant displays of native plants follow the steep, rocky contours of this site before descending into a ravine where carpeting ground covers set off shrubs, ferns, and perennials. Once a chicken coop, the house adds interest and testament to the usage and history of the area.

DATES & HOURS: May 22; 9 a.m. – 5 p.m.

DIRECTIONS: *From the Massachusetts Turnpike/Route 90,* take Route 128 north to Route 20 West. Turn left at the traffic light onto School Street. Take first left onto Maple Road, one block long. Go past stop sign onto Meadowbrook Road. Pass a "No Trespassing" sign. Hidden Road is the second left at the Weston Golf Club House. Number 8 is the second house on the left. Please park in the lot across the street.

Proceeds shared with The New England Wildflower Society.

Parker Garden, WESTON, MA

Established by Bob Harrison and enhanced by Gary Koller, this woodland garden invites easy yet satisfying exploration of the well-defined spaces. Wrapped around extensive granite ledges, golden foliage brings sunlight into all parts of the garden, while the careful juxtaposition of plants chosen for their form and texture offers a rich visual experience year round.

DATES & HOURS: May 22; 9 a.m. – 5 p.m.

DIRECTIONS: *Park as directed for Dumaine Garden.* Follow signs down the hill to tennis court roadway and into garden.

Pine Rock — The Friedlander Garden, WESTON, MA

The sound of falling water and the dappled shade of pine woods provide the backdrop for my collector's garden of plants, many of which are rarely found in New England gardens. There are species of rare trilliums, primroses, tricyrtis, ornamental grasses, rhododendrons, dwarf conifers, ferns, Japanese maples...the list goes on and on. All the plants are clearly labeled. Meandering through the stone-edged paths, one has a feeling of tranquility coupled with the excitement of discovering the many treasures.

DATES & HOURS: May 22; 9 a.m. – 5 p.m.

DIRECTIONS: *Take I-95/Route 128* to Exit 24/Route 30 West toward Framingham. Stay on Route 30 for about 2 miles until you get to a traffic light at Wellesley Street. Turn right, go past Regis College, and take first left onto Chestnut Street. Turn right on Chadwick Road, and then take first left into Baldwin Circle. Number 6 is the second house on the left.

The Spencer – Scott Garden, WESTON, MA

Having been blessed with a sun-drenched site with deep loam, we set out to create a garden to satisfy our varied interests in flowering trees, shrubs, vines, ground covers, perennials, and bulbs. We designed, created, and maintain the garden. Included are rock gardens, partial shade gardens, dwarf evergreens, and perennial beds with walking paths, all set against an open meadow. Of special interest are many varieties of peonies, species and old roses, iris, hardy geraniums, alliums, liliums, wildflowers, clematis, lilacs, daylilies, azaleas, and rhododendrons. It is amazing to us that we have collected more than 1,500 varieties over the years. Our efforts have been rewarded with delights for all our senses.

DATES & HOURS: May 22; 9 a.m. – 5 p.m.

DIRECTIONS: *From I-95,* take Exit 26 to Route 20 East toward Waltham. Go past a traffic light and turn left at the first street toward Route 117. When the street ends, turn left onto Route 117 West. Drive 1.8 miles and turn right onto King's Grant Road. Take the first left onto Myles Standish Road. The Spencer – Scott Garden is the second house on the left, #12. Please park along the road.

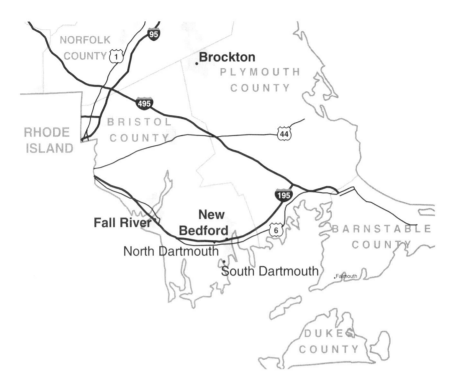

SOUTH DARTMOUTH AREA: *July 10, 1999*

Frances & Clinton Levin's Garden, NORTH DARTMOUTH, 10 A.M. – 2 P.M.

Betsy & Greer McBratney, SOUTH DARTMOUTH, 10 A.M. – 2 P.M.

Sea Thrift — Apponagansett Watch, SOUTH DARTMOUTH, 10 A.M. – 2 P.M.

Frima & Gilbert Shapiro's Garden, SOUTH DARTMOUTH, 10 A.M. – 4 P.M.

❖ The Rotch-Jones-Duff House & Garden Museum,

396 COUNTY STREET, NEW BEDFORD, MA 02740. (508) 997-1401.

The property encompasses a full city block of urban gardens surrounded by a traditional board fence. The centerpiece of the gardens, a wooden pergola, is surrounded by a formal cutting garden, a wildflower walk, and a boxwood and rose parterre garden. Restoration of the rose garden was initiated in 1996 under the direction of Stephen Scaniello, noted rosarian at the Brooklyn Botanic Garden, with the planting of more than 200 rose bushes.

DATES & HOURS: Open daily, 10 a.m. – 4 p.m. Closed major holidays and Mondays, January – May.

DIRECTIONS: *From I-195 east,* take Exit 15/Route 18 south to the second set of traffic lights. Turn right at the lights onto Union Street to the top of the hill. Turn left onto County Street and go four blocks to the large yellow house on the left.

Frances & Clinton Levin's Garden, NORTH DARTMOUTH, MA

The Gold Medal citation from the Massachusetts Horticultural Society in 1996 described the garden as "an estate of unusual design and horticultural features where surprises frequent every corner." An enclosed rose garden, shade garden, and serpentine lawns surround the house designed in the Frank Lloyd Wright tradition. Stone walls set off species of daylilies and lily cultivars. A natural pond area is a highlight.

DATES & HOURS: July 10; 10 a.m. – 2 p.m.

DIRECTIONS: *Going east on I-195,* take the first New Bedford Exit to Route 140. Turn right at end of Route 140 onto Route 6 East. Turn left at first traffic light, Slocum Road. Continue for .25 mile to first right, Patton Street. Turn right at end of block to Truman Avenue and the driveway of the Levin's home. This is the rear of the property with ample parking, view of the house and gardens.

Proceeds shared with The Rotch-Jones-Duff House & Garden Museum.

Betsy & Greer McBratney, SOUTH DARTMOUTH, MA

Our house, overlooking Buzzards Bay, was built in 1964 on four acres of dairy farm pasture. In thirty-four years, its fine trees and shrubs have matured. Vegetable gardens are surrounded by espaliered fruit trees. We have heath and heather gardens and a sunken garden featuring alpine troughs. Small raised perennial beds have an unusual color scheme of wine, yellow, and gray foliage. We also have a caged blueberry patch, a state-of-the-art compost area, and a large daffodil collection succeeded by ornamental grasses in the summer.

DATES & HOURS: July 10; 10 a.m. – 2 p.m.

DIRECTIONS: *Take I-195 to Route 140 East* to a right onto Route 6 West to Slocum Road. Turn left at first traffic light onto Slocum Road to Russells Mills and bear right. Go a short distance to the police station and turn left onto Elm. Take Elm to the village center and turn right onto Bridge Street to cross Padanaram Bridge. Turn left immediately onto Smith Neck Road. Go 1 mile and turn left at the sign for Birchfield Farm. Come to a slight rise and take the first right onto Grinnell Road. It's the second house on the left with a red door, post-and-rail fence, and gray mailbox with name on it.

Proceeds shared with The Rotch-Jones-Duff House & Garden Museum.

Sea Thrift — Apponagansett Watch, SOUTH DARTMOUTH, MA

In Alfred Walker's garden fine plantings of ornamental trees and shrubs blend harmoniously with an 1868 whaleship owner's house. The gardens, conceived ten years ago, are situated at the head of the Apponagansett River. A splendid view opens behind the Italianate-style house; hostas emerge beside and underneath shrubs and trees. Plantings around outbuildings reflect the historical nature of the property, as does an eighteenth-century burial ground in the undulating landscape between the house and the river. A woodland walk meanders back to the most dramatic feature of the garden, a great lawn surrounded by stone walls and boxwood hedges that features unusual trees and shrubs.

DATES & HOURS: July 10; 10 a.m. – 2 p.m.

DIRECTIONS: *From the end of Route 140,* turn right onto Route 6. Go left at the first traffic light onto Slocum Road. Continue past traffic lights at Allen Street. Slocum Road becomes Russells Mills Road at Friendly's Pizza. Keep straight, bearing right, pass the Dartmouth Police Station on the right. Number 288 is the fifth house on the left after the police station. Park on the adjacent streets on the right (Utica Lane) just past the house.

Proceeds shared with The Rotch-Jones-Duff House & Garden Museum.

Frima & Gilbert Shapiro's Garden, SOUTH DARTMOUTH, MA

Overlooking Padanarum Harbor, our garden has many different feelings as one walks around. The front of the house is formal, with shaped boxwood and espaliered yews. Inside the pool gate, there are large perennial borders, a rose bed which complements the borders, and a large espaliered pear tree. The house and garden follow the terrain of the land, with many unusual plantings in place. The lower patio has creeping thyme which is over thirty years old. New plantings of lilies, boxwood, and caryopteris add contrasts. A pond enhances trees, some old and some newly propagated by the owners.

DATES & HOURS: July 10; 10 a.m. – 4 p.m.

DIRECTIONS: *Take I-195 to Route 140 West* to a right onto Route 6 to Slocum Road. Turn left at the first traffic light onto Slocum Road to Russell Mills Road and turn right. Go a short distance to Elm Street and turn left at the police station. Take Elm to the village center, and turn right onto Bridge Street to cross Padanarum Bridge. Turn left immediately onto Smith Neck Road. Go 1 mile and turn left at the sign for Birchfield Farm. Continue up that road bearing left at the fork, and go down hill on Birchfield until you come to a field on the right marked for parking. The house is through the stone fence at the white open gate.

Proceeds shared with The Rotch-Jones-Duff House & Garden Museum.

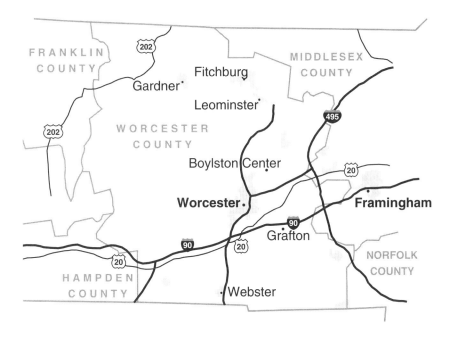

WORCESTER AREA: *June 19, 1999*

Maple Grove, BOYLSTON, 10 A.M. – 6 P.M.

Mapel & Libuda Garden, GRAFTON, 10 A.M. – 6 P.M.

Brigham Hill Farm, NORTH GRAFTON, 10 A.M. – 6 P.M.

Mole Hill — Richard & Alan Emmet, WESTFORD, 10 A.M. – 4 P.M.

Maple Grove, BOYLSTON, MA

Designed around a late-eighteenth-century half-Cape house, Maple Grove is framed by mature sugar maples. Located within the historic district of Boylston, the garden is adjacent to an eighteenth-century cemetery, giving it charming borrowed scenery. A true collector's garden, Maple Grove has a wide assortment of choice woody and herbaceous plants in a connected series of borders, beds, and islands, with sculpture and water features.

DATES & HOURS: June 19; 10 a.m. – 6 p.m.

DIRECTIONS: *From Route 290 East,* take Exit 23B for Route 140 North. Go 1.8 miles to the first traffic light and turn right onto Route 70. Go 1 mile to historic Boylston Center. Make a sharp right, circling around the old cemetery, and turn onto School Street. The house is the first on the right, a gray Cape. *From Route 290 West from Boston,* take Exit 24. Turn right at the end of the ramp and go to the blinking light. Turn left onto Route 70. Travel .25 mile to the center of Boylston (gazebo on the left). At the fork in the road, bear left at the cemetery. Go to the first house on the right. Please park along the street.

Proceeds shared with The Worcester County Horticultural Society.

❖ Tower Hill Botanic Garden,

11 FRENCH DRIVE, BOYLSTON, MA 01505. (508) 869-6111.
WWW.TOWERHILLBG.ORG

Located on 132 rural acres, Tower Hill Botanic Garden features a spectacular spring bulb display, a lawn garden of over 350 varieties of trees and shrubs, secret and cottage gardens filled with colorful perennials and unusual annuals, a vegetable and a wildlife garden, an orchard of heirloom apple varieties, walking trails, and a panoramic view. The Stoddard Education and Visitors Center hosts lectures, workshops and demonstrations, flower shows and exhibits, an 8,000 volume library, garden shop, and weekend cafe.

DATES & HOURS: Year round. Tuesday – Sunday and holiday Mondays, 10 a.m. – 5 p.m. Closed Thanksgiving, Christmas Eve and Day, and New Year's Day.

DIRECTIONS: *Located in Central Massachusetts,* 10 miles northeast of Worcester. *From I-290* take Exit 24. Travel 3.25 miles toward Boylston to 11 French Drive with entrance on right.

Mapel & Libuda Garden, GRAFTON, MA

Our seven-year-old garden has been an exciting undertaking. With an eclectic 1910 stone bungalow as a backdrop, a unique collector's garden has developed. Perennial gardens around the house anchor it to the surrounding site. Bluestone terraces lend ample space for sitting and displaying our container plants. A vegetable garden with small fruits and woodland gardens blend into the mix. The water garden and meadow areas are enjoyed by wildlife. Also, a small greenhouse has opened new realms of gardening possibilities. Set back from a country road, our garden is truly peaceful and relaxing.

DATES & HOURS: June 19; 10 a.m. – 6 p.m.

DIRECTIONS: *From the East and West,* take the Mass Pike to Exit 11 for Route 122 Millbury/Worcester. Bear right after the tollbooth to Route 122 South. Travel .5 mile and turn right onto Brigham Hill Road, directly across from Wyman Gordon plant entrance. Travel .2 mile to an intersection and continue straight across on Brigham Hill Road. Travel 1.5 miles toward Grafton Center. Number 95 Brigham Hill Road is on the right side after a sharp curve. Two mailboxes mark the driveway directly across from a fire hydrant. The garden is at the end of a 400-foot driveway. Please park along the road. *From the South,* take Route 495 to the Mass Pike westbound and follow above directions.

Proceeds shared with The Tower Hill Botanic Garden.

Brigham Hill Farm, NORTH GRAFTON, MA

Brigham Hill Farm is on the crest of historic Brigham Hill. "Gentleman Johnny" Burgoyne marched his troops past the Georgian farmhouse in the Revolution. Complete with resident ghost, and the "Irish Curse," the garden folds around the house and barn, each part different from the rest. Shaded by 100-year-old sugar maples, paths lead to a kitchen herb garden then to a raised vegetable garden flanked by fragrant lilies and hollies. A walled perennial garden leads to hillside pools, ledges and woodland paths with many interesting native plants. A meadow houses the one remaining pony, "Jelle Chatter," who eats our strawberry patch!

DATES & HOURS: June 19; 10 a.m. – 6 p.m.

DIRECTIONS: *From the Massachusetts Turnpike.* Exit 11, take a right onto Route 122 and go for .25 mile and then take a right on Brigham Hill Road (across from the entrance to Wyman Gordan Co.) Go 1.5 miles to the top of the hill. We are the yellow house and barn on the left, #128. Parking is in the field across from the drive.

Proceeds shared with The Tower Hill Botanic Garden.

Mole Hill — Richard & Alan Emmet, WESTFORD, MA

Forty-five years ago we took over an historic house with an old walled garden centered around an apple tree. We plant old-fashioned perennials that we love, concentrating on those that do well. Beyond the walled garden are old roses, clematis, peonies, and a vegetable garden. Naturalized narcissi carpet the small rounded hillside, as well as the ground beneath pear and crab apple trees. A mown path crosses a flowery meadow toward an eye-catcher in the woods. Follow a woodland path about 100 yards to another folly, this one with a bench, a welcoming destination.

DATES & HOURS: June 19; 10 a.m. – 4 p.m.

DIRECTIONS: *From Route 495 North,* take Exit 31 to Littleton Common and Route 119. Turn left off the exit ramp and go to traffic light. Turn left at light onto Route 110 toward Chelmsford. After 1.6 miles bear right onto Route 225 toward Carlisle for .3 mile to a blinking light and stop sign. Continue onto Route 225 for .7 mile to a yellow house and barn on the left. Please do not park along the road. *From Route 128,* take Route 225 West through Bedford and Carlisle. Cross Route 27 at a traffic light and go 1.9 miles to the "R. S. Emmet" sign on the right.

Proceeds shared with The New England Garden History Society.

MICHIGAN

1999 MICHIGAN OPEN DAYS

May 15: ANN ARBOR AREA
May 16 & July 17: BLOOMFIELD HILLS AREA
June 13: GROSSE POINTE AREA

ANN ARBOR AREA: *May 15, 1999*

Baker Garden, ANN ARBOR, 10 A.M. – 4 P.M.

Cochrane's Garden, ANN ARBOR, 9 A.M. – 6 P.M.

❖ Inglis Garden Walk, ANN ARBOR, 10 A.M. – 6 P.M.

Kelsch Garden, ANN ARBOR, 10 a.m. – 4 P.M.

The Reznicek Garden, ANN ARBOR, 10 A.M. – 4 P.M.

Sloan Garden, ANN ARBOR, 10 A.M. – 4 P.M.

Van Dyke Garden, ANN ARBOR, 11 A.M. – 6 P.M.

Borek Janik's Garden, CHELSEA, 10 A.M. – 2 P.M.

Guerin Wilkinson, CHELSEA, 10 A.M. – 4 P.M.

Baker Garden, ANN ARBOR, MI

Sunny mixed borders are the heart of our suburban garden, set formally amid lawns, brick paths, hedges, and surrounding woodland. Plantings in this framework are informal, emphasizing color, foliage, and seasonal change. Ours is a collector's garden, stuffed with unusual woody and herbaceous plants— there are more than twenty varieties each of shrub roses and hardy geraniums. A naturalistic border under black walnuts shows the variety of plants which can thrive there. Peak season is June through October, but even winter months have interest and a few flowers. In May, the purple-pink haze of redbuds suffuses the surrounding woods, creating a spectacular setting for spring-blooming shrubs, bulbs, and emerging perennials.

DATES & HOURS: May 15; 10 a.m. – 4 p.m.

DIRECTIONS: *From U.S. 23,* take Plymouth Road (Exit 41) west 1 mile toward downtown Ann Arbor. Turn left onto Huron Parkway. Take Huron 1 mile south to Glazier Way. Turn left onto Glazier (dirt road), ascend hill, and turn left onto Wolverhampton. Turn right onto East Dobson. The house, #3300, and garden are on the corner of Wolverhampton & East Dobson. Park on East Dobson and enter the garden to the left of the house.

Cochrane's Garden, ANN ARBOR, MI

Welcome to our woodland garden. The thirty-three-year-old traditional white Colonial is nestled beneath towering oaks. There is a display of viburnum, Japanese maples, redbuds, a pink dogwood, rhododendrons, and azaleas. The uniquely contoured site with sloping side banks has been maintained in a natural state with thousands of naturalized tulips and daffodils, many varieties of wildflowers, ferns, more than 150 named hostas, companion plants, and ground cover. Numerous partial shade perennials and lilies are located in the front- and back-yard gardens. We seek unusual plants and continuous bloom.

DATES & HOURS: May 15; 9 a.m. – 6 p.m.

DIRECTIONS: *From U.S. 23,* take Exit 37B. Go west on Washtenaw .8 mile. Turn right onto Glenwood for 2 blocks, then turn right onto Exmoor. Take the first left onto Edinborough to the second house on the left, #1530.

Kelsch Garden, ANN ARBOR, MI

The garden is naturalistic, its form and contents determined by chance, topography, and relatively transient enthusiasms. In many areas, with the passage of time, it has become a shade garden. There are remnants of the earlier sun garden in the older, no longer "dwarf" conifers and ornamental grasses. Currently, hostas, hellebores, and their companion plants dominate. A landscaped lap pool, rustic in style, has been worked into the garden (The pool is not open in May).

DATES & HOURS: May 15; 10 a.m. – 4 p.m.

DIRECTIONS: *The garden is located in northwest Ann Arbor,* off West Huron River Drive. Take a left off North Main Street just before it enters M14 (the left is well marked but is on the ramp to M14). Drive 1.75 miles on West Huron River Drive. The river is on the right. The second possible left is Warrington;take it. The subdivision is River Ridge. Take the second left off Warrington, calledLincolnshire Lane. The Kelsch residence is the second house on the right, #1977. Please park on the street. Walk up the drive to enter the garden.

The Reznicek Garden, ANN ARBOR, MI

Our yard is entirely garden; we have no lawn. It gently slopes around the house and consists of rock gardens, areas of shade- and sun-loving plants, some acid soil beds with rhododendrons and other species with similar needs, plus a small pond. The house is bordered with perennials on the south and west sides and shade-tolerant plantings on the north and east sides. Our back yard then climbs about thirty feet in elevation, with the lower portions terraced mostly as rock gardens and the steep slope planted with shrubs and ground covers. At the top is a small developing wooded area, with a pleasant overlook platform at the edge of the slope. We specialize in rock gardening, emphasizing native American, Japanese, and Chinese alpine and woodland species, complemented by interesting shrubs and small trees. Since our garden is not large we concentrate on the unusual.

DATES & HOURS: May 15; 10 a.m. – 4 p.m.

DIRECTIONS: *Take M14* to Exit 4 to Barton Drive. Turn left at the stop sign at the end of the ramp, following Barton for .5 mile to the first traffic light. Turn left onto Pontiac Trail and immediately right onto Starwick. The next street on the left is Wickfield. Follow to the very end, #890.

Sloan Garden, ANN ARBOR, MI

This rhododendron and azalea "garden" is located in a wooded area just outside Ann Arbor. It represents about thirty years of work and contains plants which are winter hardy and (with help) deer resistant in this part of Michigan. Many of the hybrids came from Shammarello's nursery. From mid-May to mid-June the garden is ablaze with color. The woods and Huron River provide a delightful background.

DATES & HOURS: May 15; 10 a.m. – 4 p.m.

DIRECTIONS: *Take the Whitmore Lake Exit* on M14 just outside Ann Arbor. Proceed up Whitmore Lake Road .9 mile to two stone pillars on the left. Turn through the pillars and immediately turn right onto Barton North Drive. Proceed .9 mile (over two speed bumps) to 3 mailboxes on the right. Turn left down the lane for 100 yards to the house, grey with an orange door.

Van Dyke Garden, ANN ARBOR, MI

My eight-year-old garden utilizes a predominantly sunny one-acre site to display a wide range of shrubs, perennials, grasses, and bulbs. The plantings were designed to accommodate as wide a range of garden plants as could be grown in southeast Michigan and I have supplemented them with annuals. Shade-loving plants are featured under deciduous trees on the east side. Because of the generally flat site, island beds are used to screen the house from surrounding roads and flow around the house.

DATES & HOURS: May 15; 11 a.m. – 6 p.m.

DIRECTIONS: *Take Route 23* to the Plymouth Road Exit on the east side of Ann Arbor. Take Plymouth Road east for 2.5 miles through the community of Dixboro to the Tanglewood subdivision. The subdivision is located on the left side of Plymouth Road where Ford Road is on the right. Turn left into the Tanglewood subdivision, travel one block and turn right onto Creekside Drive. The house is the first on the right, #3488. Please park on the shoulder or in the driveway.

❖ Inglis Garden Walk, ANN ARBOR, MI

Inglis House, built in 1927 by Mr. & Mrs. James Inglis and gifted to the University of Michigan in 1950, overlooks the Huron River and is situated on beautifully landscaped eight-and-one-half acres of rolling ground adjacent to the Nichols Arboretum. Renovations in the early 1990s were aimed at restoring the estate to its original beauty. The formal garden is part of the original gardens designed by Mrs. Inglis, an avid gardener and horticulturist. There is the rose garden, Korean mum garden, wildflower woodland, the meadow with a picturesque view of the Arboretum beyond, and the herb garden

DATES & HOURS: May 15; 10 a.m. – 6 p.m.

DIRECTIONS: *Take Route 23* to the Geddes Road Exit. Go west on Geddes Road for 1 mile to the traffic light at Huron Parkway. Turn left onto Huron Parkway across the Huron River. Turn left immediately after crossing the bridge. A small sign indicates Geddes Road. Curve around under the bridge. Go 1.3 miles west on Geddes Road to Highland Road. Turn right and go .3 mile to #2301 Highland Road. *From Central University of Michigan Campus,* take Huron Street/Washtenaw Avenue. Go east on Geddes Road .5 mile to Highland Road. Turn left .3 mile to #2310 Highland Road.

❖ The University of Michigan Matthaei Botanical Gardens,
1800 NORTH DIXBORO ROAD, ANN ARBOR, MI 48105. (313) 998-7061.
The University of Michigan Matthaei Botanical Gardens' mission is to study and disseminate knowledge of plants as they exist in nature, contribute to human culture, and support life on Earth. Our conservatory, formal gardens, and trails allow us to show the dynamic interactions between human cultures and the plants of their environments. The conservatory includes tropical, warm temperate, and desert environments. The formal gardens include the Gateway Garden of New World Plants, the Marie Azary Rock Garden, the Alexandra Hicks Herb Knot Garden, and the Rose and Perennial Garden. Interpreted areas along the trails include a constructed wetland, Sam Graham's Trees, the Ethnobotanical Trail and Ridge Garden, and the Helen Smith Woodland Wildflower Garden. An active year-round sculpture exhibition has been completed.

DATES & HOURS: Year round, daily, 8 a.m. – dusk. Conservatory open daily, 10 a.m. – 4:30 p.m.

DIRECTIONS: *Located just east* of Ann Arbor on Dixboro Road. From Route 23, take either the Plymouth Road or Geddes Road Exits. Go east, turn onto Dixboro Road and follow the blue and white directional signs.

Borek Janik's Garden, CHELSEA, MI

The rock garden is packed with diversified settings such as scree, ledges, crevices, limestone, tufa, sandstone, granite, sun, and protected places which create the appropriate environment for the alpines. It is primarily a place for alpines, but it also has small shrubs and accent plants. Altogether there are close to 500 different labeled species. The rest of the grounds contain landscaping arrangements, natural areas, a trail through a wetland, and a pond.

DATES & HOURS: May 15; 10 a.m. – 2 p.m.

DIRECTIONS: *From I-94* about 15 miles west of Ann Arbor, take Exit 159 and go north on M-52 through Chelsea. At the blinking light 1 mile north of the town, turn right onto Werkner Road. After .75 mile, turn right onto Waterloo Road (the first crossroad, it is a dirt road). The house, #13805, is on the right side, 1.2 miles from Werkner Road. It is important to measure the distance from Werkner Road; ignore the house numbers in between. *Traveling on I-96,* exit on M-52 and travel south through Stockbridge for 30 miles to the blinking traffic light described above.

Guerin Wilkinson, CHELSEA, MI

My home and gardens are set within a lovely wooded area of western Washtenaw County. Each year I push back another section of Cornus racemosa *to expand my beds of woodland and shade-loving plants or to add on to the mosaic of rock-garden outcrops. My gardens reflect the taste of someone who almost chose a career in botany — it's a collector's garden that includes: many choice and underutilized woody species, both native and introduced; curious "belly plants" (i.e., you've got to get on your belly to appreciate them); lots of fabulous alpines which I've grown from seed; and shade-loving perennials, including a selection of rarities from China.*

DATES & HOURS: May 15; 10 a.m. – 4 p.m.

DIRECTIONS: *Head west from Dexter,* under the narrow railroad bridge, straight onto Island Lake Road, then take the first road to the left (Waterloo) after the pavement ends. The house, #13765, is 1.5 miles down Waterloo on the left.

BLOOMFIELD HILLS AREA:

May 16, 1999

Betty Sturley, BEVERLY HILLS, 10 A.M. – 6 P.M.

The Knutson Garden, BIRMINGHAM, 10 A.M. – 2 P.M.

Aerie Gardens, BLOOMFIELD HILLS, 10 A.M. – 4 P.M.

Dunstan Garden, BLOOMFIELD HILLS, 10 A.M. – 2 P.M.

July 17, 1999

Betty Sturley, BEVERLY HILLS, 10 A.M. – 6 P.M.

Aerie Gardens, BLOOMFIELD HILLS, 10 A.M. – 4 P.M.

Dunstan Garden, BLOOMFIELD HILLS, 10 A.M. – 2 P.M.

Jack Krasula, BLOOMFIELD HILLS, 10 A.M. – 6 P.M.

Larry & Sandy Mackle, BLOOMFIELD HILLS, 10 A.M. – 4 P.M.

Hickory Hill, FRANKLIN, 10 A.M. – 4 P.M.

Pine Lake Perennial Rock Garden, ORCHARD LAKE, 10 A.M. – 4P.M.

Betty Sturley, BEVERLY HILLS. MI

In 1984 we built our present home, a Williamsburg-style Colonial, on a heavily wooded one-acre lot with the idea of reproducing the feel and sense of the old eighteenth-century Virginia capital. Adding to the impression is the hand-made picket fence surrounding the propagation garden that replicates an actual Colonial Williamsburg design. The finishing touch is the clapboard garden shed that resembles an eighteenth-century outbuilding. Although I love the formal, Colonial-garden style, I have only maintained that tradition in the front of the house. As a professional artist with a passion for plants, diversity, beauty, and freedom of form have dominated the development of my gardens. I have an extensive collection of old-fashioned and David Austin roses, a hosta garden, a new rock garden, a perennial garden designed in the English-garden style, and a four-tiered water garden, complete with two waterfalls and a bridge.

DATES & HOURS: May 16, July 17; 10 a.m. − 6 p.m.

DIRECTIONS: *From Lodge Expressway/Route 10* take the Evergreen Road Exit. Go north on Evergreen Road for 3 miles to 14 Mile Road. Go .5 mile west to Eastlady, then one block south to Smallwood Court. From Telegraph Road/Route 24 take the 14 Mile Road Exit. Go 1.6 miles east to Eastlady and proceed one block to Smallwood Court.

The Knutson Garden, BIRMINGHAM, MI

Inspired by years of living in Mexico, we have created a festive garden where we can enjoy the many birds and colorful flowers. Intense warm hues contrasted with blues and purples give the garden its Mexican feel. Brick walks lined with tulips meander past a flowering dogwood and apricot azaleas. Adjacent to the perennial beds in the back, we grow orchids. An arbor for climbing roses leads to a brick patio nestled among evergreens. Surrounding this cozy spot is a birdbath, several bird feeders, and a raised garden filled with brightly colored annuals.

DATES & HOURS: May 16; 10 a.m. − 2 p.m.

DIRECTIONS: *Take Woodward Avenue/M-1 or Telegraph/Route 24* to Maple/15 Mile Road. The home, #232 Pilgrim, is located in the Quarton Lake area of Birmingham, four houses north of Maple Road between Southfield and Evergreen/Cranbrook Road. Please park on the street.

Aerie Gardens, BLOOMFIELD HILLS, MI

Aerie Gardens are situated on a five-and-a-half-acre hilltop vista which includes two-and-a-half acres of woods and a small pond and stream. Wetland gardens and woodland gardens, hillside gardens, sunshine gardens, and shade gardens are all connected by paths, trails, and stone stairways. Sculptures by Marshall Fredericks are incorporated into the gardens.

DATES & HOURS: May 16, July 17; 10 a.m. – 4 p.m.

DIRECTIONS: *Lone Pine Hill* runs north of Lone Pine Road midway between Woodward Avenue and Cranbrook Road in Bloomfield Hills. The entrance to Aerie Gardens is at the top of Lone Pine Hill. Please park along one side only of Lone Pine Hill.

Proceeds shared with the Endowment Fund, Cranbrook House & Gardens Auxilliary.

Dunstan Garden, BLOOMFIELD HILLS, MI

This four-and-a-half-acre garden features a multi-terraced perennial garden surrounding a two-tiered waterfall, several clusters of rhododendrons, azaleas, and hydrangeas, several specimen trees including a weeping beech, metasequoia, and weeping Norway spruce. This entire garden is surrounded by many varieties of conifers for privacy. The grounds have several beautiful sculptures enhancing the gardens.

DATES & HOURS: May 16, July 17; 10 a.m. – 2 p.m.

DIRECTIONS: *On Lone Pine Road* between Woodward and Cranbrook Road.

Jack Krasula, BLOOMFIELD HILLS, MI

This beautiful home in a four-and-one-half-acre park-like setting was designed and planted with more than 150 different conifers, many specimen trees, and shrubs. There are more than 350 hostas, including many of the newest varieties. Paths have been made throughout the raised beds. Flower beds are included, with many different varieties. A truly spectacular garden.

DATES & HOURS: July 17; 10 a.m. – 6 p.m.

DIRECTIONS: *Take Woodward Avenue north of Big Beaver/16 Mile Road* to Charring Cross (just south of Lone Pine). Turn east through blinking traffic light to home and door just shy of Wattles Road. Garden is on the north side.

Larry & Sandy Mackle, BLOOMFIELD HILLS, MI

In 1972 we moved into our home built in 1929. The landscaping on the two acres was 1929 vintage, overgrown and included what nature planted. Our garden displays more than 500 hostas, 1000 plus daylilies, 140 conifers, and a large number of companion plants, perennials, and annuals. There is a pond and rock garden and garden statuary, most of which is in dappled sunlight.

DATES & HOURS: July 17; 10 a.m. – 4 p.m.

DIRECTIONS: *Heading north of Detroit* take Woodward Avenue to Lone Pine Road. Turn west past the Cranbrook Road traffic light to Goodhue. Turn south on Goodhue to the first house on the left.

❖ Congregational Church of Birmingham,

1000 CRANBROOK ROAD, BLOOMFIELD HILLS, MI 48301.

Within a nine-acre property we have created the most interesting group of gardens, blooming from early spring with bulbs to asters in the fall. We have award-winning displays of tree and herbaceous peonies. Included are five kinds of irises, lilium beds, several hosta beds, daylily beds, and a memorial garden. Rose beds complement specimen trees and shrubs. This is a must-see, all-season garden.

DATES&HOURS: Year round, daily, dawn – dusk

DIRECTIONS: *Take Woodward Avenue North* to Cranbrook Road. The garden is at #1000 Cranbrook Road at Woodward Avenue.

❖ Cranbrook Gardens, 380 LONE PINE ROAD, P.O. BOX 801,

BLOOMFIELD HILLS, MI 48303-0801. (248) 645-3147.

Stroll through the forty acres of gardens that surround historic Cranbrook House, the 1908 Arts and Crafts-style manor home of Cranbrook's founders, George and Ellen Scripps Booth. The formal gardens and terraces are enhanced by sculptures, fountains, paths, lakes, and streams. Tended solely by volunteers, the gardens are even more exquisite today than when the Booths created them.

DATES & HOURS: May through August, Monday through Sunday, 10 a.m. – 5 p.m.; September & October, call for hours. Guided tours may be arranged.

DIRECTIONS: *Lone Pine Road is* north of Quarton Road about 16 miles, east of Telegraph/Route 24 and west of Woodward Avenue/M-1.

Mary Sue Ewing, FRANKLIN, MI

Designed around our historic 1894 Greek Revival-style farmhouse, our gardens at Hickory Hill capture the imagination in all seasons. Our three and one-quarter-acre property features a spring garden, an iris and peony border, a rose garden, a midsummer "hat" perennial bed, and a treasured sunken white garden, complete with flowering fountain, wisteria arbor, and black stone paths. Further afield from our house is an organic raised-bed vegetable garden, a meadow for our bee hives, a small wood and large pond with a developing bog garden. Near our backporch, a classic herb garden provides fragrance and culinary herbs for the kitchen. Boxwood hedges, a 1930 Lord & Burnham greenhouse, old stone walls, and stairwells charm us to keep up the hard work.

DATES & HOURS: July 17; 10 a.m. - 4 p.m.

DIRECTIONS: *From the corner of Telegraph Road* and Maple/Fifteen Mile Road, go west approximately 2 miles to Franklin Road. Turn south, pass Cider Mill, cross Fourteen Mile Road (flashing red light) continuing past gas station to Wellington Road. Turn west onto Wellington to fourth street, Irving Road. Turn right onto Irving. Hickory Hill is the second house on the left side of the street, #26705.

Proceeds shared with the Franklin Garden Club.

Pine Lake Perennial Rock Garden, ORCHARD LAKE, MI

Our perennial rock garden tumbles down the hill twenty-four feet toward Pine Lake. It starts with a small pool at the top, containing koi and water plants. The water cascades down the rocks, emptying in a larger pool filled with water plants. The garden consists of shade perennials — astilbe, hostas, hybrid lilies, anemones, foxglove, coneflowers, and other flowering perennials. Adjoining this garden is a large outdoor sculpture.

DATES & HOURS: July 17; 10 a.m. – 4 p.m.

DIRECTIONS: *West of Telegraph Road.* Located on the west side of Middlebelt Road .5 mile north of Long Lake Road. Hidden Drive sign on right. Turn left into the driveway. Park across the street, "Long Lake Shores." South of Square Lake Road and Pine Lake Road.

GROSSE POINTE AREA: *June 13, 1999*

The Day Garden, GROSSE POINTE, 11 A.M. – 4 P.M.

The Oetting Garden, GROSSE POINTE, 11 A.M. – 4 P.M.

The Jagger Garden, GROSSE POINTE CITY, 11 A.M. – 4 P.M.

The Booth Garden, GROSSE POINTE FARMS, 11 A.M. – 4 P.M.

The Finkenstaedt Garden, GROSSE POINTE FARMS, 11 A.M. – 4 P.M.

Mrs. William S. Hickey Garden, GROSSE POINTE FARMS, 2 P.M. – 6P.M.

The McKean Garden, GROSSE POINTE SHORES, 11 A.M. – 4 P.M.

❖ Frederik Meijer Gardens,

3411 BRADFORD NE, GRAND RAPIDS, MI 49525. (616) 957-1580.

The Frederik Meijer Gardens feature the largest tropical conservatory in the state of Michigan. There are more than seventy sculptures by world-renowned artists. Indoor specialty gardens include a Victorian garden, an arid garden, and a specialty greenhouse. Outdoor gardens include an English perennial and bulb garden and a new American garden, designed by James vanSweden. The garden also includes an outdoor nature trail and boardwalk overlooking wetlands, woodlands, and meadows. A new woodland garden was recently added to honor well-known Michigan artist, Gwen Frostic. Special exhibits throughout the year include a spectacular Christmas exhibit with thirty-two Christmas trees from around the world and a live butterfly exhibit in the spring, as well as a February flower exhibit and outdoor color and tram tours in the fall.

DATES & HOURS: Year round, Monday – Saturday, 9 a.m. – 5 p.m.; Sunday, noon – 5 p.m.

DIRECTIONS: *Take I-96* to the East Beltline Exit. Go north on East Beltline one block to Bradford Street. Go east on Bradford Street .5 mile to the gardens on the left.

The Day Garden, GROSSE POINTE, MI

Handling this long, narrow and relatively tiny outdoor space so that house and garden became one presented the challenge. Privacy was also a priority. As you look to the outside, the garden is as important in the winter as it is in other seasons. Changing colors and textures and varying heights of plant material provide interest and charm. An informal plunge pool in its brick deck are seen from one room, the irregular flagstone terrace provides the living room view and an informal grassy area gives background for the master bedroom and its little terrace. A stand of hemlocks secludes the garden from its neighbor buildings less than 2 feet from its fence lines.

DATES & HOURS: June 13; 11 a.m. – 4 p.m.

DIRECTIONS: *From I-94* take Moross Road Exit and go south to Lake Shore Road. (The name will change to Jefferson Avenue.) Turn right and drive 2.1 miles on Lake Shore/Jefferson, passing two traffic lights. One block beyond the second light is block long Woodland Place on your left. Number 3 Woodland place is the last house on your right, but not "on the Lake." Parking is available on Jefferson.

The Oetting Garden, GROSSE POINTE, MI

One side of our English-style garden includes a perennial border near the patio and a statue bed backed by arborvitae and box hedge. Dwarf spirea and three large blue spruce lead to a wild area on the other side with two large dogwoods, rhododendrons, azaleas, mountain laurel and leather leaf viburnum.

DATES & HOURS: June 13; 11 a.m. – 4 p.m.

DIRECTIONS: *From I-94* take Moross and go south to Lake Shore. Turn right. It becomes Jefferson. Soon after Grosse Pointe Memorial Church, turn left onto Island Avenue. We're #5 Island Avenue. Park on Jefferson.

The Jagger Garden, GROSSE POINTE CITY, MI

Our house sits on one of the original 200-year-old French ribbon farms stretching back from Lake St. Clair. There are two perennial borders close to the lake with roses and lilies. Nearer the house are two more perennial beds with many varieties of lilies, iris, peonies, and allium. These gardens flank a classically designed pool. A circular driveway in front of the house leads you around a huge stand of forty-year-old rhododendrons planted by the original owner. These tall shrubs are heavy flowering in a lavender pink and quite magnificent.

DATES & HOURS: June 13; 11 a.m. – 4 p.m.

DIRECTIONS: *From I-94* take Moross and go south to Lake Shore Road. Turn right. Continue on Lake Shore Road which becomes Jefferson Avenue about .75 mile down. Stay on Jefferson to Donovan Place, about .5 mile on the left. Park on Jefferson. The house is the last on the lake, #1 Donovan Place.

The Booth Garden, GROSSE POINTE FARMS, MI

I have created individual vignettes on a fairly small piece of land, a series of private rooms. Each green space has been interpreted differently and reflects its own feeling and purpose. A gravel driveway leads you past an open lawn bordered with tulips and many ornamental trees. Beyond the house, an enclosed garden has been created, with an elevated pool and pergola with wisteria. Behind the tenant house lies a lush overgrown country garden with a footpath to the Hunt Club.

DATES & HOURS: June 13; 11 a.m. – 4 p.m.

DIRECTIONS: *From I-94* take Moross and go south to Kercheval Avenue. Turn left onto Provencal. From Jefferson Avenue to Lake Shore Road, turn onto Provencal. Proceed past guardhouse to #274. Park on the grass.

The Finkenstaedt Garden, GROSSE POINTE FARMS, MI

Beyond a path of spring-blooming trees and shrubs, a large rambling terrace along the back of this white clapboard house spills over with tubs of jasmine, annuals, and passion flowers climbing up the screened porch. Dappled sunlight filters through an old birch tree, sending a soft gentle light over this informal and inviting private space nestled at the end of a little lane. A shady secret garden hides next to the driveway.

DATES & HOURS: June 13; 11 a.m. – 4 p.m.

DIRECTIONS: *From I-94* take Moross and go south to Grosse Pointe Boulevard. Turn right onto Hendrie Lane (9 blocks) on your left. *From Jefferson Avenue* to Lake Shore Road, turn left onto Moross and right onto Grosse Pointe Boulevard. Please park on Grosse Pointe Boulevard. The house is the last on Hendrie Lane, #32.

Mrs. William S. Hickey, GROSSE POINT FARMS, MI

My half-acre garden has evolved over the past thirty years from the time when four children and three dogs lived here but were away in July and August. What started as a child/dog-proof plain yard became a low-maintenance garden. Because it is north-facing — with huge elms, an oak, and maple — emphasis has been placed on shade-tolerant perennials, shrubs, and ornamentals. A small naturalistic pond and curvilinear borders feature a large variety of spring bulbs, wildflowers, ferns, unusual perennials and variegated foliage surrounding a large, brick-walled terrace and pillared gallery of this American Georgian home.

DATES & HOURS: June 13; 2 p.m. – 6 p.m.

DIRECTIONS: *From I-94 East,* take Moross Road Exit. Turn right off ramp onto Moross. Go 2 miles past Mack, past Chalfonte to Kercheval light. Turn right. Pass Kerby light (four blocks). Second street after Kerby is Touraine. Turn left. Number 80 is red-brick/white clapboard Georgian, in the middle of block. Please park along the street.

❖ The Lottie Crawley Memorial Garden,

171 LAKE SHORE ROAD, GROSSE POINTE FARMS, MI 48236. (313) 881-0322. *This generous formal French herb garden is designed in the form of the stained glass window of the historic Grosse Pointe Academy Chapel. The garden is outlined with an arborvitae hedge and gray pavers. Seven raised beds comprise the garden, planted with many unusual herbs. Each bed has a theme. There is a fragrance cutting garden, a French culinary garden, a botanical studies and herbaria collection, Mary's Garden (a religious garden), lemon-scented herbs, a fairy-tale garden, and a rose window and knot garden.*

DATES & HOURS: May 13 through November 1, daily, dawn – dusk.

DIRECTIONS: *From I-94 East* take the Moross Road Exit and turn right onto Moross Road. Go 2 miles, crossing Mack Avenue and passing Chalfonte and Kercheval, to Grosse Pointe Boulevard. Turn right onto Grosse Pointe Boulevard and continue 9 blocks, turning left onto Moran Road. Go .1 mile to driveway with a sign for "Grosse Pointe Academy." Turn right and follow arrows around building to the herb garden, which is bordered by evergreens.

❖ Grosse Pointe Garden Center's Trial Garden,

32 LAKE SHORE DRIVE, GROSSE POINTE FARMS, MI 48236. (313) 881-4594. *Established in 1952, the trial garden is a unique feature of the Garden Center's contribution to the community. It is managed by the Garden Center and supported by the Vincent DePetris Fund and private contributions. The garden is laid out in the form of a wheel, with spokes forming ten garden plots. An old millstone surrounded by herbs forms the hub of the garden. The trial garden is listed in* Arboreta and Botanical Gardens of Michigan, *published in 1995 through the courtesy of Zonta Club of Northwest Wayne County and Nicholas Arboretum.*

DATES & HOURS: May through October, daily, dawn – dusk.

DIRECTIONS: *From I-94* take the Moross Road Exit to Lake Shore Road. Turn right onto Lake Shore and proceed .75 mile to the Grosse Pointe War Memorial at #32 Lake Shore Drive.

The McKean Garden, GROSSE POINTE SHORES, MI

This garden features a lush 150-foot mixed perennial and annual border in continuous bloom with more than sixty varieties of hybrid teas, abundant Oriental lilies, and many varieties of phlox, all bordered with a box hedge and adjacent to a pool and poolhouse. Nineteenth century hand-carved stone urns create an architectural accent on the terrace beneath huge window boxes. Two state-of-the-art working greenhouses are home to many highly unusual and rare orchids. Please enter through the antique iron gate at the left of the house.

DATES & HOURS: June 13; 11 a.m. – 4 p.m.

DIRECTIONS: *From I-94* take Moross and go south to Lake Shore Road. Turn left and go .09 mile to Deeplands. Turn left onto Shelden (first corner). The house is #524. Please enter garden through antique iron gate at the left side of the house.

❖ Edsel & Eleanor Ford House,

1100 LAKE SHORE ROAD, GROSSE POINTE SHORES, MI 48236. (313) 884-4222.
The master design for the Edsel and Eleanor Ford House garden was created between 1926 and 1932 by one of America's foremost landscape designers and conservationists, Jens Jensen. The eighty-seven-acre estate features a rose garden, perennial flower lane, wildflowers in the spring, and superb colors in the fall.

DATES & HOURS: April through December, Tuesday through Saturday, 10 a.m. – 4 p.m.; Sunday, noon – 4 p.m.; January through March, Tuesday through Sunday, 1 p.m. – 4 p,.m.

DIRECTIONS: *From I-94 East* exit at Vernier/Exit 225. Turn right onto Vernier and continue to its end at Lake Shore Road. Turn left onto Lake Shore Road; the Ford House is 1 mile on the right. *From I-94 West,* exit at Nine Mile Road/Exit 227. Turn left onto Nine Mile Road and continue to Jefferson (called Lake Shore in Grosse Pointe). Turn right onto Jefferson; the Ford house is 1 mile on the left.

MINNESOTA

Minneapolis

1999 MINNESOTA OPEN DAYS

July 10: MINNEAPOLIS AREA

MINNEAPOLIS: *July 10, 1999*

Mary Aamoth's Garden, WAYZATA, NOON – 4 P.M.

Martha Atwater, WAYZATA, NOON – 4 P.M.

Mary Lee Dayton, WAYZATA, NOON – 4 P.M.

Ned & Sherry Dayton's Garden, WAYZATA, NOON – 4 P.M.

Garden of Susan & Ray Johnson, WAYZATA, NOON – 4 P.M.

Patt O'Neil, WAYZATA, NOON – 4 P.M.

The Gardens at Peary Pond — Ronnie Winsor, WAYZATA, NOON – 4 P.M.

Heli & Gunther Roth, WAYZATA, NOON – 4 P.M.

Janet Spoor, WAYZATA, NOON – 4 P.M.

❖ Minnesota Landscape Arboretum,

3675 ARBORETUM DRIVE, CHANHASSEN, MN 55317. (612) 443-2460.
The Minnesota Landscape Arboretum features beautiful display and demonstration gardens as well as tree specimens. Both prairie and forest are highlighted by colorful annuals and perennials. There are home demonstration gardens and a Japanese garden, hosta gardens, a rose garden, a woodland wildflower garden, and a prairie garden.

DATES & HOURS: Year round, daily, 8 a.m. – dusk.

DIRECTIONS: *Located 9 miles west of I-494 on Highway 5* in Chanhassen (4 miles west of downtown Chanhassen).

❖ Minneapolis Sculpture Garden at Walker Art Center,

VINELAND PLACE AT LYNDALE AVENUE, MINNEAPOLIS, MN 55403.
(612) 375-7622. FAX: (612) 375-7595.
The largest urban sculpture park of its type in the country, the eleven-acre Minneapolis Sculpture Garden houses more than forty sculptures. At its center is the soaring, playful fountain-sculpture Spoonbridge and Cherry, *now a beloved Twin Cities landmark. The Minneapolis Sculpture Garden is a collaboration between the Walker Art Center and the Minneapolis Park and Recreation Board.*

DATES & HOURS: Year round, daily, 6 a.m. – midnight. Admission is free.

DIRECTIONS: *Located directly across the street from the Walker Art Center* on Vineland Place, where Lyndale and Hennepin Avenues merge. *If heading west on I-94,* take Exit 231B and go north on Lyndale/Hennepin. *If heading east on I-394,* take Exit 8A and go south on Lyndale/Hennepin. Bus lines 1, 4, 6, 12, and 28 serve the Walker.

❖ Noerenberg Memorial Park,

2840 NORTH SHORE DRIVE, ORONO, MN 55391. (612) 559-6700.

Situated on Lake Minnetonka, the park's formal flower gardens are open for tours, informal viewings, and weddings. The gardens include a wide variety of unusual annuals and perennials, an assortment of grasses, and a large daylily collection. The park features accessible brick pathways and an ornamental boathouse/gazebo overlooking the lake.

DATES & HOURS: May 15 through October 15, daily; 9 a.m. – dusk.

DIRECTIONS: The park is located approximately 30 minutes from downtown Minneapolis, Minnesota. From I-494, take I-394 west to County Road 15 West. Turn right onto County Road 15 and follow approximately 1 mile to the park entrance on the left.

Mary Aamoth's Garden, WAYZATA, MN

This Connecticut colonial house sited on south-facing property with generous sloping lawn is flanked on three sides by the Ferndale Marsh. Two oval-shaped perennial beds change at the whim of the owner to make room for a "never-seen-before" specimen. A wildflower and hosta border runs along the western edge of the property. Ephemerals are abundant in early spring to be replaced by an ever-growing hosta collection.

DATES & HOURS: July 10; noon – 4 p.m.

DIRECTIONS: *Take I-394* west from Minneapolis to the 101 South/Wayzata Exit, to Wayzata Boulevard. At the second light veer left onto Superior Boulevard/County Road 15. At the bottom of the hill veer right onto Lake Street. After three stop signs turn left onto Ferndale, cross railroad tracks and continue south on Ferndale Road for 1 mile. The house is #629. Street parking is available on Ferndale Road, please park on the shoulder, not the lawn. Limited driveway parking is also available.

Martha Atwater, WAYZATA, MN

Protected from the lake breezes, this large perennial garden is contained within the "U"-shaped driveway and bounded by Ferndale Road itself. The broad brick paths invite a leisurely stroll through a garden that looks wonderful no matter what the season. Filled with a succession of bloom, daylilies, hardy roses, baby's breath, bee balm, and astilbe are the backbone of Martha's summer garden.

DATES & HOURS: July 10; noon – 4 p.m.

DIRECTIONS: *Please use directions to the Aamoth garden.* This house is #636.

Mary Lee Dayton, WAYZATA, MN

Three separate gardens encompass this contemporary prairie-style house. A kitchen door triangle yields herbs for the cookpot while a sunny raised bed shows off roses, dahlias, zinnias, and snapdragons. A cutting garden with both flowers and vegetables completes this lovely yard.

DATES & HOURS: July 10; noon – 4 p.m.

DIRECTIONS: *Please use directions to the Aamoth garden.* This house is #510.

Ned & Sherry Ann Dayton's Garden, WAYZATA, MN

Our house and garden, built in 1994, are located on Lake Minnetonka. The frontyard pond has water lilies, irises, marsh marigolds, and hosta plantings. The backyard overlooks the lake and a rock wall provides a backdrop for a shade garden with native Minnesota plants. In the perennial garden we have planted flowers to attract birds and butterflies — birds abound but the butterflies haven't found us yet.

DATES & HOURS: July 10; noon – 4 p.m.

DIRECTIONS: *Please use directions to the Aamoth garden.* This house is #686.

Garden of Susan & Ray Johnson, WAYZATA, MN

This charming lakeside garden is planted in eight formal boxwood-lined beds. Each bed is entirely different, with hundreds of plants, including perennials, bulbs, grasses, and small trees. The gardens here represent a fine example of the mixed border in Minnesota.

DATES & HOURS: July 10; noon – 4 p.m.

DIRECTIONS: *Please use directions to the Aamoth garden.* This house is #646.

Patt O'Neil, WAYZATA, MN

Guests step inside the tall white classic wooden fence and find themselves in a turn-of-the-century colonial setting. This lovely old house has a side garden consisting of five circles of pink roses centered around an ancient stone statue of a small boy holding a snake. Trellises mark both the entry and exit of this romantic space.

DATES & HOURS: July 10; noon – 4 p.m.

DIRECTIONS: *Please use directions to the Aamoth garden.* This house is #532.

The Gardens at Peavey Pond — Ronnie Winsor, WAYZATA, MN

The yard is rich with variety and unusual plantings of trees and shrubs. Visit the quiet, cool, shady wildflower garden and the annual and perennial garden near Peavey Pond. Notice the exquisite sculpture and granite bench. Hidden behind the fence is the "practical" area with compost bins, flower supports, and garden tools. Also, there are two raised beds and a new simple garden that came about in 1998 to house plants that need special care or do not fit in the more formal garden. Look for the containers which were made by the gardener and planted with alpine plants, her new interest in horticulture. On your way to the east side of the house enjoy the clematis arbor. See the lap pool, tulip tree, fringe tree, ginkgo, and redbud tree.

DATES & HOURS: July 10; noon – 4 p.m.

DIRECTIONS: *Please use directions to the Aamoth garden.* This house is #513.

Heli & Gunther Roth, WAYZATA, MN

Precise, symmetrical, beautiful, and curving could describe this newly constructed contemporary house and garden. Two-dimensional metal sculptures enhance the garden, a wall of arborvitae ensures privacy, but nothing distracts the eye from the serene view of the lake.

DATES & HOURS: July 10; noon – 4 p.m.

DIRECTIONS: *Please use directions to the Aamoth garden.* This house is #552.

Janet Spoor, WAYZATA, MN

This charming garden features two pairs of English borders with a handsome stone bench as its focal point. Delphinium, peonies, and miniature roses are combined with annual lantanas, impatiens, and a sea wall border of snapdragons to create a colorful scene with the lake beyond.

DATES & HOURS: July 10; noon – 4 p.m.

DIRECTIONS: *Please use directions to the Aamoth garden.* This house is #622.

❖ James J. Hill Depot & Garden,
LAKE STREET, WAYZATA, MN 55391.

James J. Hill built this quaint stucco and half-timbered depot alongside Lake Minnetonka in 1906. Today the restored building sits surrounded by lovely perennial and annual gardens tended by the Lake Minnetonka Garden Club. Brick walks lead the visitor to a pier where the newly restored streetcar launch "Minnehaha" rests between excursions to Excelsior, a small lakeside town.

DATES & HOURS: Year round, daily; dawn – dusk.

DIRECTIONS: Take I-394 west from Minneapolis to the 101 South Wayzata Exit, to Wayzata Boulevard. At the second light, turn left to Superior Boulevard/County Road 15. At the bottom of the hill turn right onto Lake Street. Turn left at the second stop sign andpark in the Depot parking lot.

NEW JERSEY

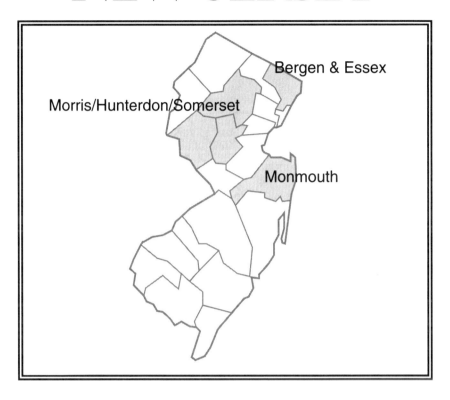

Bergen & Essex

Morris/Hunterdon/Somerset

Monmouth

1999 NEW JERSEY OPEN DAYS

May 15: MORRIS/HUNTERDON/SOMERSET COUNTIES,
BERGEN & ESSEX COUNTIES,
MONMOUTH COUNTY

June 12: MORRIS/HUNTERDON/SOMERSET COUNTIES,
BERGEN & ESSEX COUNTIES,
MONMOUTH COUNTY

September 11: MORRIS/HUNTERDON/SOMERSET COUNTIES

BERGEN & ESSEX COUNTIES:

May 15, 1999

Proctor Garden, ENGLEWOOD, 10 A.M. − 2 P.M.

John & Lyn Scott, ENGLEWOOD, 10 A.M. − 4 P.M.

 ❖ The James Rose Center, RIDGEWOOD, 10 A.M. − 6 P.M.

George Sternlieb, SHORT HILLS, 10 A.M. − 2 P.M.

Winter's Garden, SHORT HILLS, 10 A.M. − 4 P.M.

Tall Trees Garden of Jane Schulz, WYCKOFF, 10 A.M. − 4 P.M.

 ❖ Van Vleck House & Garden, MONTCLAIr, 1 P.M. − 5 P.M.

June 12, 1999

Peggy & Walter Jones, ENGLEWOOD, 10 A.M. − 4 P.M.

The Handley Garden, RIDGEWOOD, 10 A.M. − 4 P.M.

George Sternlieb, SHORT HILLS, 10 A.M. − 2 P.M.

Winter's Garden, SHORT HILLS, 10 A.M. − 4 P.M.

Richard & Ronnie Klein, TENAFLY, 10 A.M. − 4 P.M.

Tall Trees Garden of Jane Schulz, WYCKOFF, 10 A.M. − 4 P.M.

 ❖ Van Vleck House & Garden, MONTCLAIr, 1 P.M. − 5 P.M.

❖ The Emilie K. Hammond Wildflower Trail,

McCAFFREY LANE, BOONTON, NJ 07962-1295. (973) 326-7600.

The Dutch word tourne, *meaning "lookout" or "mountain," aptly describes this 463-acre park of hilly terrain and huge granite boulders. Several mountain trails wind their way through a forest of white oaks, maples, beeches, and hemlocks. A series of niches provides specific microclimates suitable for a wide variety of plant life. There are low, boggy spots and drier upland areas, moist slopes in sun and others in heavy shade, and a fast-flowing brook. Suitable habitats have been found for more than 250 different wildflowers and shrubs native to the eastern United States.*

DATES & HOURS: Year round, daily, 8 a.m. – dusk.

DIRECTIONS: *From Route 80 West,* take Route 46/Denville Exit. Take Route 46 East to Mountain Lakes Exit. Turn left onto the Boulevard. Bear left onto Powerville Road. Take first left, McCaffrey Lane.

Peggy & Walter Jones, ENGLEWOOD, NJ

A rolling hillside encompassing a variety of gardens, ranging from a formal rose garden to a wild woodland garden where the Japanese primrose and shooting stars dance with the hellebores. Other highlights include a rock garden, a living wall, a small enclosed courtyard with wonderful climbing hydrangeas and an elliptical herb garden in the center of the back lawn. Come and discover a wealth of unique trees, shrubs, and perennials. Find the split-leaf beech in the expansive front lawn. In the rear of the garden look for the old moss-covered stone steps that lead to the outdoor fireplace nestled under a canopy of large oaks. Look to the left and you will see the sorrel tree.

DATES & HOURS: June 12; 10 a.m. – 4 p.m.

DIRECTIONS: *From Route I-95/I-80 East* (local lanes). Exit at Broad Avenue/ Englewood. Follow Broad Avenue north until it ends at a traffic light at Palisades Avenue. Turn left onto Palisades Avenue and make a quick right at traffic light onto Lydecker Street. Follow Lydecker to four-way stop. Turn right onto Booth Avenue. Head up hill and take first left onto Morrow Road. Go to top of the hill. The house, #401 Morrow Road, is on the right. *From Palisades Interstate Parkway,* take the Englewood exit. Turn right onto Palisades Avenue and go to the fifth traffic light. Turn right onto Lydecker Street and follow as above.

Proctor Garden, ENGLEWOOD, NJ

Our small flag-lot property starts with a long, uphill driveway. The garden evolved in stages from 1956. Three levels with rock walls and steps lead the way through the various areas of the Ericaceae family, conifers, and a collection of chamaecyparis specimens. Two pools circulate, creating water flowing downhill to the lower level. It is a collector's garden with as many limestone rocks as plants. The design was created for year-round beauty.

DATES & HOURS: May 15; 10 a.m. – 2 p.m.

DIRECTIONS: *From the Palisades Interstate Parkway* take Exit 1 to Palisades Avenue. Go down the hill, through five lights. At the fifth light/Lydecker Street, turn right. Follow north to third street, which is Chestnut. Turn left and go downhill to the first street on the right. Number 215 King Street is the driveway after the second house on the right. Two iron posts mark the driveway. *From I-95,* take Exit 71/Broad Avenue. Go north to Palisades Avenue. Go left and make a quick right onto Lydecker Street. Follow as above. Please park on street.

John & Lyn Scott, ENGLEWOOD, NJ

Ours is a garden for evening barbecues, daytime frisbee throwers and pleasurable views. On one acre, with a Victorian-style home in the middle, the front is dominated by an immense rhododendron, while the back garden is surrounded by shrubs and trees. There are oaks, an elegant weeping beech, arborvitae, witch hazel, Japanese maples, and azaleas. Perennial borders on three sides give areas for play and relaxation.

DATES & HOURS: May 15; 10 a.m. – 4 p.m.

DIRECTIONS: *From I-95 south,* cross the George Washington Bridge's upper level. Stay to right, exiting onto the Palisades Parkway north. Take Exit 1 to Englewood. Turn right onto Palisades Avenue. Go five stoplights and turn right onto Lydecker Street. The house is #40. Please park along Lydecker Street.

❖ Van Vleck House & Garden,

21 Van Vleck Street, Montclair, NJ 07042. (973) 744-4752.

Begun at the turn of the century, these gardens have been developed by several generations of a family of committed horticulturists. The plan is largely formal, responding to the Mediterranean style of the house. The extensive collection of rhododendrons and azaleas, including several named for family members, is renowned. Also of note are the many mature plant specimens.

DATES & HOURS: May 1 – 9, May 24 – October 31, daily, 1 p.m.– 5 p.m.

DIRECTIONS: *From the Garden State Parkway North,* take the Watchung Avenue Exit. Turn left off the exit and go to the fifth traffic light. Turn left onto Grove Street. Proceed to the second traffic light and turn right onto Claremont Avenue. Proceed .9 miles to the fifth traffic light and turn right onto North Mountain Avenue. The first street on left is Van Vleck Street.

The Handley Garden, Ridgewood, NJ

John and Sue Handley's garden is set on a one-acre property. The front foundation planting is a mixed border of ornamental trees, shrubs, and flowers and prepares you only somewhat for the beauty of the garden behind the house. A water and rock garden is situated beside the deck. Sunny perennial borders punctuated by garden ornaments extend the length of the lawn path that draws you to the open lawn. Sue Handley has planted a great variety of wonderful plants, some of which may be new to you. Roses and a shade garden complete this varied landscape.

DATES & HOURS: June 12; 10 a.m. – 4 p.m.

DIRECTIONS: *From Route 17 South,* proceed past Ramsey, Allendale, and Waldwick to the right turn at Hohokus/Racetrack Road Exit. Proceed west for 3 blocks and turn left onto Nagel. Proceed to the Franklin Turnpike and make a right. The garden is on the left. *From Route 17 North,* go approximately 4 miles from Route 4 to the Linwood Avenue overpass. Go under the overpass and make a right. Continue to the second red light at Pleasant Avenue and make a right turn. Follow Pleasant to the end and turn right onto Glen Avenue. Pass the cemetery on the left to a hairpin turn at the beginning of Franklin Turnpike. The Handley Garden is approximately .75 mile on Franklin Turnpike on the left. Please park on the front lawn.

❖ **The James Rose Center,**

506 EAST RIDGEWOOD AVENUE, RIDGEWOOD, NJ 07450. (201) 444-2559. *James Rose (1913-1991) was one of the pioneers in bringing modern design principles to landscape architecture in the 1930s. Built in 1953, his house and garden were designed to change over time and now reflect more than forty years of evolution at the hands of this creative genius. Stabilization of the house and garden has begun with the assistance of the Garden Conservancy. The property is a unique environment of interwoven garden spaces formed by structure, plants, and water that create a strong fusion between house and garden. In the garden there are scrap metal sculptures and reflecting pools on a floor of fractured bluestone that can only be seen after one has entered the confines of the compound, which seems a world apart from the surrounding suburban landscape.*

DATES & HOURS: *Special Open Day:* May 15, 10 a.m. – 6 p.m.

DIRECTIONS: *From New York City* take the George Washington Bridge to Route 4 West to Route 17 North. Take 17N to Ridgewood Avenue/Ridgewood Exit. Follow East Ridgewood Avenue towards Ridgewood. House is on the corner of East Ridgewood Avenue and Southern Parkway.

George Sternlieb, SHORT HILLS, NJ

Raised beds, troughs, and more than 100 outdoor pots house a broad range of hardy and non-hardy plants, many of which have been seed-raised in the two greenhouses. Among the features are a circular rose garden, a sixty-plant dwarf conifer collection, and a variety of orchids, banana trees, datura, and vines.

DATES & HOURS: May 15, June 12; 10 a.m. – 2 p.m.

DIRECTIONS: *From Route 78,* take Millburn Exit. Go right on Vauxhall Road to end, and then turn left onto Millburn Avenue. Turn right onto Mail Street and go four blocks to driveway on the right at #66 Old Short Hills Road. Please park in driveway.

NEW JERSEY

Winter's Garden, SHORT HILLS, NJ

This garden is densely packed with conifers ranging from miniature and dwarf to intermediate and full size. Ground covers, perennials, shrubs, and deciduous trees are incorporated. Weathered limestone is extensively integrated throughout for its sculptured effect. The arrangements are personal choices for spiritual and esthetic effect.

DATES & HOURS: May 15, June 12; 10 a.m.– 4 p.m.

DIRECTIONS: *From Route 24 West,* take the Hobart Avenue Exit. Go to the light and turn right. Go about 6 blocks and turn left onto Dryden Terrace. *From Route 24 East,* take Exit 8. Travel along service road to second light (Hobart Avenue). Turn left and go about 6 blocks and turn left onto Dryden Terrace. Please park on the street.

Richard & Ronnie Klein, TENAFLY, NJ

An informal, one-acre, plant collector's garden with many rare and unusual flowering shrubs and trees (the garden's primary focus), including collections of magnolias, cercis, styrax, and dogwoods. There are also Japanese maples, fruit trees, and perennial borders in both sun and shade. One-third of the garden is a shady woodland and bog area with paths and elevated walks. Garden gates and paths lead the visitor into the next, unseen part of the garden.

DATES & HOURS: June 12; 10 a.m. – 4 p.m.

DIRECTIONS: *From the Palisades Interstate Parkway* take Exit 1/Englewood Cliffs. Circle under the highway and continue straight to first traffic light. Turn right at the light onto Route 9W North. Travel north on Route 9W to the fourth traffic light (approximately 1.6 miles) to East Clinton Avenue. Turn left onto East Clinton and travel one short block and take the next left onto Essex Drive. Go to the second house on the right, #133 Essex Drive. *From the Tappan Zee Bridge* take first exit on the right after crossing bridge onto Route 9W South. Follow Route 9W into New Jersey and turn right at East Clinton Avenue. Follow directions above. *From Route I-95/I-80 East* (local lanes) exit at Broad Avenue/Englewood. Follow Broad Avenue north until it ends at a stoplight at Palisades Avenue. Turn right onto Palisades Avenue and travel 1-2 miles to second traffic light at Route 9W. Follow directions above. Please park on the street.

Proceeds shared with Trout Unlimited.

❖ Davis Johnson Park & Gardens,

137 ENGLE STREET, TENAFLY, NJ 07670. (201) 569-7275.

Featuring an award-winning rose garden recognized by the American Rose Society, this seven-and-one-half-acre park has many floral beds, paths and benches. Our gazebo is a favorite place for wedding ceremonies and photos. This former estate has several mature beech trees.

DATES & HOURS: Year round, daily, dawn – dusk.

DIRECTIONS: *Take Route 9W* to East Clinton Avenue. Go west down hill to first traffic light (Engle Street). Turn left. Park entrance is on right, .25 miles from Clinton Avenue.

Tall Trees Garden of Janet Schulz, WYCKOFF, NJ

My creation Tall Trees, is a wonderful woodland garden featuring shade-loving perennials, bulbs, vines, and shrubs. There is an extensive collection of hosta as well as trough gardens, homemade arbors and garden statuary. Places to sit have been created so that the many garden features can be enjoyed from many areas. Almost all of the plants are labeled. Many of the clematis are growing in other shrubs which produces an elongated season of interest in plants that would have bloomed at another time. An avid plant collector, I am always searching for, and trying to find, plants that may do well in my garden. Plants must be strong to succeed here at Tall Trees for I do not believe in growing plants that require a lot of spraying or staking.

DATES & HOURS: May 15, June 12; 10 a.m. – 4 p.m.

DIRECTIONS: *From NYC and east,* take the George Washington Bridge to Route 4 West to Route 208N/Oakland. Approximately 7.5 miles to Ewing Avenue-Franklin Lakes. Go down ramp and turn right (Ewing Avenue). Proceed to traffic light. Turn right (Franklin Avenue). Proceed through two traffic lights (second is Godwin Avenue) to first street on right, Godwin Drive. Turn right. First left is Colonial Drive. Number 16 is on the right. *From points south,* Route 287 North to Route 208S. Exit on Ewing Avenue. Turn left at stop sign and proceed to traffic light (Franklin Avenue). Proceed through two traffic lights (second light is Godwin Avenue) to first street on right. Proceed as above. *From points north of Ramsey, NJ,* Route 17 South exit Lake Street/Ramsey. Follow sign for Crescent Avenue (directly across from exit). Proceed 3.4 miles to fourth traffic light and turn right (Wyckoff Avenue). Go nine blocks on left and turn onto Shadyside Avenue (Approximately 1 mile). Colonial Drive is the first right. Number 16 is on the left. Park on street. Do not block driveways, do not park on any grass.

MONMOUTH COUNTY:

May 15, 1999

Mrs. Sverre Sorensen, ATLANTIC HIGHLANDS, 10 A.M. – 4 P.M.

Linden Hill, RUMSON, 10 A.M. – 4 P.M.

June 12, 1999

Mrs. Sverre Sorensen, ATLANTIC HIGHLANDS, 10 A.M. – 4 P.M.

Rita & Bob Boyle, RUMSON, 10 A.M. – 4 P.M.

Linden Hill, RUMSON, 10 A.M. – 4 P.M.

Gail & Charles Slingluff, RUMSON, 10 A.M. – 4 P.M.

King & Leigh Sorensen, RUMSON, 10 A.M. – 4 P.M.

Mrs. Sverre Sorensen, ATLANTIC HIGHLANDS, NJ

Nestled in the hills (the highest coastal point from Maine to Florida) overlooking Sandy Hook Bay to New York City is a mature, natural woodland garden created by the owner and her late husband, Sev. Years ago plants were started by cuttings and seeds (many by daughter Sandy Sorensen Henning). Today, charming paths flanked with brunnera, epimediums, and phlox wind in and about rhododendrons, azaleas, skimmias, laurel, and dogwood — all with spectacular vistas of the ocean beyond.

DATES & HOURS: May 15, June 12; 10 a.m. – 4 p.m.

DIRECTIONS: *Take the Garden State Parkway south to Exit 114.* Turn left after the ramp and right onto Nutswamp Road. Turn left on Navesink River Road, across Route 35, onto Locust Point Road. *Do not go over the Oceanic Bridge to Rumson.* Go straight through the intersection with the Red Country Store entrance on your right, bear right downhill, through a traffic light at Route 36, up Grand Avenue, under Stone Bridge, and turn right on Ocean Boulevard (also called Scenic Drive). Make the second right onto Hill Road to #1, the first driveway on the right. Look for high stone walls and gravel driveway. Please park along the street.

Rita & Bob Boyle, RUMSON, NJ

Enter this garden through a unique wooden gate wearing a crown of lavender wisteria. Azaleas, rhododendrons and primulas — a rich color blend of white, pink and rose — abound in mid-spring. High shade is a hallmark of this two-acre garden. There is a woodland walk amid collections of hostas, conifers, shrubs, ferns and perennials — anything that catches the fancy of the owners, who enjoy tending this garden themselves. A koi pond and rock garden are featured in a book of feng shui design.

DATES & HOURS: June 10 a.m. – 4 p.m.

DIRECTIONS: *From the Garden State Parkway* take Exit 109. Take Route 520 East to a "T" in Red Bank. Turn left, cross the railroad tracks, and go to the second traffic light. Turn right and go 2.8 miles (name of road changes from Harding to Ridge Road). At Buena Vista Avenue where there is a flashing light, turn left and go one block to Orchard Lane on your right. Turn right onto Orchard Lane. The house is the first on your right, #7.

Linden Hill, RUMSON, NJ

Linden Hill provides a special and unexpected landscape with numerous garden areas that spread over seven and one-half acres. Great specimen trees rise over the level property. No one structure, garden, or style dominates the terrain. The colonial-style house, built in the early 1890s, is gracefully surrounded by garden beds, impeccably maintained lawns, and arbors of fruit trees. More than 2,500 varieties of flowers, plants, shrubs, and trees infuse this horticulturally rich landscape. Although flowers permeate the entire property, there are ten garden sections that stand out. Reaching beyond traditional forms, Linden Hill provides a horticultural impression that is inventive and pleasurable through an overall effect of cultivated informality.

DATES & HOURS: May 15, June 12; 10 a.m. – 4 p.m.

DIRECTIONS: *From the New Jersey Turnpike South* take Exit 11/Garden State Parkway South. At the toll after the Raritan River stay right on road marked "Local-All Exits." Take Exit 109/Red Bank, turn left at the light after paying toll and follow Newman Springs Road/Route 520 to the end. Turn right onto Broad Street. Turn left at the first light onto White Road. Take White Road to end. Turn left at the stop sign onto Branch Avenue. Turn right at blinking light onto Rumson Road. Go about 3.2 miles and you will see a sign for Route 8A. Turn left onto Bingham Avenue. Linden Hill is the third driveway on the left, #138. Park on the street.

Gail & Charles Slingluff, RUMSON, NJ

Our brick Georgian house has a 270-degree view of the Shrewsbury River and acres of marshlands. At the entrance to the house is a courtyard with climbing hydrangea and a fishpond that leads into a walled perennial garden. We have also created a terraced garden, a wetlands garden by the dock, and several other gardens that take advantage of the spectacular views. We have chosen plant material that is compatible with our special ecosystem.

DATES & HOURS: June 12; 10 a.m. – 4 p.m.

DIRECTIONS: *From the Garden State Parkway* take Exit 109. At Newman Springs road, turn left if from the north, turn right. If from the south, continue to Newman Springs Road for 2.1 miles to Broad Street/Route 35. Turn right onto Broad Street and go .1 mile to the light at White Road. Turn left and go .8 mile to Branch Avenue. Turn left and go .1 mile to Rumson Road/Route 520. Turn right and go 3.3 miles to Osprey Lane. Turn right and go one block to Shrewsbury Drive. Turn left and go one block to the Avenue of Two Rivers South. Turn right and go to the last house on the road. Please park at house and along the street.

King & Leigh Sorensen, RUMSON, NJ

The house is a former windmill adjacent to a river. The landscape design includes a raised perennial bed with shrubs and flowering trees in the background. The garden was featured in the January 1983 issue of House Beautiful. *There are espaliered apple trees near King's vegetable garden, which features five varieties of lettuce. Leigh has a collection of bonsai and King raises honey bees. Many ornamental grasses are incorporated into the gardens, which flood at times of extreme high tides.*

DATES & HOURS: June 12; 10 a.m. – 4 p.m.

DIRECTIONS: *Exit 109 on the Garden State Parkway.* Turn left onto Newman Springs Road and after 1.5 miles turn left onto Broad Street. After .75 mile turn right onto Harding Place and continue east for 5 miles (the road name changes to Ridge, then Hartchorne.) At the end, turn left onto North Ward Avenue. Our driveway is a continuation of North Ward Avenue. The house, #7, is marked on an oar in a grass garden.

MORRIS/HUNTERDON/SOMERSET COUNTIES:
May 15, 1999

Riverwood Corners, BEDMINSTER, 10 A.M. – 2 P.M.

Frog Pond Farm, CALIFON, 10 A.M. – 4 P.M.

Dan & Jeanne Will – Hedgerows, CHESTER, 10 A.M. – 4 P.M.

Pitney Farm, MENDHAM, 10 A.M. – 4 P.M.

Watnong Gardens, MORRIS PLAINS, 10 A.M. – 4 P.M.

Felix Kaufman's Garden, MORRISTOWN, 10 A.M. – 4 P.M.

The Hay, Honey Farm, PEAPACK, 10 A.M. – 4 P.M.

Mrs. T. M. McDonnell, PEAPACK, 10 A.M. – 4 P.M.

Kallas Garden, STANTON, 10 A.M. – 4 P.M.

Allen Garden, SUMMIT, 10 A.M. – 2 P.M.

June 12, 1999

Riverwood Corners, BEDMINSTER, 10 A.M. – 2 P.M.

❖ Devereaux Deerhaven, CHESTER, 10 A.M. – 4 P.M.

September 11, 1999

Pitney Farm, MENDHAM, 10 A.M. – 4 P.M.

The Hay, Honey Farm, PEAPACK, 10 A.M. – 4 P.M.

Mrs. T. M. McDonnell, PEAPACK, 10 A.M. – 4 P.M.

Riverwood Corners, BEDMINSTER, NJ

Year-round interest is found in this space-limited garden. The four separate planting areas also incorporate peastone paths, brick terraces, trellis work, arbors, container gardens, and antique garden furniture.

DATES & HOURS: May 15, June 12; 10 a.m. – 2 p.m.

DIRECTIONS: *Take I-287* to Exit 22 (or 22B from I-287 South). Follow 206N to the third traffic light. Turn right onto Lamington Road. Go to the next traffic light. Turn left onto Hillside Avenue. Turn right at the second street, Wildwood Avenue. The entrance to the garden is on the left beyond the fence. Please park along the street.

❖ Oakeside — Bloomfield Cultural Center,
240 BELLEVILLE AVENUE, BLOOMFIELD, NJ (973) 429-0960.

A three-acre garden near the center of the Township of Bloomfield, Oakeside is on the state and national registers of historic places. The grounds are currently undergoing restoration with assistance from the New Jersey Historic Trust. The Colonial Revival-style mansion was built in 1895. A formal rose garden (1913) and large kitchen garden (1922) were designed by Vitale, Brinckerhoff and Geiffert. A naturalistic water garden and terrace garden near the solarium date from approximately 1929.

DATES & HOURS: Daily, dawn – dusk except during private events. Groups by appointment.

DIRECTIONS: *From the Garden State Parkway South* take Exit 148. Stay straight on J.F. Kennedy Drive to end, then turn left and a quick right back onto JFK Drive. At first traffic light, turn right onto Belleville Avenue. Take the second entrance on the right for parking. *From GSP North,* take Exit 149. Make a right off the ramp onto JFK Drive. Follow as above.

Frog Pond Farm, CALIFON, NJ

Frog Pond Farm was created for all-season beauty by my husband and me in a peaceful countryside hollow. Native trees are the backdrop for small flowering trees, introduced shrubs, perennials, and wildflowers. Azaleas, rhododendrons, and primulas are most prominent in mid-spring. The scene is reflected in a half-acre pond filled by several spring-fed brooks. If you cross one brook on a small bridge, the fenced-in section of a cleared field becomes visible, the site of several curved perennial and shrub borders, raised beds of rock plants, and a blueberry house. Many of the garden's plants were grown from seed and cuttings in my small greenhouse, some of the materials obtained on our world travels. A collection of subtropicals adds interest to the flag patio in midsummer.

DATES & HOURS: May 15; 10 a.m. – 4 p.m.

DIRECTIONS: *Take I-78* to Exit 24. Turn onto Route 523 heading toward Oldwick. Continue straight ahead; road becomes Route 517. Go through the village of Oldwick and on to traffic light. Turn left onto Route 512, go about 1 mile to Beavers Road. Turn right onto Beavers Road and go about 1 mile to the foot of the hill. There is a mailbox with #26 on it. Please park on Beavers Road.

Dan & Jeanne Will —— Hedgerows, CHESTER, NJ

The landscape surrounding this nineteenth century farmhouse unfolds to reveal several acres of gardens with different themes, set in meadows where a flock of sheep graze. There are perennial borders, a formal herb garden, and woodland gardens with a reflecting pool and stream. The owners are enthusiastic collectors, and many rare plant species are growing on their property. Island beds showcase unusual shrubs and trees, and a series of trough gardens contain rock and alpine plants. The gardens are planned to create interest throughout the year.

DATES & HOURS: May 15; 10 a.m. – 4 p.m.

DIRECTIONS: *North on Route 206;* turn left onto Old Chester-Gladstone Road before entering the town of Chester. The house is .7 miles on left. *From the Intersection of Routes 24 and 206* in Chester, take 206 south and immediately turn right onto road that angles off main road. This is the Old Chester-Gladstone Road. The house is .7 miles on right. Please park in driveway.

❖ Devereux Deerhaven,

230 POTTERSVILLE ROAD, CHESTER, NJ 07930. (908) 879-4500.

Devereux Deerhaven, a rural residential treatment center for adolescent girls with emotional disorders, was once Elizabeth and Alfred Kay's estate, "Hidden River Farm." The original 1920s design was inspired by Lutyens, Jekyll, and the Cotswolds cottages. Original fieldstone walls, terraces, fountains, pools, a pergola, and a moongate are largely intact. The garden was replanted and is cared for by students in the landscape and horticulture program. Visitors will see our large collection of shrub roses around an aquatic garden of lotus and water lilies. There are two cottage gardens filled with late-spring-blooming perennials near a stream with naturalized plantings. The greenhouse is filled with plants, and a selection will be for sale. Garden Design magazine recognized our program with a Golden Trowel Award for the "Best Healing Garden" in 1995-1996.

DATES & HOURS: Open for *Directory* visitors on June 12, 10 a.m. − 4 p.m.

DIRECTIONS: *Pottersville Road* is just off of Route 206, south of the intersection of Routes 206 & 24 in Chester, New Jersey.

❖ Colonial Park Arboretum, Perennial Garden and Rudolf W. van der Goot Rose Garden,

METTLER'S ROAD, EAST MILLSTONE, NJ. (732) 873-2459.

A variety of horticultural displays are found in Colonial Park. The 144-acre Arboretum contains labeled specimens of flowering trees, evergreens, shade trees, and flowering shrubs that grow well in central New Jersey, making this area a valuable source for homeowners and landscape professionals. The Perennial Garden, located near parking lot F, provides year-round interest for the enjoyment of gardeners and park visitors alike. A gazebo in the center of the garden is surrounded by beds displaying a selection of flowering bulbs, perennials, annuals, and flowering trees and shrubs. The Rudolf W. van der Goot Rose Garden offers a formal display of more than 3,000 roses of 285 varieties. From late spring into autumn, this accredited All-America Rose Selections Garden features labeled specimens of a wide variety of roses. Located behind the Rose Garden is a Fragrance and Sensory Garden. This circular garden with raised beds is accessible for persons with disabilities so that all of our visitors can enjoy the flowers, shrubs, herbs, and scented plants that grow there.

DATES & HOURS: Year round, daily, dawn – dusk. Rose Garden, year round, daily, 8 a.m. – dusk.

DIRECTIONS: *From I-287* take Exit 12 at Weston Canal Road, go south on Canal Road. Do not cross the canal, turn left before the bridge and continue along canal until road turns left onto Weston Road. Make first right onto Mather's Road. Continue ahead to Colonial Park.

❖ Leonard J. Buck Garden,

11 LAYTON ROAD, FAR HILLS, NJ. (908) 234-2677.

The Leonard J. Buck Garden is a nationally known rock garden, developed by its namesake in the 1930s. Designed to be ecologically correct and visually appealing, the garden is as pleasant to walk through as it is to sit in. Buck Garden lies in a woodland stream valley where natural rock outcroppings have been uncovered, providing visual interest as well as planting niches. There are extensive collections of pink and white dogwoods, azaleas, rhododendrons, wildflowers, ferns, alpines, and rock-loving plants. The many rock outcroppings provide different microclimates and exposures, making this a year-round garden.

DATES & HOURS: Monday through Friday, 10 a.m. – 4 p.m.; Saturday, 10 a.m.– 5 p.m.; Closed weekends and major holidays in December through February.

DIRECTIONS: *From I-287,* take Exit 22. If approaching from the south the exit is marked 228. If approaching from the north, the exit is marked 22. From exit ramp, take Route 202/206 North, staying right to continue north on 202. Follow signs to Far Hills and Morristown. At Far Hills train station, turn right before the tracks onto Liberty Corner - Far Hills Road. Travel .9 mile to Layton Road, turn right. Garden is on the left side.

❖ Moggy Hollow National Landmark,

LARGER CROSS ROAD, GLADSTONE, NJ 07934. (908) 234-1852.

Moggy Hollow was once the outlet of the ancient Lake Passaic before the last glacier receded. Of interest to visitors are the rock outcroppings that formed a spillway for the outflow. The swamp below and the concentric rings of vegetation around the quaking bog are of special interest.

DATES & HOURS: Year round, daily, dawn – dusk.

DIRECTIONS: Moggy Hollow is located next to the Leonard J. Buck Garden, listed above. Please see the Buck listing for directions.

❖ Durand-Hedden House & Garden,

523 RIDGEWOOD ROAD, MAPLEWOOD, NJ 07040. (973) 763-7712.

The house is being restored to reflect the continuum of its life as a farmhouse and residence from the late eighteenth through the mid-twentieth centuries. The Durand-Hedden House sits on two picturesque acres that include a sloping meadow edged by trees, shrubs, and annuals, and perennial beds. The centerpiece is the award-winning educational herb garden maintained by the Maplewood Garden Club. It boasts one of the largest herb collections in the Northeast, with many species and cultivated varieties of thyme, sage, lavender, and mint.

DATES & HOURS: Year round, daily, dawn – dusk.

DIRECTIONS: *From Routes 78 and 24,* take Exit 50B/Millburn/Maplewood. At the top of the ramp, turn right onto Vauxhall Road. Continue to the intersection of Millburn Avenue at the third light. Cross Millburn Avenue onto Ridgewood Road. Go 1 mile, past the blinking light. The house is the first on the left after Durand Road and opposite Jefferson School. Please park on the street.

Pitney Farm, MENDHAM, NJ

The house has been in the same family since the early 1700s. The present-day property has a cutting garden in front of the house where cows once grazed. There is a bird garden off the breakfast room, espaliers on three sides of the wood shed, and a garden featuring evergreens off the screened porch. Further off are a walled garden and a vegetable garden adjacent to the greenhouse.

DATES & HOURS: May 15, September 11; 10 a.m. – 4 p.m.

DIRECTIONS: *From I-287 South take Exit 32.* Follow Route 510 around Morristown Square to old Route 24/Route 510. Six miles from the square at the light, turn right onto Cold Hill Road. The second right is Pitney Farm. Park on the side street or in development.

Watnong Gardens, MORRIS PLAINS, NJ

Watnong Gardens is the former Watnong Nursery made famous by Don and Hazel Smith. The garden now consists of two and one-half acres of collections including conifers, shrubs, hosta, ferns, perennials, and a water garden. Special plants are added each year. A train, complete with four railroad cars, was made into six- and eight-foot-long troughs, all handcrafted by the owner and planted with mini plants and alpines.

DATES & HOURS: May 15; 10 a.m. – 4 p.m.

DIRECTIONS: *From Route 80 West,* take Exit 43 to Route 287 South. Take Route 287 South to Route 10 West/Exit 39B. Go approximately 3 miles west to the third light (Powdermill Road). Take "jughandle" turn and head east on Route 10. After passing Mountain Club Garden Homes go slow. Watnong Terrace angles off to the right. It parallels Route 10 like a service road. It is .7 miles from the "jughandle" turn.

Felix Kaufman's Garden, MORRISTOWN, NJ

My garden features specimen shrubs and conifers — particularly the latter. Among the plants that deserve mention are Cryptomeria, *weeping hemlock, atlas blue cedar, umbrella pine, weeping white pine, Lebanon cedar, stone pine,* Pinus glauca, *Alaskan cedar,* Chaemocyparis pisifera, *weeping spruce, and a variegated beech. The plants are arranged around the periphery of the back of my property, with most in beds containing evergreen and deciduous plants. The planting emphasis is a pleasing variety of texture and color. There are good sight lines from most viewing spots in the garden.*

DATES & HOURS: May 15; 10 a.m. – 4 p.m.

DIRECTIONS: *From I-287 North* take Exit 35. At the top of the ramp at traffic light, turn right onto South Street. Go about 1 mile, passing baseball fields on left and office buildings on the right. Turn left onto Spring Valley Road. Go about .25 miles to #43 Spring Valley Road. The house, a beige-colored Cape Cod, is on the left. Street number is on the mailbox. *From I-287 South* take Exit 35/Madison Avenue. Bear right as you exit! Get over to the left immediately once you are on Madison Avenue. Go left at the traffic light which you come to immediately. You are on South Street. Proceed as above. *From points east* take I-24 to its terminus at I-287. Stay left on I-24 and follow Somerville sign onto I-287 South. Proceed as above.

❖ **Acorn Hall,** 68 MORRIS AVENUE, MORRISTOWN, NJ (973) 267-3465.
Acorn Hall, the headquarters of the Morris County Historical Society, is a Victorian Italianate mansion (c. 1853-1860). The gardens have been restored by the Home Garden Club of Morristown to be reflective of the 1853-1888 period. Features include spring flowering trees, shrubs and bulbs; more than 30 varieties of authentic Victorian roses; an herb garden and traditional knot garden; and a fern garden.

DATES & HOURS: Year round, daily, dawn – dusk.

DIRECTIONS: *From I-287 South,* take Exit 37/Route 24 East/Springfield to first exit (2A) and follow signs to Morristown. Follow Columbia Road to the end traffic light (in front of the Governor Morris Hotel). Make a left at the traffic light to the second driveway on your right. *From I-287 North,* take Exit 36A onto Morris Avenue. Take first right-hand fork onto Columbia Turnpike and make an immediate left to traffic light. Turn left to second driveway on right.

❖ **Delbarton,**
MENDHAM ROAD, MORRISTOWN, NJ 07960. (973) 538-3231.
Delbarton, the largest estate of Morris County's Gilded Age, was the country home of Luther Kountze, international banker. Now a private boys school run by the Benedictine Fathers of Saint Mary's Abbey, the campus occupies 340 acres of the original 4,000. A splendid Italian garden with a pergola and statuary flanks the west side of Old Main, the imposing residence built for the Kountze family. Also on the grounds is the striking Abbey Church, designed by Victor Christ-Janer and completed in 1966.

DATES & HOURS: Year round, weekdays, 9 a.m.–5 p.m.; weekends, 9 a.m. – dusk.

DIRECTIONS: *From I-287,* take Exit 35/Route 124/Madison Avenue. Bear right at the end of the ramp onto Route 124 West/South Street. Proceed straight to the Morristown Green. Follow signs for 510 West/Washington Street. This becomes Route 24/Mendham Road. Delbarton is on the left, 2.5 miles from the Morris-town Center.

❖ The George Griswold Frelinghuysen Arboretum,
53 EAST HANOVER AVENUE, MORRIS TOWNSHIP, NJ 07962-1295.
(973) 326-7600.

The 127-acre Frelinghuysen Arboretum in Morris Township displays a wide range of native and exotic plants in home demonstration gardens of perennials, annuals, plants for shade, ferns, vegetables and roses. Collections include peonies, dogwoods, crab apples, cherries and a pinetum. Interpretive materials are available in the Education Center.

DATES & HOURS: Year round, daily, 8 a.m. – dusk. Closed Thanksgiving, Christmas, and New Year's Day.

DIRECTIONS: *From I-287 North,* take Exit 36A. Proceed to Whippany Road. At second traffic light turn left onto East Hanover Avenue. Entrance is on left. *From I-287 South,* take Exit 36. Make right onto Ridgedale Avenue. Make right at first traffic light onto East Hanover Avenue. Entrance is on the left.

The Hay, Honey Farm, PEAPACK, NJ

Set between the hills at the end of a pasture, the gardens include an early spring patio garden and a summer-to-fall perennial border. A walk along the nearby stream leads through flowering trees and shrubs and a rhododendron glade with year-round interest. There is also a large vegetable and cutting garden.

DATES & HOURS: May 15, September 11; 10 a.m. – 4 p.m.

Directions: *Take I-78 West* from the New Jersey Turnpike. Take I-287 North to Exit 22B (or Exit 22 if coming from the north.) Stay on 206 North. At fourth light, go right onto Holland Avenue. At the end, go left into Peapack. Go right on Willow Avenue. Go 1 mile and turn left onto Branch Road. Follow signs to garden.

Mrs. T. M. McDonnell, PEAPACK, NJ

Nestled in the heart of Pleasant Valley near a tributary of the Raritan River, this beautifully landscaped farmhouse is surrounded by gardens and mature trees. Most notable is the French potager, planted with many varieties of vegetables and flowers. Other special features include artistically pruned apple trees, and a cool, quiet shade garden, as well as a pergola covered with grape vines which is by the swimming pool. Garden statuary, inviting benches, and many warm and gracious touches add immeasurably to the enjoyment of this seasonally changing garden.

DATES & HOURS: May 15, September 11; 10 a.m. – 4 p.m.

DIRECTIONS: *Take I-78 West* from the New Jersey Turnpike. Take I-287 North to Exit 22B (or Exit 22 if coming from the north.) Stay on 206 North. At fourth light, go right onto Holland Avenue. At the end, go left into Peapack. Go right on Willow Avenue. Go 1 mile and turn left onto Branch Road. Follow signs to garden.

Kallas Garden, STANTON, NJ

Approximately one and one-half acres under cultivation. Herbaceous borders, annuals, woody ornamentals. The main feature is approximately 1,000 specimens of 200 different Rhododendron *and* Azalea *cultivars.*

DATES & HOURS: May 15; 10 a.m. – 4 p.m.

DIRECTIONS: *From Flemington circle,* take 31 North. Travel 5.6 miles to Route 618 East (branches at an angle on the right just past Park Department buildings). Turn right onto 618 East .4 mile to 629 South (end of 618 East). Turn right onto 629 South to the first left (Stanton Mountain Road). Turn left and proceed to the first right (Dreahook Road). Turn right and travel .9 mile to Kallas, #91 Dreahook Road. The driveway is on the left between Cushetunk Road and Springtown Road. Please park on Cushetunk Road (unless handicapped).

Allen Garden, SUMMIT, NJ

Until four years ago, this garden, with a mix of sun and shade, was a flat, square, suburban backyard featuring a boggy corner, piles of rocks, and a few stately trees. Realizing the potential of a low stone wall and a good borrowed landscape, the owners asked Ann Granbery, of New Vernon, to design a garden for three seasons only: fall, winter, and spring. Two rock gardens, two perennial gardens, apple trees espaliered against the garage, a topiary garden "gate," and unusual plants are features.

DATES & HOURS: May 15; 10 a.m. – 2 p.m.

DIRECTIONS: *From Route 24,* take the Summit Avenue Exit. Go one block. Turn right onto Bellevue Avenue. Go around the bend to a brick ranch at #107. Please park on the street. Walk down the driveway; the garden is in the back.

❖ Reeves-Reed Arboretum,

165 HOBART AVENUE, SUMMIT, NJ 07901-2908. (908) 273-8787.

A twelve and one-half-acre former country estate, the Reeves-Reed is a national and state historic site and nature conservancy with a focus on horticultural and environmental education for children and adults. It features the newly restored historic 1889 Wisner House. There are azalea, rock, and herb gardens. Thousands of April daffodils are widely naturalized. A double perennial border flowers April through October. Naturalistic areas, a pond, and a glacial kettle provide wildlife habitat.

DATES & HOURS: Year round, daily, dawn – dusk.

DIRECTIONS: *From the New Jersey Turnpike,* take Exit 14/Newark Airport onto I-78 West. After traveling several miles on I-78 West, take Exit 48/Springfield/ Millburn onto Highway 24 West. Take the Hobart Avenue exit off Route 24 (Route 124 runs parallel). Go left over the highway and continue straight past the traffic light. Up the hill on the left will be signs for "Reeves-Reed Arboretum."

❖ The Presby Memorial Iris Gardens,

474 UPPER MOUNTAIN AVENUE, UPPER MONTCLAIR, NJ. (973) 783-5974.
The Presby Memorial Iris Gardens, the world's largest display garden of irises, is located in Mountainside Park in Upper Montclair. The collection of more than 4,000 varieties, mostly tall bearded, also contains species Louisiana, Siberians, and Japanese as well as remontants and a group of historic irises. All varieties, from miniature dwarf bearded to tall bearded, are represented in twenty-nine beds. A display bed, new in 1998, demonstrates the varied landscapes in which irises can grow. The Gardens adjoin the Victorian Walther House property, headquarters of the Presby Memorial Iris Gardens, and its beautiful surrounding gardens, also open to the public. A small sales area offers iris motif and garden items. Rhizomes may be obtained for a small donation.

DATES & HOURS: Year round, daily, dawn – dusk.

DIRECTIONS: *Upper Mountain Avenue* is bounded by Route 46 on the north, Route 23 to the west, Bloomfield Avenue, Montclair, on the south and is easily reached from Routes 3, 80, 280, 287, and the Garden State Parkway.

❖ Mindowaskin Park,

425 EAST BROAD STREET, WESTFIELD, NJ 07090. (908) 233-8110.
Mindowaskin Park, in the heart of Westfield, was named for a Lenni-Lanape Indian Chief and was established in 1918. In 1994, concerned citizens, The Friends of Mindowaskin Park, raised money to improve the facilities and continue its care. Individuals, corporations, and foundations contributed toward the new Victorian iron lamps, iron and mahogany benches, new signage, and various gardens planted with shrubbery, trees, perennials, and annuals. A large lake, fountains, waterways, winding paths, hardwood trees, a bird sanctuary, new playground equipment, flowering gardens, and a large gazebo offer opportunities for walking and watching, ice skating, model boat sailing, performances, art shows, picnics, and relaxation.

DATES & HOURS: Year round, daily, 7 a.m. – 10 p.m.

DIRECTIONS: *From the Garden State Parkway,* take Exit 137 and head toward Westfield on North Avenue. After 3.1 miles, turn right on Elmer Street and right again onto East Broad Street. Mindowaskin Park is within one block on the left.

NEW YORK

1999 NEW YORK OPEN DAYS

June 19: ALBANY AREA

May 16, June 13, July 11, July 25, September 12:
DUTCHESS & COLUMBIA COUNTIES

May 1, June 19, July 17, September 18: SUFFOLK COUNTY/
EASTERN LONG ISLAND

July 31: LAKE CHAMPLAIN AREA

May 16: ORANGE COUNTY

*April 25, May 2, May 16, May 30, June 13, June 27, July 11, July 25,
September 12, October 17:*
WESTCHESTER & PUTNAM COUNTIES

ALBANY AREA: *June 19, 1999*

Longwood Gardens, DELMAR, 2 P.M. – 6 P.M.

Joan & Henry Ferguson, LOUDONVILLE, 10 A.M. – 4 P.M.

Phyllis & Peter Heerwagen, LOUDONVILLE, 10 A.M. – 4 P.M.

Ginny & Ernie Kopp, LOUDONVILLE, 2 P.M. – 6 P.M.

Bullock House Garden — Larry & Denise Becker, SLINGERLANDS,
     10 A.M. – 4 P.M.

❖ Ten Broeck Mansion,

9 TEN BROECK PLACE, ALBANY, NY 12210. (518) 436-9826.

This Federal-style historic house and museum is situated on three acres in downtown Albany. The surrounding gardens include lilacs, hydrangea, hawthorne, crab apple, perennial beds, herbs, and annual plantings. There are unusual dawn redwoods (Metasequoia) *as well as a 100-year-old beech, ancient maples, horse chestnuts, and plane trees.*

DATES & HOURS: Year round, daily, dawn – dusk.

DIRECTIONS: *From I-90* take Exit 6 for Arbor Hill. Travel east on Livingston Avenue. The entrance to the Ten Broeck Mansion parking lot is on the south side of Livingston Avenue between North Swan and North Pearl.

Longwood Garden, DELMAR, NY

This garden, on a suburban corner lot, is in its fifth year of development. The primary emphasis is on combining a naturalistic "under-tree" setting with English cottage-style perennial beds, utilizing organic husbandry. A permanent four-bay composting system is utilized. The garden features sixty-two varieties of hosta, more than two dozen ground covers, and sweeping perennial beds.

DATES & HOURS: June 19; 2 p.m. – 6 p.m.

DIRECTIONS: *From the east,* take Route 85 to its end. Turn right on New Scotland Avenue. Turn left at the next traffic light (Route 140). Go past two traffic lights to Longwood Drive on the left. Ours is the last property on the right at the end of the street, #43.

❖ George Landis Arboretum,

P.O. BOX 186, LAPE ROAD, ESPERANCE, NY 12066. (518) 875-6935.

The George Landis Arboretum is a ninety-seven-acre public garden, arboretum and woodland located about twenty-five miles west of Albany, NY. Included are beech, oak, maple, and crab apple collections, as well as a significant lilac collection. The Arboretum also includes the Van Loveland Perennial Garden, a large terraced collection of three-season bulbs and perennials. Trails traverse the Arboretum collections and the native woodland. The George Landis Arboretum is a naturalistic garden in a rural setting, on the site of founder Fred Lape's family farm.

DATES & HOURS: Year round, daily, dawn – dusk.

DIRECTIONS: *West from Albany, NY* on Highway 20 to the village of Esperance. The Arboretum is located about 1 mile outside the village, and the route is well marked. *From the New York State Thruway,* south on Route 30 to Route 20, and then west of Route 20.

Joan & Henry Ferguson, LOUDONVILLE, NY

Intrigued by Japanese gardens, we have researched, designed, and built entirely by ourselves, three separate, visually spacious gardens filling our residential lot of less than half an acre. Each is carefully reflective of Japanese garden tradition in form, philosophy, and the aesthetic principles of antiquity, mystery, and surprise. To step into these gardens to find oneself is the philosophical purpose of this purely American creation. As in Japan, these gardens are for all seasons — winter included. Thus, forms, textures and colors of foliage are more important than blossom.

DATES & HOURS: June 19; 10 a.m. – 4 p.m.

DIRECTIONS: *From I-90,* take Route 9 north 2 miles to Chestnut Hill Road, the second left after the first traffic light. At the top of a short hill, bear right and park on the street before reaching the "Dead End" sign. Please do not enter or block the driveway. Gardens begin at the head of the driveway to the right of the "Dead End" sign. Do not go beyond the sign.

Phyllis & Peter Heerwagen, LOUDONVILLE, NY

Spring and early summer bloom is the goal of this small suburban garden. The property is private and serene in a backyard woodland setting. A feeling of indoor living which extends to the outside is achieved with brick patio and planters, a very small pond, and a curved stone wall, all near the house. The wooded area beyond is planted with rhododendrons, azaleas, shade-loving hostas, spring bulbs, and lilies, all amid birch trees. There is a sunny perennial border and herb garden. The tiny front garden enclosed with a fence allows for annuals. The gardener loves most shrubs and flowers and tries to grow a little bit of everything within her own limitations, workload, busy lifestyle, and size of her property.

DATES & HOURS: June 19, 10 a.m. − 4 p.m.

DIRECTIONS: *From Albany* (Route 90 or 787), take Route 9 North. Go several miles and through two traffic lights. After the second light, go .5 mile and turn right onto Turner Lane. Follow for .25 mile and turn right onto Schuyler Hills Road. Make your first right onto Fenway Drive. Go a short distance to Fenway Court and turn right. The house is directly in front, in the middle of the circle. It is gray with a pink door.

Ginny & Ernie Kopp, LOUDONVILLE, NY

Upon entering our garden through a wooden arched gate, a feeling of warm welcome, seclusion, and privacy is immediately experienced. The site is enhanced by the tranquil sound of a trickling waterfall as it enters a rock-framed water garden. Plantings, which include a variety of ferns, hosta, effusive holly, are capped by a weeping cherry. An espaliered pear tree is encountered on one side, a flowering quince on the other. A grouping of rhododendrons and finally, a colorful flower garden of primarily perennials complete the garden. The lot is small, but the love is large.

DATES & HOURS: June 19; 2 p.m. - 6 p.m.

DIRECTIONS: *From Route 87 North* take Exit 5/Latham/Route 155. Turn left at the traffic light and take the first right onto Old Niskayuna Road. Turn right at the second traffic light onto Osborn Road. Take the first right onto Reddy Lane. *From Route 9* turn left onto Osborn Road. Take the first right onto Reddy Lane. It is the third house on the right, #5. Please park along the road.

❖ **Pruyn House,** 207 OLD NISKAYUNA ROAD, NEWTONVILLE, NY 12128.
(518) 783-1435.

Centrally placed between the 1830 Federal/Greek revival-style Pruyn House, the 1850 Buhrmaster Barn, and the 1910 Verdoy Schoolhouse are lovely and complementary gardens designed and maintained by two garden clubs. There is a traditional herb garden appropriate to the nineteenth century. The other garden includes perennials and annuals, providing cut flowers for the house and demonstrating plant material that thrives in sandy soil and the severe winters of upstate New York.

DATES & HOURS: Year round, daily, dawn – dusk.

DIRECTIONS: *From I-90,* take Exit 24 to I-87 North. Take Exit 5 and turn right at the traffic light to Route 155. Take the second left, Old Niskayuna Road, before the bridges. Proceed 1 mile; the Pruyn House complex is on the left.

❖ **Jackson's Garden,**
UNION COLLEGE CAMPUS, SCHENECTADY, NY 12308. (518) 388-6103.

Developed in the early 1800s by Isaac W. Jackson, professor of mathematics and natural philosophy, Jackson's Garden is an eight-acre historic landscape on the Union College Campus in Schenectady, New York. The Formal Garden, Amphitheater, and Van Voast Evergreen Garden form a historic landscape that retains the original designed boundary, topography, grading, and circulation. Based on an autumn 1995 National Education Institution Garden Survey, Jackson's Garden is the oldest garden in continuous cultivation on an American college or university campus.

DATES & HOURS: Year round, daily, 9 a.m. – 4 p.m.

DIRECTIONS: *From the New York Thruway,* take Exit 24. Take the Northway (I-87) north to Exit 6, marked for Route 7 West. Follow Route 7 West for 6.5 miles and bear right onto Union Street. Continue on Union Street for 2.7 miles and enter the campus through the Payne Gate on the right.

Bullock House Garden — Larry & Denise Becker,
SLINGERLANDS, NY

This rambling, English-style country flower garden is in a historic setting which includes a stone house (circa 1787). The property features rolling lawns, barns, a stone smoke house, stone walls, sculptures, and ponds. The plantings emphasize hardy perennials and shrubs.

DATES & HOURS: June 19; 10 a.m. – 4 p.m.

DIRECTIONS: *Take I-90* to Route 85/Slingerlands Exit. Travel west on Route 85 through the hamlet of Slingerlands into the town of New Scotland. Continue on Route 85 to Bullock Road. This will be a left turn just past the railroad overpass. Go uphill for .8 mile to a large red barn on the left. The house, #183, is .9 mile on the left. Please park near the barn.

DUTCHESS & COLUMBIA COUNTIES: *May 16, 1999*

Garden of Margaret Roach, COPAKE FALLS, 10 A.M. – 4 P.M.

❖ Beatrix Farrand Garden at Bellefield, HYDE PARK, dawn – dusk.

Mark McDonald, LINLITHGO, 10 A.M. – 4 p.m.

❖ Springside, POUGHKEEPSIE, dawn – dusk.

June 13, 1999

Maxine Paetro, AMENIA, 10 A.M. – 4 P.M.

Abby Adams–Westlake, ANCRAM, 10 A.M. – 4 P.M.

Garden of Margaret Roach, COPAKE FALLS, 10 A.M. – 4 P.M.

David Lebe & Jack Potter, HARLEMVILLE, 10 A.M. – 6 P.M.

Hudson Bush Farm, HUDSON, 10 A.M. – 6 P.M.

 ❖ Beatrix Farrand Garden at Bellefield, HYDE PARK, dawn – dusk.

Mark McDonald, LINLITHGO, 10 A.M. – 4 P.M.

Tailings — David Whitcomb & Robert Montgomery, LINLITHGO,
      10 A.M. – 2 P.M.

Starr Ockenga & Donald Forst, LIVINGSTON, 10 A.M. – 2 P.M.

 ❖ Springside, POUGHKEEPSIE, dawn – dusk.

July 11, 1999

 ❖ Beatrix Farrand Garden at Bellefield, HYDE PARK, dawn – dusk.

John Whitworth, MILLBROOK, 2 P.M. – 6 P.M.

 ❖ Springside, POUGHKEEPSIE, dawn – dusk.

Amy Goldman, RHINEBECK, 10 A.M. – 4 P.M.

Ellen & Eric Petersen, STANFORDVILLE, 10 A.M. – 2 P.M.

Zibby & Jim Tozer, STANFORDVILLE, 10 A.M. – 2 P.M.

July 25, 1999

Sue & Art Bassin, ANCRAMDALE, 10 a.m. – 4 p.m.

 ❖ Beatrix Farrand Garden at Bellefield, HYDE PARK, dawn – dusk.

 ❖ Springside, POUGHKEEPSIE, dawn – dusk.

September 12, 1999

Abby Adams–Westlake, ANCRAM, 10 A.M. – 4 P.M.

Sue & Art Bassin, ANCRAMDALE, 10 A.M. – 4 P.M.

Garden of Margaret Roach, COPAKE FALLS, 10 A.M. – 4 P.M.

Hudson Bush Farm, HUDSON, 10 A.M – 6 P.M.

 ❖ Beatrix Farrand Garden at Bellefield, HYDE PARK, dawn – dusk.

Mark McDonald, LINLITHGO, 10 A.M. – 4 P.M.

Farmstead Garden, PATTERSON, 2 P.M. – 6 P.M.

 ❖ Springside, POUGHKEEPSIE, dawn – dusk.

Cedar Heights Orchard, RHINEBECK, 10 A.M. – 4 P.M.

Maxine Paetro, AMENIA, NY

Broccoli Hall is an English-style cottage garden featuring an apple tunnel, a brick courtyard, a peony border with a facing iris walk, an extensive rose border, a tree house with long views, a secret woodland garden, and a formal vegetable and herb garden.

DATES & HOURS: June 13; 10 a.m. – 4 p.m.

DIRECTIONS: *From Route 22 north,* go toward Amenia. Go west on Route 44 to County Route 83 North/Smithfield Road. Go 2.5 miles to dirt road on right, Flint Hill Road. Turn right. The house, #464, is the first on the left. Please park on Flint Hill Road. Be careful of ditches.

Proceeds shared with the Amenia Library.

❖ Wethersfield,

PUGSLEY HILL ROAD, AMENIA, NY 12501. (914) 373-8037.
Ten acres of formal and outer gardens surround Chauncey D. Stillman's Georgian-style brick home. The original garden around the perimeter of the house was created in 1940 by Bryan J. Lynch. Evelyn N. Poehler oversaw the maintenance of the garden from 1952 on and designed the formal classical-style garden over a twenty-year period.

DATES & HOURS: June through September, Wednesday, Friday, & Saturday, noon – 5 p.m.

DIRECTIONS: *From Route 44* east of Millbrook take Route 86 and turn right onto Pugsley Hill Road. Follow the signs for 1.3 miles to the estate entrance on left.

Adams — Westlake, ANCRAM, NY

Various gardens — including a walled swimming pool garden, a long perennial border, a small frog pond, an herb garden, and an exuberant potager with vegetables and flowers spilling out of raised beds — surround an 1835 farmhouse in a pastoral Columbia County valley. Our latest project: a large spring-fed pond in a beautiful natural ravine. Abby Adams is the author of The Gardener's Gripe Book. *Donald Westlake is the author of mystery novels and screenplays.*

DATES & HOURS: June 13, September 12; 10 a.m. – 4 p.m.

DIRECTIONS: *From the Taconic Parkway,* exit at Jackson Corners; go east on Route 2. At first "Y" take the left onto Route 7, following signs for Ancram. At the second "Y" take the right, staying on Route 7. Approximately seven minutes from the Taconic, the Gallatin Town Hall will be on the left. The house is next, on the left; look for #681 on a red mailbox. Park across the road.

Sue & Art Bassin — Cricket Hill Farm, ANCRAMDALE, NY

An 1844 house and horse farm sit amid rolling fields with distant views. From the house, with a native fieldstone terrace, an informal garden of herbs and vegetables flows naturally to barns and mailbox. Lawn, grass paths, stone walls and paths provide access to fifteen individual beds on five acres. Interesting plant collections include bulbs, perennials, shrubs, evergreens, grasses, herbs, fruits, and vegetables. The gardens, incorporating new rock features, are planned for ease of maintenance, four-season interest, food and cover for birds. The equestrian center will be open to visitors.

DATES & HOURS: July 25, September 12; 10 a.m. – 4 p.m.

DIRECTIONS: *From the Taconic Parkway*, take the Jackson Corners Exit. Turn right at the stop sign. Follow signs to Ancram and Gallatin, going on Route 2 and then Route 7. In Ancram, go straight past the blinking light onto Route 82. Go over small bridge about 100 yards from the center of town. Go .8 mile to first left onto Wiltsie Bridge Road; there is a brown house on the corner. Go 1.3 miles to the first right; there is a yellow house on the corner. Go .5 mile to Cricket Hill. *From Route 22,* going north from Millerton or south from Hillsdale, turn onto Route 3 by the Mobil station toward Ancramdale. After about 3 miles, passing the "Pond" restaurant, turn right onto Roche Drive. Go .5 mile to the right fork, then .7 mile to Cricket Hill. Please park across the road from the house.

Proceeds shared with Adolescent Sarcoma Patients Intense Rehabilitation with Exercise (ASPIRE).

❖ Montgomery Place,

RIVER ROAD, ANNANDALE-ON-HUDSON, NY 12504. (914) 758-5461.

This two-hundred-year-old estate enjoys a picturesque landscape, extolled by Andrew Jackson Downing. Included are ancient trees, and vistas of the Hudson River and Catskill Mountains. The early-twentieth-century garden includes a wide variety of plants, many unusual. There are also hiking trails, pick-your-own orchards, and waterfalls.

DATES & HOURS: Please call for a calendar of events.

DIRECTIONS: *From I-87* take Exit 19 for Kingston onto Route 209/199 east across the Kingston-Rhinecliff Bridge. Go left onto Route 9G for 3 miles and left again onto Annandale Road, bearing left onto River Road to the estate entrance.

Garden of Margaret Roach, COPAKE FALLS, NY

This ten-year-old homemade garden reflects my obsession with plants, particularly those with good foliage or of interest to wildlife (no, not deer!). Sixty species of birds visit. Informal mixed borders, water gardens, paved gardens, and meadow cover this two-and-one-half-acre hillside — a former orchard and pastureland dotted with simple Victorian farmhouse, barn, outbuildings, surrounded by the Taconic State Park. Recent collaborations with Glenn Withey and Charles Price of Seattle have smoothed rough edges and helped me begin to realize my hopes for the garden. Expansion continues, with several new areas to be created in the fall of 1999, and more dreams in mind.

DATES & HOURS: May 16, June 13, September 12; 10 a.m. – 4 p.m.

DIRECTIONS: *Off of Route 22* (5 miles south of Hillsdale, 13 miles north of Millerton), take Route 344 toward Taconic State Park signs. Bear right after the park and blue deli over the metal bridge, past the camp. After the High Valley Road intersectons on the left, continue right 100 feet more to the barn and house on the left.

David Lebe & Jack Potter, HARLEMVILLE, NY

Our one-acre hillside meadow of native wildflowers and prairie grasses is nestled in woodland but offers wide views across Hawthorne Valley to the Taconic Hills. Wild lupines and coreopsis light the meadow in June. A gravel courtyard, small pond, and areas of improved soil near the house include a wide range of deer-resistant plants (especially alliums, poppies, roses, and euphorbias). A stone garage and garden walls link our efforts to May Hill's mysterious network of ancient (probably Native American) walls. Jack Potter was the curator of the Scott Arboretum; David Lebe is a photographer and garden designer.

DATES & HOURS: June 13; 10 a.m. – 6 p.m.

DIRECTIONS: *From the Taconic Parkway,* take the Philmont/Harlemville Exit. Turn right (west) toward Harlemville on Route 21C. Go 1 mile to the first left, May Hill Road, then .5 mile to #104 on the right. Please park on May Hill Road.

Proceeds shared with AIDS Council of Northeastern New York, Hudson Office.

❖ East Fishkill Community Library Garden,

380 ROUTE 376, HOPEWELL JUNCTION, NY 12533. (914) 221-9943.
Implemented, designed, and maintained by Mary Alice King, the gardens surrounding the library include a fragrance garden, which contains a vine-covered "secret garden" arbor where one can sit among statuary and fragrant plants. Additional gardens include two large perennial and annual borders, a bed of ornamental grass specimens, and a butterfly garden.

DATES & HOURS: Year round, daily, dawn – dusk. Garden maps are available.

DIRECTIONS: *From the intersection of I-84 and the Taconic Parkway* go north on the Taconic for 1.5 miles to the NYS Route 52 Exit. Turn left (west) onto Route 52 and travel for 1 mile to the traffic light at Route 376. Turn right onto Route 376. The Library is 1.5 miles on the right.

Hudson Bush Farm, HUDSON, NY

Formal gardens surrounding the eighteenth-century house include color-oriented parterres, a double red border, a rock garden, and a long walk leading to a summer house, small pool, and vegetable garden on three acres surrounded by old-growth woods.

DATES & HOURS: June 13, September 12; 10 a.m. – 6 p.m.

DIRECTIONS: *From the Taconic Parkway,* take the Hudson-Ancram Exit. Take Route 82 west to traffic light/Bells Pond. Continue west on Route 9/Route 23 to Yates Road, about 1 mile. Turn right onto Yates Road. Go .25 mile to drive on the right at old brick house. Park at the top of, or along, the drive.

Proceeds shared with The Hudson Opera House.

 ❖ **Beatrix Farrand Garden at Bellefield,**
ROUTE 9, HYDE PARK, NY 12538. (914) 229-9115.
This enclosed formal garden and surrounding wild garden were designed by the acclaimed landscape gardener Beatrix Farrand in 1912. Thought to be her earliest surviving residential project, it is now being restored. Adjacent to a magnificent eighteenth century house that was remodeled by the architects McKim, Mead & White in 1911, the garden evidences both colonial American and formal European influences. Typical of Farrand's work, the subtle elegance of the plan and built elements are set off by lush borders in sophisticated color schemes.

DATES & HOURS: Year round, daily, dawn – dusk.

DIRECTIONS: Bellefield is part of the Roosevelt-Vanderbilt National Historic Sites and is located adjacent to the Franklin Delano Roosevelt Home Library. Please call (914) 229-9115 for more information.

❖ Vanderbilt National Historic Site: Italian Gardens,

ROUTE 9, HYDE PARK, NY 12538-0698. (914) 229-6432.

The three-level formal garden covers three acres. The rose garden has more than 1,200 plants. The perennial garden, along the cherry walk, includes several hundred perennials, and thousands of annuals are planted each year in the upper beds.

DATES & HOURS: Year round, daily, dawn – dusk. Group tours available by appointment.

DIRECTIONS: Located on Route 9, on the left side of the road, just north of the Hyde Park Post Office.

Mark A. McDonald, LINLITHGO, NY

The sound and motion of rocky creek lend seasonal rhythm to the Japanese spirit of this intimate, multi-level garden. Rising above the lower creekside beds, the naturalized walls of a curving ravine open to reveal a sudden view of distant Catskill peaks. A weathered fence and baffle of evergreens define the perimeter of the upper garden, affording privacy and furnishing a backdrop for the compact trees, mature shrubs, and extensive perennial beds. Notable structural features include a sculptor's entry gate, a wisteria arbor, a rustic garden shed, and steps, walls, and terraces of stone.

DATES & HOURS: May 16, June 13, September 12; 10 a.m. – 4 p.m.

DIRECTIONS: *The garden is located in Linlithgo, NY, in southern Columbia* County, 3 miles south of Olana on Wire Road, just off County Route 10.

Tailings — David Whitcomb & Robert Montgomery,
LINLITHGO, NY

The gardens at Tailings comprise a series of bulb, perennial, and rose plantings closely integrated with the natural landscape and joined to each other by woodland paths. Axial cuts have been made through the woods to offer views in all directions and to complement the architecture. These culminate in a prospect of the Hudson River and entire Catskill Mountain range.

DATES & HOURS: June 13; 10 a.m. – 2 p.m.

DIRECTIONS: *From Germantown,* take Route 9G north from stoplight to intersection of Route 10; turn right. Go .25 mile to White Birch Road; turn left. Go 1 mile to Tailings drive on the right. Look for #404 on the mailbox. Please park at the top of the driveway.

Proceeds shared with The Olana Historic Site.

Starr Ockenga & Donald Forst, LIVINGSTON, NY

Country gardens surround a complex of barn-like buildings, including a teahouse, a potting shed, and a new studio/greenhouse. Because of the heavy deer population, the gardens are enclosed with fencing that is both practical and ornamental. Features include a main garden — which is terraced on three levels by stone walls — a white garden, a gold garden, various mixed borders, a kitchen garden, and two ponds with natural plantings. The hilltop location provides dramatic views of both the Berkshires and the Catskills.

DATES & HOURS: June 13; 10 a.m. – 2 p.m.

DIRECTIONS: *From the intersection of the Taconic Parkway and Route 82* go northwest on Route 82 (toward Hudson and the Rip Van Winkle Bridge) 1.9 miles to Willow Brook Road. (Willow Brook is the first road on the left after the Taconic Orchards farmstand.) Turn left on Willow Brook Road. Follow it .7 mile to the end. Turn left on Church Road. Turn into the second driveway on the right, where there are two posts and a green metal farm gate. The mailbox reads #786. Follow the driveway to the end. Please park where directed.

John H. Whitworth, MILLBROOK, NY

Far A-Field, most of all, is a collection of trees planted in a large open space, created in part when the house was built in 1931 and enlarged when the property was acquired in 1975. The surrounding woods contain a wide variety of indigenous trees, mainly deciduous hardwoods. The principal garden feature is a long, curving mixed border richly planted atop and beneath an old stone retaining wall. There is also a long pink rose hedge bordering the west lawn, a yellow-flower and silver-foliage garden, a large conifer collection, cutting/kitchen gardens, and a hidden hot colors bed. Finally, as you walk toward the gate leading to the parking area, don't miss the small garden of dwarf conifers planted in moss beneath native gray birch trees.

DATES & HOURS: July 11; 2 p.m. – 6 p.m.

DIRECTIONS: *From the traffic light at the intersection of Routes 343/44 and Route 82 in Millbrook,* go east on Route 343, passing the Golf and Tennis Club and a cemetery on the left. Turn right onto Route 96. Follow for 1.7 miles, bearing left at the fork onto Overlook Road. Go .3 mile. Turn left into gravel drive marked "Far A-Field." Please park as posted.

Proceeds shared with Saint Peter's Episcopal Curch, Lithgow, NY.

❖ Innisfree Garden,

TYRREL ROAD, MILLBROOK, NY 12545. (914) 677-8000.

Innisfree reflects an Eastern design technique called a cup garden which draws attention to something rare or beautiful by establishing the suggestion of enclosure around it. A cup garden may be an enclosed meadow, a lotus pool, a waterfall or a single dramatic rock covered with lichens and sedums. The visitor to Innisfree strolls from one three-dimensional garden picture to another.

DATES & HOURS: May 1 through October 20. Closed Mondays and Tuesdays except holidays, Wednesday through Friday, 10 a.m. – 4 p.m., Saturdays, Sundays & holidays, 11 a.m. – 5 p.m.

DIRECTIONS: *Innisfree is on Tyrell Road,* 1 mile from Route 44 and 1.75 miles from the Taconic State Parkway overpass on Route 44.

❖ Institute of Ecosystem Studies — Mary Flagler Cary Arboretum, ROUTE 44A, MILLBROOK, NY 12545. (914) 677-5359.

The three-acre perennial garden includes ecological demonstration beds. The fern glen is a two-acre display of native plants in natural communities. The greenhouse, open year round, is a tropical plant paradise and includes an "Economic Botany Trail." There are also hiking trails, a picnic area, and an Ecology Shop with a plant room.

DATES & HOURS: Year round except holidays. Monday through Saturday, 9 a.m. – 4 p.m.; Sunday 1 p.m. – 4 p.m. Grounds open until 6 p.m. May through September. Greenhouse closes at 3:30 p.m.

DIRECTIONS: *From the Taconic State Parkway* take Route 44 east for two miles. Turn onto Route 44A. The Gifford House Visitor and Education Center is 1 mile along Route 44A on the left. *From Massachusetts and Connecticut* take Route 22 to Route 44. Where Route 44 takes a sharp left to the village of Millbrook, continue straight on Route 44A. The Gifford House Visitor and Education Center is on the right, just before Route 44A (the Millbrook bypass) rejoins Route 44.

 ## ❖ Springside Landscape Restoration,

185 ACADEMY STREET, POUGHKEEPSIE, NY 12602. (914) 454-2060.

Springside is the only unaltered, documented work of Andrew Jackson Downing, one of the most influential landscape architects in American history. Once the summer home of Matthew Vassar (founder of Vassar College), the site was an "ornamental farm." Although unrestored, the landscape bears Downing's undeniable influence, illustrating the principles of the beautiful and the picturesque.

DATES & HOURS: Year round, daily, dawn – dusk.

DIRECTIONS: *From the Taconic State Parkway* take the Poughkeepsie/Route 44 Exit and then Route 44 west through Poughkeepsie until just before the bridge. Stay in the right lane for Route 9 South/Wappingers Falls for 1 mile to the Academy Street exit. At bottom of ramp, turn left. Proceed to first entrance on the right at bottom of hill.

❖ Vassar College,

124 RAYMOND AVENUE, POUGHKEEPSIE, NY 12601. (914) 437-5686.
The Vassar College campus has a Shakespeare Garden, first planted in 1918 with plants represented in Shakespeare's writings. The garden has brick walks, statuary, knot beds, rose beds, heath and heather beds, and twelve raised-brick beds containing herbs and cottage garden plantings. A hemlock hedge encloses the garden. There is also an arboretum with 220 species of native and non-native trees and shrubs. Arboretum maps are available.

DATES & HOURS: Year round, daily, dawn – dusk.

DIRECTIONS: *From Route 44/55 in Poughkeepsie* turn onto Raymond Avenue to the Main Gate.

Cedar Heights Orchard — William & Arvia Morris,

RHINEBECK, NY
Our garden begins with mixed borders of shrubs, perennials and annuals that connect the house with a pool pavilion. From there a mown path leads past a vegetable and cutting garden, through fields of wildflowers to a bridge spanning two ponds. This path continues into a woodland garden leading to five small ponds surrounded by extensive woodland plantings which were greatly expanded in 1998. The terrain of about ten acres is very diverse and is crowned by a hillside of orchards.

DATES & HOURS: September 12; 10 a.m. – 4 p.m.

DIRECTIONS: *From the Taconic State Parkway,* exit at Rhinebeck/Red Hook and take Route 199 west to the traffic light (approximately 4 miles). Take Route 308 straight for 2 miles to Cedar Heights Road on the right. Turn right and take the second right onto Crosby Lane. Take Crosby all the way to the dead end and into Cedar Heights Orchard. Please park in the barnyard and in marked areas.

Proceeds shared with Hudson River Heritage.

Amy Goldman, RHINEBECK, NY

Maps dated 1734 for the partitioning of the Great Nine Partners Patent, label this property as "bad" agricultural land. The landscape is wooded overall, with a scattering of open meadows. Situated on a large pond is the Abraham Traver house, a late eighteenth-century farmhouse with an irresistible presence. Improvements to the landscape include a terraced garden and pergola, an Alitex greenhouse, an Adirondack-style lean-to with views of the Catskills and two large gardens featuring heirloom vegetables.

DATES & HOURS: July 11; 10 a.m. – 4 p.m.

DIRECTIONS: *From the Taconic Parkway* take Bull's Head Road exit heading west towards Rhinebeck. Go 4.2 miles on Bulls Head (also known as Slate Quarry Road or County Route 19) until you see Mountain View Road on your left. Turn left and go 1.5 miles until you see 1000 feet of split-rail fence on your left and mailbox #313. Turn left into the driveway, go past the red buildings, .5 mile to the house.

Ellen & Eric Petersen, STANFORDVILLE, NY

This is a sprawling country garden maintained by enthusiastic weekend gardeners. We have been trying to add some structure and some shelter over the last few years with rocks, walls, and arbors. I try to blend the garden into its wild surroundings with vigorous native shrubs and perennials, such as bottlebrush buckeye, Joe Pye weed and butterfly weed. I like plants that seed in: feverfew, poppies, dill, chamomile, anise hyssop and native bleeding heart, bluebells, columbine, goldenrod, and white wood aster. They provide continuity and act as informal ground covers. I'm trying to plant for winter interest with beautiful bark and conifers; broad-leaved evergreens really struggle on this windy exposed site. I love yellow, purple, silver, and variegated foliage and any perennial that tops six feet.

DATES & HOURS: July 11; 10 a.m. – 2 p.m.

DIRECTIONS: *From Route 82 North,* pass firehouse in Stanfordville. Go 5 miles to Conklin Hill Road, turn right, go 2 miles up hill. The house is on the right after a sharp turn. Please pass the drive and pull into the field. The entrance will be marked.

Proceeds shared with The Rainforest Alliance.

Zibby & Jim Tozer, STANFORDVILLE, NY

The gardens at Uplands Farm are surrounded by rolling hills, horse paddocks with romping miniature horses, grand old trees, and a lush meadow of alfalfa. Among the gardens, the Romantic Garden, with its forget-me-nots and trape-zoidal loveseats by Madison Cox, is of special interest. The Wedding Folly, built in 1998, was inspired by the teahouses at Kykuit and has latticed walls and pagoda lanterns. Large arches, covered with William Baffen roses, create a path to the meadow. The Playhouse has a charming garden and its own rhubarb patch. The main garden is a seventy-foot-long herbaceous border filled with flowering perennials and grasses. Other smaller gardens dot the property. The enclosed cutting garden is filled with colorful annuals and tomatoes and squash.

DATES & HOURS: July 11; 10 a.m. – 2 p.m.

DIRECTIONS: From the Taconic State Parkway, take the Millbrook/Poughkeep-sie Exit. Turn right at the end of the ramp onto Route 44. Go about .2 mile. Turn left onto Route 82. Stay on Route 82 for about 8 miles. At the "Y" intersection i from of Stissing National Bank, bear right onto Route 65. Go 2 miles, passing Hunns Lake on your left. The main house is the third house past the lake on the right. Please park where indicated.

Proceeds shared with The Dutchess County Land Conservancy.

LAKE CHAMPLAIN AREA: *July 31, 1999*

Irwin Garden Farm, ESSEX, 10 A.M. – 2 P.M.

Woodland Gardens of Mr. & Mrs. Wynant D. Vanderpoel, KEENE VALLEY, 2 P.M. – 6 P.M.

PLEASE NOTE: *The following gardens in Vermont are participating as part of the Lake Champlain Open Day.*

Converse Bay Farm, CHARLOTTE, VT, 10 A.M. – 4 P.M., *page 387*

Robin Price & Robert Coleburn — The Gardens at Golden Apple Orchard, CHARLOTTE, VT, 10 A.M.. – 4 P.M., *page 387*

The Gardens of Peter Morris & Pennie Beach, West Ferrisburgh, VT, 10 A.M. – 4 P.M., *page 389*

❖ Colonial Garden at Adirondack History Center,

ELIZABETHTOWN, NY. (518) 873-6466.

A formal garden adjacent to the Adirondack Center Museum, the Colonial Garden borrows brick paving and walls, decorative fencing and gates, a summer house, fountain and sundial from Colonial Gardens of Williamsburg. A formal arrangement of hedges, flowering trees, shrubs, and perennials enclose the annual borders that are planted and maintained by the Essex County Adirondack Garden Club.

DATES & HOURS: Year round, daily, dawn to dusk.

DIRECTIONS: *Northway (I-87)* to Exit 31. Proceed west on 9N approximately 4 miles to Elizabethtown. Turn left at the flashing light. Take the first left onto Church Street. *From Essex Ferry via Westport:* Exit the ferry parking lot. Turn left onto Route 9 and proceed south (the road is also called Lake Shore Drive in Westport). At the stop sign, turn left. Turn right onto Sisco. Follow to stop sign. Bear right (fair-grounds are on your right) onto 9N and continue past Westport Depot to I-87. Continue as above.

Irwin Farm Garden, ESSEX, NY

This garden surrounds a late 1800s farm house. Perennial beds on the south, east, and west form a floral setting on a site overlooking Lake Champlain. A patio planted with hardy azaleas, Russian sage, and herbs graces the approach to the house. A bed of peonies lies on the east side of the lawn. North of the house there is a vegetable garden and a nursery of shrubs.

DATES & HOURS: July 31; 10 a.m. – 2 p.m.

DIRECTIONS: *From the ferry* turn left and follow the lake road south 2.6 miles turning at the first major crossroad onto Whallons Bay Road. Proceed west to the first major driveway on the right, "Irwin Farm." Park behind the garden shed (corn crib).

Woodland Gardens of
Mr. & Mrs. Wynant D. Vanderpoel, KEENE VALLEY, NY

Overlooking an alpine brook with a scenic mountain view and framed by a stand of towering white pines, the gardens cascade down three levels displaying mixed shrub and perennial beds with annual borders. Flower colors range from blue, purple, white, and deep pink to chartreuse and burgundy shrubs.

DATES & HOURS: July 31; 2 p.m. – 6 p.m.

DIRECTIONS: *From Northway (Route 87)* take Exit 31, Route 9N, west through Elizabethtown to intersection with Route 73. Go left on Route 73 to Keene Valley, approximately 3 miles. Take a right onto Adirondack Street just past the Ausable Inn, also on the right. Go up Adirondack Street (turns into Interbrook Road) 1 mile. Do not bear off the street. The house is on the left at Camp Comfort sign.

❖ The Depot Theatre Gardens, WESTPORT, NY

Framing the Westport landmark railroad station, which underwent major restoration in 1997-1998, are flower beds with a mixture of annuals, perennials, and shrubs. The station, also known as the Depot Theatre, seats 135 for its summer season equity actor's performances between mid-June and mid-September. Overlooking Lake Champlain, the site is truly unique.

DATES & HOURS: June – September, daily, dawn – dusk.

DIRECTIONS: *From the Northway (I-87)* take Exit 31. Go east on Route 9N approximately 3 miles until 9N passes under railroad tracks. Westport Railroad Station, aka The Depot Theatre, is on the right on the west side of the tracks. *From the town of Westport,* take Route 9N west approximately 2 miles until 9N passes under the railroad tracks. Westport Railroad Station is on the left on the west side of the tracks.

ORANGE COUNTY: *May 16, 1999*

Cedar House — Garden of Dr. Margaret Johns & Peter Stern, MOUNTAINVILLE,
10 A.M. – 6 P.M.

Cedar House — Garden of Dr. Margaret Johns & Peter Stern, MOUNTAINVILLE, NY

Mixed perennial borders, "enhanced" meadows, informal flowerbeds,specimen trees, berries, lilacs, tree peonies, old clipped boxwood, espaliered fruit trees, and a white wisteria-draped pergola are connected by stone walls, trellises, and grass paths. The garden overlooks 200 acres of orchard, farmland, and dog-wood-rich forest, as well as the Hudson Highlands to the east and the Moodna Valley to the west.

DATES & HOURS: May 16; 10 a.m. – 6 p.m.

DIRECTIONS: From the New York State Thruway/I-87 North, take Exit 16/Harriman/Monroe. Turn right onto Route 32. Travel north for 10 miles to the green metal bridge. Cross the bridge and immediately turn left onto Orrs Mills Road. Take the third left onto Otterkill Road. Follow Otterkill Road .6 mile to Anders Lane (the driveway on the right). Go up the driveway to the house. From the Hudson Valley & Connecticut, travel west on I-84 cross the Newburgh-Beacon Bridge. Take Exit 10 South. Travel south on Route 32 for 7 miles. Before you cross the green metal bridge, turn right onto Orrs Mills Road. Take the third left onto Otterkill Road. Follow Otterkill Road .6 mile to Anders Lane (the driveway on the right). Go up the driveway to the house.

Proceeds shared with The Cornwall Garden Club.

❖ Storm King Art Center & Mountainville Conservancy, OLD PLEASANT HILL ROAD, MOUNTAINVILLE, NY 10953. (914) 543-3423.

Surrounded by the undulating profiles of the Hudson Highlands, this museum celebrates the relationship between sculpture and nature. Five hundred acres of lawns, maple allees, terraces, fields, and woodlands provide the site for more than wildflowers are being introduced, alongside magnificent rhododendrons, dogwood, and specimen trees.

DATES & HOURS: April through November, daily, 11 a.m. – 5 p.m.

DIRECTIONS: *From the New York State Thruway/I-87 North,* take Exit 16/Harriman/Monroe. Turn right onto Route 32. Travel north for 10 miles. Follow signs to Storm King Art Center. From the Hudson Valley & Connecticut, travel west on I-84 cross the Newburgh-Beacon Bridge. Take Exit 10 South. Travel south on Route 32 for 7 miles. Follow signs to Storm King Art Center.

❖ Anna B. Warner Memorial Garden,

CONSTITUTION ISLAND AT THE UNITED STATES MILITARY ACADEMY, WEST POINT, NY 10996. (914) 446-8676.

Old-fashioned perennial and annual border garden lining a fifty-yard path. Planted in nineteenth-century style with flowers described by Anna Warner in her book Gardening by Myself *written in 1872. Cared for by dedicated volunteers, this garden received the Burlington House Award. Tours to Constitution Island are available on Wednesdays and Thursdays, mid-June to September. Reservations required.*

DATES & HOURS: Mid-June to October, Wednesday and Thursday afternoons.

DIRECTIONS: *From the south,* take Route 9W or Palisades Parkway to Bear Mountain Bridge Circle. Go 2 miles north on 9W, then take Route 218 through Highland Falls to West Point. After Hotel Thayer take first road right (Williams Road) down hill. Cross railroad tracks. Park north of South Dock. *From the north,* take Route 9W. Take first sign to West Point. Drive through West Point on Thayer Road. After road goes under stone bridge, take first road left (Williams Road) down hill. Follow as above.

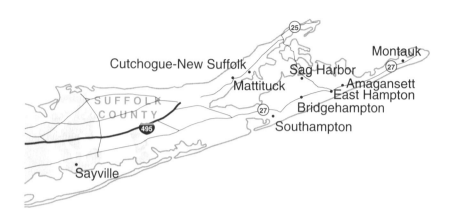

SUFFOLK COUNTY/EASTERN LONG ISLAND:

May 1, 1999

Mrs. Manfred Lee, CUTCHOGUE, 10 A.M. – 4 P.M.

Dianne Benson, EAST HAMPTON, 10 A.M. – 2 P.M.

Margaret Kerr & Robert Richenberg, EAST HAMPTON, 10 A.M. – 4 P.M.

❖ LongHouse Reserve, EAST HAMPTON, 10 A.M. – 2 P.M.

Ann Stanwell & Emily Cobb, EAST HAMPTON, 2 P.M. – 6 P.M.

Richard Kahn & Elaine Peterson, MONTAUK, 10 A.M. – 4 P.M.

June 19, 1999

Tina Raver & Chris Meltesen, BRIDGEHAMPTON, 10 A.M. – 2 P.M.

❖ Bridge Gardens Trust, BRIDGEHAMPTON, 2 P.M. – 6 P.M.

Mrs. Manfred Lee, CUTCHOGUE, 10 A.M. – 4 P.M.

Alice & Charles Levien's Garden, CUTCHOGUE, 10 A.M. – 2 P.M.

Margaret Kerr & Robert Richenberg, EAST HAMPTON, 10 A.M. – 4 P.M.

Ann Stanwell & Emily Cobb, EAST HAMPTON, 2 P.M. – 6 P.M.

Kathe & Bob Levenson, EAST HAMPTON, 10 A.M. – 2 P.M.

Mary Riley Smith, SAGAPONACK, 10 A.M. – 2 P.M.

Mr. & Mrs. Robert Meltzer, SOUTHAMPTON, 10 A.M – 2 P.M.

Milford Garden, SOUTHOLD, 10 A.M. – 2 P.M.

SUFFOLK COUNTY/EASTERN LONG ISLAND:

July 17, 1999

Ngaere Macray & David Seeler, AMAGANSETT, 10 A.M. – 4 P.M.

❖ Bridge Gardens Trust, BRIDGEHAMPTON, 2 P.M. – 6 P.M.

Alice & Charles Levien's Garden, CUTCHOGUE, 10 A.M. – 2 P.M.

Dianne Benson, EAST HAMPTON, 10 A.M. – 2 P.M.

Ina Garten, EAST HAMPTON, 10 A.M. – 2 P.M.

Carol Mercer, EAST HAMPTON, 10 A.M. – 4 P.M.

Bob & Mimi Schwarz, EAST HAMPTON, 10 A.M. – 2 P.M.

❖ LongHouse Reserve, EAST HAMPTON, 10 A.M. – 2 P.M.

Maurice Isaac & Ellen Coster Isaac, MATTITUCK, 10 A.M. – 2 P.M.

Dennis Schrader & Bill Smith, MATTITUCK, 10 A.M. – 6 P.M.

Richard Kahn & Elaine Peterson, MONTAUK, 10 A.M. – 4 P.M.

Susan & Louis Meisel, SAGAPONACK, 10 A.M. – 2 P.M.

Mac Keith Griswold, SAG HARBOR, 10 A.M. – 4 P.M.

Dr. & Mrs. William L. Donnelly, SOUTHAMPTON, 10 A.M. – 4 P.M.

Mack & Nancye Radmin, SOUTHOLD, 10 A.M. – 4 P.M.

September 18, 1999

❖ Bridge Gardens Trust, BRIDGEHAMPTON, 2 P.M. – 6 P.M.

Dianne Benson, EAST HAMPTON, 10 A.M. – 2 P.M.

Ira & Calista Washburn, EAST HAMPTON, 10 A.M. – 2 P.M.

Dennis Schrader & Bill Smith, Mattituck, 10 A.M. – 6 P.M.

Mary Riley Smith, SAGAPONACK, 10 A.M. – 2 P.M.

Lois Beachy Underhill, SAG HARBOR. 2 P.M. – 6 P.M.

Ngaere Macray & David Seeler at The Bayberry,
AMAGANSETT, NY

Four simple gardens surround the house. Unconnected to each other, they were planned to extend the interior living space into the outdoors. They include a garden of hollyhocks with shrubs and vines, a shaded courtyard leading to a terrace overlooking a wildflower meadow, a cutting flower garden, and an enclosed courtyard and pool.

DATES & HOURS: July 17; 10 a.m. – 4 p.m.

DIRECTIONS: *From Montauk Highway/Route 27,* go 2 miles past East Hampton village. Look for Honest Diner and Bayberry Nursery on the right. Turn right into Bayberry Drive and go to the house directly behind the nursery. Please park at the house.

Proceeds shared with The Madoo Conservancy.

Tina Raver & Chris Meltesen, BRIDGEHAMPTON, NY

The early American farmhouse is surrounded by an acre of informal gardens. Some trial plantings of unusual plants influence Tina's design for her clients. The rose garden is Chris' favorite, while Tina tends to focus on the perennial beds, the pond, a small woodland garden, and the flowering meadow. The guest cottage is a small haven unto itself, surrounded by scented lavender.

DATES & HOURS: June 19; 10 a.m. – 2 p.m.

DIRECTIONS: *Heading east on Route 27* after leaving Watermill, pass the "Milk Pail" apple stand on the left and take the next right onto Mecox Road. Continue for 1.1 miles to #507 Mecox Road. It is a gray shingle farmhouse directly opposite Paul's Lane.

Proceeds shared with The Madoo Conservancy.

❖ **Bridge Gardens Trust,** 36 MITCHELL LANE, P.O. BOX 1194,
BRIDGEHAMPTON, NY 11932. (516) 537-7440.

*The gardens on these five acres were designed and installed by Jim Kilpatric and
Harry Neyens. They include a formal knot surrounded by herbal beds; perennial
mounds; topiaries; specimen trees; expansive lawns; aquatic plantings; woodland
walks; a bamboo "room;" a lavender parterre; and hundreds of roses. A 750-foot
double row of privet hedge — with fifteen viewing ports in its fifteen-foot-high
walls — encloses a pavilion-like garden house (not open to the public). Bridge
Gardens Trust, a charitable foundation, was created in 1997 to preserve the
gardens and to encourage the accumulation of gardening knowledge.*

DATES & HOURS: Saturdays, 2 p.m. − 6 p.m., from late May to late September.
Open for *Open Days Directory* visitors on June 19, July 17, and September 18.

DIRECTIONS: *From the Montauk Highway/Route 27,* go to Bridgehampton. At
the blinking traffic light at the western edge of the village, turn left onto Butter
Lane. Go .25 mile and under the railroad bridge; turn left immediately onto
Mitchell Lane. Bridge Gardens, #36, is the first driveway on the left. Please park
along Mitchell Lane.

Manfred & Roberta Lee, CUTCHOGUE, NY

*Located in the village of Cutchogue, these two and one-half acres of gardens
complement the Victorian house and the outbuildings. Four large tulip trees
punctuate the front lawn. Deep perennial gardens surround the property. Mature
azaleas, rhododendrons, roses, hydrangeas and lilacs are spread throughout the
garden. There are unusual conifers and Japanese maples as well as golden chain
trees.*

DATES & HOURS: May 1, June 19; 10 a.m. − 4 p.m.

DIRECTIONS: *Take the Long Island Expressway* to Exit 73 for Route 58 which
leads into Route 25. Continue to Cutchogue. We are five houses past the North
Fork Country Club on the right (south) side of Route 25, #26850 Main Road.

Alice & Charles Levien's Garden, CUTCHOGUE, NY

This garden is designed for living – children, grandchildren, guests, frequent outdoor parties. A two-acre mixed border and woodland garden has been planted to provide year-round privacy, continuous blooms in season, many-faceted views, and tranquility during winter. Multilevel decks with a variety of container plantings serve the main house, guest houses, elevated gazebo and pool and children's playhouse. Occasional salt water flooding from a Peconic Bay creek made the swimming pool, fish pond, lotus pond, and lawn areas a creative challenge for the designer, Alice Levien.

DATES & HOURS: June 19, July 17; 10 a.m. – 2 p.m.

DIRECTIONS: *Traveling east on Route 25,* turn right at the second traffic light in Cutchogue, Eugene's Road. Turn right at Beebe Road. Bear right at the fork in the road and Antler Lane is the first street on the right. Look for a hemlock hedge. Please park along the road.

Proceeds shared with The Horticultural Alliance of the Hamptons.

Dianne Benson, EAST HAMPTON, NY

There are no annuals, no vegetables, and no bedding plants here. Dianne has removed herself from the fashion world, where she was known as Dianne B., and applied her taste to a very personal garden. It is a mélange of color coordination, texture variation, idiosyncratic plants, and a chamber-like backdrop for an assemblage of statuary and other treasures that has been culled from around the world. This continually evolving acre totally engages its gardener twelve months a year. Not only is there the endless search for distinguished and exotic plants, but the rigors of caring for a high-summer tropical garden in Zone 6 are non-stop. Many gorgeous specimen trees too.

DATES & HOURS: May 1, July 17, September 18; 10 a.m. – 2 p.m.

DIRECTIONS: *From the Montauk Highway/Route 27* you will pass signs for the Town of East Hampton, then the Village of East Hampton. At the blinking light (Georgica Getty station on the left), turn right onto Baiting Hollow Road. On the second corner on the right, #6 Baiting Hollow, you will find the garden. Please park on adjacent roads and NOT against the direction of traffic (East Hampton police adore giving tickets for that).

Proceeds shared with The Watermill Center, Byrd Hoffman Foundation.

Cobb & Stanwell Garden, SPRINGS, EAST HAMPTON, NY

An informal cottage garden, its landscaping has occurred by chance and whim. In the spring all of the flowerbeds are filled with tulips and a few choice daffodils, which give way to perennials such as you might see in an English cottage garden, with an assortment of annuals. The driveway and the woods are scattered with countless varieties of daffodils. The graves of our pets are planted as little individual gardens.

DATES & HOURS: May 1, June 19; 2 p.m. – 6 p.m.

DIRECTIONS: *From the Montauk Highway/Route 27,* go east through the village of Amagansett, past the firehouse on your left. The Amagansett Railroad station will appear on the left, and a Railroad Crossing sign ahead. Bear left at the sign, cross the tracks and turn left immediately onto Old Stone Highway. The golf course is on the right. After 1.5 miles from the railroad crossing, there is a fork. Keep left. Pass St. Peter's Chapel on the right and after just under 1 mile there is another fork with a sign that reads "Louse Point Road." Keep left on the Old Stone Highway for .4 mile. Number 239 will be on the right just after a stockade fence and driveway. Number 239 is displayed on a big wooden gate. The house is 2.8 miles from the railroad crossing. Please park on Old Stone Highway outside of the gate.

Proceeds shared with The Horticultural Alliance of the Hamptons.

Ina Garten, EAST HAMPTON, NY

This garden, designed by Edwina von Gal, is arranged in squares like a kitchen garden, but is planted with perennials, annuals, roses, vegetables and herbs. It includes a crab apple orchard and rose and hydrangea gardens and is designed to feel like a traditional East Hampton garden.

DATES & HOURS: July 17; 10 a.m. – 2 p.m.

DIRECTIONS: *From the pond in East Hampton,* go north on Route 114 towards Sag Harbor. This is called Buell Lane. The house is third on the left, #23, past the field. Park on the street.

Margaret Kerr & Robert Richenburg, EAST HAMPTON, NY

The garden, designed by Kerr, surrounds their house and studios on two acres that extend down to the wetlands of Accabonac Harbor. Kerr's brick rug sculptures, inspired by tribal Middle Eastern carpets, are placed throughout the garden. One of them, a brick prayer rug, lies in a contemplative glade below the studios. Kerr collects plants grown in the Middle Ages in a courtyard around a fountain and lily pool highlighted with espaliered pear trees. In the spring drifts of thousands of daffodils bloom in the fields around the house and are left unmowed until late fall. Native grasses and wildflowers make islands of meadow during the summer.

DATES & HOURS: May 1, June 19; 10 a.m. – 4 p.m.

DIRECTIONS: *From Montauk Highway/Route 27,* turn left at light in East Hampton. Pass town pond. Continue .9 mile past next traffic light, taking immediate left onto North Main Street. Pass windmill on the right. Go .3 mile, bearing right at fork onto Springs Fireplace Road. Go 5 miles. The driveway is marked by mailbox #1006. Please park along Springs Fireplace Road, and walk down dirt road to second house on the left.

Proceeds shared with The Horticultural Alliance of the Hamptons.

Kathe & Bob Levenson, EAST HAMPTON, NY

While the emphasis is on roses (there is a separate "rose department") there are two perennial borders that have lots of everything, including roses. One highlight is an arbor of four ginkgos with roses and clematis growing through it, which is why June is prime time.

DATES & HOURS: June 19; 10 a.m. – 2 p.m.

DIRECTIONS: *From Montauk Highway/Route 27,* follow east through the village of East Hampton. Go straight to traffic light at Egypt Lane. Go 1 mile, bearing right onto Skimhampton Road. Go .3 mile to Marley Lane. The house, #20, is at the dead end. Please park on Skimhampton Road.

Carol Mercer, EAST HAMPTON, NY

An undeniable partnering of pattern, movement, and color, makes this garden seem to glow and come alive. Mercer and her partner, Lisa Verderosa, have a thriving garden design business called The Secret Garden, and they have received several gold medals at New York City flower shows. The garden was a cover story in Garden Design *magazine. It appeared in* Better Homes and Gardens *magazine,* Design Times *magazine,* Time/Life book series' Beds and Borders, Gardening Weekends, *and* Shade Gardening, *as well as in* Martha Stewart Living, The Natural Shade Garden *and* Seaside Gardening. *It was also featured in* Newsday '99.

DATES & HOURS: July 17; 10 a.m. – 4 p.m.

DIRECTIONS: *From Montauk Highway/Route 27,* follow east through Water Mill, Bridgehampton, and Wainscott to East Hampton. At traffic light at head of pond, turn right onto Ocean Avenue. The house, #33, is fourth on the left. The white stone driveway is marked by a small gray sign. Please park as directed.

Proceeds shared with East End Hospice Inc.

Bob & Mimi Schwarz, EAST HAMPTON, NY

An explosion of color! The rainbow daylily garden is a sight to see in mid-July. More than six hundred named varieties of daylilies grow in undulating herbaceous borders, backed by cedars, hemlocks and masses of rhododendrons. More than five thousand of our own seedlings bloom in the seedling patch. There is also an ornamental grass garden with clumps of miscanthus, panicum and other grasses. The entire garden has inviting benches and shade.

DATES & HOURS: July 17; 10 a.m. – 2 p.m.

DIRECTIONS: *From Montauk Highway/Route 27*, go to East Hampton. Pass movie theater and continue to traffic light. Turn left after the light, going under the railroad bridge, leaving windmill on right. Continue .5 mile, bearing right at fork, onto Springs/County Road 41. Go 3 miles and turn right on Hildreth Place. At end, turn left onto Accabonac. Go .25 mile and turn right onto Lilla Lane. The house, #8, is 200 yards down on the right. Please park on street.

Ira & Calista Washburn, EAST HAMPTON, NY

The garden is small and informal and filled with a wide variety of unusual plants collected from near and far, many started from seed. A spectacular, three-story, espaliered pear tree dominates the terrace. A large lath house provides shade for young plants.

DATES & HOURS: September 18; 10 a.m. – 2 p.m.

DIRECTIONS: *From Montauk Highway/Route 27,* go to downtown East Hampton. From the flagpole on the Green, take Dunemere Lane, which becomes Further Lane past the golf course. Continue up hill to Windmill Lane. The house (#23) is the sixth drive on the left. Please park on Windmill Lane.

❖ LongHouse Reserve, 133 HANDS CREEK RD., EAST HAMPTON, NY 11937. (516) 329-3568. WWW.HAMPTONS.COM/LONGHOUSE

Sixteen acres of gardens are punctuated with contemporary sculpture. Landscape features include a pond, numerous allées and walks, a dune garden, and a 1,000-foot hemlock hedge that follows boundaries of farm fields that occupied the site until it was abandoned for agricultural use in the nineteenth century. There are collections of bamboo and grasses, 200 varieties of daffodils with more than one million blooms, and numerous irises, conifers, and broadleaf evergreens. The large new house (not open to the public) was inspired by the seventh-century Shinto shrine at Ise, Japan. LongHouse Reserve was established in 1991 to reflect founder Jack Lenor Larsen's professional interests and his desire to encourage creativity in gardening, collecting and everyday living with art. A majestic twenty-five-feet-tall, thirty-three-feet-in diameter Fly's Eye Dome by Buckminster Fuller has been added to a selection of almost fifty sculptures throughout the gardens.

DATES & HOURS: May through mid-September, Wednesdays and 1st & 3rd Saturdays. Open for *Directory* visitors on May 1 & July 17, 10 a.m. – 2 p.m.

DIRECTIONS: *From East Hampton Village,* turn onto Newtown Lane from the intersection at Main. Go to Cooper Street, turn right and go to the end. Turn left onto Cedar Street and bear right at fork in the road onto Hands Creek Road. Go .7 mile to #133 on the left.

❖ Rachel's Garden of the East Hampton Historical Society, 101 MAIN STREET, EAST HAMPTON, NY 11937. (516) 324-6850.

Located on the landmark eighteenth-century Mulford Farm, Rachel's Garden, an authentic "period setting" garden (circa 1790) was created by Isabel Furlaud and the Garden Club of East Hampton. The dooryard garden is planted with more than 126 heirloom seeds and plants grouped according to use (medicinal, edible, dyes, housekeeping). An eight-page self-guided tour is available.

DATES & HOURS: Year round, daily, dawn – dusk.

DIRECTIONS: *Mulford farm is located* in the heart of the historic district, across James Lane from the village green next door to the Guild Hall Museum on Route 27.

Maurice Isaac & Ellen Coster Isaac, MATTITUCK, NY

This early-1900s country farmhouse has been designed with two major borders incorporating extensive plantings of unusual combinations of bulbs, perennials, trees, shrubs, and annuals. A pond well stocked with koi and water plants adds a beautiful and soothing touch. A path leads you to a newly designed swimming pool and planting and to an old restored barn adjacent to an arbor planted with wisteria, clematis, and several vines offering tranquility, shade, and a view of the extensive nearby farm fields.

DATES & HOURS: July 17; 10 a.m. – 2 p.m.

DIRECTIONS: *Take the Long Island Expressway* to the last exit, Exit 73 for Route 58. Take Route 58 to Route 25. Go through the town of Mattituck past Love Lane to Wickham Avenue. Turn left on Wickham, go past the train tracks and traffic light. Stay straight on Wickham and it will turn into Grand Avenue. Take Grand Avenue about .25 mile to East Mill. Turn right onto East Mill, keeping to the left, and this will turn into Oregon Road. Look for signs for parking.

Dennis Schrader & Bill Smith, MATTITUCK, NY.

Set in the heart of the north fork wineries, the two-plus-acre garden surrounds a restored 1850 farmhouse. The gardens are encircled by fourteen acres of fields. There are perennial borders, ponds, a rustic arbor, a hosta collection, and many groupings of container plantings. We make extensive use of annuals, tender perennials, and tropicals in our landscape.

DATES & HOURS: July 17, September 18; 10 a.m. – 6 p.m.

DIRECTIONS: *Take the Long Island Expressway* to the last exit, Exit 73 for Route 58. Take Route 58 to Route 25. Go through the town of Mattituck past Love Lane to Wickham Avenue. Turn left on Wickham, go past the train tracks and traffic light. Stay straight on Wickham and it will turn into Grand avenue. Take Grand Avenue about .25 mile to East Mill. Turn left onto East Mill and look for #1200. Please park along the street.

Proceeds shared with The Horticultural Alliance of the Hamptons.

Richard Kahn & Elaine Peterson, MONTAUK, NY

Stately old oaks and maples frame our three-acre property on Lake Montauk. The gardens meander around a romantic brick and shingle Tudor house built in 1930. A diversity of species reveals itself in collections of hosta, heath and heather, conifers, broadleaf evergreens, alpines and iris. An upper garden contains herbs, a potager and various flowering shrubs and trees, beyond which is a meadow with a mowed labyrinth. All plants are chosen for their ability to withstand the persistent challenges of heavy wind and salt spray. Year-round residents, we design and maintain the gardens ourselves, with deference to the ecology of the lake.

DATES & HOURS: May 1, July 17; 10 a.m. – 4 p.m.

DIRECTIONS: *From Montauk Highway/Route 27* go past the village of Montauk about 1 mile. Turn left at West Lake Drive (signs for Montauk Harbor, Route 77, Montauk Downs). The house, #224, is 1.2 miles on your right. Please park along the road, not on the grass.

Susan & Louis Meisel, SAGAPONACK, NY

Our property encompasses more than 100 specimen trees, with a focus on special beeches. I use flower color of several hundred perennials as if it were paint on canvas to create the visual effects I enjoy seeing.

DATES & HOURS: July 17; 10 a.m. – 2 p.m.

DIRECTIONS: *From Montauk Highway/Route 27,* go to intersection at Sagg Main Street. Turn south. Go past the red schoolhouse on right and the general store. Turn left on Hedges Lane. Go .5 mile and take the next left onto Wilkes Lane. The house, #81, is the second house on the right. Please park along the road.

Mary Riley Smith, SAGAPONACK, NY

The entrance of the house exhibits a small garden with several perennial/annual borders, two shrub/perennial borders, and a small cottage garden. The mood is loose and romantic, blending into the agricultural landscape of the area.

DATES & HOURS: June 19, September 18; 10 a.m. – 2 p.m.

DIRECTIONS: *From Montauk Highway/Route 27,* travel east 1 mile past monument in Bridgehampton. Turn right at light onto Sagg Main Street, (South Fork Realty on corner). Go .9 mile. The house, #444, is on the left across from the school. Please park along the road.

Proceeds shared with The Horticultural Society of New York.

❖ **Madoo Conservancy,** 618 MAIN STREET, P.O. BOX 362,
SAGAPONACK, NY 11962. (516) 537-8200.

This two-acre garden is a virtual compendium of major garden styles, including oriental bridge, a box-edged potager, a Renaissance-perspective rose walk, a knot garden, laburnum arbor, hermit's hut and a grass garden, as well as an Italianate courtyard and a user-friendly maze. It is fountained, rilled and pooled. It is noted for its bold and innovative pruning techniques and striking colors (a gazebo is in three shades of mauve). Sculptures are by Matisse, Bourdelle, and Soriano. Rare trees and plants abound. A copse of fastigiate ginkos rises above box balls like the handles of mallets about to strike boules or hedgehogs. A staircase going nowhere is another of its whimsical features. The garden has been much published.

DATES & HOURS: May through September, Wednesdays and Saturdays, 1 p.m. – 5 p.m. Admission is $10. Tours of 10 or more may be arranged at other times.

DIRECTIONS: *From the Long Island Expressway,* take Exit 70 and follow signs to Montauk. Sagaponack is on Route 27, 1 mile east of Bridgehampton. Make a right at the traffic light (the first light east of Bridgehampton on Route 27). The Madoo Conservancy is a little over 1 mile from the highway and is three driveways after the post office on the right.

Mac Keith Griswold, SAG HARBOR, NY

This village garden is composed of three parts. The front yard greets visitors and protects our privacy with a privet hedge and picket and lattice fences covered with irises and roses. The square side garden is a full-sun, hot micro-climate filled with experiments — how much drought can these plants stand? Figs, Rosa banksia *'Lutea' and* Rosa chinensis *'Mutabilis' grow in side beds. Behind the house is a forty-foot long perennial border fourteen feet deep planted in four bays. At the end of the lawn, two mulberries make an arch over the garden shed, and under our neighbor's privet hedge, a shade bed surrounds an old 'Clapp's Favorite' pear tree.*

DATES & HOURS: July 17, 10 a.m. – 4 p.m.

DIRECTIONS: *From Montauk Highway/Route 27,* travel to Bridgehampton. Take the Sag Harbor Turnpike north 5 miles to Sag Harbor. On entering town, pass the Cove Deli on the right and Bayview Street on the left. Take the next left onto Howard Street. The house, #57, is the third from the end on the left. Please park on the street or in the municipal parking lot behind Main Street.

Lois Beachy Underhill, SAG HARBOR, NY

A series of brick paths and terraces are bordered by beds planted for year-round foliage color. Pink flowers echo the soft tones of the old bricks. The south and west terraces overlook the harbor. An old granite retaining wall built from ships' ballast forms an "L" around the south corner of the house. Its border emphasizes blues and yellows. The outlying hillside includes old apple trees, a nineteenth-century chestnut, lilacs, grapevines, as well as the more recent plantings of an orchard, a bamboo allée, and a series of boundary borders.

DATES & HOURS: September 18; 2 p.m. – 6 p.m.

DIRECTIONS: *From Montauk Highway/Route 27,* go to Bridgehampton. At the monument, take the Sag Harbor-Bridgehampton Turnpike to Sag Harbor. From Main Street, continue to Long Wharf. Turn right onto Bay Street. Go through blinker, past harbor and yacht yard on left. The house, #68, is a two-story shingle structure on the right. From East Hampton, turn onto Route 114 towards Sag Harbor and follow directions above. Please park along Bay Street.

Proceeds shared with The Committee for Sag Harbor's Old Burying Ground.

❖ Meadow Croft — The John E. Roosevelt Estate,

MIDDLE ROAD, SAYVILLE, NY 11701. (516) 472-9395.

This nature preserve, consisting of seventy-five acres of woods and tidal wetlands, was the summer home of John E. Roosevelt, a first cousin of President Theodore Roosevelt. The privet-and-lattice-enclosed "kitchen garden" adjacent to the Colonial Revival home was planted and maintained by the Bayport Heritage Association and contains plant material that would have been available in 1910, the year to which the house is restored. Included are twenty-four varieties of heirloom roses, heirloom vegetables, annuals, and more than sixty varieties of perennials.

DATES & HOURS: June 20 through October 24, Sundays, noon – 5 p.m. Closed July 4, September 5, & October 10.

DIRECTIONS: *Take Sunrise Highway/Route 27* to Lakeland-Ocean Avenue (CR 93) and exit southbound. Proceed south on Lakeland-Ocean Avenue for approximately 2 miles to Main Street. Make a left onto Main Street and immediately bear right to South Main Street/Middle Road. Continue on Middle Road for .5 mile and make a left at estate entrance.

Dr. & Mrs. William L. Donnelly, SOUTHAMPTON, NY

This informal one-acre garden was designed, planted, and maintained by the owners. It features unusual plants, many that are grown from seed and cuttings.

DATES & HOURS: July 17; 10 a.m. – 4 p.m.

DIRECTIONS: *From the west,* take Route 27 to Southampton College Exit. Turn right (south) and go one block. Turn left (east) onto Montauk Highway which becomes Hill Street after passing blinking light. Turn right at the third street, Halsey Neck Lane. After second stop sign, turn left onto Meadowmere Lane. The house, #156, is on the corner of Halsey Neck Lane and Meadowmere Lane. Please park on Meadowmere Lane.

Mr. & Mrs. Robert Meltzer, SOUTHAMPTON, NY

Our garden has developed since 1987 and consists of a sculpted lawn and woodland walk designed by A.E. Bye. Since 1990 Edwina von Gal has consulted with us on an herb garden, a rose garden, wildflower meadows, and numerous shrub and flower borders.

DATES & HOURS: June 19; 10 a.m. – 2 p.m.

DIRECTIONS: *From Montauk Highway/Route 27,* take Exit 7/Southampton College. Turn right, go over railroad tracks, and continue to end. At stop sign, turn left onto Montauk Highway, which becomes Hill Street. Go approximately 1.7 miles; turn right onto Halsey Neck Lane. At second stop sign, turn left onto Great Plains Road. Take first right onto Cooper's Neck Lane. The house, #137, is the third on the left. Sign on white gate reads "RMM." Please park along Cooper's Neck Lane.

Milford Garden, SOUTHOLD, NY

Our garden is an integral part of our old farmhouse, barn, and field complex. We have a little pond, a number of perennial gardens, a rose garden, a vegetable garden, an orchard, and an herb and cutting garden.

DATES & HOURS: June 19; 10 a.m. – 2 p.m.

DIRECTIONS: *Located between the hamlets of Peconic and Southold,* just off of Route 25 on Bay View Road. Turn at the Gulf Station and drive .3 mile until you reach the Indian Museum on the right. We are the next house, #1200. Please park along the road.

Mack & Nancye Radmin, SOUTHOLD, NY

A seaside location with informal plantings of perennials, annuals and roses. The upper garden is accented with stone containers overflowing with blooming annuals. The lower gardens are terraced with plants and grasses that Nancye has cultivated over the years with an emphasis on plant material which blooms heavily and withstands salt spray and wind.

DATES & HOURS: July 17; 10 a.m. – 4 p.m.

DIRECTIONS: *From east or west* go to Town of Southold. Then take Oaklawn Avenue to first stop sign, which is Pinencak Road. Make a left and go 5 blocks to North Bayview — make right, cross over small bridge — water is on your left. Immediately after bridge on left is North Park Drive. The house is on the left, #1415.

WESTCHESTER & PUTNAM COUNTIES:

April 25, 1999

John & Penelope Maynard, BEDFORD, 10 A.M – 4 P.M.

Judy & Michael Steinhardt, MOUNT KISCO, 10 A.M. – 4 P.M.

May 2, 1999

Mr. & Mrs. Coleman Burke, BEDFORD, 10 A.M. – 4 P.M.

Cross River House, KATONAH, 10 A.M. – 2 P.M.

May 16, 1999

Cobamong Pond, ARMONK, 10 A.M. – 6 P.M.

John & Penelope Maynard, BEDFORD, 10 A.M. – 4 P.M.

Phillis Warden, BEDFORD HILLS, 10 A.M. – 4 P.M.

❖ Stonecrop, COLD SPRING, 10 A.M. – 6 P.M.

Cross River House, KATONAH, 10 A.M. – 2 P.M.

❖ The Wildflower Island at Teatown Lake Reservation, OSSINING,
    10 A.M. – 4 P.M.

WESTCHESTER & PUTNAM COUNTIES:

May 29, 1999
Henriette Suhr, MOUNT KISCO, 2 P.M. — 6 P.M.
For additional garden tour on May 30 see, Peonies at Poverty Hollow.

June 13, 1999
Mrs. John C. Sluder, ARMONK, 10 A.M. — 2 P.M.
Ann Catchpole–Howell, BEDFORD, 10 A.M. — 4 P.M.
Phillis Warden, BEDFORD HILLS, 10 A.M. — 4 P.M.
Vivian & Ed Merrin, CORTLANDT MANOR, 10 A.M — 2 P.M.
Cross River House, KATONAH, 10 A.M — 2 P.M.
Roxana Robinson, KATONAH, 10 A.M — 4 P.M.
Page Dickey, NORTH SALEM, 10 A.M. — 4 P.M.
Keeler Hill Farm Gardens, NORTH SALEM, 10 A.M. — 6 P.M.

June 27, 1999
❖ Stonecrop, COLD SPRING, 10 A.M. — 6 P.M.
Mr. & Mrs. Robert Cresci, GARRISON, 10 A.M — 6 P.M.
Ross Gardens, GARRISON, 10 A.M. — 6 P.M.

July 11, 1999
Cross River House, KATONAH, 10 A.M. — 2 P.M.
White Garden, LEWISBORO, 10 A.M. — 4 P.M.
Judy & Michael Steinhardt, MOUNT KISCO, 10 A.M. — 4 P.M.
Sara & Martin Stein, POUND RIDGE, 10 A.M. — 4 P.M.

July 25, 1999
Mrs. John E. Lockwood, BEDFORD, 10 A.M. — 2 P.M.
Phillis Warden, BEDFORD HILLS, 10 A.M. — 4 P.M.

September 12, 1999
Ann Catchpole–Howell, BEDFORD, 10 A.M. — 4 P.M.
Mrs. John E. Lockwood, BEDFORD, 10 A.M. — 2 P.M.
John & Penelope Maynard, BEDFORD, 10 A.M. — 4 p.m.
❖ Stonecrop, COLD SPRING, 10 A.M. — 6 P.M.
Dick Button — Ice Pond Farm, NORTH SALEM, 10 A.M. — 6 P.M.
The Farmstead Garden, PATTERSON, 2 P.M. — 6 P.M.
James & Susan Henry, WACCABUC, 10 A.M. — 2 P.M.

October 17, 1999
Cobamong Pond, ARMONK, 10 A.M. — 6 P.M.

Cobamong Pond, ARMONK, NY

This is one of the great woodland gardens of the world — a twelve-acre pond surrounded by twelve acres of naturalistic woodlands that have been enhanced for almost forty years. It is now featured in The Beckoning Path, *with eighty color photographs. The garden has an abundance of rhododendrons, flowering trees, shrubs, and Japanese maples. The garden was also developed to emphasize New England fall color.*

DATES & HOURS: May 16, October 17; 10 a.m. – 6 p.m.

DIRECTIONS: *From I-684 southbound,* take Exit 4/Route 172. Turn left (east). Follow to end. Turn right (south) at Shell station onto Route 22. Go 2.2 miles, then turn left onto Middle Patent Road. Take second driveway on right, marked by four mailboxes. The house, #15, is at end of a long driveway. Please park near house or along driveway. *From I-684 northbound,* take Exit 3N and go north on Route 22 for 4 miles then turn right on Middle Patent Road and proceed as above.

Proceeds shared with Mount Kisco Day Care Center.

Mrs. John C. Sluder, ARMONK, NY

This garden is modeled on a French "jardin potager," with a decorative mixture of vegetables and flowers. The French-Norman house is surrounded by a home orchard with raspberries, apples, peaches, plums, and northern kiwi. Tubbed citrus and bay laurel trees thrive in the warmth around the swimming pool.

DATES & HOURS: June 13; 10 a.m. – 2 p.m.

DIRECTIONS: *From I-684,* take Exit 2. Turn left onto Route 120 to Whippoor-will Road. Turn right on Whippoorwill Road, go .7 mile to Half Mile Road (first right). The house, #9, is the first driveway on the right. Please park in circle and in driveway.

Mr. & Mrs. Coleman Burke, BEDFORD, NY

This is a simple, formal, country garden with old stone walls complementing a nineteenth-century house. A rock garden frames a naturalistic swimming pool with views of the perennial garden and the Aspetong River.

DATES & HOURS: May 2; 10 a.m. – 4 p.m.

DIRECTIONS: *From I-684,* take Exit 4 north. Follow Route 172 to Route 22 north through Bedford Village. Bear left on Route 22 and continue to Hook Road, on the right beyond the golf course. Follow .25 mile. The house, #52, is on the left. It is beige with black shutters and a cobblestone driveway. Please park along Hook Road.

Ann Catchpole-Howell, BEDFORD, NY

This garden features large perennial borders. It is designed on a central axis, with terraces, stone walls, and hidden steps leading to an unusual shrub garden. It was featured in Melanie Fleischmann's American Border Gardens. *Tea and plants are for sale.*

DATES & HOURS: June 13, September 12; 10 a.m. – 4 p.m.

DIRECTIONS: *From Bedford Village,* take Route 172 toward Pound Ridge. Turn right at Mobil station onto Long Ridge Road (road to Stamford). Follow 2 miles to the house, #448, on the right. Please park in the meadow as directed.

Mrs. John E. Lockwood, BEDFORD, NY

An unusual and interesting garden that makes use of its varied terrain. The path from the house leads through the apple orchard to a parterre-like garden of perennials and herbs. Specimen trees, a beautiful woodland, a collection of clematis, a large vegetable garden, and a wildflower meadow enhance the property.

DATES & HOURS: July 25, September 12; 10 a.m. – 2 p.m.

DIRECTIONS: *From I-684,* take Exit 4/Route 172 Exit. Go east on Route 172 to Route 22. Turn left onto Route 22. In Bedford Village, go right, staying on Route 172 East. Go about .5 mile and turn right at the Mobil Station onto Route 104/Long Ridge Road. Go .7 mile, making a right onto Miller's Mill Road. Make the first left onto Mianus River Road. Go 1.5 miles to Saint Mary's Church Road. Turn right onto Saint Mary's Church Road and go .3 mile to beige farmhouse on the right, #32. There is a pond across the street. Please park at Saint Mary's Church at top of hill or along road.

Penelope & John Maynard, BEDFORD, NY

We created a garden among rock ledges and oak woods on the steep shoulder of Mount Aspetong. The site is fragmented; thus the garden areas are designed to flow from one to another, linked together by a ribbon of stone walls. The greatest challenge has been to create some flat, restful spaces. The wide variety of plants must meet one criterion — to prove themselves in dry woodland conditions.

DATES & HOURS: April 25, May 16, September 12; 10 a.m. – 4 p.m.

DIRECTIONS: *From I-684,* take Exit 4. Turn east onto Route 172. Go 1.6 miles to Route 22. Turn left and drive through Bedford. Just beyond the Bedford Oak Tree, 2.1 miles from Route 172 and Route 22, turn right onto Hook Road. The house (#210) is almost at the top of the hill. Please park along road.

Phillis Warden, BEDFORD HILLS, NY

This garden of many facets includes perennial borders, two water gardens, a formal vegetable garden, a wildflower garden, a moss and fern garden, a marsh garden, a woodland walk, and a formal croquet court on seven acres.

DATES & HOURS: May 16, June 15, July 13; 10 a.m. – 4 p.m.

DIRECTIONS: *From Bedford Village,* take Route 22 towards Katonah to the intersection at Bedford Cross. The garden is on the left. Please park at Rippowam School.

❖ New York Botanical Garden, 200TH STREET & KAZIMIROFF BOULEVARD, BRONX, NY 10458-5126. (718) 817-8700.

The New York Botanical Garden is one of the foremost public gardens in America and a National Historic Landmark. It has some of the most beautiful natural terrain of any botanical garden in the world, with dramatic rock outcroppings, a river and cascading waterfall, undulating hills, wetlands, ponds, and forty acres of historic, uncut forest. Within this grand 250-acre setting in the north Bronx, many gardens and special plantings offer stunning seasonal displays, from rainbows of tulips and azaleas in the spring to the rich tapestries of fall foliage. Several noteworthy buildings include America's most beautiful Victorian green-house, the Enid A. Haupt Conservatory.

DATES & HOURS: Year round, Tuesday through Sunday, and Monday holidays. Closed Christmas. April through October, 10 a.m. – 6 p.m., November through March, 10 a.m. – 4 p.m.

DIRECTIONS: *From Westchester County,* take the Cross County Parkway East or West to Bronx River Parkway South. Take Parkway Exit 7W/Fordham Road and continue on Kazimiroff Boulevard to Conservatory Gate on the right. *From Connecticut* take I-95 to Pelham Parkway West. Continue for three miles. Across from the Zoo entrance, bear right on Kazimiroff Boulevard to Conservatory Gate entrance on right. *From New Jersey:* Take the George Washington Bridge and Henry Hudson Parkway North to Mosholu Parkway Exit. Continue on Mosholu Parkway to Kazimiroff Boulevard, turn right, and continue to Conservatory Entrance gate on left. This site is also accessible by public transportation. Please call for details.

❖ Wave Hill,

249TH STREET & INDEPENDENCE AVENUE, BRONX, NY 10471. (718) 549-3200. *Often called "the most beautiful place in New York," Wave Hill is a twenty-eight-acre public garden in a spectacular setting overlooking the Hudson River and Palisades. Formerly a private estate, Wave Hill features several gardens, greenhouses, historic buildings, lawns, and woodlands, and also offers programs in horticulture, environmental education, land management, landscape history, and the arts. All programs focus on fostering relationships between people and nature.*

DATES & HOURS: Mid-October through mid-April, Tuesday through Sunday, 9 a.m – 4:30 p.m. Mid-April through mid-October, Tuesday through Sunday, 9 a.m. – 5:30 p.m. and Fridays, 9 a.m. – dusk.

DIRECTIONS: *From the West Side and New Jersey* take the Henry Hudson Parkway to Exit 21 (246-250th Street) Continue north to 252nd Street. Turn left at overpass and left again. Turn right at 249th Street to Wave Hill Gate. *From Westchester* take the Henry Hudson Parkway southbound and exit at 254th Street (Exit 22). Turn left at the stop sign and left again at the light. Turn right onto 249th Street to Wave Hill Gate.

❖ Stonecrop Gardens,

ROUTE 301, COLD SPRING, NY 10516. (914) 265-2000. *At its windswept elevation of 1100 feet in the Hudson Highlands, Stonecrop enjoys a Zone 5 climate. The display gardens cover an area of approximately nine acres and include a diverse collection of gardens and plants, woodland and water gardens, a grass garden, raised alpine stone beds, a cliff rock garden, perennial beds, and an enclosed English-style flower garden. Additional facilities include a conservatory, a display alpine house, a pit house with an extensive collection of choice dwarf bulbs, and a series of polytunnels for overwintering half-hardy plants.*

DATES & HOURS: April through October: Tuesday, Wednesday, & Friday as well as the first Saturday of each month, 10 a.m. – 4 p.m. Always by appointment. Open for *Directory* visitors on May 16, June 27, & September 12, 10 a.m. – 6 p.m.

DIRECTIONS: *From the Taconic Parkway* take Route 301/Cold Spring Exit. Travel 3.5 miles to Stonecrop's driveway on the right. Just before the drive on the left, there is a wooden wheel and a cream-colored house with blue shutters.

Vivian & Ed Merrin, CORTLANDT MANOR, NY

Overlooking a small lake, this garden has unfolded over a rocky wooded site over the last ten years, under the guidance of designer Patrick Chassé. Mixed borders line garden rooms that flow among the landforms. Native plants form the framework for a collection that embraces many unusual and exotic plants. Several water gardens enhance the site, and greenhouses and a formal kitchen garden provide additional plants ornamental and edible.

DATES & HOURS: June 13; 10 a.m. – 2 p.m.

DIRECTIONS: *From the Taconic Parkway,* exit at Route 202. Turn left (west) towards Peekskill. Go 2.5 miles, then turn left at traffic light onto Croton Avenue, just past Cortland Farm Market. Go 1.2 miles to blinking light/stop sign, and turn right onto Furnace Dock Road. Go .8 mile to blinking light/stop sign, and make left onto Maple Avenue. Go .9 mile to private road on right. Go .2 mile to #2547 on left. Please park at house.

❖ Van Cortlandt Manor,

SOUTH RIVERSIDE AVENUE, CROTON-ON-HUDSON, NY 10520. (914) 271-8981.
This restored Federal-period manor complex includes a border of period ornamentals of interest throughout the growing season, a large tulip display, a vegetable garden, an orchard, and narcissi naturalized at woodland edge. An extensive culinary and medicinal herb garden is also noteworthy.

DATES & HOURS: April through October, daily except Tuesdays, 10 a.m. – 5 p.m.

DIRECTIONS: *Take Route 9* to Croton Point Avenue. Go east on Croton Point Avenue to traffic light. Turn right at traffic light onto South Riverside. Van Cortlandt Manor is at the end of the road, past the Shop Rite shopping center.

Mr. & Mrs. Robert Cresci, GARRISON, NY

This property is situated on the Hudson with a southern view of the river and the Bear Mountain Bridge. The grounds comprise almost twenty acres and include sweeping lawns and specimen trees. Behind the house is a recently redesigned sunken garden with fieldstone retaining walls surrounding perennial borders, a swimming pool, pergola, and bentgrass croquet lawn.

DATES & HOURS: June 27; 10 a.m. – 6 p.m.

DIRECTIONS: *The house is located in Garrison, NY*, approximately 3 miles north of the Bear Mountain Bridge and 1.25 miles south of the intersection of Route 403 and Route 9D. The driveway entrance is at the north end of a long white wooden fence. It has stone pillars and three black mailboxes, one of which is #721. Once on the property, bear left in the driveway. Please park by the basketball backboard in the driveway.

Ross Gardens, GARRISON, NY

This series of vignette gardens flows one onto another on five acres overlooking the Hudson River. The gardens are designed and maintained by owner Arthur Ross and include a water garden, a moon (white) garden, a meditation garden, a rock garden, a fern garden, a shrub garden, and cutting gardens and garden sculptures. Garden paths give easy access to many unusual flowers.

DATES & HOURS: June 27; 10 a.m. – 6 p.m.

DIRECTIONS: *From Route 9*, go to Garrison Golf Course. Turn west onto Snake Hill Road. The garden is .25 mile on the left. Parking is available for 30 cars at any one time.

Proceeds shared with The Philipstown Garden Club.

❖ Boscobel Restoration,

1601 ROUTE 9D, GARRISON, NY 10524. (914) 265-3638.

Boscobel is a museum of the Federal era, built between 1804 and 1808. Sixteen acres of landscaped grounds overlook the Hudson River and West Point and feature a formal rose garden, an orangery, and an herb garden. The herb garden is maintained by the Philipstown Garden Club. A one-mile woodland trail was opened to the public in October 1997.

DATES & HOURS: April through October, daily, 9:30 a.m. – 5 p.m.; November & December, daily, 9:30 a.m. – 4 p.m.

DIRECTIONS: *From the New York Thruway* go to Route 84 to Route 9D south to Boscobel. *From the Taconic Parkway* to Route 301 to Cold Spring traffic light. Turn left on Route 9D. *From New Jersey,* take the upper level of the George Washington Bridge to the Palisades Parkway north to the Bear Mountain Bridge to Route 9D.

Cross River House, KATONAH, NY

Cross River House's gardens are situated on seventeen acres overlooking the Cross River Reservoir in northern Westchester County. The gardens unfold through woodland paths filled with ferns, wildflowers, and large rhododendrons. From the paths you enter the first of the garden rooms. The hosta or shade garden is surrounded by trellises covered in clematis and wisteria. From the hosta garden you enter the perennial garden. The border was recently redesigned out. Low fencing and stonework separate the border from a white azalea allée and a tiny crescent shade area under the magnolias.

DATES & HOURS: May 2, May 16, June 13, July 11; 10 a.m. – 2 p.m.

DIRECTIONS: *From Bedford Village:* As you come into Bedford, go right (north) on Route 22. Take Route 22 approximately 3.3 miles. Maple Avenue is a right turn onto a dirt road at a curved intersection. There are signs for Caramoor at this point, although you *don't* go towards Caramoor, which is a hard right turn. Once on Maple Avenue, we are .5 mile down on the right, #129. *From New York City:* Take 684 North to Exit 6, "Route 35, Cross River, Katonah." At the end of the ramp, take a right onto Route 35 east. Take the next right on Route 22 south. Go 1.8 miles. Make a left at the intersection in the curve on Maple Avenue (a dirt road), go .5 mile and the house is on the right, #129. Park along Maple Avenue on either side of the white gates.

Roxana Robinson, KATONAH, NY

A writer's garden, Willow Green has old-fashioned perennial borders, a white garden, an herb/kitchen border, a summer border, a woodland border, meadows, and stone walls on the grounds of a nineteenth-century farmhouse. All organic.

DATES & HOURS: June 13; 10 a.m. – 4 p.m.

DIRECTIONS: *From I-684,* exit at Route 35 East (toward Cross River) approximately 2 miles. Turn left onto North Salem Road (a dirt road). Willow Green Farm, #159, is 1 mile on the right, past Mount Holly Road. Please park along the road.

Proceeds shared with The Natural Resources Defense Council.

❖ Caramoor Gardens,

P.O. Box 816, KATONAH, NY 10536. (914) 232-1253.
Located throughout the 100 acres are the Sunken Garden, the Spanish Courtyard, the Butterfly Garden, the Sense Circle, the Cutting Garden, the Medieval Mount, the Woodland Garden, the Cedar Walk, and numerous antique containers planted in creative ways.

DATES & HOURS: May through October, Tuesday through Sunday, 1 – 4p.m. Group tours with luncheon available every Tuesday. Call to reserve.

DIRECTIONS: *Girdle Ridge Road is off Route 22.* Enter through Main Gate.

❖ John Jay Homestead State Historic Site,

400 ROUTE 22/JAY STREET, KATONAH, NY 10536. (914) 232-5651.

Five garden areas are maintained by local garden clubs in styles ranging from formal to natural/wilderness. The Bedford and Rusticus Garden Clubs use plantings that were popular in the 1920s and 1930s, with formal gardens following the plans of the last Jays to live on the site. The New York Unit of the Herb Society of America maintains an herb garden in a style traditional of herb gardens since medieval times. Hopp Ground Club is establishing gardens that will incorporate selections of plantings not accessible to all patrons in present garden areas, and Pound Ridge Garden Club is planting the field areas surrounding the newly opened Beech Allée.

DATES & HOURS: Year round, daily except holidays, 8 a.m. – dusk.

DIRECTIONS: *From I-684* take Exit 6. Take Route 35, heading east, for .25 mile to the next light. Turn right onto Route 22 (sign for John Jay Homestead). Continue for 2 miles. The site is on your left.

❖ Muscoot Farm Park,

ROUTE 100, KATONAH, NY 10536. (914) 232-7118.

Muscoot is a Westchester Country Gentleman's Farm circa 1880-1950. The herb garden on the property is cared for by the Muscoot Naturalist. The garden is currently undergoing restoration to install beds with tea, dye, fragrance and cooking herbs to be used for programs and workshops.

DATES & HOURS: Year round, daily, 10 a.m.– 4 p.m.

DIRECTIONS: *From Route 684* take Exit 6 (Route 35/Katonah) west on Route 35 for 1.3 miles. Take a left (south) on Route 100. The Muscoot Farm is on the right after 1.5 miles.

White Garden, LEWISBORO, NY

The hardwood forest and native plants provide a "Sacred Grove" setting for this Greek Revival home. The gardens, designed by Patrick Chassé, are classically inspired near the house, including a nymphaeum, a pergola garden, a labyrinth, a theater court. More exotic surprises are hidden in separate garden rooms. Sculptures and water features enrich the gardens.

DATES & HOURS: July 11; 10 a.m. – 4 p.m.

DIRECTIONS: *From the Merritt Parkway* take Exit 38 and follow Route 123 North through New Canaan to the New York state line. The town of Lewisboro and the village of Vista are the first signs encountered. Go past the Vista Fire Department (on right) about .25 mile. Just after the shingled Episcopal church on the right, Route 123 will bear left, and Elmwood Road will fork right. Go about another .25 mile just over a hill. At the beginning of a gray stockade fence on the right is the driveway at #199 Elmwood Road.

Judy & Michael Steinhardt, MOUNT KISCO, NY

The Steinhardts' love of plants is evident throughout this fifty-five-acre estate. More than 2,000 species of trees, shrubs, and perennials have been incorporated into the gardens. Landscape designer Jerome Rocherolle has created a naturalistic setting with walkways, stream beds, bridges, and ponds where plants can be appreciated and nurtured. There are diverse orchards, a mature perennial bed, and a newly-developed alpine and wall garden. Much of the plant material is labelled for the viewer's benefit. Look for extensive use of ferns, moss (a moss bridge), more than 200 cultivars of Japanese maples. Wildlife and not-so-wild-life include exotic waterfowl, cranes, and peacocks.

DATES & HOURS: April 25, July 11; 10 a.m.– 4 p.m.

DIRECTIONS: *From the Saw Mill Parkway* take the Kisco Avenue Exit (1 exit beyond Mount Kisco). Turn right at end of exit and after a few hundred feet, turn right onto Croton Lake Road. Number 433 is 1.8 miles to the mailbox on the left. Please park where directed.

Henriette Suhr, MOUNT KISCO, NY

"Rocky Hills" is an appropriate name for this property — with hills, rocks of all sizes, and a lovely brook. The garden was started by the owner and her late husband about forty years ago. The azalea *and* rhododendron *plantings number in the thousands. There is an extensive tree peony collection, a woodland garden, a fern garden, a wildflower garden, lots of bulbs, and irises of all descriptions. An interesting group of evergreens is planted among rocks. This is a most varied garden in all seasons.*

DATES & HOURS: May 29; 2 p.m. – 6 p.m.

DIRECTIONS: *From the Saw Mill Parkway,* travel north to Exit 33/Reader's Digest Road. At the traffic light, make a left and then a sharp right onto Old Roaring Brook Road. "Rocky Hills," #95, is 1 mile on the right. *From the Merritt Parkway,* travel to the Cross County/Route 287 West. Exit the Cross County at the Saw Mill Parkway North. Travel to Exit 33/Reader's Digest Road. Follow directions above. Please park along Old Roaring Brook Road or Lawrence Farms Crossways as directed.

Proceeds shared with Friends of Lasdon Arboretum.

Dick Button, Ice Pond Farm, NORTH SALEM, NY

Ice Pond Farm has beautiful views over meadow and pond. There is a kitchen garden — a mixture of vegetables, annuals, perennials and roses. A bocce court has an allée of crab apples. A long flower border by the swimming pool, references to the fine art of figure skating, and a wildflower walk complete this lovely garden.

DATES & HOURS: September 12; 10 a.m. – 6 p.m.

DIRECTIONS: *From the north:* take I-684 to Exit 8/Hardscrabble Road. Take Hardscrabble Road east about 5 miles to June Road (Old Route 124). Turn right on June Road and go .5 mile to #115 June Road. *From the south:* take I-684 to Exit 7/Purdys. Take Route 116 east for about 3 miles to North Salem. Turn left onto June Road (Old Route 124). Go .5 mile to #115 June Road. Park in field as directed.

Page Dickey, NORTH SALEM, NY

A series of hedged-in gardens are related to the nineteenth-century farmhouse they surround. They include an herb garden, white garden, and nasturtium garden, described in Duck Hill Journal *and* Breaking Ground *by the author/owner.*

DATES & HOURS: June 13, 10 a.m. – 6 p.m.

DIRECTIONS: *From I-684,* take Exit 7. Follow Route 116 east to North Salem. After Route 121 joins Route 116 go approximately .5 mile. Turn left onto Baxter Road. Go to the top of the hill and turn right onto a private road. Duck Hill, #23, is the second house on the left. Please park along the road.

Keeler Hill Farm Gardens, NORTH SALEM, NY

Although the land has been farmed since 1731, it is just in the last ten years that gardens have been developed. The perennial, the green, and the white gardens were designed by Page Dickey. A friendship garden, which provides swimming pool privacy, was planted with friends' castoffs. The vegetable, fruit, and cutting gardens were placed among the farm buildings. With horses, a cow, and fowl roaming so near, a working farm atmosphere has been created.

DATES & HOURS: June 13; 10 a.m. – 6 p.m.

DIRECTIONS: *From Route 684 North* take Purdy's/Exit 7. Turn right off exit ramp onto Route 116 East. Stay on Route 116 East for approximately 5 miles. Cross over Old Route 124/June Road. Route 116 will join up with Route 121 about 1 mile after the June Road intersection. Bear left at that intersection. About 1 mile up the road turn right onto Keeler Lane. Proceed up Keeler Lane .5 mile. On the left you will see seven yellow barns. Turn in the gate with the sign on the left pillar that reads "Keeler Hill Farm" and "Keeler Homestead" on the right pillar. Proceed up driveway to parking.

Proceeds shared with The North Salem Open Land Foundation.

❖ Hammond Museum Japanese Stroll Gardens,

DEVEAU ROAD, NORTH SALEM, NY 10560. (914) 669-5033.

A three-and-one-half-acre garden with thirteen different landscapes, there is a stroll garden, a waterfall garden, a garden of the Rakan, a fruit garden, a red maple terrace, and an azalea garden. The terrace restaurant serves lunch and provides a chance to dine among the trees and flowers.

DATES & HOURS: Through October 24, Wednesday through Saturday, noon – 4 p.m., November 1 through December 6, Friday & Saturday, noon – 4 p.m.

DIRECTIONS: *From 684 North* take Exit 7/Route 116/Purdys/Somers. Go right at stop sign for .2 mile to Route 22. Turn left onto Route 22 North, bear right after .5 mile to Route 116 East and travel for 4 miles. After passing the North Salem Library, turn left at Salem center to Route 124/June Road. Take the first right, Deveau Road, and follow to museum at end of street.

❖ The Wildflower Island at Teatown Lake Reservation,

1600 SPRING VALLEY ROAD, OSSINING, NY 10562. (914) 762-2912.
WWW.BESTWEB.NET\TEATOWN

The Island is a woodland garden of more than 200 species of native flowers. Several hundred pink lady's slippers make a spectacular display in May. In late summer, the sunny shores of the Island are ablaze with cardinal flowers, lobelia, iron weed, and other bright, moisture-loving flowers. A small interpretive museum is at the entrance to the bridge leading to the island. Visitors are guided along narrow paths by experienced volunteers. Call for a tour schedule.

DATES & HOURS: Teatown Reservation: May to September, Tuesday – Saturday, 9 a.m. – 5 p.m., Sunday, 1 p.m. – 5 p.m. Closed Mondays. **Wildflower Island tours:** April to June, Saturday and Sunday, 2:p.m.; May, Saturday 11:30 a.m., 2 p.m., Sunday 2 p.m., Wednesday 7 p.m.; July – September, Sunday, 2 p.m. Open for Directory visitors on May 16, 10 a.m. - 4 p.m.

DIRECTIONS: *Take the Major Deegan Expressway* to Route 87 North to Exit 9 for Tarrytown (last exit before the Tappan Zee Bridge). Take Route 9 north to Ossining. Watch for Route 133 on right. At third traffic light after Route 133, turn right onto Cedar Lane. Cedar Lane will become Spring Valley Road. Teatown is on the left 3.8 miles from Route 9.

The Farmstead Garden, PATTERSON, NY

This garden, located on historic Quaker Hill, was planned as a rural landscape in keeping with its 1740 farmstead beginnings. A master plan was commissioned by the owners in 1985 to define the site's woodlands, wetlands, house gardens, and agricultural fields into a harmonious native plant landscape while preserving the property's horticultural heritage. An heirloom apple orchard greets you as you enter the fieldstone entrance. The driveway is the old Stagecoach Road, which connected Pawling, NY with Danbury, CT. Native wildflower meadows now grace the upper and lower fields after decades of haying. A grove of more than eighty mature blueberry bushes tell the story of the acid soil and summers of picking and tasting. The original vegetable garden is anchored by an old majestic quince, and the kitchen herb garden is filled with flowering thyme, catnip, lavender, with a border of germander. A two-acre wetland can be traversed to experience plant and aquatic wildlife. The roadside sloping fields have been mowed to create welcoming paths and sculptural grasslands.

DATES & HOURS: September 12; 2 p.m. – 6 p.m.

DIRECTIONS: *From NYC:* Route 684 to Pawling, about 65 miles. At the junction of Route; 311 take a sharp right up a hill, which is South Quaker Hill Road. At the first stop sign (2.5 miles) turn right onto Birch Hill Road. Follow the road to Box 590. The property is on the left. *From CT,* take Route 37 through Sherman and continue to Wakeman Road. Turn right onto Wakeman and continue to Quaker Hill Road. The Akin Hall Library is on your right and the Hill Farm is on your left. Turn left and continue going south. This road becomes Birch Hill Road. Continue about .25 mile to Box 590. Please park in the driveway. The garden is wheelchair accessible.

Proceeds shared with The Conservancy for Historic Battery Park.

❖ Kykuit, POCANTICO HILLS, NY 10591. (914) 631-9491.

The extraordinary early-twentieth-century gardens at Kykuit, the Rockefeller Estate, were designed by William Welles Bosworth. Included are a formal walled garden, woodland gardens, a rose garden, fountains, and spectacular Hudson River views. Important contemporary sculptures were added by Governor Nelson Rockefeller.

DATES & HOURS: May through October, daily except Tuesdays, 10 a.m. – 5 p.m. Reservations required.

DIRECTIONS: *All tours begin at historic Phillipsburg Manor,* located on Route 9 in the village of Sleepy Hollow.

Sara & Martin Stein, POUND RIDGE, NY

This four-acre site, an ecological restoration by the author of Noah's Garden *and* Planting Noah's Garden, *includes upland and wetland meadows, woodlands and thickets. Many native species important to wildlife but not often used in landscaping have been planted. Other features include a stone terrace that houses a dryland community of shrubs, forbs, grasses, as well as sedges, red maple swamp, a moss garden, and a pond. Numerous paths lead through the various habitats.*

DATES & HOURS: July 11; 10 a.m. – 4 p.m.

DIRECTIONS: *From I-684,* take Exit 4/Route 172 through the town of Bedford. Go 1 mile past Bedford Village Green. At light turn right onto Long Ridge Road toward Stamford. Continue 2.3 miles to Fox Hill Road. Turn right. Number 8 is the first drive on the left. *From the Merritt Parkway,* take Exit 34/Long Ridge Road/Route 104. Continue 6 miles toward Bedford. Turn left onto Fox Hill Road. Number 8 is the first drive on the left. Please park along road.

❖ Donald M. Kendall Sculpture Gardens at PepsiCo,

700 ANDERSON HILL ROAD, PURCHASE, NY 10577. (914) 253-2900.

One hundred and twelve acres of landscape designed by Russell Page surround the world headquarters of PepsiCo, Inc. Spacious lawns and shrubs, plantings of trees, and small gardens provide settings for forty-five sculptures by renowned twentieth-century artists.

DATES & HOURS: Year round, daily, dawn – dusk.

DIRECTIONS: *From I-84 East or West,* take Route 684 South to the Westchester Airport exit. Take Route 120 South to Anderson Hill Road to PepsiCo on the right. *From the Merritt Parkway South* (which becomes the Hutchinson River Parkway) take Exit 28 (Lincoln Avenue/Port Chester). Turn left onto Lincoln Avenue and proceed 1 mile to PepsiCo on the right.

❖ Philipsburg Manor,

ROUTE 9 NORTH, SLEEPY HOLLOW, NY 10591. (914) 631-3992.

This colonial-period working farm with water-powered grist mill is on the banks of the Pocantico River. The farm interprets the agricultural practices of the Hudson Valley. A recreated kitchen garden contains culinary, herb, and medicinal crops appropriate to the period. The gardens feature heirloom varieties of eighteenth-century plants.

DATES & HOURS: April through December, daily except Tuesdays.

DIRECTIONS: *From I-87* take Exit 9 for Tarrytown and proceed north for 2 miles.

❖ Lyndhurst,

635 SOUTH BROADWAY, TARRYTOWN, NY 10591. (914) 631-4481.

The grounds at Lyndhurst are an outstanding example of nineteenth-century landscape design. Elements include sweeping lawns accented with shrubs and specimen trees, a curving entrance drive revealing "surprise" views, and the angular repetition of the Gothic roofline in the evergreens. The rose garden and fernery are later Victorian additions.

DATES & HOURS: Mid-April through October, Tuesday through Sunday, 10 a.m.– 4:15 p.m. November through mid-April, weekends, 10 a.m.– 3:30 p.m.

DIRECTIONS: *From the Taconic State Parkway* take the Saw Mill River Parkway south to the exit for Route 287 West.* Follow signs to the Tappan Zee Bridge. (Do not take Exit 1 for Tarrytown.) Continue to Exit 9. Turn left at the end of the ramp. Turn left at the next traffic light. The entrance is .25 mile on the right. *From Westchester and Connecticut,* take I-95 south to Connecticut to Route 287 West. Follow directions above.*

❖ Sunnyside,

WEST SUNNYSIDE LANE, TARRYTOWN, NY 10591. (914) 591-8763.

The picturesque mid-nineteenth-century landscape is among the earliest, most important, and best preserved in America. It has a large, diverse collection of narcissi in April. A large kitchen garden with a varied collection of ornamentals and edibles was re created in 1995.

DATES & HOURS: Year round, daily except Tuesdays.

DIRECTIONS: *From I-87* take Exit 9 for Tarrytown and proceed south for 1 mile.

James & Susan Henry, WACCABUC, NY

A nineteenth-century farm is the setting for perennial gardens, specimen trees, a walled garden, cordoned apple trees, a vegetable garden, berries and fruits, a pond in a meadow, and a vineyard producing red and white wines.

DATES & HOURS: September 12; 10 a.m. – 2 p.m.

DIRECTIONS: *From I-684/Saw Mill Parkway,* take Exit 6. Follow Route 35 east for 5 miles. After a long hill, look for Mead Street sign on the left. Take Mead Street .25 mile to #36 on the left. Turn left into driveway and left into parking area. *From Connecticut,* Mead Street is 4 miles from the traffic light at Route 35 and Route 123. Please park in the field behind the vineyard.

OHIO

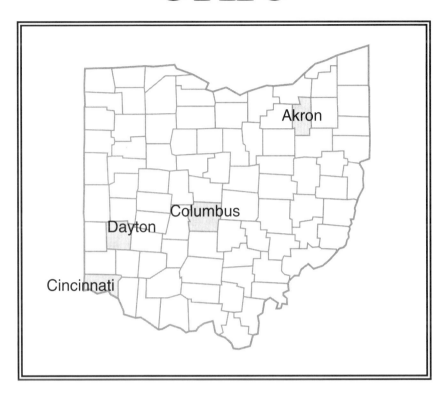

1999 OHIO OPEN DAYS

June 5: COLUMBUS AREA
June 19: AKRON AREA
June 19: CINCINNATI AREA
September 25: DAYTON AREA

AKRON: *June 19, 1999*

Retta & Charles Billow, AKRON, 10 A.M. – 2 P.M.

Ruth Evan's Garden, AKRON, 10 A.M. – 2 P.M.

Dorothy Francis, AKRON, 10 A.M. – 2 P.M.

Mary Stark, AKRON, 10 A.M. – 2 P.M

Retta & Charles Billow, AKRON, OH

"Gardening Forever — Housework Whenever." This whimsical statement is
found on a slate plaque that adorns the entranceway to the patio area of this old
English manor home built in 1928. The owners call this glorious work of art a
Friendship Garden, as many of the specimens have been given to them by friends
and lovingly transplanted into this picturesque setting, nestled under a stately oak
tree. They have worked with hearts and hands and designed and planted the
entire garden. Development of the present garden has taken place over the past
four years. Seventy-year-old sandstone patio slabs that had been covered over
many years ago and long forgotten were unearthed during extensive renovation of
the home and now outline the stunning red brick patio area. Brilliantly colored
poppies, iris, delphinium, and bleeding heart offer a rich tapestry for the seasonal
display. The grade slopes gently from the patio to the lush green grounds surrounded by towering arborvitae and bounded by the eighth fairway of a local
country club. There, it is separated by a handsome barnstone wall designed and
executed by landscape architect Rick Young. Overall harmony of the garden is
achieved through the repetition of lush foliage plants and key perennials such as
sedum and vibrant Stella de Oro lilies. These, along with hydrangeas, weeping
red maples, golden yews, and other shrubs and trees, form the garden's basic
structure. While hostas border the perimeter of the garden, pink and white
impatiens, and Early Sunrise coreopsis add color.

DATES & HOURS: June 19; 10 a.m. – 2 p.m.

DIRECTIONS: *From I-77* take exit 132 (White Pond Drive – Mull Avenue).
Follow signs to Stan Hywet Hall and Gardens. The house is located 2 blocks
south of Stan Hywet at #474 N. Portage Path.

Proceeds shared with the Akron Volunteer Center.

Ruth Evan's Gardens, AKRON, OH

These small gardens for condominium living are designed to enhance walls and terraces. A variety of plants are used to keep blooms all summer long. The beds are small but interesting, from a mixture of peonies and annuals to wall climbing vines. I try to plant so there will be a reflection of color in our pond, which also has pink and white water lilies (as well as ducks and geese). We have little beds of fragrant flowers all around the patio. One feels as though one were sitting in a bower far away from the city.

DATES & HOURS: June 19; 10 a.m. – 2 p.m.

DIRECTIONS: *Take West Market Street* (Route 18) to the Summit Mall. At the Mall, take Ghent Road to the 1st light and turn right onto Smith Road. Drive past 2 traffic lights and, in about .5 miles, turn right into Brookwood Village. Stay on the main road and at the end of the tennis courts turn right to #1782. Please park in the parking spaces.

Dorothy Francis, AKRON, OH

An English-style garden for all seasons. A spectacular display of daffodils, Japanese primula and azaleas in the spring is followed through summer and fall with annuals and perennials. A mature, naturalized pond with goldfish and Koi is also to be discovered. Many large English urns, wire baskets and hanging baskets adorn the site. Wildlife is welcomed with a fountain, several bird baths, feeders and nesting boxes.

DATES & HOURS: June 19; 10 a.m. – 2 p.m.

DIRECTIONS: *From I-77,* Exit 133 (Ridgewood Road – Miller Road). Travel east on Ridgewood to Ely Road. Turn left on Ely to #114.

Proceeds shared with the Akron Volunteer Center.

Mary Stark, AKRON, OH

This wonderfully diverse garden started as a little plot and just kept on growing. Now half of the front yard is border and the enthusiastic owner is wondering where to spill over next. There is a White Garden, a Rock Garden, a North Garden, Shade Garden, Sun Garden, Daylily Garden, Hosta Garden, and much more on a corner lot. Borders feature shrub roses, climbing roses, old roses and English roses plus numerous specimen trees and shrubs, including Franklinia, *fringe tree, Seven Sons Flower Tree, Mountain Silver Bell, magnolias, and many more. The joy of the unexpected is very evident in passersby who just have to wander in to see more.*

DATES & HOURS: June 19; 10 a.m. – 2 p.m.

DIRECTIONS: *From I-77,* Exit 133 (Ridgewood Road - Miller Road). Travel east on Ridgewood to stop sign at Halifax. Turn left and go down the hill. Cross West Market Street and you are on Overwood Road. Go to second block on right, #155.

Proceeds shared with the Akron Volunteer Center.

❖ Stan Hywet Hall & Gardens,

714 NORTH PORTAGE PATH, AKRON, OH 44303. (330) 836-5533.
Designed between 1911 and 1915 by Warren Manning, one of the fathers of American landscape design, Stan Hywet's landscaped grounds are of national historic significance. A walk through the more than seventy acres will take you through the Great Meadow, the Japanese Garden, the Formal West Terrace, a noted Ellen Shipman English Garden, a rose garden, lagoons, vistas, and allées of birch and London plane trees.

DATES & HOURS: End of January through March, Tuesday through Saturday, 10 a.m.– 4 p.m., Sunday, 1 p.m.– 4 p.m.; April through January, daily, 9 a.m.– 6 p.m.

DIRECTIONS: *Take I-77 South* to Ghent Road/Fairlawn Exit (138). Turn right from ramp onto Ghent Road and continue 1.25 miles to Smith Road. Turn left onto Smith Road at the traffic light and continue 2.5 miles to the end at Riverview/Merriman Road. Turn right at the traffic light onto Riverview/Merriman and continue for 1 mile to light at Portage Path. Turn right onto Portage Path and continue for 1.25 miles to Stan Hywet on the right-hand side.

❖ Ohio State University/Ohio Agricultural Research & Development Center's Secrest Arboretum,

1680 MADISON AVENUE, WOOSTER, OH 44691. (330) 263-3761.

A major research arboretum planted with 2,000 species, varieties, and cultivars of trees and shrubs for evaluation and viewing. Collections of note: 200 crab apple selections, 100 rhododendron selections, forest plantation, pinetum, John Ford Azalea Allée, Ollie Diller Holly Display (100 selections), and Garden of Roses of Legend and Romance (500 varieties of old garden roses).

DATES & HOURS: Year round, daily, dawn – dusk.

DIRECTIONS: *From Columbus and Cleveland,* take I-71 to Route 30 East to the exit for Route 83 South.

CINCINNATI: *June 19, 1999*

William & Mary Bramlage, CINCINNATI, 10 A.M. – 4 P.M.

Krombholz Gardens, CINCINNATI, 10 A.M. – 4 P.M.

The Rose Garden, CINCINNATI, 10 A.M. – 4 P.M.

Mr. & Mrs. John G. Sloneker, CINCINNATI, 10 A.M. – 2 P.M.

William & Mary Bramlage, CINCINNATI, OH

Informal cottage garden of wildflowers, bulbs, perennials, and annuals in five acres of a beech forest. Garden accents include antique iron fence, a pond with a Robinson iron fountain, stone benches and urns, bridges and creeks, and meandering paths through the woods and gardens.

DATES & HOURS: June 19; 10 a.m. – 4 p.m.

DIRECTIONS: *From I-75 or I-71* take 275 East to Loveland/Indian Hill Exit. Turn right to Loveland Madiera Road (pass major intersection at Remington Road). Proceed .25 mile past Remington, turn left to Spooky Hollow Road. Turn right (at stop sign) continue on Spooky Hollow. Turn right (at stop sign) to Given Road. Go 2.4 miles to #6900 Given Road to the Bramlage Gardens. Park in Driveway.

Proceeds shared with the Cincinnati Horticultural Society.

Krombholz Gardens, CINCINNATI, OH

My one acre shade garden features gently curving flower beds surrounded by mature plantings of white pines, blue spruces, arborvitaes and hemlocks. Collections of ferns, astilbes, hosta, and ivies share garden space with hundreds of fancy-leaf caladiums, impatiens, begonias, and salvias. Broadleaf evergreens include boxwoods, southern magnolias, pieris japonicas, azaleas, rhododendrons and hellleborus. Large window boxes and dozens of hanging baskets add additional summer color to my garden.

DATES & HOURS: June 19; 10 a.m. – 4 p.m.

DIRECTIONS: *North on the 71 Expressway* to Exit 11 (Kenwood Road). Turn right off of ramp at light. At first light turn left (Euclid Road). Drive 1 mile on Euclid Road to first light (Miami Drive). Turn right and drive 1.3 miles to #5650 Miami Road (Krombholz Garden). *South on the 71 Expressway.* Drive to Exit 12 (Montgomery Road). Turn left off of ramp at light. Drive past Bob Evans on left to first light (Hosbrook Road). Turn right on Hosbrook and drive to dead end of street (Euclid Road). Turn left and drive to first light (Miami Road). Krombholz Garden is 1.3 miles from corner of Euclid and Miami Roads. Look for large brown concrete basket next to driveway, number #5650 Miami Road.

Proceeds shared with the Cincinnati Horticultural Society.

The Rose Garden, CINCINNATI, OH

Voted the Best Residential Rose Garden (1993) in America, our garden now features more than 1000 rose bushes with more than 600 different cultivars. It is designed with soft curves which lead the eye to view the more than twenty rose beds. Our rose hybridizing skills are evident throughout the garden. Multiple large areas of annuals, perennials, conifers and tropical plants grace the estate. More than 150 varieties of hostas are planted. Strolling the brick path will finally lead the visitor to a spectacular view of the Ohio River. Still a baby of thirty years, our garden grows in splendor every year.

DATES & HOURS: June 19; 10 a.m. – 4 p.m.

DIRECTIONS: *Take I-75 south or north* to 50 West (River Road). Turn right on Anderson Ferry Road. Turn left on Palisades Drive. The house is the last on the right, #5584 Palisades Drive. Park on Palisades Drive. Approximate distance from the center of Cincinnati, 11 miles.

Proceeds shared with the Cincinnati Horticultural Society.

Mr. & Mrs. John G. Sloneker, CINCINNATI, OH

Hemlocks and hollies line the curved driveway up to the entrance to this lovely house. The terrace at the back of the house faces a sweep of lawn that visually melds with the golf course beyond. To the left of this magnificent open vista is a path which invites as it disappears around a wall of beautifully clipped hemlocks. Following the path, the visitor comes upon a charming asymmetrical pool and garden nestled into a hollow in the landscape. A lovely weeping beech stands as a graceful and appropriate sentry. The twists and turns of the path move the visitor through the garden, revealing one surprise after another. Cotoneaster and blue-tinted juniper cascade down the gentle slope and spill over the low retaining walls. Tree peonies, herbaceaous peonies, roses and long-spurred columbine bloom in profusion. Bright-colored annuals are added to provide color between the perennials of June and the blooms of fall. Dwarf cut-leaf Japanese maples, one with green leaves and one with red, add a different texture, as do several varieties of dwarf chamaecyparis. Exotic-shaped pines droop gracefully over the narrowing at the middle of the pool, dividing it visually into two spaces. It is altogether an intriguing and titillating combination of plant material.

DATES & HOURS: June 19; 10 a.m. – 2 p.m.

DIRECTIONS: *North on I-71* take Exit 11 (Kenwood Road). Turn right. At the first light turn left onto Euclid Road. Drive 1 mile to the first light (Miami Road) and turn right. Drive approximately 1 mile to intersection of Miami and Shawnee Run Road. Turn left on Shawnee Road. Proceed 1 mile to Drake Road (four-way stop). Turn right. Go past Indian Hill Church (on left). The next left is Camargo Club Drive. Proceed to # 8400. *South on I-71* take 275 East. Exit Loveland/Indian Hill Exit. Turn right on Loveland – Madeira Road. (Cross major intersection at Remington Road). Approximately .25 mile past Remington turn left onto Spooky Hollow Road. Turn right at stop sign. Continue to Given Road. Approximately 2.5 miles turn right on Shawnee Run Road. At four-way stop sign turn left onto Drake Road. Go past Indian Hill Church (on right) to next left, Camargo Club Drive. The house is #8400.

❖ The Cincinnati Zoo and Botanical Garden,

3400 VINE STREET, CINCINNATI, OH 45220. (800) 94-HIPPO.

Among the finest horticultural display gardens in the country, the Cincinnati Zoo and Botanical Garden features over 2,800 varieties of trees, shrubs, tropical plants, bulbs, perennials and annuals. Arranged in extensive landscaped gardens and in naturalistic settings simulating animal habitats, many of the plants are labeled, providing identification and interesting information for the garden enthusiast. The Zoo boasts one of the largest and finest spring gardens in the country with over a million spring bulbs and thousands of colorful, early-blooming shrubs and trees. Home to the largest collection of hardy bamboo species in any Midwest botanical garden, the Zoo also has one of the largest plantings of perennials and ornamental grasses in Ohio.

DATES & HOURS: Year round, daily. Summer hours (Memorial Day – Labor Day) 9 a.m. – 6 p.m. Winter hours (Labor Day – Memorial Day) 9 a.m. – 5 p.m.

DIRECTIONS: *From I-74,* go east to I-75 North. Take I-75 North to Mitchell Avenue exit. Turn right onto Mitchell Avenue. Turn right onto Vine Street. Turn left onto Forest Avenue. Turn right onto Dury Avenue. The Auto Entrance is on the right. *From I-75 North,* take Mitchell Avenue exit. Turn right onto Mitchell Avenue. Turn right onto Vine Street. Turn left onto Forest Avenue. Turn right on Dury Avenue. The Auto Entrance is on the right. *From I-75 South,* take Mitchell Avenue exit. Turn left onto Mitchell Avenue and follow as above.

❖ Civic Garden Center of Greater Cincinnati,

2715 READING ROAD, CINCINNATI, OH 45206. (513) 221-0981. FAX (513) 221-0961.

The Civic Garden Center of Greater Cincinnati is located in the Hauck Botanic Gardens, also known as "Sooty Acres." The property was donated to the CGC by Cornelius Hauck, who developed the property into an urban oasis. The garden includes rare, historic trees, an herb garden, a hosta garden, a dwarf conifer collection and a children's and butterfly garden.

DATES & HOURS: Year round, daily, dawn – dusk.

DIRECTIONS: *From I-71 South,* take the William Howard Taft Exit to Reading Road. Turn right and proceed one block to Oak Street. Turn left onto Oak Street and take an immediate left into the CGC parking lot. *From I-71 North,* take the Reading Road exit and proceed north on Reading Road to Oak Street. Turn left onto Oak Street and take an immediate left into the CGC parking lot.

❖ Spring Grove Cemetery and Arboretum,

4521 SPRING GROVE AVENUE, CINCINNATI, OH 45232. (513) 681-6680.
Since its founding over 150 years ago, Spring Grove has remained a leader in cemetery design and management. The landscape "lawn plan" concept was created here and, although it was considered a radical concept of cemetery design at that time, it later became accepted almost universally as the model plan. Spring Grove remains a masterwork of the landscaping art, studied by horticulturists and admired by thousands of visitors. The Cincinnati Chamber of Commerce lists it among the city's outstanding attractions, proudly quoting the praise of an artist who once said, "Only a place with a heart and soul could make for its dead a more magnificent park than any which exists for the living." With over 733 acres, fourteen lakes and one waterfall, three expansive floral borders, twenty-three Champion Trees and over 1,000 labeled woody plant specimens within the Arboretum, Spring Grove truly is one of Cincinnati's best-kept secrets.

DATES & HOURS: Front gate: daily, 8 a.m. – 6 p.m.; North Gate: daily, 8 a.m. – 5 p.m.

DIRECTIONS: *From downtown,* I-75 North. Proceed to Mitchell Avenue Exit #6. Turn left (west) onto Mitchell Avenue. Travel Mitchell Avenue to Spring Grove Avenue, turn left onto Spring Grove (in center lane) past three traffic lights (including the light at Mitchell). Pass under third light (Winton Road) and get into curb lane as you pass under light. Entrance to cemetery is approximately 500 feet ahead on the right. *From Dayton,* I-75 South to Mitchell Avenue, Exit #6. Bear to your right (west) on Mitchell Avenue. Follow as above. *From Indiana,*
I-74 East to I-75. Continue North on I-75 to Mitchell Avenue Exit #6. Proceed as previously instructed. *From Columbus,* I-71 North to Norwood Lateral Exit E562. Follow lateral to I-75 South to Mitchell Avenue Exit #6. Turn right (west) onto Mitchell Avenue and proceed as above.

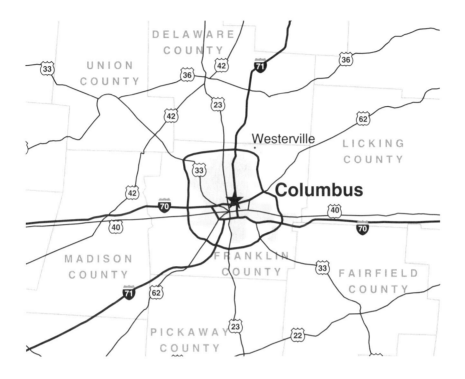

COLUMBUS: *June 5, 1999*

Jeff & Diane Keeler Garden, COLUMBUS, 10 A.M. – 4 P.M.

Ed Miller Garden, COLUMBUS, 10 A.M. – 2 P.M.

Garden of Jack & Sue Dingle, UPPER ARLINGTON, 10 A.M. – 4 P.M.

The Hadley Garden, UPPER ARLINGTON, 10 A.M. – 4 P.M.

Jeff & Diane Keeler Garden, COLUMBUS, OH

Our hillside rockery-type garden is a peaceful oasis from the hectic pace of city living. A 365-day-a-year garden of all perennials with specimen dwarf conifers integrated throughout, planted with an eye to contrasting texture, size, shape, color, and bloom time so that each element shows off to best advantage. Recirculating fish ponds accent the hillside rock garden which slopes down to an open, sunny meadow. The meadow is surrounded by woods on three sides, creating a garden sanctuary. An oriental gazebo anchors a quiet corner at the edge of the woods and is planted for shade. Azaleas, rhododendrons, columbine and a large collection of variety irises bloom in late spring, followed by masses of daylilies, butterfly bushes and hostas in mid-June.

DAYS & HOURS: June 5; 10.a.m. – 4 p.m.

DIRECTIONS: *Driving north on Riverside Drive* (Route 33) from downtown Columbus, pass the intersections at Fishinger Road and McCoy Road. Just past the next turn at Lane Road, turn right (east) at the fourth driveway (just past the four mailboxes) at the lighted stone pillars and white-fenced pasture. Proceed up the private .25 mile lane to the top of the hill, past the old barn, and park around the circular driveway at edge of grass. *Driving south on Riverside Drive* from Route 161, pass the intersection at Hayden Run Bridge, pass the traffic light at Henderson Road, (put on left turn signal at driveway with white boulders) and turn left (east) at the driveway with the stone pillars and white-fenced pasture. Proceed as above.

Ed Miller Garden, COLUMBUS, OH

This heavily wooded, informal hillside garden has been thinned and limbed-up to allow the development of an understory of dogwoods, serviceberries, redbuds and other flowering shrubs and trees. A small pond and stream is present. Many wildflowers native to the central Ohio region, as well as ferns, ornamental grasses, more than 300 varieties of hostas and numerous shade-tolerant perennials provide color from February to November.

DATES & HOURS: June 5; 10 a.m. – 2 p.m.

DIRECTIONS: *From Route 315* take Henderson Road Exit and go west on Henderson 2.6 miles to Chevy Chase Court. Turn right (go north). House is the third on the left side of the road with a wooden bridge over the stream. *From Riverside Drive* along the Scioto River turn east at the Henderson Road traffic light and go 1.1 miles to Chevy Chase Court and turn left (go north). Park in the driveway on the road.

❖ Franklin Park Conservatory & Botanical Garden,

1777 EAST BROAD STREET, COLUMBUS, OH 43203. (614) 645-8733.

The Conservatory features the original Victorian Palm House, which was placed in the National Register of Historic Places in 1974. A large addition, which features a tropical rain forest, a desert environment and a bonsai collection, was completed in 1992. The Conservatory is surrounded by a five-acre formally landscaped Grand Mallway, fountains, sculpture, a Japanese Garden, a Victory Garden and innovative educational displays.

DATES & HOURS: Year round, daily, dawn – dusk.

DIRECTIONS: The Conservatory and Garden are located approximately 2 miles east of the center of downtown Columbus, on the south side of Broad Street.

❖ The Topiary Garden at the Deaf School Park,

480 E. TOWN STREET, COLUMBUS, OH 43215. (614) 645-0197.

George Seurat's famous post-impressionist painting, "A Sunday Afternoon on the Island of La Grande Jatte," is recreated in topiary of taxus or yews. There are fifty topiary people, three dogs, a monkey, and boats in a real pond representing the Seine. The largest figure is twelve feet tall.

DATES & HOURS: Year round, daily, dawn – dusk.

DIRECTIONS: *From I-71 South,* take the Broad Street Exit, go west and pass Washington Avenue (no left turn). Turn left on 9th Street and left again on Oak Street to Washington Avenue. Turn right and go one block to East Town Street. *From I-71 North,* take the Main Street exit and go to Rich Street (one block). Turn right onto Washington Avenue and go one block to Town Street.

❖ The Dawes Arboretum,

7770 JACKSONTOWN ROAD S.E., NEWARK, OH 43056-9380. (800) 44-DAWES. *Established in 1929, the Dawes Arboretum is dedicated to education in horticulture, natural history, and arboretum history. It includes 1,149 acres of horticulture collections, gardens, natural areas, a Japanese garden, the Daweswood House, and collections of hollies, crab apples, rare trees, and rhododendrons. A four-and-one-half-mile auto tour and eleven miles of trails provide easy access.*

DATES & HOURS: Year round, grounds open dawn – dusk. Visitor's Center open Monday through Saturday, 8 a.m. – 5 p.m.; Sundays & Holidays, 1 p.m. – 5 p.m. Closed Thanksgiving, Christmas, and New Year's Day.

DIRECTIONS: *Located 30 miles east of Columbus* and 5 miles south of Newark on Route 13, north of I-70, off of Exit 132.

Garden of Jack & Sue Dingle, UPPER ARLINGTON, OH

This is a gently sloping, partially wooded and informally terraced garden. Large trees provide a canopy for woodland plantings of shrubs, spring perennials, and a garden pond. Stone walls are topped by perennial beds and rock gardens. There is also a heath garden and terrace plantings around a lovely swimming pool.

DATES & HOURS: June 5; 10 a.m. – 4 p.m.

DIRECTIONS: *Take Route 315* to Henderson Road. Go left on Henderson about 3 miles to the intersection of Sawmill Road. Turn left on Sawmill Road. Squires Ridge is a private road that goes to the right. Number 2875 is 100 yards from the entrance, on the left. *From Route 33* go north to Henderson Road. Go east on Henderson to the intersection with Sawmill Road. Turn right on Sawmill and continue as above.

The Hadley Garden, Upper Arlington, OH

A welcoming informal city garden constructed over thirty years by the owners. Planned originally to provide vistas from inside their home, the garden has become their center for relaxation and entertaining. Dominated by an old white oak and tall shagbark hickory, the path invites you to wander from wisteria-topped wall fountain to a former vegetable garden gone to shade, shadbush, and Exbury azaleas. A morning patio and rock garden with blue-and-white garden containers, small fountain and bird feeders is juniper-hedged for privacy and quiet and features a niger magnolia and tricolored beech.

DATES & HOURS: June 5; 10 a.m. – 4 p.m.

DIRECTIONS: *Take Route 315* to North Broadway exit. Head west for .75 mile on North Broadway to Kenny Road (traffic light). Turn right on Kenny. At next light (.25 mile), turn left on Tremont Road. The Ohio State University golf course will be on your right. Turn left at the third entrance to Trueville-Fountaine Drive. The house is the 5th on the right, #1401 Fountaine Drive. Park on the street.

❖ Inniswood Metro Gardens, 940 South Hempstead Road, Westerville, OH 43081-3612. (614) 895-6216.

Originally the home of Grace and Mary Innis, Inniswood is a balance of colorful, landscaped gardens and natural areas, yet it captures the warmth and serenity of a long-established estate garden. The herb, rock, and rose gardens fit the contours of the land and are in harmony with the meadow and woodlands. Cultural and educational programs and tours are offered for all ages. Fall is celebrated with "An Affair of the Hort," held the last week of September.

DATES & HOURS: Year round, daily, 7 a.m. – dusk.

DIRECTIONS: *Take Route 270* to the Westerville exit. Turn left onto Westerville Road. Turn left at the first traffic light onto Dempsey. Turn left at the second traffic light onto Hempstead Road. The road will veer to the right after the fire station, and the entrance to the park is on the right. Look for brown-and-white park signs.

DAYTON: *September 25, 1999*

The Beiser Garden, DAYTON, 10 A.M. – 4 P.M.

Barbara S. Rion, DAYTON, 10 A.M. – 4 P.M.

Ellie Schulman, DAYTON, 10 A.M. – 4 P.M.

Jean Woodhull, DAYTON, 10 A.M. – 4 P.M.

Sara E. Woodhull, DAYTON, 10 A.M. – 4 P.M.

 ❖ Aullwood Gardens, DAYTON, 8 A.M. – 7 P.M.

The Bieser Garden, DAYTON, OH

Surrounding our white "Connecticut Colonial" house, the garden meanders from shaded areas of hosta and ferns to sunny perennial borders and on to woodland beds. A stone path leads around the house to a white garden in the pool area. We have attempted to encompass all moods and seasons so there's lots of variety. Currently we are adding more perennials and shrubs for fall color and texture. Our ultimate goal is to develop a four-season gardenscape that is beautiful to the eye, satisfying to the soul and supportive of the environment.

DATES & HOURS: September 25; 10 a.m. – 4 p.m.

DIRECTIONS: *Exit I-75* at Edwin Moses Boulevard/University of Dayton. Turn east and proceed to Stewart Street. Turn right, cross the bridge and proceed to third traffic light. Turn right onto Brown Street and proceed to third traffic light. Turn left through stone pillars onto East Schantz Avenue. Drive several blocks and up a steep hill. The garden is at the top of the hill on the left at #790 East Schantz Avenue.

Proceeds shared with The Van Cleve Garden.

Barbara S. Rion, DAYTON, OH

A garden that drifts through two acres includes large perennial and fall beds (very large beds indicating passionate plant collector at work). A path winds into the woods where wildflowers are daring to emerge since the removal of the Japanese honeysuckle. Vegetable and three white flower gardens flank a grass path that leads to a small shade garden nestled among understory trees and a view of the fall beds. It is all just too much fun!

DATES & HOURS: September 25; 10 a.m. – 4 p.m.

DIRECTIONS: *From I-75* take the Main Street Exit. Go south on Route 48/Far Hills to Peach Orchard (4 miles). Turn right and go two blocks. Turn left on Ridgeway Road to #2325, the second house on the right.

Proceeds shared with The Van Cleve Garden.

Ellie Shulman, DAYTON, OH

My garden style has been influenced by extensive English, French, and American garden touring and by collaboration with garden designer Ziggy Petersons. In front is a shaded "garden within a garden" — all green plant material but no lawn. Challenges of difficult terrain and mostly full sun to the south and west have resulted in a terraced rose garden and several "garden rooms" with perennials, topiary, espalier, and a start at pleaching. There is an unusually large amount of plant material on less than an acre of property, and I am always working toward that elusive goal of "continuous color, bloom, and fragrance."

DATES & HOURS: September 25; 10 a.m. – 4 p.m.

DIRECTIONS: *From I-75* take Edwin Moses Boulevard/University of Dayton Exit and go east on Edwin Moses .8 mile to Stewart Street (first traffic light). Turn right on Stewart and proceed .6 mile (third traffic light). Turn right on Brown Street and proceed .7 mile (four traffic lights plus two more streets). Turn left on Schenck Avenue and proceed to #253.

Proceeds shared with The Van Cleve Garden.

Jean Woodhull, DAYTON, OH

My garden surrounds our family home, both of which have been brought to this time by much loving care, work, and use by four generations. My mother taught me, my husband dug with me, my children planted along with us, now grandchildren work a bit and play a lot. The garden has grown in many ways through these years — its bones are a pleasure through the seasons. Autumn is an especially rewarding time.

DATES & HOURS: September 25; 10 a.m. – 4 p.m.

DIRECTIONS: *From I-75* take the Main Street Exit and turn south on Main Street to Route 48 – Far Hills Avenue. At the top of the hill, look for Dixon Avenue. Turn toward the west onto Dixon Avenue, which dead ends into Runnymede Road. Turn left onto Runnymede and travel .25 mile. The house, #1200, is on the left (it's yellow). Please park on Runnymede Road.

Proceeds shared with The Van Cleve Garden.

Sara E. Woodhull, DAYTON, OH

This is a small urban garden. It specializes in the use of the entire space — especially the front yard. This garden has been in constant evolution, from no children, to little children, and now a very friendly and digging dog. This garden is a blend of shade and sun, perennials, annuals, and a few vegetables. Its fall beauty comes more from the textures of what is left, mixed with fall colors and a small demonstration area of possible materials to use in larger spaces. This garden is done by the gardener herself and shows what is possible with a small space.

DATES & HOURS: September 25; 10 a.m. – 4 p.m.

DIRECTIONS: *From I-75,* take Exit 50B. Turn left at the end of the ramp onto Route 741 South. Proceed to the third traffic light to Kettering-Dorothy Lane and turn left. Go through five traffic lights, past the golf course on the left, to a major intersection at Far Hills Avenue. Turn north onto Far Hills Avenue. Drive to the ninth street on the left side, Grandon Road. There is a Unitarian Fellowship building on the left corner. Turn left onto Grandon and go to the second house on the left. Please park in front of the house.

Proceeds shared with The Van Cleve Garden.

❖ Aullwood Gardens,

930 AULLWOOD ROAD, DAYTON, OH 45414. (937) 898-4006.
Aullwood Gardens MetroPark is an estate garden. The shady woodland combines native wildflowers, bulbs, and exotic plants. A meadow has some native prairie species. Peak bloom is in spring, especially April and May. There is something in bloom most of the year from Helleborus, Narcissus, Mertensia, *and* Syringa *to* Echinacea, Lycoris, Hosta, *and* Colchicum.

DATES & HOURS: March 1 through November 30, Tuesday through Sunday, 8 a.m. – 7 p.m.

DIRECTIONS: *From I-75,* take Route 40 West, take Aullwood Road South by Englewood Dam. Pass Aullwood Audubon Center, turn right into garden parking via sign.

❖ Cox Arboretum & Gardens,

6733 SPRINGBORO PIKE, DAYTON, OH 45449. (937) 434-9005.

The Cox Arboretum exhibits landscaped and natural areas on 175 rolling acres. Garden features include the Edible Landscape Garden, Herb Garden, Founders Water Garden, and the Shrub Garden. Woody plant collections include crab apple, magnolias, lilacs, maples, oaks and conifers. Hiking trails traverse approximately seventy acres of woodlands and ten acres of prairie and wetland. Tulips and daffodils afford a major spring display.

DATES & HOURS: Year round, daily, 8 a.m – dusk. Closed Christmas and New Year's Day.

DIRECTIONS: *From I-75* go to Exit 44. Go east on Route 725 1 mile to Route 741/Springboro Pike, south 2 miles to the entrance.

❖ Wegerzyn Horticultural Center/ Stillwater Gardens Metropark,

1301 EAST SIEBENTHALER AVENUE, DAYTON, OH 45414-5397. (513) 277-6546.

The Horticultural Center offers education in horticulture and the natural sciences to all ages. The Stillwater Gardens are comprised of children's, rose, Federal, English, and Victorian gardens, with a central mall featuring a "Cimmaron" white ash allée. These formal gardens are bordered on the west by the scenic Stillwater River and on the east by a mature lowland forest of sycamore, oak, red and silver maple, hickory and ash, through which a 350-foot boardwalk meanders.

DATES & HOURS: Year round, daily, 8 a.m. – dusk. Closed Christmas and New Year's Day. The center is open Monday – Friday, 9 a.m. – 5 p.m. Closed major holidays.

DIRECTIONS: *The Stillwater Gardens and Wegerzyn Horticultural Center are located 1.5 miles west of I-75,* approximately 4 miles south of I-70. Take I-75 to Siebenthaler/Wagner Ford Road Exit (57B). Go west on Siebenthaler Avenue to Dewese Parkway. Go north on Dewese Parkway for .5 mile to Stillwater Gardens.

PENNSYLVANIA

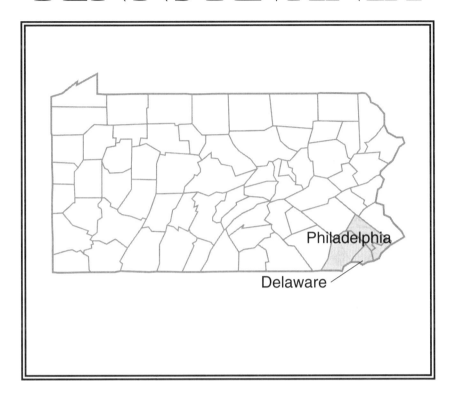

1999 PENNSYLVANIA OPEN DAYS

May 9: WILMINGTON, DELAWARE AREA
May 15: PHILADELPHIA AREA

PHILADELPHIA AREA: *May 15, 1999*

Overfields, BERWYN, 10 A.M. – 6 P.M.

David Culp, DOWNINGTOWN, 10 A.M. – 6 P.M.

Northrop Garden, MALVERN, 10 A.M. – 6 P.M.

Tunnel Farm, NORTH WALES, 10 A.M. – 4 P.M.

Stoneleigh, VILLANOVA, 10 A.M. – 4 P.M.

The S. M. V. Hamilton Estate, WAYNE, 10 A.M. – 2 P.M.

Overfields, BERWYN, PA

In the 1930s and 1940s, Overfields was a lovely garden, but by the time we bought it in 1973 it was badly out of shape. We spent our first years clearing and removing thirty-three trees. Frederick Peck, ASLA, gave us guidelines to strengthen existing axes and angles. Along the way we tackled a huge old vegetable garden. As our children grew and our needs changed, this area went through many transformations. At present it is open space surrounded by looping perennial beds. We have had a wonderful time developing these four acres.

DATES & HOURS: May 15; 10 a.m. – 6 p.m.

DIRECTIONS: *Berwyn is on the Lancaster Pike/Route 30,* approximately 2 miles east of Paoli and 2.5 miles west of Wayne. From the center of Berwyn, at the post office and train station, going west on Lancaster Pike, it is .3 mile to a left on Leopard Road. Go .9 mile to Sugartown Road. Turn right onto Sugartown and immediately left into the driveway with a black mailbox marked "Overfields 1200." Note: This is a very busy road. Exercise care when entering and exiting drive. Also, there is another Sugartown Road in Malvern and another Leopard Road in Paoli. Please ignore them.

David Culp, DOWNINGTOWN, PA

The garden is my version of a Pennsylvania country garden, with mixed borders of native and exotic species for both shade and full sun. There are rock, woodland, rose, and vegetable gardens. In the ruins of an old carriage house, stone walls contain alpine plants and provide a site for my container garden. Species include both native and exotics planted in a naturalistic design.

DATES & HOURS: May 15; 10 a.m. – 6 p.m.

DIRECTIONS: *From Route 202 North or South,* take Route 30 West (30 Bypass) to the Thornedale Exit. Turn right from the ramp to the second road on the right, Osborne Road. Make a right over a one-lane bridge. Go up the hill to the house on the right side behind a stockade fence. It is #1158 Osborne Road.

Northrop Garden, MALVERN, PA

When we purchased this challenging hillside, the field was depleted by corn and divided by black walnuts. The chief charm lay in its view: the receding hills of Chester County. We began gardening at the top of the property and have been slowly landscaping downhill, terracing with intermittent stone walls that structure the connected gardens. Stone steps from the upper herb garden and summer house lead past a lily pond, by a dry shade garden under the walnuts, to the pergola in the lower, more formal garden. Further down the hill the view has been augmented by a pond where a wet woodland area is being established.

DATES & HOURS: May 15; 10 a.m. – 6 p.m.

DIRECTIONS: *From the Valley Forge Exit off the Pennsylvania Turnpike,* take Route 202 South and exit at Route 29 North/Great Valley. Turn right at the second traffic light onto Route 29 North. Go 1.8 miles through four more traffic lights. At the traffic light after the railroad tracks, go straight on Charlestown Road for .5 mile, up a hill. Bear left after the school onto Pikeland Road. Go 1.6 miles to the second road on the left. Turn onto Wells Road. Go .5 mile to two driveways on the left at the top of the hill. Number 3104 is the second driveway. Park along the drive.

❖ Meadowbrook Farm & Greenhouse,

1633 WASHINGTON LANE, MEADOWBOOK, PA 19046. (215) 887-5900.
This beautiful garden is the life work of J. Liddon Pennock. Designed as a series of outdoor rooms, each garden is unique and very comfortable, with the emphasis on design. The public display garden leads to the greenhouse where plants and garden gifts of all types are available. Meadowbrook Farm has long been known for special horticulture activities including lectures and workshops to visiting groups.

DATES & HOURS: Year round, Monday – Saturday, 10 a.m. – 5 p.m. Tours by appointment.

DIRECTIONS: *From Pennsylvania Turnpike:* take Exit 27. Take Route 611 south, turn left onto Route 63, in approximately 1.5 miles turn right onto Washington Lane. Meadowbrook Farm sign is located approximately .75 mile on left side.

Tunnel Farm, North Wales, PA

In June 1961, two weeks before the first of our children was born, we moved into Tunnel Farm. The roofs of the dark-red stone Welsh farmhouse (oldest part – circa 1735) and bank barn leaked, vines crawled into the trees, the ha-has were crumbling, and my husband and I were hooked. Since then we have raised four children and many animals, added a wing, redone the barn, rebuilt ha-has, added stone and brick terraces, gardens and sculpture, a pond, and many species of trees, creating different habitats to welcome a variety of plant and animal life. From our grape allée to our courtyard between the springhouse and the house where our espaliered Camellia japonica, Hibiscus syriacus 'Diana', *and* Nandina domestica *keep company with a red stone St. Francis fountain, we have kept the spirit and simple charm of a Welsh farmhouse and garden.*

DATES & HOURS: May 15; 10 a.m. - 4 p.m.

DIRECTIONS: *Take Route 476/Blue Route* to the Plymouth Meeting Exit. Take Exit 9 to a dead end at Plymouth Road. Turn right onto Plymouth to the first traffic light at Butler Pike. Turn left onto Butler Pike to Broad Axe Route 73 (2.6 miles). Turn left onto Route 73/Skippack Pike to Center Square Route 202 (3 miles). Turn right onto Route 202 to Township Line Road. Turn left and take the first road on the right, Swedesford Road. Turn right onto Swedesford Road and go 1 mile to the house after the red barn on the right.

❖ Fairmount Park Horticulture Center & Arboretum,

Belmont Avenue & North Horticultural Drive, Philadelphia, PA 19131. (215) 685-0096.

The Arboretum covers twenty-two acres and boasts an assortment of trees, many of which have been labeled with both common and botanical names. The display house is the first greenhouse you enter from the lobby. Its permanent display includes olive and fig trees, oleander, and bougainvillea. The next greenhouse contains a magnificent collection of cacti and succulents. There are also many statues and perennial gardens on these grounds. Come and visit!

DATES & HOURS: Year round, daily, 9 a.m. – 3 p.m.
DIRECTIONS: *From I-76 West,* take Exit 35 for Montgomery Drive. Turn left at the light onto Montgomery Drive and travel one block, turning left onto Horticultural Drive. Drive through the front gates on the left; the building is on the right.

❖ Historic Bartram's Garden,

54TH STREET AND LINDBERGH BOULEVARD, PHILADELPHIA, PA 19143.
(215) 729-5281.

Historic Bartram's Garden is America's oldest living botanical garden, founded in 1728 by John Bartram, America's first great botanist, naturalist, and plant explorer. The forty-five acre site on the banks of the Schuylkill River includes the furnished Bartram house and other unique eighteenth-century farm buildings, a botanical garden, historic trees, a fifteen-acre wildflower meadow, a water garden, a wetland, a parkland, and a museum shop.

DATES & HOURS: Year round, daily, dawn – dusk.

DIRECTIONS: *Located less than fifteen minutes from Center City Philadelphia* and convenient to I-76 and I-95. Please call for detailed directions.

❖ Morris Arboretum of the University of Pennsylvania,

100 NORTHWESTERN AVENUE, PHILADELPHIA, PA 19118. (215) 247-5777.

The Morris Arboretum of the University of Pennsylvania is an historic public garden and educational institution. Its programs integrate science, art, and the humanities to promote an understanding of the relationships between plants and people. The Living Collection is the Arboretum's defining collection. Sited in a 166-acre landscape, it contains approximately 2,330 taxa and over 9,000 accessioned and labeled plants from the temperate Northern Hemisphere, parts of Asia, Europe, and North America. The collection consists primarily of woody plants, trees, and shrubs adapted to our region.

DATES & HOURS: Year round, daily, 10 a.m. – 4 p.m.

DIRECTIONS: *Take I-76/Schuylkill Expressway* to the Blue Route/476 North. Take Exit 8/Plymouth Meeting and follow signs for Germantown Pike East. Continue on Germantown Pike for 4 miles and turn left onto Northwestern Avenue. The Arboretum entrance is .25 miles on the right.

❖ The Scott Arboretum of Swarthmore College,

500 COLLEGE AVENUE, SWARTHMORE, PA 19081. (610) 328-8025.

The Scott Arboretum is a green oasis uniquely situated on the Swarthmore College campus. More than 300 acres create the college landscape and provide a display of the best ornamental plants recommended for Delaware Valley gardens. There are more than 3,000 different kinds of plants grown on the campus. Major plant collections include: flowering cherries, coreopsis, crabapples, hydrangeas, lilacs, magnolias, rhododendrons, tree peonies, viburnums, wisteria, and witch-hazels. Special gardens include the Rose Garden, Fragrance Garden, Teaching Garden, Entrance Garden, Winter Garden, Nason Garden, Harry Wood Court-yard Garden, and Cosby Courtyard.

DATES & HOURS: Year round, daily, dawn – dusk.

DIRECTIONS: *From I-95* take Exit 7 for I-476 North/Plymouth Meeting. Take I-476 to Exit 2 for Media/Swarthmore. Turn right onto Baltimore Pike and follow signs for Swarthmore. Stay in the right lane for .25 mile and turn right onto Route 320 South. Proceed through the second traffic light at College Avenue to the first driveway on the right.

Stoneleigh, VILLANOVA, PA

Stoneleigh, built in 1900, comprises approximately thirty-nine acres and includes an area designed in 1925 by the Olmsted Brothers, vestiges of which remain. The main delights are marvelous old trees, lovely sweeps of lawn, and areas of azaleas, which, along with the house, evoke an English manor house and "park" which were all the rage in 1900. We moved to Stoneleigh in 1964 with our young family, added the pool and the poolhouse and resurrected the tennis court. Much of the property is under conservation easement, therefore, it will never be developed. The preservation of Stoneleigh is a work in progress and a labor of love.

DATES & HOURS: May 15; 10 a.m. – 4 p.m.

DIRECTIONS: From I-476 South, take Exit 5 for Villanova/St. Davids, and turn right onto Route 30. Proceed east on Route 30 for .25 mile and turn left at the Coastal Gas Station onto Route 320 North (also called Spring Mill Road). Proceed north through the traffic light at County Line Road and travel .5 mile to the first entrance on the left, #330 North Spring Mill Road.

S. M. V. Hamilton Estate, WAYNE, PA

The Hamilton Estate features many garden areas. There is an English rose garden planted with David Austin shrub roses and other climbing roses and a formal annual garden adjacent to the house. The poolhouse and pool area are surrounded by a more relaxed perennial garden. A perennial border surrounds the parking area. The rest of the eight-and-one-half-acre estate, accented with garden ornaments and a Lodge Pole from Vancouver, British Columbia, includes a formal rose garden, an espaliered orchard, vegetable gardens, and a state-of-the-art greenhouse complex.

DATES & HOURS: May 15; 10 a.m. – 2 p.m.

DIRECTIONS: *Take Route 476* to Exit 5/Villanova/St. David's. Continue west on Route 30 for 2 miles, passing through the heart of Wayne. Continue to Lancaster County Farmer's Market. Turn right at the traffic light onto Eagle Road. Turn left at the blinking light onto Stafford Avenue. Number 218 will be the second driveway on the left, before the stop sign. Proceed up the driveway, past the garage on the right, and turn left into the field through the gates. *From I-95* proceed north to I-476, Exit 5 and follow above directions.

❖ Chanticleer, 786 CHURCH ROAD, WAYNE, PA 19087. (610) 687-4163.

This thirty-acre pleasure garden was formerly the home of the Rosengarten family. Emphasis is on ornamental plants, particularly herbaceous perennials. The garden is a dynamic mix of formal and naturalistic areas, collections of flowering trees and shrubs, a pond, a meadow, wildflower gardens, and a garden of shade-loving Asian herbaceous plants.

DATES & HOURS: April 1 to October 31, Wednesday through Saturday, 10 a.m. – 5 p.m.

DIRECTIONS: *Take Route 76 West* to Route 476. Turn south onto Route 476 toward Chester. Take Exit 5 toward Villanova. Turn right at the intersection of Route 30 and Route 320 South. Turn right at the next traffic light onto Conestoga Road. Turn left at the second traffic light onto Church Road. Go .5 miles to Chanticleer.

WILMINGTON, DELAWARE AREA: *May 9, 1999*

Glenderro, COATESVILLE, 10 A.M. — 4 P.M.

Runnymede, COATESVILLE, 10 A.M. — 4 P.M.

Primrose Paths, FAIRVILLE, 10 A.M. — 2 P.M.

PLEASE NOTE: *These above gardens are participating as part of the Wilmington Delaware Area Open Day.*

Meown Farm, CENTREVILLE, DE, 10 A.M. — 2 P.M., *page 121*

Mt. Cuba, GREENVILLE, DE, 10 A.M. — 6 P.M., *page 121*

Larke Stowe, WILMINGTON, DE, 10 A.M. — 4 P.M., *page 122*

❖ Gibraltar, WILMINGTON, by appointment only.

❖ **Brandywine Conservancy Wildflower & Native Plant Gardens,** US ROUTE 1, CHADDS FORD, PA 19317. (610) 388-2700.

Begun in 1974, the gardens feature indigenous and some naturalized plants of the greater Brandywine region displayed in natural settings. The gardens use wildflowers, trees, and shrubs in landscaped areas. Plants are selected to provide a succession of bloom from early spring through the first killing frost. Each is located in a setting akin to its natural habitat: woodland, wetland, flood plain, or meadow.

DATES & HOURS: Year round, daily, dawn – dusk.

DIRECTIONS: *From I-95 North,* take exit marked for Route 141 North to Route 52 North. Follow Route 52 until it intersects with Route 1. Turn right onto Route 1 North. Travel 2 miles to the Museum.

Glenderro Farm, COATESVILLE, PA

Our horse farm is under conservation easement, surrounded by Cheshire fox-hunting country. Descending into a glen through an orchard underplanted with spring bulbs, one comes upon the house and small terraced garden. A more formal brick terrace and old iron fenced rugosa rose garden overlooks two spring-fed ponds. The smaller is surrounded by clethra and other shrubs to attract birds. The much larger one is our "swimming pool," shared with a great blue heron, trout and large frogs.

DATES & HOURS: May 9; 10 a.m. – 6 p.m.

DIRECTIONS: *From Kennett Square,* take Route 82 north through Unionville and Doe Run to Route 841 (about 8 miles). Turn left onto Route 841 to the first road on the right (Chapel Road). Follow for 2 miles to the dead end. Turn left onto Gum Tree Road, and go .25 mile to village of Gum Tree. Take the first right, Five Points Road, and go .25 mile to the first driveway on the right. Look for two white mailboxes. Turn right into Glenderro Farm.

Proceeds shared with The Delaware Center for Horticulture.

Runnymede, COATESVILLE, PA

On a hill overlooking the Doe Run Creek and the serene pasture beyond sits the perennial spring garden bordering the swimming pool area. It is partially surrounded by a stone wall and contains many varieties of roses and peonies. Flagstone steps descend to a wisteria-covered terrace with a small ornamental pool. Many species of lovely old trees and shrubs surround the house, which was built for Mr. & Mrs. J. Stanley Reeve in 1931 to resemble a Cotswold hunting "box" in Leicestershire, England. The architect was Shepherd & Stearns, Boston. The contractor was J.S. Cornell. A wing was added in 1963. The architect was Walter Durham of Ardmore, and the landscape architect was Owen Schmidt of Gladwyne. Also be sure to enjoy the handsome stone stud barn, delightful waterwheel, vegetable garden, wildflower garden, greenhouse, and apple orchards.

DATES & HOURS: May 9; 10 a.m. – 4 p.m.

DIRECTIONS: *From Route 1,* exit at Route 82 North and proceed through Unionville to the stop sign at Route 841. Turn left onto Route 841 and proceed to second road, Springdell Road, and turn right. Take the first left onto Runnymede Road. This is a narrow, one-lane road. At the first fork, bear left over the bridge. At the second fork, turn right and go through iron gate. At the third fork, turn right and go to the main house.

Proceeds shared with The Delaware Center for Horticulture.

Primrose Paths, FAIRVILLE, PA

I acquired this property for its dramatic topography and varied natural surroundings. My aim is to create different sorts of garden spaces which can be enjoyed from the inside as well as the outside throughout the year. Wooden decks on the southwest side of the house overlook a woodland gorge. Below, a sea of Primula japonica *covers a delta between two streams. On the northeast side, there is an upward-inclining wildflower field rich in poppies. Beyond the house and its surrounding perennial beds, mass plantings of daylilies and caryopteris, among others, engage the eye.*

DATES & HOURS: May 9; 10 a.m. – 2 p.m.

DIRECTIONS: *Go north on Route 52* from Winterthur. One mile after crossing the Pennsylvania border, turn right on Fairville Road. Go 1 mile to the joint driveway on the left with three mailboxes, marked #1201-1221. Turn left here, go .1 mile. My driveway is the first left, marked #1219.

Proceeds shared with The Delaware Center for Horticulture.

❖ Longwood Gardens,

ROUTE 1, P.O. BOX 501, KENNETT SQUARE, PA 19348-0501. (610) 388-1000.
WWW.LONGWOODGARDENS.ORG

One of the world's premier horticultural displays, Longwood offers 1,050 acres of gardens, woodlands, and meadows; twenty outdoor gardens; twenty indoor gardens within four acres of greenhouses; 11,000 types of plants; spectacular fountains; extensive educational programs, including career training and internships; and 800 events each year, including flower shows, gardening demonstrations, courses, children's programs, concerts, musical theater, and fireworks displays.

DATES & HOURS: Year round, daily, 9 a.m.– 5 p.m. (6 p.m. April through October). Open many evenings, call for details.

DIRECTIONS: *Located on Route 1,* 3 miles northeast of Kennett Square, Pennsylvania and 12 miles north of Wilmington, Delaware.

❖ Doe Run, P.O. BOX 367, UNIONVILLE, PA 19375. (610) 384-5542.

Doe Run was a thoroughbred horse farm for many years, without a garden and with only five trees. Sir John Thouron proceeded in 1953 to plant trees and design herbaceous borders, an alpine garden, a sunken garden, and pebble and moss gardens on this 300-acre estate. With its many rare plants in the garden and the greenhouses, it is now rated as one of the premier private gardens in America and can be seen by appointment only. The tours are usually escorted by the owner and last about an hour.

DATES & HOURS: Tours by appointment only from June through August; Monday, Wednesday & Friday.

DIRECTIONS: *Located 10 minutes from Longwood Gardens* and 30 minutes from Winterthur.

RHODE ISLAND

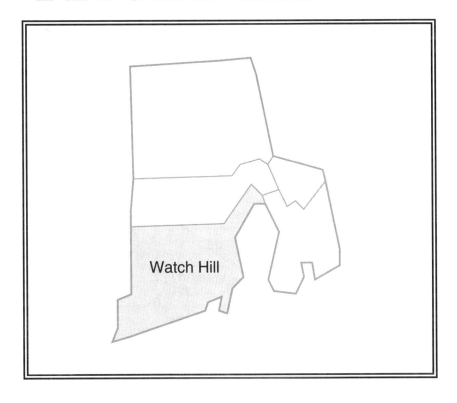

1999 RHODE ISLAND OPEN DAYS

July 11: WATCH HILL AREA

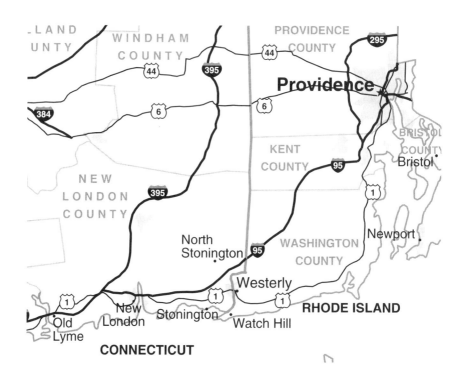

WATCH HILL: *July 11, 1999*

The Garden at Graigie Brae, WATCH HILL, 10 A.M. – 4 P.M.

Mr. & Mrs. Thomas D. O'Connor.— Bayberry Ridge, WATCH HILL, 10 A.M. – 4 P.M.

PLEASE NOTE: *The following gardens in New London County, Connecticut are also open on this day.*

Barbara & Peter Block - Stewart Hill, NORTH STONINGTON, CT, 10 A.M. – 2 P.M., *page 111*

Mr. & Mrs. Thomas F. Moore, STONINGTON, CT, 10 A.M. – 4 P.M., *page 113*

❖ Blithewold Mansion, Gardens & Arboretum,

101 FERRY ROAD (ROUTE 114), BRISTOL, RI 02809. (401) 253-2707.
Former summer estate of Pennsylvania coal baron Augustus Van Wickle features thirty-three acres of historic landscape overlooking Narragansett Bay. More than 2,000 trees and shrubs, varied gardens, a bamboo grove and a ninety-foot tall Giant Sequoia, the tallest of its kind east of the Rocky Mountains. A property of the Heritage Trust of Rhode Island.

DATES & HOURS: Year round, 10 a.m. – 5 p.m. Admission charged; group rates available. Guided garden tours by appointment.

DIRECTIONS: *Take Route I-95 East* out of Providence. Take Exit 2 in Massachusetts for Route 136 South. Go through the towns of Warren and Bristol. Pass the Bristol Police Station on your right and go approximately 1 mile to Griswold Avenue on the right. Take Griswold to the end and turn left on Route 114. Blithewold is just ahead on the right.

The Garden at Graigie Brae, WATCH HILL, RI

My gardens fill a rather small piece of property overlooking Foster's Cove on Little Narraganset Bay facing west. The terrain is varied, so we have created "garden rooms." By the front door I have a "walk-through" English garden, followed by a green garden with a small fish pond for quiet repose. Through a pergola and a gate there is a wide perennial border — across from which is a large herb garden featuring a knot garden backed with old fashioned roses. Below the swimming pool is a small shady retreat.

DATES & HOURS: July 11; 10 a.m. – 4 p.m.

DIRECTIONS: *From Thomas Moore's home in Stonington, CT:* Turn left from Moore's driveway. Go to the stoplight. Turn left onto A-1-A. Go about 3 miles until you reach the stop sign in Westerly. Turn right and follow signs to beaches. Going about 2 miles up a hill to Beach Street go past Smith's Florist and keep going to stop sign. Go straight through approaching Watch Hill. Proceed to a yellow house on the right. The second street after the house will be Neowan Avenue on the right. Take this one block to Aquidneck Avenue. Turn left. The house is the second on the right. There is a #6 on the door.

Mr & Mrs. Thomas D. O'Connor — Bayberry Ridge,
WATCH HILL, RI

Overlooking the Pawcatuck River with views to Stonington, this garden is a classic summer garden befitting an 1890 Watch Hill House. The plantings, designed in 1987 by landscape architects Susan and T. P. Plimpton, yield maximum interest during the warmer months. A large horseshoe-shaped perennial garden is colorful throughout the season. Viewed from the house is an enchanting white garden. At a lower level, dwarf English boxwood edge a rose garden. A cutting garden, daylily collection, and seasonal potted plants further enrich this interesting property. The perimeter plantings achieve privacy and contain many salt-tolerant trees and shrubs.

DATES & HOURS: July 11; 10 a.m. – 4 p.m.

DIRECTIONS: *From New London,* take Exit 92 off of I-95. Turn right at end of ramp and proceed to Route 78. Turn right and go to the first traffic light at Route 1. Cross Route 1 and go to second stop sign and turn left. Pass Route 1A and Avondale Road will be the third street on the right. The house is the first on the left, surrounded by a low stone wall.

Proceeds shared with the Women's Resource Center of South County, RI.

TENNESSEE

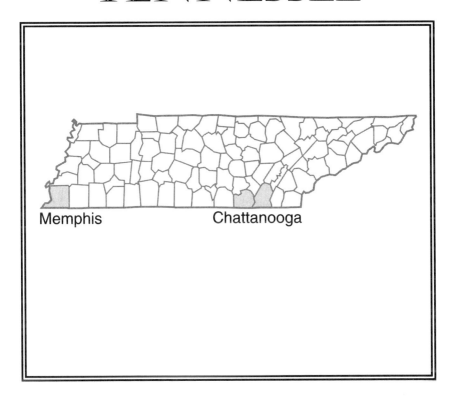

Memphis   Chattanooga

1999 TENNESSEE OPEN DAYS

April 17: MEMPHIS AREA
May 22: CHATTANOOGA AREA

CHATTANOOGA: *May 22, 1999*

Holmberg Garden, CHATTANOOGA, 2 P.M. – 6 P.M.

McDonald–Elder Garden, CHATTANOOGA, 10 A.M. – 4 P.M.

The Garden at Skillet Gap, CHATTANOOGA, 2 P.M. – 6 P.M.

Mr. & Mrs. Edward L. Mitchell, LOOKOUT MOUNTAIN, 2 P.M. – 6 P.M.

Teeta's Garden, LOOKOUT MOUNTAIN, 2 P.M. – 6 P.M.

Warner's Garden, LOOKOUT MOUNTAIN, 2 P.M. – 6 P.M.

PLEASE NOTE: *The following garden in Georgia is participating as part of the Chattanooga Area Open Day.*

Susan & Steven Bradley, LOOKOUT MOUNTAIN, GA, 2 P.M. – 6 P.M., *page 145*

Holmberg Garden, CHATTANOOGA, TN

This pool and terrace-side garden offer a spectacular view of downtown Chattanooga, the Tennessee River and the distant Smokey Mountains. There is sculpture interspersed on the lawn and viewing areas. Plantings are informal, and the view dominates.

DATES & HOURS: May 22; 2 p.m. – 6 p.m.

DIRECTIONS: *Leave downtown Chattanooga on I-24* heading south to Nashville/Birmingham. The Tennessee River will be on your right. Exit to the right at Brown's Ferry Road. Go 1 mile and turn left on Elder Mountain Road. There is a quick-stop grocery on the corner. Follow the road up the mountain to the top (2-3 miles). At the guardhouse, turn right. The house is the second on the right side.

McDonald – Elder Garden, CHATTANOOGA, TN

Our house and gardens, located on the brow of Elder Mountain, reflect the work of two families more than fifty years. The gardens, with the exception of the woodland garden, have been developed to frame the mountain stone house and spectacular views of Chattanooga, the Tennessee River, and Lookout Mountain. Native plants — rhododendrons, azaleas, laurel, dogwoods, redbuds, ferns, wildflowers, and vines — grow around terraces, ponds, and rock outcroppings on the brow and in the woods. Winding paths lead to large native hollies, hydrangeas, old peonies and English boxwoods, a vegetable garden and many specimen trees, including towering spruce and hemlocks.

DATES & HOURS: May 22; 10 a.m. - 4 p.m.

DIRECTIONS: *I-24 north of Chattanooga* to Browns Ferry Road Exit. Turn right (east) on Browns Ferry. Go .8 mile to Elder Mountain Road on left. Follow this to top of mountain. Directions to garden will be posted at the guardhouse.

The Garden at Skillet Gap, CHATTANOOGA, TN

This meandering garden sprawls from the shady front pond to a rock garden full of blue and purple flowers at the side of a woodsy, contemporary home. There are three outdoor garden "rooms" as well. On the south side, in back of the home, are three paths at varying levels above the Tennessee River. Each one offers a different perspective — from natural woodland to cultivated lilies, hydrangeas, and azaleas. Although the gardens were installed in 1994, they exude a feeling of a more established setting.

DATES & HOURS: May 22; 2 p.m. – 6 p.m.

DIRECTIONS: *From I-24 West or East* take Browns Ferry Exit. Proceed north about 1 mile. Take a left on Elder Mountain Road (at the Quick Stop). Travel about 2 miles to the guardhouse. Turn right on Cumberland Road. Go about 2.5 miles. Take a left on Skillet Gap. The gardens are at the end of the road. Signs will lead the way.

Mr. & Mrs. Edward L. Mitchell, LOOKOUT MOUNTAIN, TN

An English garden, terraced with wildflower and perennial beds, of which the most outstanding specimen is an old tree peony. There are beds of indigenous species of rhododendron and laurel, and groupings of four separate varieties of hydrangeas. Large plantings of hosta edge the lawn. A restored fish pond is nestled in a garden of fern and Japanese maple. A rose garden is centered in a perennial border.

DATES & HOURS: May 22; 2 p.m. – 6 p.m.

DIRECTIONS: *Take I-124* through Chattanooga. Take Lookout Mountain Exit, follow signs to Ruby Falls. Pass Ruby Falls and go to the top of the Mountain. *At top take hard right* (East Brow Road). Go about 1 mile. Morrison Street turns off to the left, beside a large green bus garage. (If you come to the top of the Incline Railroad, you went 1/2 block too far). Take Morrison Street to the last house on the left, #206 Morrison St. (stone-and-stucco Tudor house.) Park on Morrison Street.

Teeta's Garden, LOOKOUT MOUNTAIN, TN

A typical mountain garden — uphill and downhill on several levels. Enter along a drive bordered with laurel, rhododendron, leucothoe and fern. Paths lead by plantings of native azalea, pieris Japonica, groups of hydrangea, including native hydrangea bordered by hosta, astilbe, different forms of ground cover. A rustic bridge leads across a stream bed to the cutting garden and beds of cuttings being grown for future plantings. This is a garden grown for the pleasure of gardening!

DATES & HOURS: May 22; 2 p.m. – 6 p.m.

DIRECTIONS: *From downtown Chattanooga* follow Scenic Highway 148 up Lookout Mountain. At top of the mountain, continue straight ahead until you see a mountain stone fountain in the center of the road. Take a left and continue past stores and post office. The house is on the left directly across from Dogwood Drive on the right. Park on Dogwood Drive or a bit further down along the Scenic Highway.

Warner's Garden, LOOKOUT MOUNTAIN, TN

The name of our street announces our property's most wonderful asset: its spectacular view. In our efforts to enhance this and to add softness and coolness, we are adding pockets of small shade trees, and groupings of unusual evergreens. We are liberal in our use of ground covers and vines. A pathway through a hillside planted in native rhododendrons provides a natural transition to adjoining National Forestry property. Waterfalls in swimming and lily pools add the sound of music. We hope our garden provides a peaceful bench where the panorama surrounding us can be enjoyed.

DATES & HOURS: May 22; 2 p.m. – 6 p.m.

DIRECTIONS: *From downtown Chattanooga* follow Highway 148 up Lookout Mountain, passing by Ruby Falls and over Incline tracks. At the flashing caution light, turn right onto East Brow Road. Note signpost toward Point Park. After a left and right curving there will be a long, low, serpentine white brick wall on the right. Shortly, turn right at Grandview (signposted). We are the second house on the right (cobblestone courtyard, slate roof). From flashing light to Grandview, distance is .6 mile. Park on the street in front of the house.

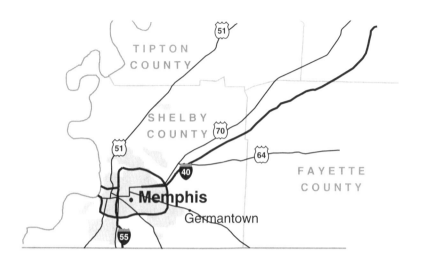

MEMPHIS: *April 17, 1999*

Hillbrook, GERMANTOWN, 10 A.M. – 4 P.M.

Mr. & Mrs. Michael McDonnell, MEMPHIS, 10 A.M. – 2 P.M.

Irene & Joe Orgill's Garden, MEMPHIS, 10 A.M. – 4 P.M.

Hillbrook, GERMANTOWN, TN

Hillbrook is an informal, country oasis in the middle of town. The predominant area is a woodland park with a recirculating stream flowing into a pond and a lovely waterfall by the dock. Along one side of the stream is a deep border full of a wide variety of perennials, flowering shrubs, and trees. The features on the sunny part of the property are a rose garden and large perennial beds that are along the pasture fence on the other side of the pool. The whole atmosphere is of peace and serenity, with the slight burbling sounds of the water. Neighbors' children are quite often found fishing at the pond

DATES & HOURS: April 17; 10 a.m. – 4 p.m.

DIRECTIONS: *Take Poplar Avenue* (Highway 72) to Germantown. At West Street turn south and go to 2nd right past the railroad – Second Street. Turn right (west) one block to dead end into McVay Road. Turn left, go around a sharp curve, past Sleepy Hollow Lane on the right, to #7398 McVay Road (mailbox on right just after McVay). *From I-40* (East of Memphis) take the Germantown Exit south, cross Poplar Avenue, go south across the railroad track, turn right on Second Street across from Germantown Commissary, go two blocks to dead end into McVay Road, turn left and continue as above.

Mr. & Mrs. Michael McDonnell, MEMPHIS, TN

Designed by Tom Pellett, the McDonnell is a three-acre suburban garden that is particularly pretty in early spring with a wildflower dell and woodland walk. A sunny flower border provides summer color. There is a rose garden beside the pool gazebo and a raised bed vegetable garden in the same area.

DATES & HOURS: April 17, 10. a.m. – 2 p.m.

DIRECTIONS: *Take the Perkins exit south off I-240* to a stop light at Walnut Grove Road, then east on Walnut Grove. Norval is a small dead-end street off of Walnut Grove Road, east of Perkins and west of Mendenhall. The house is #110 Norval. Park along Norval.

Irene & Joe Orgill's Garden, MEMPHIS, TN

It has been said that gardening is a very competitive sport; not so for me. My father was a farmer, and I've inherited his respect for growing things. I love digging in the soil and find peace in observing the growth cycles of the plants in my garden. Happily, our house came with an established 1930s garden, and over time I've been able to add my ideas and blend the old with the new. I think of my garden as a family garden; we've all enjoyed it over the years and have had two daughters married in it!

DATES & HOUSES: April 17; 10 a.m. – 4 p.m.

DIRECTIONS: *From the traffic light at Walnut Grove and Perkins,* turn north on Perkins; second driveway on west side of street, #71 North Perkins Road. Park on the street.

TEXAS

1999 TEXAS OPEN DAYS

March 20: HOUSTON AREA
September 25: AUSTIN AREA

AUSTIN: *September 25, 1999*

James deGrey David, AUSTIN, 10 A.M. – 6 P.M.

Deborah Hornickel, AUSTIN, 10 A.M. – 6 P.M.

Anne McGrath & David Schade, AUSTIN, 10 A.M. – 6 P.M.

Frances Judson Smith, AUSTIN, 10 A.M. – 6 P.M.

Dr. Gordon L. White, AUSTIN, 10 A.M. – 6 P.M.

James deGrey David, AUSTIN, TX

This is a collector's garden with Mediterranean elements. It includes a series of terraces and courtyards. Water features include a native limestone water staircase extending to a creek bed. A special feature is a vegetable garden with a collection of exotic, hard-to-find edibles. The garden integrates and flows with this architecturally acclaimed home.

DATES & HOURS: September 25; 10 a.m. – 6 p.m.

DIRECTIONS: *Travel south on Loop 1.* Go west on 2244, commonly known as Beecave Road. Turn right on Edgegrove at the Texaco Station. Turn right on Rollingwood Drive and then a quick left onto Gentry. Turn right on Sugar Creek and park along the road.

Deborah Hornickel, AUSTIN, TX

Rows of shaped English boxwoods lead you to the front door. To the left of the walkway, the garden is shaded by a southern magnolia tree. On the right side is a wilder, sunny area for growing annuals and perennials. Roses lead you down the driveway to the garden surprise — a Pyrus calleyera *tunnel located in the back garden.*

DATES & HOURS: September 25; 10 a.m. – 6 p.m.

DIRECTIONS: Travel north on Loop to the 35th Street exit. Go east on 35th Street and turn right on Oakmont Boulevard. Please park along the road.

Anne McGrath & David Schade, AUSTIN, TX

This suburban garden consists of several distinctive theme gardens. Woodland, wildlife, white, herb, and water gardens are some of the special areas. There is a strong use of vertical accents with a vast array of plant species.

DATES & HOURS: September 25; 10 a.m. – 6 p.m.

DIRECTIONS: *From Loop 1,* take Beecave Road to Westbrook Road, which will become Briarwood and finally Brookhaven Trail. Look for #501 Brookhaven Trail. Please park along the road.

Frances Judson Smith, AUSTIN, TX

This is a plantsman's garden whose location focuses on the entrance to the residence. It combines a central shaded woodland environment and a more peripheral sun-drenched setting with a strong western United States' plants selection uniquely arranged.

DATES & HOURS: September 25; 10 a.m. – 6 p.m.

DIRECTIONS: *From Ranch Road 2222* turn south on Mt. Bonnell Road. Continue past Mt. Bonnell Park to the second house on the right. *From 35th Street,* travel west, curving around Albert Davis Water Treatment Plant. The first right is Mt. Bonnell Road. Go over a bridge and up a hill. The house is on the left before reaching the park. Please park along the road.

Dr. Gordon L. White, AUSTIN, TX

This is a relatively small garden designed as a series of rooms, each with an intimate relationship with the house and surrounding mature tree species. Formal as well as informal plantings of native and exotic flora coexist in several different microclimates, each influenced by sun, shade, and differing soil and water conditions. Hand-crafted native stonework acts to unify the design hardscape.

DATES & HOURS: September 25; 10 a.m. – 6 p.m.

DIRECTIONS: *From I-35,* exit Downtown (12th – 15th Streets). Head west on 15th Street, which changes into Enfield Road. Turn right and travel north onto Exposition Road. Bridle Path is the first street on the right. The garden is on the right side of the street, the fifth house from the corner, with a gravel and stone front courtyard.

❖ Lady Bird Johnson Wildflower Center,

4801 LaCrosse Avenue, Austin, TX 78739. (512) 292-4100.
WWW.WILDFLOWER.ORG

The Lady Bird Johnson Wildflower Center maintains a native plant botanical garden with acres of designed gardens and courtyards showcasing the magnificent native plants of the Texas Hill Country in a variety of styles from naturalistic to formal. Highlights of the grounds include a Visitor's Gallery with exhibits and a video presentation, a gift store, a terraced cafe, a forty-five-foot Observation Tower, a children's discovery room, home comparison gardens, and nature trails. The Center also has North America's largest rooftop rainwater collection system, with a series of aqueducts, beautiful stone cisterns, and waterways.

DATES & HOURS: Year round, Tuesday through Sunday, 9 a.m. – 5:30 p.m.

DIRECTIONS: *From I-35,* take Exit 227 for Slaughter Lane. Bear west off of the exit and travel 6 miles west to the intersection of Slaughter Lane and Loop 1. Turn left onto Loop 1 and left again onto LaCrosse.

❖ Westcave Preserve,

General Delivery, Round Mountain, TX 78663. (830) 825-3442.

Westcave Preserve is a thirty-acre natural sanctuary protected for future generations. It is a delight for wildflower enthusiasts, hikers, birders, or anyone who loves the natural beauty of the Texas Hill Country.

DATES & HOURS: Tours year round, Saturday & Sunday, 10 a.m., noon, 2 p.m., & 4 p.m. Weekday programs scheduled in advance.

DIRECTIONS: *Take Highway 71 West* from Austin to the village of Bee Cave. Turn left onto Ranch Road 3238 (Hamilton Pool Road) and travel 14 miles, crossing the Pedernales River. Look for the first gate on the right.

HOUSTON AREA: *March 20, 1999*

❖ Peckerwood Garden, HEMPSTEAD, 1 P.M. – 5 P.M.

The Artfull Garden, Rochella Cooper, HOUSTON, 10 A.M. – 4 P.M.

Susan Cooley Family Garden, HOUSTON, 10 A.M. – 2 P.M.

Mr. & Mrs. Charles R. Gregg, HOUSTON, 2 P.M. – 6 P.M.

Garden of Karen & John Kelsey, HOUSTON, 10 A.M. – 2 P.M

Liddell Garden, HOUSTON, 10 A.M. – 2 P.M.

Garden of Donna & Ed Maddox, HOUSTON, 10 A.M. – 2 P.M.

Mr. & Mrs. Robert F. Wheless, HOUSTON, 10 A.M. – 2 P.M.

❖ **Peckerwood Garden,**

ROUTE 3, BOX 103, HEMPSTEAD, TX 77445. (409) 826-3232.

Peckerwood Garden is an artist's garden set in a natural landscape. It holds an unduplicated collection of native rarities from Texas and Mexico interspersed in the garden with their Asian counterparts. This garden also serves as a horticultural laboratory where unusual plants and innovative techniques are tested. At present the cultivated garden occupies about seven acres of the twenty-acre site and includes a woodland garden along the banks of a creek, a higher dry garden on the north slope of the creek, and a recently established meadow garden and arboretum on acreage to the south. More than 3,000 species and cultivars can be found here, including significant collections of Quercus, Acer, Magnolia, Ilex, Pinus, Clethra, Styrax, Taxus, Philadelphus, Monarda, Bauhinia, Agave, *rare bulbs, conifers, ferns, and palms.*

DATES & HOURS: Open March 20 for *Directory* visitors, 1 p.m. - 5 p.m. Also open March 19 & 21; April 16, 18, 23, 25, & 30; May 2, 7, & 9; September 24, & 26; October 15 & 17; 1 p.m. - 5 p.m.

DIRECTIONS: *From Houston,* take Highway 290 West past Prairie View. Before reaching Hempstead, take Exit FM359 toward Brookshire. Proceed through the traffic light at the intersection with Highway 290. The garden is located 1.7 mile past this intersection, on the right. Look for a small sign.

The Artfull Garden, Rochella Cooper, HOUSTON, TX

This organic garden, dotted with sixty foot Post Oaks, understory trees and native plants, includes a dry creek which flows into a self-regenerating pond and overflows into a roadside ditch. Overlooking this Texas Wildlife Habitat-certified garden is a new metal-clad home, echoing the metal used in this eclectic neighborhood, two blocks east of the "Beer Can House." The garden also serves as the home to an outdoor sculpture gallery, The Artfull Garden, with changing exhibitions every few months. Although this garden is only one year old, numerous art and gardening groups have visited.

DATES & HOURS: March 20; 10 a.m. – 4 p.m.

DIRECTIONS: *Take Westcott going north from Memorial Drive,* second right on Lacy, fifth left on Reinicke.

Susan Cooley Family Garden, HOUSTON, TX

The garden was designed in 1996 by Suzy Fischer of Fischer Schalles Co. The garden complements the Arts and Crafts bungalow-style home. Plant materials are mostly natives. The backyard garden is done using French intensive vegetable gardening principles. All plants provide either fruit, vegetable, flower, or aroma to this inviting garden. It is a haven for birds, butterflies, hummingbirds and neighborhood children. Be prepared to smile!

DATES & HOURS: March 20; 10 a.m. – 2 p.m.

DIRECTIONS: *From I-59* turn north on Buffalo Speedway, cross Richmond, West Alabama, Westheimer, and turn west at next street, Locke Lane. We are #3646.

Proceeds shared with Friends of River Oaks Park.

Mr. & Mrs. Charles R. Gregg, HOUSTON, TX

Within these four wooded acres on Buffalo Bayou we have maintained the original 1940 landscaping concept by blending pocket gardens into the natural setting. A natural pond is surrounded by Louisiana Iris and Pseudacorus. A short climb at the rear of the property leads to our Secret Garden where you will find a variety of roses, vegetables, and herbs.

DATES & HOURS: March 20; 2 p.m. – 6 p.m.

DIRECTIONS: *Going west from Loop 610 and/or downtown Houston,* turn left onto Radney Road, which is the first traffic light after the intersection of Memorial and San Felipe. Turn left at the end of Radney (.5 mile) and the house is the entrance on the right, #101. Park only on the right side of the street.

Garden of Karen & John Kelsey, HOUSTON, TX

Our garden is in an Italian design, with formal beds trimmed by boxwood and filled with old roses. Native Texas plants are used for ease of care and maintenance.

DATES & HOURS: March 20; 10 a.m. – 2 p.m.

DIRECTIONS: *Westgate runs north and south* and crosses Westheimer between Kirby and Greenbriar (where the French Gourmet Bakery is). Turn north off Westheimer onto Westgate. Stay on Westgate almost until the intersection with Avalon. Number 2112 is on the west side of the street, three lots from the corner. It is a three-story stucco house with palm trees on the third-floor terrace. Please park on street.

Proceeds shared with Urban Harvest.

Liddell Garden, HOUSTON, TX

This small cottage-style garden was developed over a period of twenty-five years by Alice Staub Liddell, and has been lovingly maintained by her husband, Frank A. Liddell, Jr., since her death in 1997. Mrs. Liddell was a noted plantswoman and landscape designer of many of Houston's most interesting gardens. Her own garden reflects her desire to try the unusual as well as native plants. Mr. Liddell welcomes visitors to this charming garden.

DATES & HOURS: March 20; 10 a.m. – 2 p.m.

DIRECTIONS: *From the traffic light at Memorial Road and Voss Road go west* .3 mile to the next traffic light at Greenbay. Turn right onto Greenbay and continue for two blocks to Hedwig Road. Turn right onto Hedwig Road and continue .5 mile to stop sign. Proceed approximately one-hundred feet to Hedwig Green and turn right. The Liddell home, #406 Hedwig Green, is the third house on the right.

Garden of Donna & Ed Maddox, HOUSTON, TX

Our garden a habitat plan for butterflies and hummingbirds (and other birds), is filled with native plants, shrubs, and colorful vines. Salvias of all sorts, cuphea, lantana, buddleia, pentas are included along with Mexican flame vines, passion vines, cypress and cardinal climbers; also several ornamental grasses. Trees include vitex, possum haw, Mexican plum, and mountain laurel. Pond and fountains and walkways of stone make a statement.

DATES & HOURS: March 20; 10 a.m. – 2 p.m.

DIRECTIONS: *Exit West Loop 610 heading south* on San Filipe and turn right, proceed approximately 1 mile to Briar Ridge. Turn left onto Briar Ridge and go one block. Turn right onto Terwilliger and proceed to #6249.

Mr. & Mrs. Robert F. Wheless, HOUSTON, TX

An English rock garden originally designed by Leonard Tharp and Charles Thomas. Espaliered magnolia trees frame the front of the brick-and-clapboard house with an enthusiastic cottage garden that spills to the street. The iron gate was designed by ironsmith Ivan Bailey and complements the garden with its hollyhock design. Ornamental cabbage and kitchen herbs are a favorite of this gardener.

DATES & HOURS: March 20; 10 a.m. – 2 p.m.

DIRECTIONS: *From Loop 610 West* exit San Filipe. Turn left, heading east to River Oaks Boulevard. Turn left, take first right onto Chevy Chase. In second block on left. *From downtown Houston* take Allen Parkway for 5 miles to Kirby Drive (Allen Parkway turns into Kirby at Shepherd Drive). Continue on Kirby to Chevy Chase (last street before light at San Filipe). Turn right and house is on the right-hand side almost at end of the block.

❖ Bayou Bend Collection & Gardens,

ONE WESTCOTT STREET, HOUSTON, TX 77077. (713) 639-7750.

Bayou Bend, now the Decorative Arts wing of the Museum of Fine Arts, Houston, is located within the fourteen-acre estate of Miss Ima Hogg. The regional bayou woodland has been interplanted with a diverse collection of native gulf coast and exotic ornamental plants. The horticultural collection is framed in a series of formal garden rooms, woodland gardens, ravines, and paths. The integrated house/garden composition is a significant example of a regional historic landscape of the American Country House movement. The gardens feature one of the most extensive collections of azaleas and camellias in Texas.

DATES & HOURS: Year round, Tuesday through Saturday, 10 a.m. – 5 p.m. Sunday, 1 p.m. – 5 p.m.

DIRECTIONS: *Approach Bayou Bend via Memorial Drive in Houston,* turning south at Westcott Street. Please park in the free lot and cross the footbridge to enter the gardens.

VERMONT

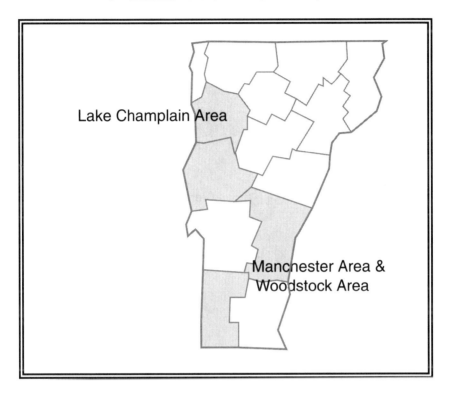

Lake Champlain Area

Manchester Area &
Woodstock Area

1999 VERMONT OPEN DAYS

June 12 & July 10: MANCHESTER AREA & WOODSTOCK AREA
July 31: LAKE CHAMPLAIN AREA

LAKE CHAMPLAIN AREA: *July 31, 1999*

Converse Bay Farm, CHARLOTTE, 10 A.M. – 4 P.M.

Robin Price & Robert Coleburn — The Gardens at Golden Apple Orchard, CHARLOTTE, 10 A.M. – 4 P.M.

The Gardens of Peter Morris & Pennie Beach, WEST FERRISBURGH, 10 A.M. – 4 P.M.

PLEASE NOTE: *The following gardens in New York are participating as part of the Lake Champlain Open Day.*

Irwin Garden Farm, ESSEX, 10 A.M. – 2 P.M., *page 385*

Woodland Gardens of Mr. & Mrs. Wynant D. Vanderpoel, KEENE VALLEY, 2 P.M. – 6 P.M., *page 386*

Converse Bay Farm, CHARLOTTE, VT

The garden is composed of several different elements on two levels, each of which focuses on the view of Lake Champlain. On the upper level, the main feature is two pergolas. There are several accesses to the next level. There are two parterre rose gardens with an iron arbor as a backdrop. A sixty by ten inch perennial border is at the next level. There also is a lily pond surrounded by shade plants and rose gardens, an herb garden, and another perennial border. In the area of the barns is a parterre potager.

DATES & HOURS: July 31; 10 a.m. – 4 p.m.

DIRECTIONS: *Take I-89 North* to Vermont Exit 13. Head south on Route 7 through the town of Shelburne approximately 5 miles to Charlotte intersection. Turn right onto F-5 going west. This is Ferry Road. Continue straight over the railroad tracks. At Lake Road intersection, turn left. Go .8 mile. Turn right onto Converse Bay Road. Fourth driveway on the left. Park along the driveway to the barn (third drive on the left)

Robin Price & Robert Coleburn — The Gardens At Golden Apple Orchard, CHARLOTTE, VT

Overlooking Lake Champlain and the Adirondacks, the house is centered within an eighteen-acre pick-your-own apple orchard. Gardens planted in front of and behind a picket fence define the public and private spaces. Robin's white clapboard studio sits within a large walled garden. This garden is divided into rooms by hedges of gray-stemmed dogwood, arborvitae, yew, blueberry, winterberry, roses and asparagus. It includes a center knot garden which is flanked on both sides by perennial borders. Korean boxwood, hardy in Vermont, is the formal hedge in the herb garden. The conifer garden, featuring many dwarf species, adds interest in the snowy landscape. Koi and many kinds of frogs survive the winter in two lily ponds. A new thyme path winds through a rock garden and leads to an arbor-covered terrace behind the main house. Most of the gardens are accessible across pebbled paths and lawns.

DATES & HOURS: July 31; 10 a.m. – 4 p.m.

DIRECTIONS: *From Route 7* in Charlotte, take Ferry Road (F-5) west toward the ferry for 1.5 miles. Turn right onto Lake Road. Go 1 mile and turn left onto Whalley Road. The Golden Apple Orchard is .5 mile down on the left.

❖ The Inn at Shelburne Farms,

1611 HARBOR ROAD, SHELBURNE, VT. (802) 985-8686. FAX: (802) 985-8123.
The gardens at the Inn at Shelburne Farms, originally designed by Lila Vanderbilt Webb, feature lush perennial borders inspired by the English cottage style of Gertrude Jekyll. The peak of the garden's bloom is early June when the Queen Victoria peonies are in their glory, through July when delphiniums bloom in front of a backdrop of tall plume poppies. Low brick walls provide the formal architectural structure to define the "rooms" within the garden and create multiple levels for the rose garden, the lily pond, surrounded by Dutch and Japanese iris, and an herb garden. Continuing Lila's tradition to welcome the community into her gardens, we invite you to visit. Shelburne Farms is a 1,400-acre working farm, national historic site and non-profit environmental education center whose mission is to cultivate a conservation ethic by teaching and demonstrating the stewardship of natural and agricultural resources.

DATES & HOURS: July 9; Please call for hours.

DIRECTIONS: *From I-89,* take Exit 13 (I-189) to Route 7 West at the stop light in the center of Shelburne. Drive 1.6 miles to the entrance of Shelburne Farms. Turn right into the Welcome Center parking area before entering the gates. Tickets may be purchased in the Welcome Center.

The Gardens of Peter Morris & Pennie Beach,
WEST FERRISBURGH, VT

These private gardens are a passion and ongoing experiment for architect and landscape designer Peter Morris. The Upper Garden is designed and laid out first to complement and "ground" Pennie and Peter's house. While many visitors stop here, the larger "garden imagined" lies to the south — into, around, and along a sinuous waterway/marsh known as "the Run," a naturalized drainage outlet into Lake Champlain from about 250 acres. Despite the challenges of building paths and gardening its steep banks, Peter is attracted to the Run's natural beauty, curves, and mystery. The overall concept is a somewhat Chinese stroll garden with distinctive "rooms," transitions, and stations. The gardens amplify the changes and contrasts of the site.

DATES & HOURS: July 31; 10 a.m. – 4 p.m.

DIRECTIONS: *From the Essex, NY – Charlotte, VT ferry:* Follow Route F-5 east to Route 7. Turn right, south on Route 7. Turn right onto Route 22A into Vergennes. Go through town, down hill, over the bridge and take second right at flashing light onto Panton Road. Follow signs to Basin Harbor Club and Lake Champlain Maritime Museum. Go west about 1 mile and turn right onto Basin Harbor Road. Proceed 6 miles to Basin Harbor Club entry sign. Take first left after grass airstrip. Park in field to right. *From Lake Champlain Bridge on Route 17:* Continue northeast on Route 17 for about 2 miles. Take left fork at Addison Gas Station and Store onto Lake Street. Follow signs to Lake Champlain Maritime Museum. Stay on paved road about 5 miles and fork left at Panton Store and gas pump. Stay left and go about 1 mile past Button Bay State Park, left onto Basin Harbor Road to Basin Harbor entry sign and Lake Champlain Maritime Museum. Take first left after grass airstrip. Park in field to right. The Upper Gardens are accessible over grass paths.

Proceeds shared with The Vermont Arts Council.

❖ The Gardens of Basin Harbor, WEST FERRISBURGH, VT

Gardens at The Basin Harbor Club are a central part of the property's history. Established in 1886, the (landscape) vision of Basin Harbor came from our grandfather, Allen Penfield Beach. Through his vision we have made the preservation of the landscape an integral part of our philosophy. Much of what you see today is from the bones laid out by our grandfather. Overlooking Lake Champlain, Basin Harbor's gardens comprise 20,000 square feet of annuals, the largest display of unusual annuals in Vermont. Spread throughout our property you will discover gardens, varying in size, color, and design. Our head gardener, Kelly Sweeney, is always looking for new and innovative ways to improve and show our gardens while keeping Basin Harbor's tradition and history alive.

DATES & HOURS: July 31; 10 a.m. – 4 p.m.

DIRECTIONS: *From the Essex, NY – Charlotte, VT ferry:* Follow Route F-5 east to Route 7. Turn right, south onto Route 7. Turn right onto Route 22A into Vergennes. Go through town, down hill, over the bridge and take second right at flashing light onto Panton Road. Follow signs to Basin Harbor Club and Lake Champlain Maritime Museum. Go west about 1 mile and turn right onto Basin Harbor Road. Proceed 6 miles to Basin Harbor Club entry sign. Follow signs to the Lodge. *From Lake Champlain Bridge on Route 17:* Continue northeast on Route 17 for about 2 miles. Take left fork at Addison Gas Station and Store onto Lake Street. Follow signs to Lake Champlain Maritime Museum. Stay on paved road about 5 miles and fork left at Panton Store and gas pump. Stay left and go about 1 mile past Button Bay State Park, left onto Basin Harbor Road to Basin Harbor entry sign and Lake Champlain Maritime Museum. Follow signs to the Lodge.

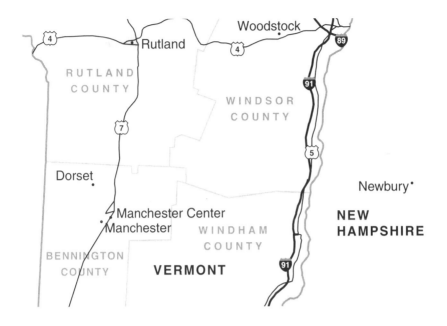

MANCHESTER AREA & WOODSTOCK AREA:

June 12, 1999

The Garden at Enfield, DORSET, 10 A.M. – 4 P.M.

The Old Stone House Garden, DORSET, 10 A.M. – 2 P.M.

❖ Alice's Flower Gardens, MANCHESTER CENTER, 10 A.M. – 6 P.M.

Glebelands, MANCHESTER VILLAGE, 10 A.M. – 5 P.M.

The Sunken Garden, MANCHESTER VILLAGE, 10 A.M. – 2 P.M.

Indian Tree Hill — The Highberg Garden, WOODSTOCK, 10 A.M. – 2 P.M.

 ❖ The Fells at the John Hay National Wildlife Refuge, NEWBURY, NH, dawn – dusk.

July 10, 1999

The Garden at Enfield, DORSET, 10 A.M. – 4 P.M.

The Old Stone House Garden, DORSET, 10 A.M. – 2 P.M.

❖ Alice's Flower Gardens, MANCHESTER CENTER, 10 A.M. – 6 P.M.

Glebelands, MANCHESTER VILLAGE, 10 A.M. – 5 P.M.

The Sunken Garden, MANCHESTER VILLAGE, 10 A.M. – 2 P.M.

Wyndhurst, MANCHESTER VILLAGE, 10 A.M. – 4 P.M.

 ❖ The Fells at the John Hay National Wildlife Refuge, NEWBURY, NH, dawn – dusk.

The Garden at Enfield, DORSET, VT

Amid breathtaking stands of white birch, our informal garden highlights our 1776 home amid the multiple springs cascading down Enfield's hill. The perennial garden is designed to have blooms from early spring through fall and is sprinkled with beautiful annual plants. Many stands of lilacs, mountain pinks, azaleas, crab apples, and towering maples complete the effect.

DATES & HOURS: June 12, July 10; 10 a.m. – 4 p.m.

DIRECTIONS: *From Dorset Green on Route 30,* proceed southwest on Church Street to the end. Turn left on Dorset West Road to Nichols Hill Road, which is the first paved road on the right. Turn right on Nichols Hill Road and .3 mile after pavement ends note driveway sign "Enfield" on the left. Turn left into the private driveway. Enfield is #821 Nichols Hill Road.

The Old Stone House Garden, DORSET, VT

Commissioned in 1914, this formal Italian garden was designed by Charles Downing Lay. The extensive flower gardens enhance a marble teahouse, marble pergola, thirty-two marble containers carved on the site in 1914 and 1915, fountains, a peony walk, marble benches, tables, urns, monuments, roses, vines, and a bucolic view of Vermont meadows. The house and garden consist of three levels surrounded by marble walls and are listed on the National Register of Historic Places.

DATES & HOURS: June 12, July 10; 10 a.m. – 2 p.m.

DIRECTIONS: *From Manchester* follow Route 30 northwest out of town to Dorset West Road. Turn left and travel 1.25 miles to the Old Stone House. There are extensive lawns with a flagpole. Please park in the west meadow and enter the garden through the front garden gate.

❖ **Hildene,** P.O. Box 377, MANCHESTER, VT 05254. (802) 362-1788.
Robert Todd Lincoln's Hildene was the home of Abraham Lincoln's descendants until 1975. This Georgian Revival mansion is situated among formal gardens that have been restored to their original beauty. Many of the original plantings remain, and the location on a promontory in the valley provides a splendid view of the mountains on either side of Hildene's meadowlands below. Cutting and kitchen gardens are in the process of being restored.

DATES & HOURS: Mid-May through October, 9:30 a.m. – 4 p.m. Tours available by appointment.

DIRECTIONS: Located just 2 miles south of the junctions of Routes 7A and 11/30.

❖ **Alice's Flower Gardens,** MANCHESTER CENTER, VT
Our cutflower gardens/nursery were featured in Organic Gardening, *November 1992;* Garden Design, *April/May 1996;* National Gardening, *December 1996. A modest ranch-style house is surrounded by two acres of immaculately kept beds and borders filled with an amazing diversity of hybrid and heirloom flowers. The planting of organic gardens began in 1954 and has been orchestrated so that something is in bloom from May to October, though the gardens are particularly spectacular in June and July.*

DATES & HOURS: June 12, July 10; 10 a.m. – 6 p.m.

DIRECTIONS: *On East Manchester Road,* .5 mile east of the intersection of U.S. Highway 7 and Vermont 11/30.

Glebelands, MANCHESTER VILLAGE, VT

The garden started in the 1930s with perennials and a long allée of peonies. Added later were marble defining walls, two gazebos (a Temple of Love and a Moorish-style one with tassels), statues, and a tiled pool. I've incorporated a large reflecting pool with fountains at each end, antique iron (New Orleans) gates and grills, urns and statuary from my former house. The grounds, totaling thirty acres, encompass an orchard underplanted with narcissus (fairyland in spring-time), a folly pavilion, two large ponds created by a 100-yard-long nineteenth-century marble dam (the area was a marble mill), two miles of woodland trails, brooks, and fine trees, including a Chamaecyparis *collection I've raised from cuttings that I propagated.*

DATES & HOURS: June 12, July 10; 10 a.m. – 5 p.m.

DIRECTIONS: *Take Route 7A* from The Equinox Hotel in Manchester Village. Travel north for .7 mile. Orvis Company will be on your right. Look for a dirt driveway within a spruce and pine grove on your left. A "Glebelands" sign will be in the middle of the drive. The house cannot be seen from the road. Please follow signs for parking. *From the north,* take Route 7A South past the junction of Routes 11 and 30 in Manchester Center. Travel .6 mile south. "Glebelands" will be on the right.

Proceeds shared with the Federated Garden Club of Vermont, Inc.

The Sunken Garden, MANCHESTER VILLAGE, VT

My sunken garden is in an area that was previously the foundation of a green-house. The glass frame was taken away years ago and only the old sunken stone wall remains. This area could easily have become an eyesore. and it presented a challenging problem. The stone wall was lovely so I decided to make a garden using the stone wall as a background. It is an old-fashioned English-style cottage garden that is attached to the brick greenhouse that is now the study. It seems to belong with the small 200-year-old cottage that is my home.

DATES & HOURS: June 12, July 10; 10 a.m. – 2 p.m.

DIRECTIONS: *From Route 7A South in Manchester* go 1 mile down River Road. The driveway is the second on the left past the entrance to The Wilburton Inn. Look for "J.B. Wilbur" on the stone pillars. Please park along the driveway.

Proceeds shared with The Federated Garden Club of Vermont, Inc.

Wyndhurst, MANCHESTER VILLAGE, VT

A century ago my family bought a Vermont farm. Later I redesigned the formal garden in a more romantic lush informal style. A new garden (replacing a vegetable garden) is a maze of curving paths of various widths forming twenty-one beds of different size and shape. I wished to create a walk where you were embraced by flowers on all sides with ever-changing views. Rules have been kept to a minimum and spontaneity has played a large part in the color scheme and design.

DATES & HOURS: July 10; 10 a.m. – 4 p.m.

DIRECTIONS: *From the north,* go south on Route 7A past the Equinox Hotel in Manchester Village. Wyndhurst, #3227 Main Street, is on the right opposite River Road. *From the South,* go north on Route 7A. Wyndhurst is on the left shortly after you enter Manchester Village, after passing Hildene and Dellwood Cemetery on the right.

Indian Tree Hill — The Highberg Garden,

WOODSTOCK, VT

This is a dynamic garden that has evolved over the past twenty years. It combines an extensive collection of plants in a natural setting, giving it year-round interest, continuity of style, and an intimate appeal. The various garden areas are defined by the meandering paths and the creative use of native stone. Explore the alpine scree, woodland garden, sunny pool area, alpine wall, and more. Each place has its own unique feature: a sculptured steel archway and gates, an echoing waterfall, mossy stone benches, and a carved fountain. The vast variety of plant material and its arrangement will interest the seasoned collector, the student of design, as well as any garden enthusiast. Hundreds of alpines, dozens of dwarf conifers, countless bulbs, interesting ground covers, native and exotic woodland species, unusual trees, and many old favorites make this garden unique. A cutting garden of mixed perennials and annuals, a vegetable garden, and apple trees provide beauty and bounty.

DATES & HOURS: June 12; 10 a.m. – 2 p.m.

DIRECTIONS: *From "The Green" in Woodstock* at the west end, go to the left of the stone Episcopal Church and take Church Hill Road for 1.5 miles. Turn left onto Randall Road, a dead-end gravel road, and go another 1.5 miles. The driveway is on the left, directly across from a red steel field gate. The house is #414 at the end of the drive.

❖ The Fells at the John Hay National Wildlife Refuge,

ROUTE 103A, NEWBURY, NH 03255. (603) 763-4789.

These extensive gardens, developed from 1914 to 1940 as a showplace country estate, had fallen into decline in recent years. After four seasons of work by Garden Conservancy staff and dedicated volunteers, the profile of this historic design has reemerged. Currently, the rock garden, in which Clarence Hay experimented with alpine plants for more than forty years, is being rehabilitated.

DATES & HOURS: Year round, daily, dawn – dusk. House tours available on weekends. Call ahead for special events and educational programs.

DIRECTIONS: *From the south and east,* take I-89 north to Exit 9/Route 103 and go west to Newbury. Take 103A north for 2.2 miles. The Fells is on the left. *From the north,* take I-89 south to Exit 12/Route 11. Turn right at the end of the ramp and immediately left onto Route 103A south. Travel 5.6 miles to The Fells on the right. Please park in the parking lot and walk down the driveway to the house and gardens.

VIRGINIA

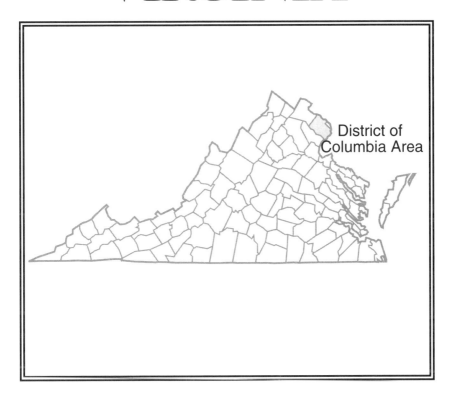

District of
Columbia Area

1999 VIRGINIA OPEN DAYS

June 26: DISTRICT OF COLUMBIA AREA

DISTRICT OF COLUMBIA AREA: *June 26, 1999*

Hilltop Cottage, MCLEAN, 10 A.M. – 4 P.M.

PLEASE NOTE: *The following gardens in the District of Columbia and Virginia are participating as part of the Washington Area Open Day.*

May 15, 1999

John & Caroline Macomber, WASHINGTON, DC, 10 A.M. – 4 P.M., *page 129*

Mr. & Mrs. Eric Weinmann, WASHINGTON, DC, 10 A.M. – 4 P.M., *page 129*

❖ Dumbarton Oaks Park, WASHINGTON, DC, 2 P.M. - 6 P.M., *page 130*

Nancy Vorhees, BETHESDA, MD, 10 A.M. – 2 P.M., *page 180*

Gay & Tony Barclay — Orchard Farm, POTOMAC, MD, 10 A.M. – 4 P.M., *page 181*

The Olson Garden, POTOMAC, MD, 10 A.M. – 4 P.M., *page 181*

Carole Ottesen's Garden, POTOMAC, MD, 2 P.M. – 6 P.M., *page 182*

June 26, 1999

The Sexton – Borgiotti Garden, CHEVY CHASE, MD, 10 A.M. – 4 P.M., *page 181*

Robert Moore & Frank Kirste, SILVER SPRING, MD, 10 A.M. – 4 P.M., *page 183*

❖ American Horticultural Society at George Washington's River Farm,

7931 EAST BOULEVARD DRIVE, ALEXANDRIA, VA 22308. (703) 768-5700. *Once part of George Washington's property, this twenty-five-acre garden overlooking the Potomac River now serves as headquarters for the American Horticultural Society. The demonstration gardens include: the Interactive Children's Gardens; the George Harding Memorial Garden; the National Capitol Daylily Society display bed; the Wildlife Garden; rose, herb, perennial, and annual display beds; the Home Composting Park; a picnic area; art exhibits; a visitor's center and gift shop.*

DATES & HOURS: Year round, Monday through Friday, 8:30 a.m. – 5 p.m.

DIRECTIONS: *River Farm is located* approximately 4 miles south of Old Town Alexandria, just off the George Washington Memorial Parkway. Exactly .5 miles after going under the Stone Bridge, make a left off the Parkway at the Arcturus/East Boulevard/Herbert Springs Exit. Turn left at stop sign. Entrance is on the right.

Hilltop Cottage, McLEAN, VA

We bought an old house with an even older, very neglected, once-great garden. Its strength was classic Virginia: One dramatic spring display of hundreds of azaleas, rhododendrons, and mountain laurel. To enjoy the garden throughout the year, we have re-designed it, adding two water gardens (one for koi; one for goldfish), two perennial gardens, shade gardens and an evergreen hillside — all connected by paths, focal points, and rest spots. The garden today is a complex series of "rooms" on different levels that have to be sought out to be enjoyed. Intentionally, one cannot "read" the garden with a single glance or from a single perspective.

DATES & HOURS: June 26; 10 a.m. – 4 p.m.

DIRECTIONS: *From Washington:* Take 66 West. Exit at Sycamore Street and turn right onto Sycamore. Go 1 mile to the light at the junction of Sycamore and Williamsburg at the Williamsburg Shopping Center. Follow Williamsburg straight ahead for five blocks. Turn left on Kensington. Go five blocks to Rockingham. Turn left. Hilltop Cottage is the second house on the right after the intersection of Rockingham and Rhode Island. *From The Beltway:* Take 66 East. Exit at Westmorland Street. Turn left onto Westmorland. At first traffic light turn right onto Williamsburg. Go .75 mile. At the light at the Williamsburg Shopping Center, turn left to continue on Williamsburg for five blocks. Follow as above.

WASHINGTON

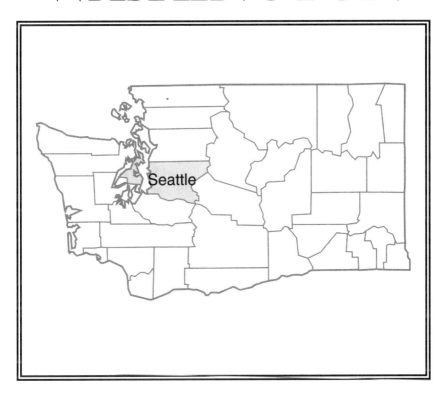

1999 WASHINGTON OPEN DAYS

June 5: SEATTLE AREA

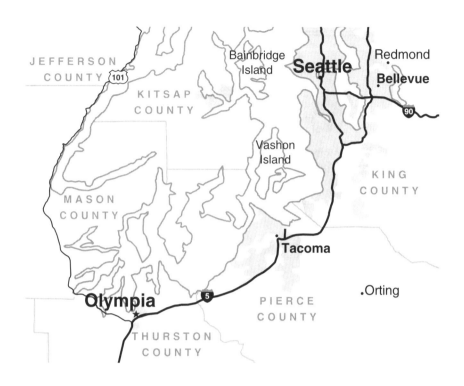

SEATTLE AREA: *June 5, 1999*

Little and Lewis, BAINBRIDGE ISLAND, 10 A.M. – 4 P.M.

Linda Cochran, BAINBRIDGE ISLAND, 10 A.M. – 4 P.M.

Dan Hinkley & Robert Jones – Heronswood, KINGSTON,
       9:30 A.M. – 3:30 P.M.

1332–232nd Place NE, REDMOND, 10 A.M. – 4 P.M.

Stone Hollow Farm, REDMOND, 10 A.M. – 4 P.M.

Geller — Irvine, SEATTLE, 10 A.M. – 2 P.M.

The Chase Garden, ORTING, 10:30 A.M. – NOON, 1:30 p.m. – 3 P.M.

Little and Lewis, BAINBRIDGE ISLAND, WA

The garden of Little and Lewis is an internationally known garden featuring the collaborative concrete sculptures of David Lewis and George Little. Their garden is filled with oversized perennials and tropical plants that act as a setting for their colorful fountains, water mirrors, dripping columns, and garden art. Featured in Horticulture, Sunset, *and* Better Homes & Gardens, *their garden is alive with visual images and contemplative sounds.*

DATES & HOURS: June 5; 10 a.m. – 4 p.m.

DIRECTIONS: *Take the Seattle – Bainbridge Island Ferry* to downtown Winslow (approximately 35 minutes). Go up to the first traffic light (Winslow Way) and turn right. Go two short blocks to Ferncliff Road. Turn left. Go two blocks to Wing Point Way. Turn right. Go approximately .5 mile. The garden is on the left. Park in the street.

Proceeds shared with Bainbridge Island Public Library – Landscape Fund.

Garden of Linda Cochran — Froggy Bottom,
BAINBRIDGE ISLAND, WA

My five-acre garden on Bainbridge Island in Puget Sound is designed to take full advantage of our relatively mild, Zone 8 climate. It has been described as "the epicenter of the tropicalismo movement," but it is not limited to tropical-looking plants. It also makes extensive use of grasses and other perennials, including many from South Africa and New Zealand. It has been the subject of articles in publications such as Horticulture *and* Better Homes and Gardens, *as well as in various books.*

DATES & HOURS: June 5; 10 a.m. – 4 p.m.

DIRECTIONS: *Take Washington State Ferry* from downtown Seattle to Bainbridge Island. After disembarking, turn left at the first stop light onto Winslow Way. Turn right at the first stop sign onto Madison Avenue. Turn left at the next stop sign onto Wyatt. Follow Wyatt until it makes a "Y" split. Take the right-hand split. That is Blakely. Follow Blakely approxmately 3 miles. Turn right on Country Club Road. Take the next right (approximately .25 mile) on Fort Ward Hill Road. Make a left on Kitsap Street. The garden is at #10132 Kitsap Street, the second house on the right.

❖ Bloedel Reserve,

7571 N.E. DOPHIN DRIVE, BAINBRIDGE ISLAND, WA 98110. (206) 842-7631.
WWW.BLOEDELRESERVE.ORG

The Bloedel reserve is a 150-acre former residence now public access garden and nature preserve. The primary purpose of the Reserve is to provide people with an opportunity to enjoy nature through quiet walks in the gardens and woodlands.

DATES & HOURS: Year round, Wednesday – Sunday (except federal holidays) 10 a.m. – 4 p.m. by reservation.

DIRECTIONS: *The Reserve is located approximately 8 miles north of Winslow* (Bainbridge Island Ferry Terminal) off Highway 305. Phone for reservations and directions.

❖ Elda Behm Highline Botanical Garden, SEATTLE, WA

In the shadow of the Seattle-Tacoma International Airport, eighty-five-year-old Elda Behm created an English country garden full of special plants grown from seed, cuttings, and the generosity of fellow gardeners. Airport expansion will destroy our local treasure so it will be moved. Species rhododendrons and azaleas crown the garden in spring. The show goes on all year. Let Elda introduce you to her "Paradise Garden."

DATES & HOURS: June 5; 2 p.m. – 6 p.m. Otherwise by appointment.

DIRECTIONS: *The garden is located on the west side of Seattle-Tacoma International Airport* midway between those cities. Approach on I-5 from the north or south and I-405 from the east. Exit to State Route 518 (airport freeway) traveling west. Take the Des Moines Memorial Drive Exit, which is after the airport access exit. Proceed about 3 miles. At Des Moines Drive turn left onto city street. Drive south on Des Moines Drive to South 160th Street. Turn left at the traffic light. Proceed one block to 9th Avenue South. Turn left and go one-half block. Park along 9th Street. The garden is clearly marked.

❖ Rhododendron Species Botanical Garden,

P.O. Box 3798, FEDERAL WAY, WA 98063-3798. (253) 661-9377.

The Rhododendron Species Botanical Garden features one of the finest collections of rhododendrons in the world. Enjoy more than 10,000 rhododendrons growing in a beautiful twenty-two-acre woodland setting with exotic and unusual companion plants. Year round features include scenic beauty, alpine, pond, and woodland gardens, a hardy fern collection, and a gazebo.

DATES & HOURS: March – May, daily (closed Thursday); 10 a.m. – 4 p.m. June – February, Saturday through Wednesday; 11 a.m. – 4 p.m.

DIRECTIONS: *From I-5,* take exit 143 for Federal Way/South 320th Street. Turn left onto 320th Street. At Weyerhaeuser Way South, turn right. Bear left at the fork and turn left at the stop sign. Take the first right and follow signs for parking.

Dan Hinkley & Robert Jones — Heronswood,

KINGSTON, WA 93346. (360) 297-4172. FAX (360) 297-8321.

Three-plus acres of unusual perennials, shrubs, grasses, vines, trees, and conifers in varied garden conditions. A large woodland shade garden, mixed shrub and herbaceous borders, wet site and bog gardens make up this partially wooded setting in rural Kitsap County. Interesting arbors and hardscape complete the design.

DATES & HOURS: June 4 & 5, July 16 & 17, September 10 & 11; 9:30 a.m. - 3:30 p.m.

DIRECTIONS: *Please call or fax for directions in advance.*

❖ Lakewold Gardens,

12317 GRAVELLY LAKE DRIVE SW, LAKEWOOD, WA 98499.
(253) 584-4106. WWW.LAKEWOLD.ORG

A beautiful ten-acre public estate garden showcasing stunning formal gardens as well as naturalistic displays. This includes woodland areas, aquatic displays, waterfalls, rock and alpine gardens, a knot garden, kitchen garden, shade garden, rose garden, and fern garden. Lakewold also is a splendid example of noted landscape architect Thomas Church's residential designs.

DATES & HOURS: April – September: Thursday, Saturday, Sunday, Monday, 10 a.m. – 4 p.m.; Friday, noon – 8 p.m. October – March: Friday – Sunday, 10 a.m. – 3 p.m.

DIRECTIONS: *Take Exit 124 off I-5* (Gravelly Lake Drive). Follow signs for 1 mile. Lakewold is only 10 miles south of the Tacoma Dome.

☀ The Emmott and Ione Chase Garden, ORTING, WA.

The core garden surrounding this contemporary house (dating from the early 1960s), was influenced by Japanese and modernist design principles. Subsequently, the Chases have added an alpine meadow and woodland paths inspired by views of the valley and Mount Rainier beyond.

DATES & HOURS: Open for *Directory* visitors on Saturday, June 5, 10:30 a.m. – noon; 1:30 p.m. – 3:00 p.m. Open by appointment mid-April – mid-May.

DIRECTIONS: *Please call (206) 242-4040 for directions.*

1332 – 232nd Place NE, REDMOND, WA

A typical suburban lot with nothing on it has been transformed into a plantsper-
son's paradise. There is a white garden leading to a "woods" of magnolias *and*
sorbus. *Alpines are in another area, and a double perennial border is full of*
surprising combinations. Containers change constantly as plants go in and out of
bloom. Irises are a feature of the garden.This garden has been featured in Fine
Gardening, *the* Seattle Times *and* The Natural Garden *by Ken Druse.*

DATES & HOURS: June 5; 10 a.m. – 4 p.m.

DIRECTIONS: The garden is east of Lake Sammamish. From Highway 520 turn
right (south) onto Redmond/Fall City Road. Go straight for about 2.5 miles. Turn
right at the traffic light at Sahalee Way (the Grey Barn Nursery at this intersection is very good). Go up Sahalee Way 3 miles where it becomes 228 Avenue NE.
Turn left onto NE 14th Street (Cimarron) just past the fire station. Turn right at
232nd Place NE. The house is the second on the right, #1332.

Proceeds shared with the Northwest Perennial Alliance.

Stone Hollow Farm, REDMOND, WA

This garden is approximately one cultivated acre, surrounded by alder woods and
a cedar grove. Arranged in three concentric tiers down to a sizable pond, the
gardens are composed of mixed borders, rock and shade gardens.

DATES & HOURS: June 5; 10 a.m. – 4 p.m.

DIRECTIONS: *From SR 520,* exit Route 202 (Redmond/Fall City Road). Stay
right to East Lake Sammamish Parkway. Go 3 miles to a left on Inglewood Hill
Road, to a right on 216, to a right on Main, up to a "T" at 214. Make a left and a
quick right on SE 1st (a private road). *From I-90,* exit at Issaquah Front Street
and proceed to East Lake Sammamish Parkway. Go under the freeway to 212
Way. Go up a windy hill (becomes 212 Avenue) to SE 8th (about 2 miles). Go
right then make a left on 214 Avenue. Go up the hill to the top and make a left
on SE 1st. The house is on the right at the end of the cul-de-sac.

Geller – Irvine Garden, SEATTLE, WA

I started the garden about sixteen years ago when there were only two trees on the property. Today, the woodland cottage garden reminds me of my native New England. The placement of the main structure of trees and shrubs naturally define the interconnected outdoor rooms. A walk through the property brings you up a steep hillside entry garden through the woodland canopy, and onto two brick terrace gardens surrounded by perennials. The sixty foot by 120' garden feels larger than it is due to the changing feeling and flow of the spaces.

DATES & HOURS: June 5; 10 a.m. – 2 p.m.

DIRECTIONS: *Take I-5 to Madison Street.* Head east on Madison toward Lake Washington. Take a right onto 25th Avenue East (heading south). Take a left onto East John Street, proceed down the hill. Take the first right onto 26th Avenue and continue a couple of blocks past East Denny and East Howell. Number 1725 26th Avenue is on the right side just past East Howell. Look for a wooden staircase.

❖ Washington Park Arboretum, 2300 ARBORETUM DRIVE EAST, SEATTLE, WA 98112-2300. (206) 543-8800.

The Washington Park Arboretum is a living plant museum emphasizing trees and shrubs hardy in the maritime Pacific Northwest. Plant collections are selected and arranged to display their beauty and function in urban landscapes, to demonstrate their natural ecology and diversity, and to conserve important species and cultivated varieties for the future. The arboretum serves the public, students at all levels, naturalists, gardeners, and nursery and landscape professionals with its collections, education programs, interpretation and recreational opportunities.

DATES & HOURS: Year round, daily, dawn – dusk.

DIRECTIONS: *From I-5 northbound or southbound,* take Exit 168-B (Bellevue/Kirkland) East. Take the very first exit, Montlake Boulevard/UW. At the traffic signal, go straight. You are now on Lake Washington Boulevard East. Follow for 1 mile until you come to the stop sign with the left-turn lane. Turn left onto Foster Island Road and follow signs to the Visitors Center.

WEST VIRGINIA

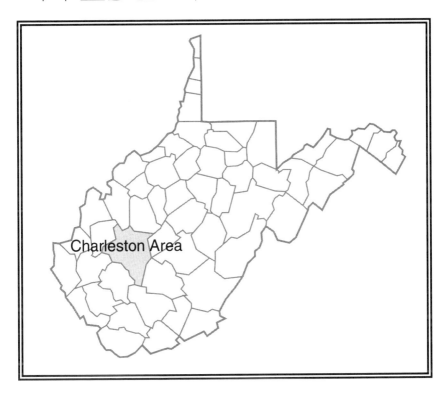

1999 WEST VIRGINIA OPEN DAYS

June 19: CHARLESTON AREA

CHARLESTON AREA: *June 19, 1999*

The Johnson Garden, CHARLESTON, 10 A.M. – 4 P.M.

Otis Laury Garden, CHARLESTON, 10 A.M. – 4 P.M.

The Garden of Bill Mills & Thomas Gillooly, CHARLESTON, 10 A.M. – 4 P.M.

Zeb Wright's Garden, CHARLESTON, 10 A.M. – 4 P.M.

Kanawha Salines — The Garden of Mrs. Turner Ratrie, MALDEN,

      10 A.M. – 4 P.M.

The Johnson Garden, CHARLESTON, WV

The Johnson Garden evolved following a meeting with well-known landscape designer Stuart Ortloff in 1955, prior to building our home. He advised a totally natural setting, using primarily native plants. We started with twelve native rhododendrons in six inch pots placed discreetly along dog paths which outlined the spring wildflower hillside in the front of the house. In the back, facing west, the summer and fall flowers are placed along brick walks. Flower beds line the terrace wall and hostas are placed in the rear of the yard to add interest to a shady, mossy area. The viewer will see strictly "hands-on" gardening.

DATES & HOURS: June 19; 10 a.m. – 4 p.m.

DIRECTIONS: *Follow signs from Oakwood and S.S. Bridge* to Kanawha State Forest. Louden Heights Road leads into Connell Road. On Connell, go .5 mile to Johnson Road (right turn). On Johnson Road go .25 mile. On the right is a red mailbox. We are across from a tennis court. The house number, #1199, follows #1203, because we built later.

Proceeds shared with The Kanawha Garden Club.

Otis Laury Garden, CHARLESTON, WV

Originally a carriage house, the home was built in the early 1900s. It has been used as office space and a hearing-aid clinic. The garden is enclosed by a brick wall and includes a wide variety of spring bulbs, perennial plants, shrubs, daffodils, jonquils, crocus, columbine, bluebell and more. The center of the garden is a circle of herbs: rosemary, thyme, basil, French sorrel, parsley, and chives, highlighted by a bright strawberry bunch border. In the later summer the garden is filled with white phlox, asters, and mums.

DATES & HOURS: June 19; 10 a.m. – 4 p.m.

DIRECTIONS: *From I-64* take the Broad Street Exit. Stay on Broad Street until you reach theKanawha River. Turn left onto Kanawha Boulevard. Drive 1 block to Brooks Street. Turn left. The garden is on the right just beyond the apartment building and is enclosed by a brick wall at #20 Brooks Street.

The Garden of Bill Mills & Thomas Gillooly, CHARLESTON, WV

As a garden designer I (Bill) greatly enjoy having my own laboratory to work in. This property of about an acre offers a pleasant range of sites, from sunny flats to hillside woodland. As one walks up the gravel drive, a series of borders, each with its own color pallet, comes into view. Through a gate, an all white circular garden with a small formal pond leads on to another border and another circular space. A walk up the hill behind the cottage rambles through many pocket gardens and on to the woodland garden. Urns, pots, and haymows are found throughout the property, rich in color and contrast.

DATES & HOURS: June 19; 10 a.m. – 4 p.m.

DIRECTIONS: Take the *Oakwood Exit of I-64* to Route 119. Turn right onto Cantley Drive. From Cantley turn right onto Wilkie Drive. Make the second left turn onto South Fort Drive. South Fort turns into Gordon Drive. Our residence, one mile further at #729 Gordon Drive, is on the left, a small cottage up a gravel drive. Additional parking may be found just past the residence at Weberwood Elementary School. The garden is not wheelchair accessble.

Zeb Wright's Garden, CHARLESTON, WV

The home of garden designer, retired garden writer, and avid collector, displaying over 1300 species and cultivars of shrubs, orchids, dwarf conifers, perennials, wildflowers, and water/bog plants sited in a figure-eight pattern that meanders among rock, mixed border, carnivorous and water gardens. Especially recom-mended are large colonies of hardy orchids and 240 species and cultivars of conifers landscaped among companion astilbes, hostas, dwarf shrubs, heathers, and ground covers. Some areas of garden go back as far as thirty years; the bog and water gardens are new additions. Most plants are labeled, and a computer printout will be available upon request.

DATES & HOURS: June 19; 10 a.m. – 4 p.m.

DIRECTIONS: *Take I-64 toward Huntington.* Take the Oakwood Exit onto Route 119 to the top of the hill and the second stoplight (approximately 1 mile). Turn left onto Oakwood Road to the George Washington High School intersection. Turn right onto Clark Road, to the fourth house on the right, #1525.

Kanawha Salines —
The Garden of Mrs. Turner Ratrie, MALDEN, WV

Kanawha Salines, one of the most historic properties in the Kanawha Valley, was built by a pioneer in the exploitation of the abundant resources of salt brine beneath the earth. The original house was built in 1815 and remodeled in 1923. The owner, Mrs. Ratrie, is a direct descendent of the first salt producers and has been the garden designer since 1958. An allée of cherry trees on either side of an old brick walk leads to an enchanting white garden surrounding a rectangular pool filled with white water lilies. There is a formal rose garden surrounded by an English boxwood hedge, an extensive vegetable garden, and a beautiful herbaceous border. The property encompasses one and-one-half acres.

DATES & HOURS: June 19; 10 a.m. – 4 p.m.

DIRECTIONS: *From I-64/I-77* take Route 60 East to the Malden Exit. Turn left after the underpass and proceed through the town of Malden. Turn right onto a gravel road east of town. Look for a sign at the gravel driveway. Please park as directed.

Proceeds shared with The Kanawha Garden Club.

WISCONSIN

Milwaukee Area

1999 WISCONSIN OPEN DAYS

July 18: MILWAUKEE AREA

MILWAUKEE AREA: *July 18, 1999*

Grossman Garden, MEQUON, 10 A.M. – 4 P.M.

Kasten, MILWAUKEE, 10 A.M. – 4 P.M.

Deerwood, RIVER HILLS, 10 A.M. – 4 P.M.

Hilltop, RIVER HILLS, 10 A.M. – 4 P.M.

❖ Boerner Botanical Gardens, 5879 SOUTH 92ND STREET, HALES CORNERS, WI 53130. (414) 425-1130.

Internationally recognized, fifty acre formal gardens set within a 1,000 acre arboretum park. Collections are displayed in beautifully landscaped settings including a Perennial Mall, Herb Garden, Rose Garden, Annual Garden, Rock Garden, and Shrub Mall. Seasonal displays of wildflowers, tulips, crab apples, peonies, iris, roses and daylilies are among the popular attractions. BBG's Trial Garden is an All-American Selections Flower Trial Judging Ground, an All-American Rose Selection's Test Site, and displays All American Flower Trial and Vegetable Trial Winners.

DATES & HOURS: Mid-April – November, 8 a.m. – dusk.

DIRECTIONS: *Located southwest of Milwaukee.* Take I-894 to Exit 5A (Forest Home). Take Forest Home southwest to 92nd Street and go south approximately 1 mile to the College Avenue entrance.

Grossman Garden, MEQUON, WI

A country retreat nestled into nine-acre maple and beech woods. Paths lead to a native prairie frequented by butterflies and hummingbirds, and many other varieties of birds. Climb over the style or open the gate to view the perennial garden, two water gardens, and a woodland garden. A trellis welcomes you to the night fragrance garden as well as the vegetable and herb gardens. Enjoy a peaceful day in the country!

DATES & HOURS: July 18; 10 a.m. – 4 p.m.

DIRECTIONS: *Take I-42* to Route 167, also called Mequon Road. Turn west on Route 167; we are about 9 miles west of I-43. Cross Route 57 and Route 181. Pass Baehmann Vegetable Stand, and then cross Granville Road. Go .5 mile west, into the woods at #11702 West Mequon Road. Turn into the woods. Go to the first driveway on the right.

Kasten Garden, MILWAUKEE, WI

This garden was once a field that yearned for ponds and gardens. The ponds, with plantings of wild roses, grasses, and wildflowers are home for ducks, geese, and a family of mate swans. The prairie restoration welcomes butterflies and song birds, while the perennial garden was designed keeping in mind the appetite of deer...trying to discourage browsing! Around the house are annual gardens with a country feeling to compliment the country house.

DATES & HOURS: July 18; 10 a.m. – 4 p.m.

DIRECTIONS: *Take I-43* to Brown Deer Road West. Go west for about 2 miles and through one traffic light to Upper River Road. Turn right following the white fence around the corner. Follow the river to River Bend Court about .75 mile on your left. Turn left and the Kasten Garden is the second driveway on the right.

Deerwood, RIVER HILLS, WI

We have created a restful woodland area bisected by a brook leading into small ponds and waterfalls. Entering the woods on a bridge over the stream, you come upon a small grassy glade with a bench framed by trees and evergreens. The area is crisscrossed with paths winding through beds of native perennial wildflowers and ground covers. We have tried to achieve a natural woodland area, very informal and unstructured. Leaving the woods you come upon a vine-covered pergola and a large lawn sloping gently toward the Milwaukee River.

DATES & HOURS: July 18; 10 a.m. – 4 p.m.

DIRECTIONS: *Take I-43* to Good Hope Road. Proceed west for .5 mile to the second road on the right, River Road. Go north on River Road to Dean Road (at a stop sign). Turn left and go west for .5 mile to the house, #2055 West Dean Road. Please park along the road.

Hill Top, RIVER HILLS, WI

The property consists of fifteen acres with a system of interconnecting paths that circumnavigate the property. There are numerous surprises of May apples, wild geraniums, and asters blooming on the forest floor. There is a man-made pond to provide water for the five acres of mowed lawn. The pond is surrounded by ferns, lilies, foam flowers, wild ginger, sweet woodruff, quaking aspeas and is home to numerous frogs and about twenty-five koi. There are two connecting ponds where a natural overflow was turned into a recirculating stream to maintain the constant flow of water and wetland area. These pathways lead to and from the more detailed boxwood-lined gardens surrounding the house at Hill Top.

DATES & HOURS: July 18; 10 a.m. – 4 p.m.

DIRECTIONS: *Take I-43* to Good Hope Road. Proceed west for .5 mile to the second road on the right, River Road. Go north on River Road to Dean Road (at a stop sign). Turn left and go west for .5 mile to #2280 on the north side of the road. Please park along the road.

Joseph De Sciose
Garden Photography
212 / 426 - 1484

CITY SPACES

There's no better way to view your garden or grow one than from a custom English conservatory or greenhouse. Call us about a design or send $12 for brochures and a planning guide.

OR COUNTRY PLACES

TOWN & COUNTRY
Conservatories

London • Chicago

5153 N. Clark St. • Suite 228-GC • Chicago, IL 60640 • ph: 773-506-8000 • fax: 773-506-8815

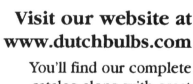

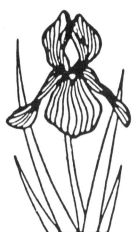

CLAIRE'S

**The Perennial Garden Center
26 Years of growing quality
perennials....over 1,000 varieties.**

**Haviland Hollow Road
Patterson, NY 12563
914-878-6632**

Morning Glory Farm

Growers of Rare & Unusual Perennials and Annuals

PO Box 423
Fairview, TN 37062

Phone: 615-799-0138
Fax: 615-799-8864

Website Address: www.morninggloryfarm.com

Over 600 varieties of shade and sun loving perennials and annuals. Many new introductions of Heuchera, Ligularia, Hosta and Pulmonaria. We specialize in growing unusual perennials and ship the majority in 1 gallon containers.

We are the premiere grower in our area. Come see why!

Catalog: $4.00

Website: Free

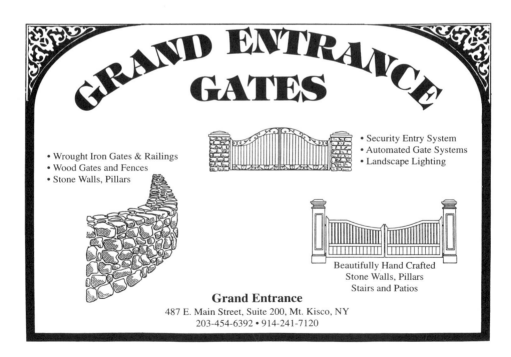
426

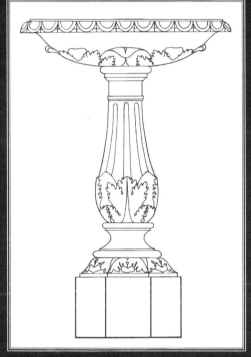

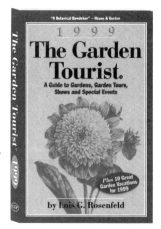

ENGLISH GARDENING TOOLS & GIFTS

Window Hayracks & Wall Baskets

Brighten up windows or railings with hayracks filled with luxuriant plants, or add splashes of color to blank walls or fences with wall planters in a variety of shapes, sizes and designs.

Hayrack Wall Trellises

Now you can grow spectacular wall displays using these elegant new Wall Trellises and English hayracks. This combination enables all kinds of climbing and trailing plants to beautify blank

walls in sun or shade. Select from 4 sizes.

Freestanding Planters

Enjoy flowers at your fingertips with urns, cradles, cauldrons and patio planters, all at various heights. Try out exciting color and texture combinations on patio or poolside.

Living Wreath Forms

Our clip-together design makes it easy for you to assemble living wreaths planted with ivies, small annuals, herbs and succulents. For walls, doors and fences—even as a tabletop centerpiece.

Hanging Floral Globes

Create striking decorations using these spherical wire forms planted with flowers, ivies, succulents, herbs or ferns. Embellish with ribbons for special occasions.

Illusion Arches & Silhouettes

These Perspective Arches, Trees & Follies make it easy to bring life to blank walls, courtyards and patios. Create striking effects when framed with plants. Add the suggestion of more

space in tight areas or on fences. Combine elements to make scenes that add a bit of fun to your garden, balcony, even indoors.

Visit our store on River Road, in historic Bucks County

KINSMAN COMPANY

River Road, Point Pleasant, PA 18950-0357
CALL TOLL-FREE: 1-800-396-1251

Call or write for our FREE full-color Catalog

Visit our website at www.kinsmangarden.com

433

Michael H. Dodge

PLANTSMAN AND HORTICULTURAL PHOTOGRAPHER

White Flower Farm's primary photographer for over twenty years is now accepting commissions in plant and garden portraiture. Also booking 1999 slide lectures, workshops and garden consultations.

telephone: 860-567-1456   e-mail: mhdodge@snet.net

© 1998 Michael H. Dodge

Oliver

How to find the nursery that the:

Massachusetts Horticultural Society,

New York Botanical Gardens,

Horticultural Society of New York,

and the North American Rock Garden Society

all visit.

42 — Merritt Pkwy — 44

Weston Rd

Cross Highway

Bayberry La

Hillside

Congress

Tpk

Black Rock

Hulls Farm Rd

Oliver ★

Bronson

I-95 — CT Tpk — 20 — Sturgess — 21

Oliver Nurseries—come and discover.
We are open 7 days a week at 1159 Bronson Road,
Fairfield, CT 06430. Call 203 259-5609.

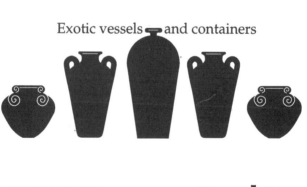

INDEX